CHALLENGING POSTMODERNISM

CHALLENGING POSTMODERNISM

PHILOSOPHY AND THE

POLITICS OF TRUTH

DAVID DETMER

an imprint of Prometheus Books
59 John Glenn Drive, Amherst, New York 14228-2197

Published 2003 by Humanity Books, an imprint of Prometheus Books

Inquiries should be addressed to
Humanity Books
59 John Glenn Drive
Amherst, New York 14228–2197
VOICE: 716–691–0133, ext. 207
FAX: 716–564–2711

07 06 05   5 4 3 2

Library of Congress Cataloging-in-Publication Data

Detmer, David, 1958–
    Challenging Postmodernism : philosophy and the politics of truth / by
    David Detmer.
        p. cm.—
    Includes bibliographical references and index.
    ISBN 1–59102–101–4 (pbk. : alk. paper)
    1. Postmodernism. 2. Truth. 3. Political correctness. I. Title.

B831.2.D475 2003
149'.97—dc21

                                                    2003008981

Printed in the United States of America on acid-free paper

CONTENTS

ACKNOWLEDGMENTS

W riting, in theory, is a solitary activity. And yet, as I now turn my attention to the pleasant task of thanking those who have helped me to write this book, I realize with full force the foolishness of such a conception.

I'll begin by thanking Steve Hendley, Christopher Norris, Ann O'Hear, Henry Rosemont Jr., and an anonymous publisher's referee for reading an earlier draft of this work, and for offering many helpful criticisms and suggestions for revision. I've followed their advice in several places, and the book is much improved as a result. Still, in some cases I've been stubborn enough to persist on my own chosen path, so I'm happy to affirm the old cliché: I alone bear full responsibility for the faults and errors to be found in this work.

I'd also like to thank the many friends and scholars (often both) with whom I've discussed this project and its ideas over the years. With heartfelt apologies to those I'm forgetting, I'll mention here Ronald Aronson, Hazel Barnes, Bill Becker, Phyllis Bergiel, Betsy Bowman, Charles (The Babbling Gourmet) Brown, Marilyn Cleland, Robert Ellis, Matt Eshleman, Jenel Farrell, Colin Fewer, Neil Florek, Tom Flynn, Lewis Edwin Hahn, William Hamrick, Leonard Harris, Lina Hartocollis, Helen Heise, Yahya Kamalipour, Ray Langley, Kathleen League, Gail Linsenbard, Ashok Malhotra, Bill Martin, Bill McBride, Adrian Mirvish, the late Phyllis Morris, Connie Mui, M. L. Rantala, John Rowan, Michel Rybalka, Ron Santoni, Eugene Schlossberger, Victoria Sherry, Amy Sprengelmeyer, Bob Stone, David Turpin, Robin Turpin, Joe Walsh, and Xia-Si Yang.

I've been fortunate in having the chance to present some of this material at conferences, as this has allowed me to benefit from the comments of audience members as well as fellow panelists. Accordingly, I wish to thank the American Philosophical Association, the Radical Philosophy Association, the North American Sartre Society, and the World Congress of Philosophy for giving me a platform, and I thank all of the participants in these sessions for listening, and for sharing ideas. Special thanks, in this regard, go to Sam and Susan Zinaich for hosting the monthly "philosophy party" at which I've had many opportunities to develop and refine some of the ideas presented here. I'm grateful to all of the participants at these events for their help and encouragement.

While a substantial majority of the material in this book has not been published previously, Chapters 1 and 6 do contain revised versions of articles that have appeared elsewhere. Chapter 1 is a revised and expanded version of "Husserl's Critique of Relativism," in Brice Wachterhauser, ed., *Phenomenology and Skepticism* (Evanston, IL: Northwestern University Press, 1996), pp. 101–111, 243–245. Chapter 6 incorporates revised versions of "The Ethical Responsibilities of Journalists," in John R. Rowan and Samuel Zinaich Jr., eds., *Ethics for the Professions* (Belmont, CA: Wadsworth, 2003), pp. 373–379; and "Covering Up Iran: Why Vital Information Is Routinely Excluded from U.S. Media News Accounts," in Yahya R. Kamalipour, ed., *The U.S. Media and the Middle East: Image and Perception* (Westport, CT: Greenwood Press, 1995), pp. 91–101. I thank the editors and publishers for permission to reprint. I am also most grateful to Noam Chomsky who generously granted permission to quote from his "Rationality/Science," *Z Papers* 1, no. 4 (October–December 1992).

Next, it is my pleasure to thank the good folks at Humanity Books for their hard work on behalf of this book. I especially thank my editor, Ann O'Hear, who has worked tirelessly to keep the project alive, and who has offered me much good advice and encouragement.

My greatest debt, of course, is to my family. I thank my sisters,

Kris and Rachel Detmer, and my parents-in-law, Eva and Rol Mommer, for their numerous acts of kindness and support over the years.

My mother, Letha Detmer, died shortly after I completed this book. I have far more to thank her for than I could ever recount here, so I'll mention just one thing. When I first learned to read our family lived in a tiny town that had no library. Still, my mother contrived to obtain for me a library card for use in a library in the nearest city, about thirty miles away. As it was clear that my sisters and I loved to read, she drove us to that library every two weeks, and I brought home a huge stack of books each time. If I've managed to learn anything of value in my life, and successfully communicated any of it here, my mother should receive a great deal of the credit.

I thank my partner in life, Kerri Mommer, and our son, Arlo Detmer, for their love and support, for their brilliance, and for their wonderful sense of fun. They make life worth living.

Finally, I offer my thanks to all people who read.

INTRODUCTION

Many people today reject the notion of "objective truth" and argue instead that "truth" is socially constructed and varies from one culture or community to another. Indeed, the establishment of such a conception of truth is supposed to be one of the principal achievements of "postmodernism," as is skepticism about the ability of modern science to transcend such limitations of subjectivity and of culture.

On the other hand, the claims of postmodernism have also given rise to a heated reaction, but this reaction tends to be defective in at least three ways, leading to an impoverished debate. It is defective, first, in that it typically fails to engage with the texts and arguments of the postmodern anti-truth squad, preferring instead simply to dismiss them all at once for failing to confirm traditional ways of looking at the world. Second, it is almost always issued from a politically conservative vantage-point, with the result that the critique of postmodern views on truth becomes entangled with disapproval of the political views of leading postmodernists, leaving it unclear what a critique emanating from a political position more in sympathy with that of most postmodernists might look like. Finally, it often displays a lack of understanding of "continental" European philosophy, the philosophical tradition from which postmodernism derives most of its inspiration.

In response to this situation I have attempted to write an accessible, nontechnical discussion of current philosophical controversies surrounding the ideas of relativism, objectivity, social constructionism, and truth. These controversies, in turn, underlie the intense ongoing quarrels over multiculturalism, tolerance, "political correctness," and kindred notions—quarrels that engage the general public, and not merely professional philosophers and their students.

This book defends the idea of objective truth and attempts to show that doing so is a matter of considerable political importance. Moreover, my approach to these issues is unusual in at least three respects:

(1) I quote extensively from the writings of postmodernists, social constructionists, assorted relativists, and other critics of the notion of objective truth, and engage directly with their arguments.

(2) While most postmodernists, relativists, social constructionists, etc., adopt a liberal/left political position and are attacked from the political right, I criticize postmodernism from a politically leftist perspective.

(3) While most postmodernists, etc., derive their central insights from continental European philosophy and are attacked from the standpoint of Anglo-American analytic philosophy, I approach these issues from a position heavily (and favorably) influenced by continental philosophy. Indeed, Edmund Husserl and Jean-Paul Sartre are two of the figures on whom I draw most in constructing my arguments. (At the same time, I devote a fair amount of attention to analytic philosophy, and the book contains substantial discussions of Richard Rorty and Noam Chomsky, among others affiliated with that tradition.)

It remains to say something about the organization of the book. In chapter 1, "Husserl's Critique of Relativism," I make use of some of Edmund Husserl's arguments developed in response to the relativists of his day—about one hundred years ago—and attempt to show how devastatingly they tell against contemporary postmodernism and social constructionism.

One of Husserl's arguments is that all forms of relativism and skepticism are incoherent and self-refuting. Contemporary postmodernists vehemently deny this charge. In chapter 2, "Self-Referential Inconsistency," I reply to their arguments and end up affirming Husserl's charge.

Many people think that relativism, or at least the denial of objective truth, follows from the simple fact of disagreement. In chapter 3, "The Argument from Disagreement," I explore this claim at some length and provide multiple grounds for rejecting it.

The next three chapters draw heavily on the ideas of Jean-Paul Sartre. Chapter 4, "Sartre's Defense of Truth," uses several of Sartre's principal ideas in an attempt to show that one can accept many of the arguments put forth by contemporary postmodernists without thereby being forced to embrace their rejection of objective truth. I argue that Sartre's position provides an alternative both to postmodern relativism and to the cruder forms of objectivity and realism (like positivism) that the postmodernists rightly reject.

Chapter 5, "Truth in Ethics and Politics: Sartre vs. Rorty," presents a detailed critique of Richard Rorty's truth-rejection and its unfortunate political consequences. In making my case I criticize Rorty's interpretation of Sartre, contrast his position with Sartre's, and make use of some of Sartre's ideas in arguing against his.

Chapter 6, "What Is Objectivity? Sartre vs. the Journalists," argues that postmodernists reject objectivity in part because they have in mind a defective version of that idea—in particular, they understand "objectivity" the way mainstream journalists in the United States do. I try to show that the postmodernists are right to reject this form of objectivity. Indeed, I attempt to demonstrate that it is partly responsible for the grotesque and utterly inadequate performance of these media. But I also argue that the postmodernists are wrong to reject objectivity outright, since that notion can be understood to mean something quite different from what the journalists take it to mean. Accordingly, I present an alternative, scholarly or scientific, concept of objectivity, which I derive in part from Sartre, and contrast it with the journalistic notion of objectivity.

In chapter 7, "The Anti-Truth Squad," I critically examine the writings of some leading social constructionists, such as Michael Bérubé, Barbara Herrnstein Smith, Walter Truett Anderson, and several others. I attempt to show that their ideas cannot withstand critical scrutiny.

Science has frequently been regarded as the one human endeavor that can consistently and reliably deliver to us objective truths about the world. It is not surprising, then, that the postmodern assault on objective truth has included, as an essential component, an attack on science. In chapter 8, "The Limitations of Rationality and Science? Noam Chomsky, O. J. Simpson, and Alan Sokal," I make use of several arguments and insights from Chomsky in defending science against postmodernist and social constructionist criticisms. I then focus on the notorious O. J. Simpson murder case, since it has often been pointed to in support both of attacks on the power of science and of denials of the possibility of objective truth. I argue that the Simpson case will not bear such weight. The chapter then concludes with a discussion of the notorious "Sokal hoax"—by far the most widely publicized and hotly debated event in the history of the postmodern "science wars." I argue that while the hoax itself has proved little, many of the comments of Sokal's critics have further illuminated the weaknesses of the social constructionist understanding of science.

In spite of my strong disagreement with the views on truth and objectivity held by those who are called "politically correct," I argue, in chapter 9, "Chomsky, 'Political Correctness,' and the Politics of Truth," that the popular criticisms of "political correctness" are misguided. In making this case I draw, once again, on key ideas of Chomsky's and discuss extensively, as a test case, the current reception of Christopher Columbus. I then bring the book to a close by restating its central themes in the light of this discussion—that it is a mistake to reject objective truth, that such rejection has disastrous political consequences, and, more specifically, that the abandonment of objective truth cannot serve a genuinely progressive and humane political agenda.

Chapter 1

HUSSERL'S CRITIQUE OF RELATIVISM

Many contemporary thinkers have abandoned "truth" entirely, viewing it as an outmoded, discredited, perhaps even dangerous concept. Others, while retaining the notion of truth, have insisted upon understanding it in a radically subjectivist or relativist sense, far removed from the robust sense of truth as something "hard" and objective.[1]

In this respect, at least, our "postmodern" condition bears a remarkable similarity to the intellectual climate confronting Husserl at the dawn of the twentieth century, when he published his *Logical Investigations*. Husserl evidently found that climate to be so pervaded by various forms of relativism, subjectivism, and skepticism as to warrant his decision to precede the presentation of his many constructive and original findings in the area of logic with a lengthy "Prolegomena," largely devoted to the refutation of such deflationary epistemologies—epistemologies the widespread acceptance of which would tend to preclude at the outset a serious appreciation of the fruits of his enormous labors.[2]

While a glance at the current intellectual scene would tend to suggest that Husserl's arguments against relativism have failed to find favor, it does not follow, needless to say, that they deserve such a fate. In fact, it may very well be that many contemporary thinkers, indeed, even amongst the ranks of philosophers, are unfamiliar with Husserl's arguments. For one thing, while the cultural split between the predominantly English speaking "analytical" philosophers, on the one hand, and those more at home in the European "continental" tradition, on the other, is nowhere near as severe as it was just a few decades ago, it remains true that a good many members of the former camp have no substantial acquaintance with the details of Husserl's thought. Furthermore, it seems to be the case even within the continental tradition that its more recent recruits tend to see no need to consult Husserl firsthand, taking it as read that he is a hopelessly old-fashioned "logocentric" rationalist who has been decisively refuted, or better, "deconstructed," by Derrida.[3] Indeed, my sense is that such a perspective on continental philosophy is also widely, and uncritically, adopted by nonspecialists in that tradition, with the result that, even when they conscientiously endeavor to keep up with currents within that field, they tend to focus almost exclusively on Nietzsche and Heidegger and their many followers, including the (variously classified) poststructuralists, deconstructionists, and (other) postmodernists. Finally, while it must of course be acknowledged, in spite of what the preceding remarks might suggest, that Husserl has exerted, and clearly continues to exert, a wide, deep, and multifarious influence on contemporary philosophy,[4] nonetheless his arguments against relativism, perhaps because they are preliminary to, rather than central and essential to, his greatest and most singular contribution to philosophy, namely, his project of phenomenology, have suffered comparative, and possibly undeserved, neglect.[5] Thus, in light of their obvious relevance to our contemporary situation, it seems worthwhile to attempt to relieve that neglect somewhat and to look again at Husserl's arguments against relativism, to see what they might yet have to teach us.

In order to keep the discussion to manageable length, however, I shall focus on just three of Husserl's many arguments, and only one in great detail, though in my own defense I might point out both that these are clearly central arguments, as evidenced by the fact that Husserl repeatedly presents them in his many different treatments of relativism and skepticism, and that I shall also be touching on several additional arguments, if only in passing, during the course of my own discussion.

As a final preliminary to that discussion, I think it will prove worthwhile to examine a substantial quoted passage representing (and, indeed, confidently summarizing and defending) the "post-modern" position against which I am eager to press Husserl's arguments. I do this in part to ward off the criticism that I am enlisting the aid of Husserl merely for the purposes of attacking a "straw man." Of course, one might always argue that I have chosen an unrepresentative example, but I am confident that students of the contemporary intellectual scene will recognize the rhetoric and position taken in the quoted passage, by Tom Bridges, as quite similar to what they have heard and read over and over again in recent years. Bridges's statement is atypical, in my judgment at least, only in its clarity and succinctness, and also, though perhaps less so, in its pugnacious tone. Bridges writes:

> [T]he failure of the Enlightenment project is by now simply a fact. . . . Of course, there are still many in our midst who out of misunderstanding, habit and resistance to intellectual change routinely make claims to objective knowledge of history and nature. The trouble is that such people cannot give us a credible account of how such knowledge is possible. Since the publication of Kuhn's *The Structure of Scientific Revolutions* in 1962, a vast arsenal of arguments has been stockpiled—arguments drawn from Dewey, Wittgenstein, Heidegger, Gadamer, Foucault, Derrida and Rorty, to name just a few—arguments entirely sufficient to persuade anyone paying attention that human knowledge is historically conditioned, that there is no privileged standpoint outside of history from which human beings can contemplate things or events as they really are in themselves. Do . . . any of the defenders of objective truth have any response to these arguments? Can they show precisely how it is that a particular human being, conditioned by gender, historical and spatial location, class, ethnicity, nationality and religion, can somehow assume the purely universal and timeless standpoint of a pure knower? Just how is this miracle possible? How do we manage to jump out of our historical skins to rub up against the cold steely surfaces of objective fact? . . . Progressive today is not a return to the foundationalist conceptions of truth and knowledge that served us in the past, but rather the new postmodernist rhetorical conceptions of discourse that alone are capable of giving pluralistic, multivocal and multifaceted critical political discourses the central place they must have in any free society.[6]

I. The Self-Referential Inconsistency Argument

One of the most persistent criticisms of postmodern forms of relativism or skepticism, and one that Husserl repeatedly pressed against earlier versions,[7] concerns their failure to deal adequately with straightforward questions concerning their self-referentiality. To illustrate this, consider the popular position which is sometimes called "cultural relativism": the doctrine that all "truth" is socially constructed and thus must be understood as obtaining only within a particular culture, which it can in no way transcend. The present objection to such a position is brought out by considering such questions as: If all "truth" is merely relative to a particular culture, then is not *this* truth merely relative to the culture in which it is asserted? If so, then how is the claim to be understood, since it appears to be a universal, transcultural claim? On the other hand, if this truth is an exception to the general rule that all truths are merely relative to a particular culture, then why cannot there be other exceptions? Similarly, if one claims that all truth is socially constructed, what is the status of *this* claim? Is it, too, simply the product of a particular culture and thus devoid of valid application outside of and beyond it? And if there is no truth, what is the nature and status of the *claim* that there is no truth?

Let us now apply all of this to our representative specimen of postmodernist thinking. Recall Bridges's assertion that we cannot "rub up against the cold steely surfaces of objective fact," since "human knowledge is historically conditioned" and also "conditioned by gender . . . , class, ethnicity, nationality," and so forth. Notice that, on Bridges's own terms, his statements must be taken not as capturing the way things really are—not as objective truths—but rather as expressions of his own peculiar perspective, which is through-and-through conditioned by his gender, ethnicity, nationality, and so on, and which, therefore, cannot be assumed to be otherwise, let alone universally or uniquely, valid. The way is left fully clear for others, with different perspectives, perhaps, as Bridges would have it, because of the different kinds of conditioning they have undergone, to deny everything he says. What seems needed, then, is a standpoint external to these opposed standpoints, from which their opposition might be adjudicated. But Bridges, of course, denies that this is possible, as when, in connection, specifically, with historical conditioning, he remarks: "there is no privileged standpoint outside of history from which human beings can contemplate things or events as they really are in themselves." So Bridges is stuck.

Part of his problem, it would seem, is that his argument depends upon, and his rhetoric also suggests, the idea that his claims are really true, or at least better than their denials, and this in turn entails, at the very least, that something more can be said for his claims than that his conditioning has *led* him to believe them and to issue them. For, with regard to his rhetoric, it is perhaps sufficient to note that he calls it "simply a fact" that the Enlightenment project has failed, only to ridicule, a scant three sentences later, those who are foolish enough to "make claims to objective knowledge of history."[8] As for his arguments, it is not only that his conclusion seems to undermine itself (e.g., "all knowledge claims are historically conditioned, and do not necessarily reflect how things really are" clearly implies that "the *claim* that all knowledge claims are historically conditioned is *itself* historically conditioned, and does not necessarily reflect how things really are"); his conclusion also seems to undermine its own premises and the pattern of its logical reasoning. For Bridges's rhetoric surely suggests—and here I will not quote again, but rather ask readers to go back, so as to verify it for themselves—that he regards the claims supporting his conclusion as true, or at least better than their denials, and holds that these claims do indeed lend support to his conclusion. And if he is not right about this, there is no need to take his argument seriously, for why should we lend our credence to a conclusion which is based upon premises that are no better than their denials, or which is not supported by its premises? Sadly, however, if Bridges's conclusion is accepted, then he is not right in his implicit claims about his premises and reasoning. He has fallen into the trap Husserl diagnosed years ago: "All genuine skepticism of whatever kind and persuasion is indicated by the essentially necessary countersense that, in its argumentations, it implicitly presupposes as conditions of the possibility of its validity precisely what it denies in its theses."[9]

How might Bridges, and other postmodernists, escape or overcome this objection? I will discuss three common strategies. One is to give up the claim that one's claims are really "true," or "warranted," or what have you, and instead frankly to admit that they have only relative, or subjective, or rhetorical merit.[10] As Husserl puts it, such a person "will not bow to the ordinary objection that in setting up his theory he is making a claim to be convincing to others, a claim presupposing that very objectivity of truth which his thesis denies. He will naturally reply: My theory expresses my standpoint, what is true for me, and need be true for no one else."[11] I will only point out, by way of reply, that such a stance relieves anyone not initially tempted to adopt the thesis in question of any obligation to refute it.[12]

A second strategy, favored especially by Heidegger, Derrida, and some of their followers, is to claim that such incoherence is at present unavoidable since, while we are able to see that the "logocentric" Western metaphysical tradition, with its characteristic understanding of, and emphasis on, truth, objectivity, reason, and kindred concepts, is thoroughly exhausted, untenable, and in need of replacement, we are not yet able to see how to think, write, and speak in the radically new way that is required, so we are forced, reluctantly, to make use of the very concepts and ways of thinking, writing, and speaking that we are simultaneously attempting to overthrow. The incoherence of this approach can be somewhat mitigated by the use of irony, and, in general, a highly literary, rather than expository and argumentative, style of presentation, together with the use of lines to cross out some of the problematical words, so that the words are both used (because written down) and not used (because crossed out). Derrida's term for this technique, which he takes over from Heidegger but develops in his own way, is writing "under erasure."

Without wishing to assert that such a technique is in principle unscrupulous, or that it cannot be used to produce intriguing literary effects, surely there is no gainsaying James Edie's quite restrained remark that "we must still ask ourselves commensensically from time to time what it means to use a vocabulary 'under erasure,' and what it all eventually comes to."[13] I think it is fair to add, however, and without wishing to advance a philistine position on the matter, or to deny in general the benefit which can accrue from avant-garde experimentation in the uses of language, that there is considerable danger that this technique can be abused so that it functions simply as an immunizing device. After all, one cannot show that a claim is mistaken if one does not know what it means.

A final response, and perhaps the most common one, which defenders of postmodern claims issue in reply to the charge that such claims are self-referentially inconsistent is to reply that those who press such claims are nitpickers who are hung up on the strictures of logic and who are either unable or unwilling to embrace a more expansive, albeit more uncertain, way of looking at things. Thus, G. B. Madison states, approvingly, that "postmodern philosophical discourse . . . often deliberately ignores the requirements of logic (e.g., the principle of non-contradiction), because what it wishes to say necessarily cannot be said in logic (in the eyes of many postmodernists it is no objection to an utterance that it be 'inconsistent' or 'improbable')."[14]

By way of reply, it is necessary to point out, once again, how readily such a position can function, whether intentionally or not, as an immunizing device. For, as Patrick Colm Hogan points out, "those who deny the Principle of Non-Contradiction quite literally allow no contradiction. There simply is no way of disputing their claim[s]."[15]

I will refrain, however, from pursuing further this line of argument here so as to point out instead, I think very much in the spirit of Husserl,[16] that an unwillingness to face up to, and to take responsibility for, that which experience reveals to be inconsistent or improbable is not a purely logical error, but rather a moral, political, and existential failing of the highest order, as is the refusal to eliminate flat contradictions from one's thinking.[17] Moreover, the fact that postmodernists tend to renounce a robust sense of logic and of truth in their more reflective, theoretical moments, only to appeal to it implicitly when they are doing so (e.g., it is true that there is no truth) and explicitly at unguarded moments in their lives (e.g., "I did *not* do that, and that is the absolute truth!—look, here is the evidence to prove it!"), strongly suggests that such a robust sense of truth (and a similar point could easily be made about their sense of evidence, of consistency, and of probability) is deeply present to them in their own experience.[18] Thus, the fault that I think Husserl, and even more so his "existentialist" followers, such as Sartre,[19] would find in many contemporary postmodernists is not merely that they fail to subject their beliefs to abstract, artificial, purely formal and logical tests, but that they fail to notice that they cannot live by those beliefs. A desire to live according to their theorizing and to theorize according to their living (experiencing)[20] would thus lead the defenders of postmodernism to reject from their thinking those relativistic or skeptical notions by which they cannot live—for who knows how to put into practice a self-contradictory idea?—or, better still, to work hard on reconciling what still seems valid in these notions with that in their experience which seems to render them untenable.

Moreover, since the more expansive stance from which logic is often rejected as overly constricting is typically a moral and political one, and since, in general, postmodern claims are frequently defended on moral and political grounds, I will close this discussion of the self-referential inconsistency objection with a brief consideration of it in precisely such a context. The point I wish to make here is that it is far from clear that any relativizing or subjectivizing of truth, or any reduction of it to multiple opinions or perspectives (recall the concluding sentence from the passage quoted from Bridges above), entails greater tolerance for diverse voices, let alone increased respect for them. For the claim that such a move does provide a rationale or justification for tolerance yields, once again, the familiar self-referential paradoxes. If the claim that we should be tolerant is to be upheld as a universal truth, how can this be squared with the idea that all truths are relative, perspectival, and thoroughly conditioned? If this claim is an exception to the general rule, what are the grounds for this, and why can there not be other universal (transcultural, transperspectival) truths? If, on the other hand, the idea that we should be tolerant is to be considered as just one perspective among others, then such relativism is inimical to the claim that everyone, irrespective of the peculiarities of their own cultural perspective and conditioning, is truly obliged to be tolerant, and leaves us powerless in the face of those whose perspective is one of opposition to tolerance. And how can such perspectivism yield respect for the other, when, on the epistemology in question, we always know beforehand that the other's perspective is just different from ours, and not inferior (as relativists are quick to insist) or superior (as they are not) to it? Thus, relativism removes one of our most powerful motives to study the views of the other—the idea that the other might be right and we might be wrong.

Here is one real-life example which illustrates some of these points, showing in particular that self-referential confusions and paradoxes should not be dismissed as of merely academic or narrowly intellectual concern (the sort of thing about which logical nit-pickers are obsessed), because in fact they bring forth significant, and often unfortunate, consequences in the social and political realm.

At an antiwar meeting held in Chicago during the 1991 Gulf War, several opponents of the war advocated the circulation of a petition documenting the rampant sexism of the policies of the government of Kuwait and condemning this sexism. A sizable group of self-proclaimed "postmodernists" opposed this, on the grounds that it would be arrogant and intolerant for "us" to make such a judgment and to impose "our" standards on the people of Kuwait. Notice: (a) the paradox of invoking the value of tolerance to justify refusing to oppose intolerance in the form of sexism; (b) the futile attempt to be neutral—"Who are we to judge them?" was a common refrain—resulting, in effect, in the taking of sides; (c) that the side taken is the repressive, intolerant one, in that the side supported, if only by means of opposing criticism of it, is that of the sexists of Kuwait, with the side opposed being those who would criticize them; (d) that the postmodernists' argument implies, though I feel certain this is unintentional, the racist assumption that all of the people of Kuwait think alike—"Who are we to judge them?"—as if there were no feminists in Kuwait who would endorse the petition; and (e) that the argument depends upon the denial of the eidetic dimension of experience (to be discussed in the final section of this paper), in that it assumes that we, not being members of the culture in question, cannot possibly be in a position to understand and judge the sexism in Kuwait, overlooking, or else denying, that the essential structure of sexism might be such that we can at least partially understand sexism in Kuwait on analogy to sexism in the United States, with this admittedly partial and fallible level of understanding of this sexism being sufficient to render us competent to judge it as wrong, and to entail that we are not acting irresponsibly in condemning it.[21]

What this example suggests, I think, is that the postmodernists' approach to defending tolerance is incoherent, uncritical, and ineffective. What is more, this is true in large part because of the self-referential inconsistencies which pervade it, and which might otherwise, though mistakenly, be dismissed as matters solely of formal and logical concern, far removed from all social and political import.[22]

II. THE EVIDENTIARY ARGUMENT

Let us next take up one of Husserl's principal arguments against "psychologism"—the thesis that logical truths are, in fact, empirical truths about the ways in which human beings happen to think.[23] According to psychologism, the argument "either A or B; not A; therefore B," reduces to something like: "all people are so constituted psychologically that if they believe that either A or B is true, and if they further believe that A is not true, then they cannot help but believe that B is true."[24]

I will not pursue the obvious objection that, as everyone who has ever taught logic knows all too well, it simply is not the case that "all people are so constituted psychologically that if they believe that either A or B is true, and if they further believe that A is not true, then they cannot help but believe that B is true."[25] I also will not linger over the point that reasoning in psychology—for example, the drawing of inferences concerning how people in fact tend to think, on the basis of empirical data of some kind—depends upon principles of logic, as does all reasoning, so that the reduction of logic to psychology appears to involve vicious circularity.

The Husserlian argument that I do wish to stress is this: On the one hand, at least some logical principles seem powerfully evident to us—it appears obvious, for example, that if A is taller than B, and B is taller than C, then A must be taller than C. On the other hand, we also have some evidence in support of certain psychological theses concerning how people in fact happen to think. But surely at least some of our logical principles, such as the one just mentioned, are far more evident and obvious to us than are any of the empirical generalizations we find in psychology, or in any of the other empirical sciences. Thus, to attempt to explain logic in terms of psychology is to explain the more certain by the less certain. It is, in short, to commit the fallacy of *obscurum per obscurius*.[26]

Now let us apply this argument to our specimen of postmodernism—the passage by Bridges quoted above. Let us concede that there is some evidence to support many of Bridges's central contentions. Certainly there is no shortage of evidence to support the conclusion that much of our thinking is, indeed, "conditioned by gender, history, class, ethnicity," and so on. Perhaps there even is evidence to support the claim that *all* of our thinking is so conditioned, together with the further conclusion that, as a result, we cannot "contemplate things or events as they really are in themselves" (let us here waive the self-referential inconsistency objection). But the presence of some such evidence, even if it be both powerful and abundant, is not yet sufficient to sustain the conclusion. For we would first have to weigh that evidence against the available evidence supporting the denial of this conclusion. Thus, the evidence that all of our thinking is thoroughly conditioned, and in such a manner as to cut us off from all knowledge of "how things really are," together with the inference from this that our belief that $2 + 2 = 4$, for example, is a thoroughly conditioned belief which, for that reason, cannot be granted transcultural and transhistorical validity, must be weighed against the evidence that, simply, $2 + 2 = 4$. Similar considerations apply to the balancing of the evidence that "q" follows from the conjunction of "p implies q" and "p," or (to turn to empirical matters) that elephants are heavier than ants, and that the sun is hotter than the Earth, or, finally (and turning now to value judgments), that happiness is intrinsically better than misery, against the evidence that all of these are conditioned and relative claims, lacking in universal validity, and telling us nothing about how things really are. It seems to me clear that, however strong may be the evidence that at least much of our thinking is conditioned in the ways described by Bridges, there are at least some logical and mathematical, and even empirical and evaluative (both moral and nonmoral), judgments for which our evidence is much stronger.[27] Thus the attempt by postmodernists such as Bridges to explain away these judgments when they run afoul of epistemological strictures less certain than are the judgments themselves is to commit an evidentiary fallacy and to reason *obscurum per obscurius*.[28]

III. THE EIDETIC ARGUMENT

Finally, it seems to me that Bridges goes wrong by assuming, without argument, that a knower must achieve a standpoint stripped of all particularity in order to have access to knowledge that is not thoroughly conditioned by the particularity of the knower. But an alternative possibility, defended at length by Husserl[29] but ignored by Bridges, is that it is possible, even from a particular standpoint, to see truths which transcend that standpoint, and which further transcend the particularities of what is seen, so that the knower "rubs up against" truths which are not only objective, but also universal and necessary.

Consider this example, provided by Erazim Kohák:

> When I try, unsuccessfully, to squeeze a tennis ball into a wine bottle, I need not try several wine bottles and several tennis balls before, using Mill's canons of induction, I arrive inductively at the hypothesis that tennis balls do not fit into wine bottles. One instance is enough. I see not only that this tennis ball won't fit into this wine bottle but that, in principle, tennis balls do not fit into wine bottles, and, for that matter, I see that large objects do not fit into small openings. . . . [O]ur ordinary experience . . . includes not only a perception of objects but a perception of principles as well.[30]

We are now in a position to turn the tables on Bridges and ask, "If I judge that tennis balls do not fit into wine bottles, can you show *precisely* how it is that my gender, historical and spatial location, class, ethnicity, etc., undermine the objectivity of this judgment? They seem quite irrelevant to *this* judgment, though, of course, not to others." Or again, "If from the fact that A is taller than B, and that B is taller than C, I draw the conclusion that A is taller than C, how, *precisely,* does the fact that I am a historical being, living in a particular time and place and culture, preclude me from rubbing up against this truth?"[31]

Thus, it would appear that Bridges's argument depends upon proceeding sweepingly on the theoretical level, and upon prescinding from a close consideration of any of the billions and billions of particular cases of experiences which, like the ones I have cited here, at least seem to fly in the face of his prescriptions. If we are to make sense of the ways in which we are influenced in our thinking by our particularity, it will not do to operate in this high-flown manner.[32] Rather, we will have to emulate Husserl in looking at specific instances carefully and in detail, remaining alive to the possibility that, while our particularity might influence our thinking here, distort it there, and utterly close us off from the truth in another instance, it might not at all undermine our ability to arrive at objective truth in yet another case.[33] All of this deserves much more careful consideration than it has usually received from contemporary postmodern relativists.[34] Should such careful consideration soon be forthcoming, it might yet become possible in the twenty-first century to dispense with the business of repeating Husserl's most fundamental insights, and instead get on with the task of criticizing, refining, and building upon them.[35]

NOTES

1. I quote from the works of many such thinkers in this book. See especially the discussions of the ideas of Tom Bridges in this chapter, those of Richard Rorty in chapter 5, and those of Barbara Herrnstein Smith, Barry Sarchett, Walter Truett Anderson, and many others in chapter 7. Several other thinkers sharing a similar outlook are treated more briefly throughout the book. Thousands of others, for reasons of space and the avoidance of redundancy, must unfortunately go ignored.

2. Edmund Husserl, "Prolegomena to Pure Logic," in his *Logical Investigations*, vol. 1, trans. J. N. Findlay (New York: Humanities Press, 1970). See especially Sections 17–51 on "psychologism," which he classifies as "a sceptical relativism." (For the most part, my references to Husserl will be to section numbers, rather than to page numbers.)

3. The most relevant text in this connection is Jacques Derrida, *Speech and Phenomena*, trans. David Allison (Evanston, IL: Northwestern University Press, 1973). But for a powerful critique of Derrida's reading of Husserl, see J. Claude Evans, *Strategies of Deconstruction* (Minneapolis: University of Minnesota Press, 1991).

4. On this point see James M. Edie, "What Is Phenomenology?" in *Edmund Husserl's Phenomenology*, ed. James M. Edie (Bloomington: Indiana University Press, 1987), pp. 1–21.

5. On the other hand, Husserl's arguments against relativism are given sustained and detailed attention in Gail Soffer, *Husserl and the Question of Relativism* (Dordrecht: Kluwer, 1991).

6. Tom Bridges, "Modern Political Theory and the Multivocity of Postmodern Critical Discourses," *Inquiry: Critical Thinking across the Disciplines* 8, no. 1 (September 1991): 3, 7.

7. For example, see Husserl, *Logical Investigations*, especially Sections 32, 35, and 36; *Ideas Pertaining to a Pure Phenomenology and to a Phenomenological Philosophy: First Book*, trans. F. Kersten (The Hague: Martinus Nijhoff, 1982), Sections 20 and 79; *Experience and Judgment*, trans. James S. Churchill and Karl Ameriks (Evanston, IL: Northwestern University Press, 1973), pp. 392–393; "Philosophy as Rigorous Science," in *Phenomenology and the Crisis of Philosophy*, trans. Quentin Lauer (New York: Harper Torchbooks, 1965), pp. 122–147; and *The Crisis of European Sciences and Transcendental Phenomenology*, trans. David Carr (Evanston, IL: Northwestern University Press, 1970), Section 6. This is but a small sample.

8. Indeed, notice that Bridges's manifesto exhibits none of the modesty and restraint that one might expect from one supposedly keenly alerted to the dangers of spurious claims to universality. For how is Bridges's account

to be understood if not as a sweeping and global one, claiming validity everywhere, for everyone, and for all times without exception? Clearly, his claim that all knowing is conditioned by history, gender, ethnicity, and the like is not itself being presented as one which has been conditioned by his own history, gender, ethnicity, and so on, nor is its application intended to be gender-specific or limited to the domain of one ethnicity or another. Nowhere does Bridges suggest that other people, having been conditioned differently, might be able to affirm legitimately that it is indeed possible to obtain objective knowledge of history and nature. Rather, the explanations he offers for the persistence of such affirmations are limited to "misunderstanding," "habit," "resistance to intellectual change," failure to "pay attention" to the arguments of some recent philosophers, and other similar cognitive shortcomings. Can it really be that Bridges wishes to suggest that the conditioning undergone by people of genders, ethnicities, and nationalities other than his own tends to produce in them these epistemic vices, which he, due to his own quite different conditioning, is mercifully spared? But no, I do not really suspect that such arrogance or bigotry underlies Bridges's claims, since the general thrust of his article is very much to celebrate, and to insist upon the legitimacy of, different ethnic, cultural, and gender perspectives. Rather, it seems to me much more plausible to understand him merely as committing a fallacy of self-referential inconsistency.

9. Husserl, *Ideas Pertaining to a Pure Phenomenology*, Section 79, p. 185.

10. This is Barbara Herrnstein Smith's strategy in *Contingencies of Value* (Cambridge, MA: Harvard University Press, 1991). But for a critique of Smith on precisely this point see David L. Roochnik, "Can the Relativist Avoid Refuting Herself?" *Philosophy and Literature* 14, no. 1 (April 1990): 92–98. See also my own discussion in chapter 7, Section XIV, below.

11. Husserl, *Logical Investigations*, Section 35.

12. Another thinker who attempts to answer the charge of self-referential inconsistency by denying that he is making truth claims is Hugh Tomlinson (in "After Truth: Post-Modernism and the Rhetoric of Science," in *Dismantling Truth*. ed. Hilary Lawson and Lisa Appignanesi [London: Weidenfeld and Nicolson, 1989], p. 57), who remarks, very near the end of his attack on truth, that "[t]his has been a story about suspending truth but it is a story which must itself suspend truth. It can make no 'truth claims', pretend to no unique status. . . . The post-modern world is without guarantees, without 'method'. After truth there is no 'dialectic', no high road to powerful and useful theories. All we can do is invent. . . . Post-modernism is paradoxical, against the common opinion, and, in terms of its ever present realist opponent, it is absurd." Note several points: (1) What a strange status these utterances must have! On the author's own terms it simply is not true, despite

what he explicitly says, that his story must itself suspend truth, that the postmodern world is without guarantees, that there is no dialectic or method, etc., etc. (2) Notice the absence of bite. Not only are these utterances not true, but they cannot even claim any "unique status." Why, then, should we accept them? (3) Note the red herring about postmodernism being paradoxical and against common opinion. This has nothing to do with the subject at hand, but appeals to the desire of many postmodernists to view themselves as beleaguered conceptual revolutionaries who are bold and bright enough to handle dazzlingly difficult insights that are beyond the ken of the ordinary person. Look, it is fine and exciting to go beyond common opinion when you've got the goods—when you can explain clearly and compellingly, and in terms of accessible evidence, that what you are saying is true. But when your insights are unclear, of no unique status, and not even true (all on your own terms), why should we go along? In any case, the argument that since one's ideas are paradoxical and revolutionary, the attacks that they face must therefore be attributable to the small-minded philistinism of the defenders of common sense has been adequately refuted many times. For example, Carl Sagan, in a quite different context, writes: "The proponents of . . . borderline beliefs, when criticized, often point to geniuses of the past who were ridiculed. But the fact that some geniuses were laughed at does not imply that all who are laughed at are geniuses." Indeed, while they laughed at Einstein, the Wright brothers, and Picasso, "they also laughed at Bozo the Clown" (*Broca's Brain* [New York: Ballantine, 1980], p. 75).

Moreover, this seemingly tough-minded response to the self-referential inconsistency objection is like a conjurer's trick. The rhetoric all along is "this is how it really is—those who believe in objective truth are simply wrong." Then, at the end, when the objection is raised, Tomlinson and those of like mind say "our position is not offered as objectively true." If you are just looking for the problem to go away, you might stop there and fail to think about the implications of this move. But think about those implications! For example, if the claim is that there is no objective truth, and that truth, instead, must be understood in terms of cultural consensus (and this is just one of the many alternatives to objective truth that has been offered), then this does not mean that there really, objectively, is no objective truth. Rather, it means only that there is a cultural consensus that there is not. (By the way, it would clarify things enormously if these thinkers would explain what, in principle, would count as evidence against their views. Would a demonstration that there is no cultural consensus that truth is a matter of cultural consensus do the trick? If not, then what?) Thus, one is obliged to go back through an essay like Tomlinson's with his disclaimers in mind, if only to see what a high price is paid by those who would shrug off the self-referential inconsistency objection in this fashion.

13. James M. Edie, "Husserl vs. Derrida," *Human Studies* 13 (1990): 116. Moreover, as James L. Marsh points out, in *Critique, Action, and Liberation* (Albany: State University of New York Press, 1995), p. 223, Derrida's "talk of the double gesture [that of simultaneously using and not using a word] just names the problem without resolving it. After all, any contradiction is as a contradiction a double gesture, affirming A and not-A simultaneously and in the same way."

14. G. B. Madison, "Merleau-Ponty's Destruction of Logocentrism," in *Merleau-Ponty Vivant*, ed. M. C. Dillon (Albany: State University of New York Press, 1991), p. 135.

It is not at all clear that it is even possible to dismiss the principle of non-contradiction in the manner recommended by Madison. What would such a dismissal even mean? After all, those who say that the law of non-contradiction should be dismissed must be prepared to swallow the implication that, once we have dismissed it, we will no longer be in a position to see the thesis that "the law of non-contradiction should be dismissed" as ruling out the thesis that "the law of non-contradiction should *not* be dismissed." Thus, the Madisonian postmodernists who would advocate dispensing with the law of non-contradiction must either covertly (and incoherently) rely on that very principle as they make their case or else say things that fail to exclude the legitimacy of everything that they are trying to undermine, such as the thesis that the law of non-contradiction must never be abandoned, come what may! (James L. Marsh, *Critique, Action, and Liberation*, pp. 61–62, makes a similar point.)

But Madison is indeed right to claim that many postmodernists make this move. For example, Malcolm Ashmore, in *The Reflexive Thesis* (Chicago: University of Chicago Press, 1989), p. 88, asserts that the self-referential inconsistency charge will disturb only those who "share a logicians' prejudice against paradox grounded in a magical belief in its evil power." This statement provokes some questions: (1) Why is it merely a prejudice? Is it not possible to give a good, well-reasoned explanation of what is wrong with self-referential inconsistency? (2) Why is an objection to incoherence a "magical" belief? (3) Why is it a belief in its evil power? Incoherent statements merely have the power of guaranteeing that they cannot possibly be true. As such, they are useless, and sometimes are confusing. That seems to me quite different from being evil or having an evil power.

In any case, another thinker who makes a similar move is Hans-Georg Gadamer (in *Truth and Method*, 2d ed., trans. W. Glen-Doepel, revised by Joel Weinsheimer and Donald G. Marshall [New York: Crossroad, 1991], p. 344): "However clearly one demonstrates the inner contradictions of all relativist views, it is as Heidegger has said: all these victorious arguments have something of the attempt to bowl one over. However cogent they may seem, they still miss the main point. In making use of them one is proved right, and yet they do not express any superior insight of value. That the thesis of skepticism or relativism refutes itself to the extent that it claims to be true is an irrefutable argument. But what does it achieve?" In reply, one can only point out that the successful employment of the self-referential inconsistency objection is not intended as a substitute for achieving a "superior insight of value" into the issue at hand, but only to rule out some purported insights as self-contradictory. That, in answer to the question posed at the end of the quoted passage, is what it claims to achieve. Gadamer disagrees, however, contending instead that (and here the quotation continues right where it left off above): "[t]he reflective argument that proves successful here rebounds against the arguer, for it renders the truth value of reflection suspect. It is not the reality of skepticism or of truth-dissolving relativism but the truth claim of all formal argument that is affected." Indeed, when one's position is exposed as illogical, it is always possible to defend oneself by condemning logic.

For more on this topic, see chapter 2, note 4.

15. Patrick Colm Hogan, *The Politics of Interpretation* (New York: Oxford University Press, 1990), p. 35.

Marsh (*Critique, Action, and Liberation*, p. 62) points out another reason, albeit a confused one, why some thinkers reject logic. Quite simply, they recognize the undeniable truth that logic is not everything. Many clear and logically consistent claims are banal, uninteresting, or false. As Marsh puts it, "[l]ogical consistency and clarity are necessary but not sufficient conditions for a sentence to be meaningful, true, and revelatory. Logic is part of science and philosophy, not the whole." Perhaps one reason why some people reject logic, then, is simply that they confuse the necessity claim with the sufficiency claim.

16. See especially *The Crisis of European Sciences and Transcendental Phenomenology*; Husserl, "Philosophy and the Crisis of European Man," in *Phenomenology and the Crisis of Philosophy*; Husserl, *Vorlesungen über Ethik und Wertlehre, 1908–1814.*, ed. Ullrich Melle (Dordrecht: Kluwer, 1988); and Edie, *Edmund Husserl's Phenomenology*, p. 72.

17. Janet Radcliffe Richards makes the point in connection with feminism:

Logic covers a much smaller area than many people think. At root it is about *consistency*. It is not just an arbitrary set of rules which might have been otherwise and which could be done without, like the Marquess of Queensberry's, or like the various rules and conventions which keep women in their traditionally subservient place. It is a set of rules presupposed by the existence of language; not just some particular language, but any language. The most fundamental rule is that of non-contradiction. Essentially, whatever is meant when something is said, . . . if the statement is to mean anything at all it must *exclude* some possibilities. In other words, to say for instance that something is red all over, in the standard use of those words, is to imply at the same time that it is *not* all kinds of other things, such as green or blue or spotted or striped. . . .

Similarly, to say 'if it's red all over, it can't be blue', making an inference from redness to non-blueness, is to rely on the same rule. . . . Being illogical is not having strong feelings, or mixed feelings, or changing your mind, or being unable to express things and prove things, or anything of the sort. It is maintaining that incompatible propositions are both true. . . . [S]ince the purpose of language is to convey information, to use language at all is to rely on logic.

Feminists therefore cannot disregard logic. . . . A feminist who thinks there is nothing wrong with inconsistency is in no position to complain if men expect women to carry heavy loads when those loads consist of children or shopping or washing, but say that they can't lift (the same) heavy loads when it is convenient to have rules excluding women from well-paid work. What is happening is that these men have . . . implied that [women] both can and cannot lift loads of a certain weight. They invent the conflicting facts as they go along, to suit their convenience. Of course feminists complain, and they complain on grounds of logic (*The Sceptical Feminist* [Boston: Routledge & Kegan Paul, 1980], pp. 20–22).

18. Indeed, if it were not it would, contrary to fact, be impossible to rely on, reason with, or even talk with postmodernists. For consider, if someone says, "My position is x, but this does not commit me to the view that it is not, not x—indeed, it may well be that, at the same time and in the same respects, it is the case that there is no position that I disclaim more vehemently or regard as more clearly and thoroughly wrong than x," you are not going to get very far in trying to reason with this person. If when this person says, "I will pick you up at the train station at six," it must be construed as not implying that he or she will pick you up at the train station at six, this is not the person you want to rely on to pick you up. This is also probably not the person you want for a friend.

19. See, for example, Jean-Paul Sartre, *Truth and Existence*, trans. Adrian van den Hoven (Chicago: University of Chicago Press, 1992).

20. The idea that we should theorize according to our experiencing seems to me quite faithful to the radically experientialist thrust of Husserl's phenomenology.

21. I am grateful to my colleague David Turpin for the information about what transpired at this antiwar meeting.

22. I shall have much more to say about the self-referential inconsistency objection in the next chapter, which is devoted to it.

23. See the "Prolegomena" to the *Logical Investigations*.

24. Here I am giving a variation on an example given in Roderick M. Chisholm, *Theory of Knowledge* (Englewood Cliffs, NJ: Prentice-Hall, 1966), p. 79.

25. And, as Edie points out, "[o]ur greater novelists and other thinkers, like Dostoevsky, Kierkegaard and Nietzsche, have always known that human beings not only can, but almost always do, hold and act on contradictory impulses and beliefs" ("On Confronting Species-Specific Skepticism as We Near the End of the Twentieth Century," *Man and World* 25 [1992]: 326).

26. As Gottlob Frege puts it, "It would be strange if the most exact of all the sciences had to seek support from psychology, which is still feeling its way none too surely" (*The Foundations of Arithmetic* [Oxford: Basil Blackwell, 1950], p. 38).

27. Here are some examples. Any object that has size must also have shape. If it is true that heavy rain last night would definitely have made the grass wet right now, and that the grass is not wet right now, it follows that it did not rain heavily last night. The pitch level at which a spoken utterance is delivered is often irrelevant to its meaning. Any number divided by itself equals one. It is easier for most human beings to see during the daytime than at night. Two people working cooperatively with one another usually can lift more weight than either of them can alone. No human being can run as fast as a billion miles per second. All human beings die. Some birds can fly. If your head, dear reader, is cut off in the year 2005, you will be dead by 2007. Giraffes are taller than ants. Most people who live to be ten years old are bigger on their tenth birthday than they were at birth. Collecting string for its own sake is not the very best way that one can spend one's life. Health is intrinsically better than sickness. Cruelty, ignorance, and cowardice are bad things. Friendship is better than war. Willie Mays was a good baseball player. It is not true that in order for a musical composition to be good it is both necessary and sufficient that it begin with an A-minor chord. There are billions of others. Moreover, perhaps it is arrogance on my part, but it seems to me that I can see, from my standpoint as a white, male American, who was born in the twentieth century (and so on for any other applicable contingencies you might care to name), that such matters of knowledge as I have just listed do not depend upon contingencies of this sort. Rather I submit that these truths are fully accessible to me, but also and equally to others who radically differ from me in terms of the factors of conditioning cited by Bridges.

28. Perhaps the reason why this fallacy is so common is that thinkers, once they notice the undeniable fact that individual acts of thinking are in

some sense historically conditioned, tend to confuse these acts of thinking with their contents—the objects of thought. From the fact that the former (e.g., individual *acts* of judging that 2 + 2 = 4) are particular and unrepeatable, it does not follow that the latter (e.g., 2 + 2 = 4) are. Edie explains this clearly in several places. See, for example, "On Confronting Species-Specific Skepticism," p. 317, and p. 336, note 31.

29. See especially "Part One" of *Ideas Pertaining to a Pure Phenomenology.*

30. Erazim Kohák, *Idea and Experience* (Chicago: University of Chicago Press, 1978), p. 16.

31. On the other hand, it must be conceded that we do, of course, err in our judgments of essential truth, sometimes in particular confusing the necessarily true with the merely culturally familiar. But this consideration is not sufficient to sustain Bridges's conclusions.

32. Thus, Bridges's approach appears to deserve such epithets as "reductionistic," "unspecific," "abstract," "not complex," "unsophisticated," "legislative," "insensitive to contingency," etc.—in short, all of the terms of abuse that postmodernists typically hurl at the heirs of the Enlightenment. For, after all, is not the position that the particularities of our conditioning sometimes do (and then to varying degrees) and sometimes do not (depending upon the specific nature of the contingency and of the truth in question) bar us from arriving at objective truth—a more complex, concrete, context-sensitive, etc., position than is the one that Bridges and so many other postmodernists endorse?

Of course, this does not show it to be closer to the truth; some sweeping, exceptionless, context-insensitive statements capture the truth perfectly, so that the introduction of nuances and qualifications could only move us into the direction of error. Thus, to revive an earlier example, I say that if A is taller than B, and B is taller than C, then it follows that A is taller than C, no matter what A and C are, no matter who you are, no matter what year it is, no matter what the weather is, etc. Moreover, saxophones, I maintain, are always, everywhere, and without exception musical instruments, ill-suited for use as dental floss. Thus, contrary to the stance of many postmodernists, subtlety, context-sensitivity, and sophistication (as they understand it) are not always markers of a superior intellectual position. Moreover, as I have tried to show here in the case of Bridges, and will have occasion to argue in connection with other thinkers, these self-proclaimed virtues are rarely achieved by the very postmodernists who advocate them. Indeed, the unsubtle insistence upon subtlety, the exceptionless demand for the acknowledgment of exceptions, the context-insensitive call for context-sensitivity, and so forth are both the hallmark and the rhetorical self-referential inconsistency of postmodernism. And the claim that everything is contextual and contingent is either itself merely contextual and contingent, or else it is a self-contradicting universalism.

33. In this way we can attempt to avoid the reductionistic tendencies of both dogmatism and skepticism, a task which, it is somewhat embarrassing to admit at this late date in history, we have yet to complete.

34. Among the points needing to be considered are these, as articulated by Jean Grimshaw: "The experience of gender, of being a man or a woman, inflects much if not all of people's lives. . . . But even if one is always a man or a woman, one is never *just* a man or a woman. One is young or old, sick or healthy, married or unmarried, a parent or not a parent, employed or unemployed, middle class or working class, rich or poor, black or white, and so forth. . . . Experience does not come neatly in segments, such that it is always possible to abstract what in one's experience is due to 'being a woman'" (*Philosophy and Feminist Thinking* [Minneapolis: University of Minnesota Press, 1986], pp. 84–85).

35. In chapter 8 I will briefly take up the question of whether or not the methods of science are especially well-suited, at least within their proper domain, to help us to overcome whatever obstacles the particularities of our conditioning might pose for us and enable us to know objective truths about the velocity of light, the behaviors of gases, the movements of the planets, the evolution of species, and the like. Bridges does not specifically address this question, though perhaps his reference to Kuhn is meant to imply that anyone "paying attention" would at this point in history reject such a suggestion as wildly implausible.

Chapter 2

SELF-REFERENTIAL INCONSISTENCY

As we observed in the last chapter, the first obstacle facing any ambitious form of relativism, subjectivism, or skepticism is the venerable objection that such theories cannot even get off the ground, let alone succeed, because they are "reflexively" self-undermining.[1] The point of this objection is that when these doctrines are subjected to the test of self-application, they appear to nullify themselves.

I. EIGHT FORMULATIONS

This point can be explained in several ways, eight of which I will pursue here in connection with one particular (albeit very broad) kind of relativism. My chosen example is the doctrine holding that all "truth" is "socially constructed."

A. Self-Referential Inconsistency

The first point to be made about this form of relativism is that it appears to be self-referentially inconsistent. In other words, when it is judged, as seems only reasonable and fair, in the light of its own explicitly stated content, it seems to contradict itself. For if all truth is indeed to be regarded as socially constructed, rather than as reflecting accurately how things "really are," then surely this claim itself—that is, the theory of social constructionism—must also be viewed merely as a social construct and precisely not as an accurate reflection of how things really are. Thus, insofar as social constructionism is itself intended as something other and more than just one more social construction—more specifically, insofar as it is advanced as a claim about what "truth" is really like, and as a debunking of rival accounts as mistaken or wrong—it simply contradicts itself.

Of course, defenders of social constructionism might not intend their theory to be construed in such a way as to result in its ensnarement in this self-referential paradox, but in that case it is unclear what the theory's meaning and point could possibly be. For in claiming that all knowledge is socially constructed, these theorists appear to be saying something like the following: "Look, for more than two thousand years philosophers have been searching for objective truths, but we can now see that they were making a mistake in doing so, for we have discovered that there are no such truths to be found. All truth is, in fact, socially constructed. So anyone, or for that matter, any culture or group, holding that there are genuinely objective, transcultural, transhistorical, unconstructed truths (let alone that such truths are, or can be made, accessible to finite and fallible human beings) is simply mistaken." Thus, the social constructionists seem to be uttering such absurdities as: "It is objectively true that there are no objective truths"; and "It is really true, and not merely a social construction, that all truths are socially constructed."

B. Incoherence

To put the point another way, social constructionism seems to be an incoherent doctrine: it asserts what it denies and denies what it asserts and thus fails to communicate any clear meaning at all.

To see this, we need only ask whether the statement that "all truth is socially constructed" asserts, or rather denies, that all truth is socially constructed.

Obviously, in one sense, if "all truth is socially constructed" is to be understood as an assertion, then it asserts that all truth is socially constructed, since any assertion asserts itself.

But on the other hand, since the assertion appears to be *about* the nature of truth, and more specifically to be an account that is hostile to claims of objectivity, universality, and cultural independence with regard to truth, it seems to undermine any assertion about what truth is *really* like, let alone any such statement about what *all* truth is like. Thus, it seems to deny such claims as, for example, that all truth is socially constructed. For if "all truth is socially constructed" is a truth claim, then it implies, once again, that it is itself merely a social construction, which can achieve, at best, a validity relative to some specific social group, and which therefore leaves untouched all truth residing outside of this group's purview. Accordingly, the statement that "all truth is socially constructed" apparently denies that *all* truth is socially constructed even as it simultaneously asserts it, and thus the statement fails to communicate any coherent meaning at all.

C. Performative Contradiction

Even if, for the sake of argument, we were to waive the objection that social constructionism is straightforwardly incoherent, we would still have to consider whether or not such a doctrine can be *articulated* without contradiction. Let us consider an analogy. There is nothing incoherent or self-contradictory about the idea of a person who never makes remarks about herself. But there is something self-contradictory about the *statement* "You know, the remarkable thing about me is that I never make remarks about myself." For then the *act*, or, if you prefer, the *performance*, of making this statement contradicts the content of the statement itself. Similarly, while there might be nothing self-contradictory about the *belief* that there is no such thing as writing, or that it is impossible to say the word "breakfast," or that I am the only person in the universe (though of course all of these beliefs would be mistaken), the act of *writing* that there is no such thing as writing is self-contradictory,[2] as are the acts of *saying* that you cannot say "breakfast,"[3] of trying to prove to other people the truth of solipsism, and of telling other people never to do what they are told.

Social constructionists seem to commit just such a performative contradiction in asserting their doctrine, and even more so in their confident reliance on it in their polemics with those who would defend objectivity. For the clear implication of these performances by the social constructionists is that they regard one position to be objectively true, namely, their theory that there are no such truths; that they consider it to be inconsistent with the way things really are to assert that it is possible to know the way things really are; and that they believe that there is one position, that of social constructionism, which achieves a transcultural validity, and a corresponding power to advance legitimate criticisms against all perspectives out of harmony with its own, that no mere construction could ever hope to rival. In short, social constructionists commit a performative contradiction whenever they treat an opposing position not simply as another construction, which might for all they know attain a certain validity relative to its own social domain (which is, of course, all that social constructionists can consistently claim for their own theory), but as really *wrong*, truly *incorrect*, and/or simply inconsistent with the relevant facts of life.[4]

D. The Epistemologist's Fallacy

Social constructionists commit a similar reflexive fallacy when they claim to know things which, according to the position on knowledge that they themselves are endorsing, neither they nor anyone else can possibly know. Errol E. Harris calls this reflexive fallacy, that of providing a self-referentially inconsistent explanation of how knowledge is obtained, "the epistemologist's fallacy." He provides three formulations: "This is the fallacy of giving an account of knowledge which could be given only by someone whose own knowledge was an exception to the theory proposed"; "The epistemologist's fallacy is that of propounding a theory of knowledge which, if generally true so that it included the theorist's own knowledge, is one which he could not possibly know or discover"; and "[I]t is the fallacy of presupposing that one has access to facts the possibility of which one's theory of knowledge excludes." Harris judges that this fallacy "is frequently committed by epistemologists and proves fatal to the majority of theories of knowledge."[5]

As an example of a theory which commits this fallacy, and which is neither relativist, subjectivist, nor globally skeptical in nature, consider an extreme version of empiricism, one holding that it is impossible to derive genuine knowledge from anything but one legitimate source—that of direct sensory experience. The reflexive problem for such a theory becomes apparent, of course, as soon as one asks how anyone could possibly know the truth of this empiricist thesis about knowledge, since the thesis that all knowledge is (in this sense) empirical is not itself (in the same sense) empirical. Thus we arrive at the paradoxical conclusion that if we can indeed know that this form of empiricism is true, then in fact it must be false.

To be sure, the objection can be overcome by giving up the claim to know the truth of the empiricist thesis and by reconstruing it as a mere proposal (e.g., "let's start thinking of knowledge exclusively as that which arises from direct sensory experience"), but this removes much of the force of empiricist criticisms of non-empirical knowledge claims. After all, a proposal can always be declined; and, more importantly, this reconstrual of empiricism would entail that empiricists can no longer assert that non-empiricists are just wrong (mistaken, in error, not in accordance with the way things are) in their views on the nature of knowledge.

Similarly, social constructionists could escape the charge of having committed the epistemologist's fallacy by admitting that they do not *know* that all "truth" is socially constructed, but then they would have to withdraw their claim that their opponents are simply mistaken in failing to face up to the relevant "facts," specifically those concerning the (allegedly) irreducibly contingent and historically and culturally situated nature of the standpoint from which we think.

E. The "Bold but Incoherent"/"Coherent but Weak" Dilemma

These considerations strongly suggest that social constructionism is trapped within the following dilemma: either it is to be understood as boldly making an objective truth claim, in which case it is self-undermining and incoherent (not to mention arbitrary, for if somehow it is possible for the "truth" of social constructionism to elude its own strictures and establish itself as an exception to its own rule that all truths are merely relative to a particular culture, then it is unclear why there cannot be other exceptions), or else it is to be construed merely as a social construction (presumably just one among many) expressing a localized cultural consensus, in which case it regains its coherence but only at the cost of losing much of its interest and critical force (in part because it leaves the way fully clear for others operating from different cultural, personal, or paradigmatic standpoints validly to assert everything that it is itself attempting so strenuously to deny).

F. Evidence and Reasoning

The same dilemma applies, moreover, when we shift our attention away from the grand *conclusions* drawn by social constructionists and instead focus on the *evidence* and *reasoning* to which they appeal in support of these conclusions.

To see this, let us briefly examine the premises underlying the social constructionist position. Typically, one of these will be a descriptive claim, perhaps based upon the findings of cultural anthropologists, that, as a straightforward matter of fact, what is believed to be true varies significantly from culture to culture; and another will be some version of the assertion that beliefs are always essentially connected to the cultures which give rise to them and to the cultural norms with reference to which they derive their intelligibility (and to which they make implicit reference).

But the question that immediately suggests itself is this: How can social constructionists, while consistently maintaining their own doctrine, claim to know the truth of these premises? For such a claim seems to imply that at least one cultural group (e.g., social constructionists and/or the anthropologists on which they rely) is sufficiently competent not only to understand and to describe accurately the beliefs held by people of another culture, but also to assert that these beliefs are different from, indeed often mutually incompatible with, those held by people in still other cultures. Even more impressively, this cultural group claims to be able to understand the beliefs of people in other cultures so well as to be able to understand the specific ways in which those beliefs are embedded in, and inextricably connected with, other practices and norms peculiar to the culture being investigated. Clearly, this cultural group claims to be able to know a great deal about the beliefs of people in other cultures!

But from what standpoint can this group of investigators claim to know so much? Surely it cannot be from some sort of universal standpoint, not essentially connected to and limited to the framework of norms and practices peculiar to the investigators' own culture, for it is precisely this group's point that no such standpoint is available. Nor can the standpoint be that of the culture under investigation, for, once again, the investigators' chief claim is that we can never escape our own cultural background, and such escape would seem to be a necessary prerequisite to our taking up as our own the standpoint of some other culture. Thus, if social constructionists are claiming in their premises, as seemingly they must if they are to get their argument off the ground, that they are able to understand what the beliefs and belief-frameworks of other cultures are really like (either in some universal or transcultural sense, or at least in the sense of faithfully capturing the self-understanding of these other cultures themselves), then in doing so they simply contradict the conclusion of their argument.

To avoid this contradiction, social constructionists would have to intend their claims about the content and cultural framework dependence of the beliefs of other cultures neither as asserting the real truth (in some culture-transcending sense) about these beliefs nor as capturing the way in which they are understood from within the cultures in question, but rather as reflecting how they are seen from within the cultural framework of the investigators themselves. But on this construal of the sociological relativist's argument, it must be seen as telling us not so much about the nature of truth, beliefs, cultures, and their interrelationships as such, as about the culture of the group issuing claims about these matters.

Thus, it is in their assertion of evidence, and in their reasoning about it, every bit as much as in their statement of conclusions, that social constructionists convict themselves either of impotence or of incoherence: either they are powerless to criticize others as mistaken (in part because they cannot achieve a standpoint from which to do so soundly), or else they simply contradict themselves.

G. The Inquirers and the Inquired-About

Thus, social constructionism's emphasis on the importance of cultural groups leads to its downfall. For social constructionism must, after all, either make, on behalf of that cultural group which seeks to understand others (anthropologists and other social scientists, for example), an arbitrary and incoherent exception to its own strictures concerning the epistemic limitations of all cultural groups, or else admit that its findings can only aspire to a culturally relative validity.

But it should also be pointed out that social constructionism can be seen to trap itself within precisely this same dilemma even when we turn our attention away from that cultural group which does the inquiring and focus it instead on those culture groups about which they inquire. For if all truth is socially constructed, and if this is established largely by the (alleged) fact that people in cultural groups other than our own tend to look at the world differently than we do, then what is to be done with the possibility that some cultural groups might (as, indeed, I believe most of them obviously do) understand "truth" in a plainly non-relativist, non-constructionist sense? Once again, the result appears to be a dilemma. When faced with such an occurrence, social constructionists would appear either to have to make an arbitrary and incoherent exception to their doctrine (e.g., "truth is always a social construction, so whenever any group constructs as truth the claim that truth itself is not a construction, we will disallow, as mistaken, *that* construction"), or else to admit that the thesis "all truth is socially constructed" is true only for those groups which construct it as such, and not for those many which do not.

H. The Incoherence/Infinite Regress Dilemma

In order to say anything intelligible, the last word, as Thomas Nagel puts it, must be an attempted statement of objective truth.[6] Otherwise, the result is an infinite regress. If "Beethoven is great" means "My culture approves of Beethoven," then either this last statement is an attempted objective truth, or else we have "My culture approves of the idea that my culture approves of Beethoven." Then either *that* is objective, or else we get "My culture approves of the idea that my culture approves of the idea that my culture approves of Beethoven," and so on, ad infinitum and ad nauseum. (Notice, incidentally, that my culture's judgments about what it approves of or believes can, if construed as objective claims, in principle be false. We might believe one thing but think that we believe another.)

The same logic applies on the meta-level. "What is true is determined by cultural consensus" is either intended to be objectively true, or else it means, "It is the consensus of my culture that truth is determined by cultural consensus." This, in turn, is either an attempted statement of objective truth (in which case it is false, in addition to being self-referentially incoherent, the latter disability being one plaguing all of these when construed as covert attempts to state objective truths), or else it means that "it is the consensus of my culture that it is the consensus of my culture that truth is determined by cultural consensus."

II. EXAMPLES

Let us now turn to a consideration of a few varieties of relativism, subjectivism, and skepticism so as to bring our discussion of reflexive fallacies to a higher degree of detail and refinement.

A. *Postmodernism*

I will begin with a passage from Michael Bérubé, in which he clearly and confidently summarizes and defends the "postmodern" rejection of objective knowledge and truth: "[F]ifty years of anti-positivism from people as diverse as Ludwig Wittgenstein, Thomas Kuhn, and Michel Foucault have led the cultural left [which I take Bérubé to be defending here] to argue that objects of knowledge are locally and historically specific, and that they become available for human understanding only within certain 'language games', 'paradigms', and 'discursive formations' (not that these are three names for the same thing, either)."[7]

Any careful attempt to understand Bérubé's position will reveal, however, that it is caught within something like the following dilemma. Either there are indeed no objects of knowledge which transcend local and historical specificity, and which escape the constraints of certain language games, paradigms, or discursive formations, or else this is not the case and there are some (or at least one) such "transcending and escaping" objects of knowledge. But if the former alternative is correct, then neither Bérubé nor anyone else is in a position to *know* it to be correct, since in that case we would not ever be able to get our hands on anything but a locally and historically specific and paradigm (or what have you)-relative "human knowledge" as an object of knowledge. We would be utterly closed off from observing "human knowledge" as such, understood in a non-specific, non-relativist sense (there being no such thing, on this view); nor would we be able to scrutinize "human knowledge" as it looks from some other locally and historically specific standpoint, or from within some paradigm other than our own. The result of affirming this horn of the dilemma is therefore that all of the critical force is subtly drained from the bold pronouncement that all "objects of knowledge are locally and historically specific." Critics like Bérubé are seen no longer to be in a position to say that those who affirm objective, universal truths are unsophisticated dupes who are *really wrong*, unless it is clearly understood that this claim can aspire only to a validity relative to a specific situation and paradigm. But since the "dupes" may, on this reading, simply be coming at the issue from within an entirely different situation and paradigm than that of their critics, and one which these critics may not even be able to *see*, let alone validly criticize, the manifesto seems to lose much of its bite.

To avoid these consequences, some might like to seize the other horn of the dilemma and insist that there is indeed one object of knowledge which transcends the relativities of geography, history, paradigm, and the like, and that is "human knowledge" itself as an object of knowledge. This move perhaps rescues Bérubé's position from the difficulties or limitations just noted, but only at the cost of incoherence. For the passage does, after all, explicitly and categorically state that "objects of knowledge are locally and historically specific" and "available for human understanding only within certain language-games, paradigms, and discursive formations." Thus, on this interpretation, the position starkly contradicts itself.

Moreover, it might be pointed out in passing that even if we were to waive this objection, the position would, on this reading, still seem to be vulnerable to charges of arbitrariness. For if geography, history, and paradigms are as important as Bérubé claims they are, then how does "human knowledge" itself as an object of knowledge escape their pervasive influence? What is so special about *this* object of knowledge? And if *it* can be an exception, why cannot there be others? No answers are forthcoming here, or, to my knowledge, elsewhere.

Similar difficulties plague Chantal Mouffe's assertion that "[i]t is always possible to distinguish between the just and the unjust, the legitimate and the illegitimate, but this can only be done from within a given tradition, with the help of standards that this tradition provides; in fact, there is no point of view external to all tradition from which one can offer a universal judgment."[8] But if "in fact, there is no point of view external to all tradition from which one can offer a universal judgment," then on what grounds, and from what standpoint, can Mouffe offer *this* straightforwardly universal judgment? And if distinctions between the legitimate and the illegitimate can be made "only from within a given tradition," then who can fail to notice that the *judgment* that it is illegitimate to claim to offer a universal judgment transcending any particular tradition must *itself* be understood as issuing from within a particular tradition, which *it* cannot transcend?

Next let us consider the position held in common by various "feminist standpoint theories," as Mary E. Hawkesworth terms them. This position holds, according to Hawkesworth's summary, that "knowledge is always mediated by a host of factors related to an individual's particular position in a determinate sociopolitical formation at a specific point in history. Class, race, and gender necessarily structure the individual's understanding of reality and hence inform all knowledge claims."[9] But once again, if the claim that "[c]lass, race, and gender necessarily structure the individual's understanding of reality and hence inform all knowledge claims" is *itself* a knowledge claim, then surely it too must be understood as issuing from an understanding that has been structured by class, race, and gender. This suggests that, for all we know, someone who has been structured differently might have a quite different understanding of this matter, perhaps even one in which the possibility of advancing legitimate knowledge claims which transcend the boundaries of class, race, and gender would be affirmed. For notice that if we suspect this to be in fact impossible, we would have no way of knowing, on the position under consideration, whether our suspicion accurately reflects how things really are (if such a concept is even intelligible on this view), or whether it is more to be explained as the result of the structuring of our understanding of reality by class, race, and gender. The reference to "an individual's particular position in a determinate sociopolitical formation at a specific point in history" suggests all the more strongly that if things were simply to change a bit—if we were to bring about some sort of sociopolitical revolution, or perhaps just wait patiently for the *Zeitgeist* to undergo some sort of transformation—then, for all we know, we might be able to understand ourselves as perfectly competent to make valid judgments that are as universal and objective as all get-out.

Finally, let us examine one more passage exhibiting many of these same patterns: "[T]he consensus of most of the dominant theories is that all thought does, indeed, develop from particular standpoints, perspectives, interests. . . . As the most powerful modern philosophies and theories have been demonstrating, claims of disinterest, objectivity, and universality are not to be trusted and themselves tend to reflect local historical conditions."[10]

Once again, the position here attributed to "most of the dominant theories" and to "the most powerful modern philosophies and theories" entails that it is *not* objectively or universally true that "all thought develops from particular standpoints, perspectives, and interests"; nor that it is objectively or universally true that "claims of disinterest, objectivity, and universality are not to be trusted and themselves tend to reflect local historical conditions." Rather, the implication of these dominant and powerful theories is that all particularist, perspectivist, and anti-objectivist conclusions and pronouncements must *themselves* be understood as developing from particular standpoints, perspectives, and interests (what might these be?), and as reflecting local historical conditions.

B. *Unqualified Skepticism*

Extreme or unqualified skepticism is, in a very direct way, self-referentially inconsistent. For notice that anyone denying that knowledge is possible would have to concede, in order to render such a denial coherent and self-consistent, that it is itself unknowable, just as anyone claiming that there is no truth would have to admit that the thesis that there is no truth is itself not true.

Skepticism is rarely defended in such stark terms today. Still, as we have seen, it is difficult to know what to make of the performances of some contemporary relativists, especially in their polemics with defenders of objectivity, if they are not to be construed as implicitly insisting that "we now *know* that nothing is really known" or that "it is simply *true* that there is no such thing as truth—at least not for mere human beings." In any case, even if this interpretation is judged unfair, it is well worth considering, in connection with any of the subtler and more refined versions of skepticism one might encounter, whether or not they succeed in overcoming the straightforwardly self-referential problems which sink the less cautious versions.

Finally, note that skeptical positions, unless they are simply baldly asserted (in which case one need not take them seriously), are usually supported by arguments of some kind. But this raises obvious reflexivity problems with regard to the status of the premises of the arguments. For if the conclusion is that nothing is known, or that nothing is true, then neither can the premises supporting such a conclusion be known or true. Thus, how can the argument even get started, let alone establish its skeptical conclusion? The central fallacy here is the attempt to claim knowledge of some sort (e.g., we should be tolerant, or all cultures are equal, or we are prisoners of language, or what have you) from the premise that no knowledge of that sort is possible.

C. Subjectivism (Personal Relativism)

Subjectivism, the doctrine that "knowledge" is relative not to cultures but to individuals, faces similar self-referential problems. For if, to take a crude version of the theory, all "knowledge" is said to be reducible to personal opinion, then who can fail to see that the truth of this subjectivist principle must itself be conceded to be reducible to personal opinion?

And what is to be said to the individual whose personal opinion is that subjectivism is false? Since truth is established by personal opinion, according to this form of subjectivism, the truth of such subjectivism would paradoxically result, in this case, in its falsity. Thus, its incoherence is clearly manifested.

While Brian Vickers's position is considerably more sophisticated than the one just described, it clearly faces similar difficulties. Vickers writes:

> Our whole act of experiencing reality is subjective, . . . and anyone in search of objective truths in a world after Nietzsche, Husserl, and Popper, say, is doomed to a dusty answer. . . . [W]e have now reached a stage in which relativism can be defended—not cynicism, not amorality, not indifference, but an honest admission that, in phenomenological terms, the acts of perceiving the world, interpreting its signs, evaluating its actions, are all irremediably personal.[11]

But this means, of course, that none of Vickers's own claims in this passage can qualify as "objective truths." Rather, they must be seen as issuing from his own "irremediably personal" perceptions, interpretations, and evaluations.[12]

D. *Historicist Relativism*

Historicist relativism is the position holding that all "truth" is historically conditioned and historically relative, there being no possibility of an objective, universal, or eternal truth which would transcend all such contingencies. Now, as we have seen, this position cannot itself coherently be asserted as an objective truth which escapes historical contingency, but let us waive that objection for a moment so as instead to examine the reasons that might be put forth in its support. One such reason is simply that all previous attempts to formulate ahistorical truths have (allegedly) failed, as all are revealed upon careful analysis to bear distinct traits which not only mark them as products of their own particular time, but also reveal their inability to apply validly to temporal periods differing significantly from their own in relevant respects.

What are we to say of this premise? First of all, it is far from clear that it is true. In what sense, for example, is the truth that "if A is taller than B, and B is taller than C, A must therefore be taller C" limited in its validity to some specific historical period? Second, note that if the conclusion that no truth can ever legitimately aspire to an ahistorical validity is to be derived solely from the premise that no past truth has ever succeeded in transcending history, the argument, even should we grant the truth of its premise, is an inductive one and therefore fails to show that the formulation of a truth which would transcend historical relativity is impossible or absurd. Third, the strength of the induction might well be questioned (again, even if we assume that its premise is true), given a future of unlimited length and the relative youth of science and philosophy.

But let us waive these objections, in order to focus instead on the self-referential problems plaguing the use of this premise in an argument purporting to establish the truth of historicism. For notice that, from a historicist perspective, the premise that no "truth" has ever succeeded in achieving transhistorical validity must itself be understood as failing to achieve such validity and as instead merely reflecting the peculiarities of our own age. Those attracted to the idea of eternal truths may thus be comforted by the thought that a new age might well be coming in which not only will several such (hitherto undreamt of) truths be discovered, but also many more from past eras, now stigmatized as achieving only a historically relative validity, will come to be recognized as such! To deny this possibility, and to insist that it is absolutely true, rather than true relatively to our own historical period, that no absolute truths have ever been discovered, is starkly to contradict not only the historicist conclusion (that there never *can be* any such truths), but also the premise supposedly used to establish it (that there never *have been* any such truths). So if this is indeed what historicists are insisting, then they are guilty of falling into the relativist vice of claiming to do precisely what they are simultaneously exerting so much energy in maintaining cannot be done.[13]

Finally, it would appear that the *logic* of the historicist argument must suffer the same fate as that confronting its premise and conclusion. For the reasoning here used—that the failure of all previous attempts to formulate transhistorical truths establishes (or at least strongly suggests) the impossibility of any such successful formulation[14]—is itself asserted either as valid in a transhistorical sense or else as valid only in a historically relative sense. If the former, the argument is self-referentially inconsistent; if the latter, its critical force is weak.

E. Cultural-Belief Relativism

Nor does the relativist argument fare any better when it is cast in an anthropological or sociological form, in which truth is said to be reducible to cultural consensus and thus to vary from one society to another, than it does in its historicist version, in which the vicissitudes of time are stressed. For, once again, either the sociological relativist's claim is asserted as a universal truth, holding equally for all cultures whatsoever, in which case the claim is incoherent and self-undermining, or it is to be understood as holding true only within the relativist's own culture, in which case it fails as an instrument of criticism of claims of absolute or universal truth, when such claims are issued from within cultures other than that of the relativist.[15]

Pursuing this latter alternative, moreover, reveals this oddity:

While the champions of cultural-belief relativism defend it, in part, on the grounds that it is allegedly a doctrine which is uniquely respectful of the convictions held by people from cultures other than our own (since it holds, after all, that we should regard such convictions as valid or true, even if only relatively to the cultural domain in which they are affirmed), a little analysis reveals it to be, at a deeper or more abstract philosophical level, profoundly disrespectful of the beliefs of those culturally at a distance from ourselves. The reason is quite simple. Most such persons reject relativist interpretations of knowledge and of truth and conceive of their own strongest convictions not as true relative to their own culture, but as true simpliciter. Thus, the assertion of cultural-belief relativism, with its consequent denial of such objective or transcultural validity to the deepest beliefs of our cultural "others," does considerable violence to their self-understanding and to their assessment of the status of their understanding of the world.

But let us look a bit closer. If truth is to be established by cultural belief, and to achieve only a validity relative to the specific culture in which such belief is affirmed, the fairly precise determination of what is to count as a "culture" would appear to take on a good deal of importance. To show this, we need only ask ourselves what is the definition of the culture relative to which cultural-belief relativism gives a sound account of the nature of truth. (Of course, cultural-belief relativists could insist that their theory holds universally and is not established by cultural belief, but then they would stand convicted of arbitrariness and incoherence). Is this "culture" to be understood as that of cultural anthropologists and other social scientists? Or, given that many scholars in these fields reject all forms of sociological relativism, should it be construed more narrowly as the culture of that subset of social scientists which accepts such relativism? Or should it be interpreted more broadly as including also all those persons who accept the relativistic doctrines of (some) social scientists, whether they themselves are social scientists or not? Or, finally, should it be understood as encompassing, in very broad terms, the culture which has given rise to these social sciences (e.g., "the West," or, perhaps, "the post-Enlightenment West")? While this problem of cultural group identification is a serious one for cultural-belief relativism, I will not here consider it further, since it is not directly relevant to the objections, based upon considerations of self-referential inconsistency, that I am presently pressing.

F. The Sociology of Science

What I mean by the "sociology of science" is the understanding of science according to which widespread agreement by scientists on the truth of a particular scientific theory is understood as reflecting, not the likely "real truth" of the theory, as revealed to the scientists' (nearly) uniformly rational assessment of the evidence concerning it, but rather the presence of sociological factors which happen at a given historical moment to push most scientists in the same direction in motivating or influencing them in the formation of their scientific beliefs. Thus, on this view, what moves scientists to accept one theory rather than another is not evidence, not "epistemic" factors of any sort, but rather, say, class interests, political considerations, or the desire for personal prestige and professional advancement.[16] If, for example, most scientists consider animal species to have arisen over time through evolutionary processes, rather than instantaneously by special creation, this, we are told, tells us less about the origin of species or about evolution (the *objects* of the scientists' beliefs) than it does about the political, economic, and professional factors which allegedly determine the beliefs of the scientists (the *subjects* who hold convictions about evolution and the origin of species).

The fatal weakness of this approach is, of course, that on its own terms it must be taken as reflecting not the real truth about the nature and causes of scientific belief, but rather the presence of non-epistemic factors which motivate sociologists of science to advance their claims about scientific belief. Thus, we would have to suppose that the explanation of the rejection, by the sociologists of science, of scientific claims to objectivity must be explained not by the real falsity of those claims, or by an objective deficiency of the evidence which the scientists adduce in their support, but rather by the class interests, political considerations, professional ambitions, and the like, of the sociologists of science. Of course, sociologists of science could escape this criticism by claiming objectivity for their studies of scientific belief-formation,[17] but then they would have to explain on what basis they can legitimately grant such an achievement to themselves in their studies of scientists, while denying it to scientists in their studies of nature.[18]

III. REBUTTALS

In the first section of the previous chapter I discussed three common replies to the charge of self-referential inconsistency. I would like to conclude this chapter by considering two additional, and rather more idiosyncratic, rebuttals: those of Marilyn Friedman and Stanley Fish.

A. Friedman

Friedman offers this response to the self-referential inconsistency objection:

> This criticism of skepticism, however, is very limited. If successful, it would undermine only an extreme skepticism that denies that *any* human assertions are true, including those of the skeptic herself. The refutation of extreme skepticism, however, does not establish that there is an objective, impartial truth to be discerned about any and every specific subject matter. That is, the failure of extreme skepticism would not establish that the truth-claims of, say, political or moral theorists were objectively or universally true. Philosophers are very familiar with qualified forms of skepticism; logical positivists, for example, reject the notions of metaphysical and moral truth while still championing scientific truth. A partial and limited skepticism that challenged a particular realm of study . . . might succeed where extreme skepticism fails. The important point is that such limited skepticisms would not have to be formulated in self-contradictory or otherwise self-defeating terms.[19]

I have two comments to offer by way of reply. First, it is not true that the only kind of skepticism that is self-contradictory is "an extreme skepticism that denies that *any* human assertions are true." Rather, what makes a skepticism self-refuting is entirely captured by the last clause in Friedman's formulation: the denial that the skeptic's own assertions are true. For example, suppose I were to say that "all unqualified generalizations are false." Notice that this statement is self-refuting, since it is itself an unqualified generalization. And yet it certainly does not claim, nor does it in any way imply or entail, that no human assertions are true. So Friedman's major claim about the limitations of the self-referential inconsistency objection is false. Indeed, her own example, that of logical positivism, makes this point quite effectively. Friedman correctly points out that logical positivism, though it denied that any metaphysical or moral claims were true, was not an absolute skepticism, since it did recognize scientific truths. Now, Friedman cites this as an example of a kind of (limited) skepticism that is not self-refuting, but in fact the undoing of logical positivism was largely due to the observation that it is self-refuting. The reason is this. The logical positivists refused to recognize metaphysical and moral claims as true because they did not even regard them as meaningful. According to their criterion of meaning, no statement can be meaningful unless it is either an analytic statement (or tautology) or else an empirically verifiable statement. Metaphysical and moral claims are neither tautologies nor empirically verifiable, according to the logical positivists; therefore, they (unlike, for example, scientific statements, which are held to be empirically verifiable) are meaningless. The self-referential inconsistency emerges as soon as one applies the logical positivists' criterion of meaning to itself. Is the claim that only tautologies and empirically verifiable statements are meaningful (and thus candidates for truth) itself a tautology? It would seem not. Is it empirically verifiable? Clearly not. Thus, the logical positivists' own statement of their own position, according to which metaphysical and moral statements are meaningless (and thus not true) is shown, by its own standard, to be itself meaningless and thus not true. Logical positivism, contrary to Friedman, is self-refuting, even though it is not a global skepticism.

My second comment is that even when limited skepticisms are not directly self-refuting in this way, often the arguments used to support such skepticisms will undo the skepticisms themselves. Thus, to give just one example, if the phenomenon of disagreement within a given intellectual domain is alleged to prove that there is no truth within that domain, then the disagreement over the validity of such a proof should establish that it is itself untrue. To make the example more specific, if moral disagreement is held to entail moral skepticism (or moral relativism), then why should not meta-ethical disagreement—that is, disagreement over, for example, whether or not objective moral knowledge is possible—entail that we should be skeptical of moral skepticism (or moral relativism)?

B. Fish

Fish defends his "anti-foundationalist" position against the self-referential inconsistency objection in the following way:

> [Anti-foundationalism] says that foundations are local and temporal phenomena, and are always vulnerable to challenges from other localities and other times. The vulnerability also extends, of course, to the anti-foundationalist thesis itself, and that is why its assertion does not involve a contradiction, as it would if what was being asserted was the impossibility of foundational assertion; but since what is being asserted is that assertions—about foundations or anything else—have to make their way against objections and counterexamples, anti-foundationalism can without contradiction include itself under its own scope and await the objections one might make to it; and so long as those objections are successfully met and turned back by those who preach anti-foundationalism . . . , anti-foundationalism can be asserted as absolutely true since (at least for the time being) there is no argument that holds the field against it.[20]

By way of reply it must be pointed out that if Fish here successfully defends his position against the self-referential inconsistency objection, he does so at the cost of reducing that position to self-evident banality. Is there anyone in the world, including the defenders of even the most hard-core versions of objectivity, who would disagree with "what is being asserted" here, namely, that "assertions have to make their way against objections and counterexamples" and that they "are always vulnerable to challenges"? Indeed, Fish goes much further than do many adherents of objectivity, in that he attributes "absolute truth" to those assertions which, at least at present, hold up best against these objections and counterexamples. In short, Fish is fighting a straw man, in this case the mythical creature who thinks that his or her assertions are indubitable.

Moreover, the success of Fish's defense here depends upon his having described his own position accurately, and it is far from clear that he has done so. His discipline-centered relativism seems to assert far more than that "assertions have to make their way against objections and counterexamples" and that they "are always vulnerable to challenges."[21] Thus, Fish's defense is doubly unfair. It is unfair to those who press the self-referential consistency objection, since it accuses them of denying what they in fact insist upon: that "assertions have to make their way" and are "always vulnerable." And it attempts to rescue those against whom the objection is pressed by reducing them to asserting nothing more than these uncontroversial banalities.

To document this last charge—that Fish here attempts to defend against the self-referential inconsistency objection not only his own position, but also those other forms of relativism or skepticism against which the objection is frequently pressed, and that he does so by conflating these different positions with his own and inaccurately reducing them all to the innocuous and trivial doctrine described above—it is sufficient to point out the following: (a) when he gives his exposition of the self-referential inconsistency objection, Fish says that it is directed against "anti-foundationalism (*or cultural relativism or radical skepticism*)";[22] (b) the specific quotation that he provides as an instance of the objection is directed against cultural relativism in ethics, and is formulated quite differently than Fish's own anti-foundationalism; (c) Fish nonetheless immediately equates it with his own position and gives to it the same name, "anti-foundationalism"; and (d) he immediately proceeds, without distinguishing between these different anti-objectivist positions, to declare that the objection "is a point easily gotten around" and presents his response as if the quotation had been directed at him.

That Fish thinks he can defend "anti-foundationalism" in this manner stems, or so it seems to me, from his confusions concerning what it means to defend objectivity. To see this, consider the following passage from his writings:

> [N]ot only is there no one who could spot a transcendent truth if it happened to pass through the neighborhood, but it is difficult even to say what one would be like. Of course we would know what it would *not* be like; it would not speak to any particular condition, or be identified with any historical production, or be formulated in the terms of any national, ethnic, racial, economic, or class traditions. In short, it would not be clothed in any of the guises that would render it available to the darkened glasses of mortal—that is, temporally limited—man. It is difficult not to conclude either (a) that there are no such truths, or . . . (b) that while there are such truths, they could only be known from a god's-eye view. Since none of us occupies that view (because none of us is a god), the truths any of

us find compelling will all be partial, which is to say they will all be political.[23]

(Fish is responding here to a statement by Lynne Cheney, in which she defines "transcendent truths" as "truths that, transcending accidents of class, race and gender, speak to us all.")[24]

In reply to Fish I would argue, first, that it is far from the case that such truths "would not speak to any particular condition"; rather, they would, presumably, speak to each and every one of them. Second, when Fish claims that they would not "be identified with any historical production," he simply commits the genetic fallacy. If there are any transcendent truths in the sense defined, there is no reason why the discovery of any given one of them might not take place at a certain point in history, at a particular geographical location, and in a specific cultural context, without these factors in any way detracting from its status as a transcendent truth. No doubt there is a (true) story to be told about the discovery of the fact that the Earth is not flat, and is instead much closer to being round, but the spatial, temporal, and cultural particularities and contingencies of the historical event of this discovery do not in any way detract from its validity or scope. Third, with regard to his claim that such a truth must not be formulated in the terms of any national, ethnic, racial, economic, or class traditions, this commits the same fallacy as would a claim that it must not be formulated in any particular language. But many things that can be said in English can be said just as well in French, Swahili, or any other language one might name. It is as if Fish were saying that no spoken utterance could ever communicate a transcendent truth since the voice uttering it would be at a specific pitch level and would be characterized by a certain timbre, to the exclusion of all others. Fourth, as to his main point, that no one could possibly recognize one, or say what it would be like, this can perhaps be refuted simply by drawing up a short list: "If A is taller than B, and B is taller than C, then A is taller than C"; "If A implies B, and A is true, then B is true"; "Any number divided by itself equals one"; "Elephants are heavier than flies" (note that nothing in the definition of "transcendent truth" provided rules out the merely empirical); "Happiness is intrinsically better than misery"; "Intelligence is better than stupidity"; "A political system that guarantees that all of its citizens die of thirst at a young age is bad"; "It is not true that all (and the only) paintings that are good are portraits of clowns on crushed black velvet"; and billions of others.

Indeed, much of Fish's work falls apart, it seems to me, as soon as one refuses to follow him in committing the fallacy of false dilemma in two specific ways. The first is his strange notion that all norms and standards must either be (a) contingent, historical, potentially revisable, and having only local validity, or (b) objective, established permanently, and having universal validity. He then gives reasons for concluding that all values and standards in fact fall under category (b), (a) being a chimera. The problem is that he ignores the possibility (c) that some norms might be objective, have more than local validity, and yet still be potentially revisable. After all, one can defend objectivity and still be a fallibilist. That is, one can believe that there are truths that transcend the particular and contingent judgments of particular individuals or cultures at particular historical moments, without thinking that all, or even many, or even any, of our beliefs concerning the identity of these truths can be known with certainty to be right. Moreover, one can be a defender of objectivity and still be a contextualist. That is, one can believe that there are objective truths—truths that are in no way dependent for their truth on what anyone happens to think—that are context sensitive.[25]

Fish's other false dilemma is his idea that all norms and standards must either be (a) experienced and produced locally and historically, and therefore—note the genetic fallacy—having only local validity, or (b) experienced in some (unfathomable and inexplicable) nonlocal and nonhistorical way; and not produced at all, but rather having the status of having always existed (perhaps in some Platonic or heavenly realm); and having universal and objective validity. He then has an easy time establishing (a) over (b). The problem, however, is that he ignores the possibility of (c) values and standards that have universal and objective validity in spite of (from his standpoint) the fact that they are instantiated and articulated and made manifest in particular, local, contingent, historical circumstances, contexts, and experiences. For example, he asserts that the claim that there are

> norms that are independently and objectively established . . . fails when one realizes that were such standards to exist somewhere—in the mind of God or in the totality of the universe—there would be no one capable of recognizing or responding to them. After all, none

of us lives in the mind of God or in the totality of the universe; rather, we all live in specific places demarcated in their configurations and in their possibilities for action . . . by transient, partial, shifting, and contingent understandings of what is and what should be.[26]

Here I will limit myself to three comments. First, like Bridges, Fish ignores or denies, without argument, the possibility that experience might contain an eidetic dimension.[27] Second, it is odd to say that standards must "exist somewhere." Finally, this means that Fish must either deny that giraffes are taller than ants, that $2 + 2 = 4$, that happiness is intrinsically better than misery, and that "none of us lives in the totality of the universe; rather we all live in specific places," etc., etc., which he does not want to do, or else assert that all of these truths have merely local validity, which he does. Thus, Fish's claim that all truth-claims must necessarily achieve no more than a local validity must be understood as itself achieving no more than a local validity. I have tried to argue, however, that it achieves less than that.

NOTES

1. This objection has been repeatedly pressed against all but the most severely qualified versions of relativism, subjectivism, and skepticism throughout the history of Western philosophy. It is at least as old as Plato's critique of the ancient Greek Sophists and continues to be much debated in connection with assessing contemporary "postmodern" forms of relativism. For Plato's version of the argument, see *Theaetetus* 169D–171D. A good translation is that of Francis M. Cornford, in *Plato's Theory of Knowledge* (Indianapolis: Bobbs-Merrill, 1957), pp. 76–80. Errol E. Harris discusses one version of the objection, which he terms "the epistemologist's fallacy," in the context of the early modern period (roughly, Descartes through Hume) in his *Fundamentals of Philosophy* (New York: Holt, Rinehart and Winston, 1969), pp. 273–274. James F. Harris, in his *Against Relativism* (La Salle, IL: Open Court, 1992), develops the objection at length and applies it against such contemporary philosophers as Willard Van Orman Quine, Nelson Goodman, Thomas Kuhn, Peter Winch, Hans-Georg Gadamer, and Richard Rorty. For the use of the argument as an instrument of criticism against one prominent version of postmodern relativism, that of Barbara Herrnstein Smith, see David L. Roochnik, "Can the Relativist Avoid Refuting Herself?" *Philosophy*

and Literature 14, no. 1 (April 1990): 92–98. Finally, for two book-length discussions of the issue which, in radical contrast to the just-cited works of James Harris and Roochnik, exhibit considerable sympathy toward postmodernism and an ambivalent attitude concerning the force of self-referential inconsistency arguments, see Malcolm Ashmore, *The Reflexive Thesis* (Chicago: University of Chicago Press, 1989); and Hilary Lawson, *Reflexivity* (La Salle, IL: Open Court, 1985).

2. This example comes from Frithjof Schuon, *Logic and Transcendence*, trans. Peter N. Townsend (New York: Harper Torchbooks, 1975), p. 7.

3. This example comes from Max Hocutt, *First Philosophy* (Belmont, CA: Wadsworth, 1980), p. 33.

4. In the section on self-referential inconsistency in the previous chapter I pointed out that some postmodernists shrug off the self-refutation objection by suggesting that there is nothing wrong with transgressing the strictures of logic. The irresponsibility of such a position is perhaps brought into an especially clear focus in the case of performative contradictions, since their structure, that of saying one thing while doing another, is familiar to us in everyday life under the heading of "moral hypocrisy." In this connection there is no gainsaying James L. Marsh's remark, in *Critique, Action, and Liberation* (Albany: State University of New York Press, 1995), p. 62, that "[i]ntegrity can hardly be described as a trivial preoccupation."

5. Harris, *Fundamentals of Philosophy*, p. 273.

6. Thomas Nagel, *The Last Word* (New York: Oxford University Press, 1997).

7. Michael Bérubé, *Public Access* (New York: Verso, 1994), p. 123.

8. Chantal Mouffe, "Radical Democracy: Modern or Postmodern?" trans. Paul Holdengräber, in *Universal Abandon?* ed. Andrew Ross (Minneapolis: University of Minnesota Press, 1988), p. 37.

9. Mary E. Hawkesworth, "Knowers, Knowing, Known," *Signs* 14 (1989): 536.

10. George Levine et al., *Speaking for the Humanities* (n. p.: American Council of Learned Societies, 1989), pp. 10, 18.

11. Brian Vickers, *In Defence of Rhetoric* (Oxford: Clarendon Press, 1989), p. 211.

12. While I will not take the time to argue the point here, it is also important not to let Vickers's reading of the three philosophers he cites go unchallenged. Husserl and Popper both strenuously oppose the sort of subjectivism or relativism which Vickers here invokes on their authority. For Husserl's views on the subject, see especially his *Logical Investigations*, vol. 1, trans. J. N. Findlay (New York: Humanities Press, 1970), Sections 17–51, and the discussion in chapter 1 of the present work. To see that nothing could be further from Husserl's position than that "in phenomenological

terms [is this supposed to be a reference to *Husserl's* phenomenology?], the acts of perceiving the world, interpreting its signs, and evaluating its actions, are all irremediably personal," consult his *Ideas Pertaining to a Pure Phenomenology and to a Phenomenological Philosophy: First Book*, trans. F. Kersten (The Hague: Martinus Nijhoff, 1982), especially Sections 52–54. A very helpful commentary is Erazim Kohák, *Idea and Experience* (Chicago: University of Chicago Press, 1978), pp. 74–83, 94–102. Popper's position is presented in Karl Popper, *Objective Knowledge* (Oxford: Oxord University Press, 1972). While Vickers is undoubtedly on much stronger ground in his reference to Nietzsche, even here the case is complicated, and there is a good deal of counterevidence. See in this regard Maudemarie Clark, *Nietzsche on Truth and Philosophy* (New York: Cambridge University Press, 1990); and John Wilcox, *Truth and Value in Nietzsche* (Ann Arbor: University of Michigan Press, 1974).

13. A more straightforward way to make this point is to construe the historicist argument as resting on the premise that a central, and indeed permanent, feature of all human knowledge is its incessant changeableness. In other words, the historicist premise is that there is one thesis, namely, that human knowledge is always and inherently revisable, which has always been true in the past and which continues to be true today. On the basis of this premise, the historicist concludes, apparently inductively, that this thesis will also always remain true in the future, and thus that historicism may legitimately be granted ahistorical validity. On this understanding of the historicist argument, not only is the historicist conclusion self-undermining and inconsistent with its supporting premise, but also it seems that this premise, with its almost oxymoronic reliance on a notion of "constant change," is self-contradictory.

14. What I am calling "the logic" of the historicist argument is the inductive inference that the (ahistorical) truth of historicism is established by the (alleged) historical failures of all previous attempts to transcend historicism. Alternatively, one might interpret the argument as containing an implied premise to the effect that these past failures imply the truth of historicism, in which case my criticism of "the logic" of the argument would simply be shifted to this implied premise.

15. Harold I. Brown, in *Rationality* (New York: Routledge, 1990), pp. 126–127, puts the point this way:

> These arguments [those of the sociological relativists] are aimed at showing that the results of Western science have no validity beyond the culture in which they have emerged, but the arguments in question are themselves dependent on our accepting the results of one particular Western science—anthropology. This is not a quibble.

Anthropology is a modern Western science, one which is not found in, say, ancient Greek or medieval cultures, nor in the societies that have provided the basis for much of the anthropological argument on behalf of relativism, and relativism is incompatible with the central beliefs of those societies. If we were to take social relativism literally, we would have to conclude that this view is true for a subculture of contemporary Western thinkers, period. Clearly, the intended scope of the doctrine is much greater than this. The thrust of the doctrine seems to be that we should, universally, recognize that people's modes of cognition are a feature of their culture, not just that this is true for anthropologists, yet it is extremely difficult to see why we have a basis for adopting _this_ view as universally true, while withholding such status from, for example, the view that the earth is not flat, that the stars are much farther away than many people think they are, that many diseases are caused by microorganisms, or that people who take psychedelic drugs do not fly. It seems that those who cite anthropological data in support of the doctrine of social relativism are, in effect, reserving a special cognitive position for their own particular science, and have done so without providing any grounds for making this exception. From a social relativist perspective, they would seem to be open to a charge of extreme ethnocentrism.

16. Works defending such a perspective include the following: Barry Barnes, _Scientific Knowledge and Sociological Theory_ (London: Routledge and Kegan Paul, 1974); David Bloor, _Knowledge and Social Imagery_ (London: Routledge and Kegan Paul, 1976); Harry M. Collins, _Changing Order_ (Chicago: University of Chicago Press, 1992); Bruno Latour, _Science in Action_ (Cambridge: Harvard University Press, 1985); Bruno Latour and Steve Woolgar, _Laboratory Life_, 2d ed. (Princeton, NJ: Princeton University Press, 1986); and Steven Shapin, "History of Science and Its Sociological Reconstructions," _History of Science_ 20 (1982): 157–211.

17. Larry Laudan lampoons this self-exempting move by attributing to his fictional relativist character, Quincy Rortabender, authorship of a book entitled _Skepticism about Everything Except the Social Sciences: A Post-Modernist Guide_. Larry Laudan, _Science and Relativism_ (Chicago: University of Chicago Press, 1990), p. xiii. The bulk of Laudan's book is cast in the form of a discussion of central issues in the philosophy of science among four fictional characters, each of whom is a composite representing a major position. The four positions represented are relativism, pragmatism, positivism, and realism.

18. Such a criticism might be rejected as unfair to sociologists of sci-

ence, since they do, most assuredly, offer considerable evidence in support of their views. But the problem remains: why should we focus on rational, evidentiary *reasons*, as opposed to reductive, sociological *causes*, in our explanations and evaluations of the views of sociologists of science, when such a focus is precisely what these same sociologists of science are asking us to abandon in connection with the beliefs of other scientists about the natural world?

Similar self-referential problems plague Stanley Fish's discipline-centered form of relativism—the position holding that, while the beliefs of scientists (and other scholars) do indeed tend to result substantially from rational considerations of evidence on their part, what *counts* as evidence and as the rational evaluation of same varies from discipline to discipline, and even from specialty to specialty. For on Fish's view, argumentation works only by appealing to implicitly agreed upon standards and criteria which arise through specialization, and which take on a stronger, more explicit, and more binding character the more narrowly specialized is the scholarly community within which they are (tacitly) invoked. See, for example, Fish's *There's No Such Thing as Free Speech and It's a Good Thing, Too* (New York: Oxford University Press, 1994), p. 24. The problem, of course, is that Fish's views on the discipline- and specialty-specific nature of rational norms must be viewed either as sound only relative to the standards of evidence prevailing in his own area of scholarly specialization, whatever that might be taken to be, in which case the rest of us need take no special note of it, or else as claiming objective or universal validity (or, more modestly, merely a validity transcending the confines of one small community of academic specialists), in which case it simply contradicts itself.

19. Marilyn Friedman, "Codes, Canons, Correctness, and Feminism," in *Political Correctness: For and Against*, ed. Marilyn Friedman and Jan Narveson (Lanham, MD: Rowman & Littlefield, 1995), pp. 17–18. I might add parenthetically that, despite my disagreement with Friedman on this point, I think she makes a fine contribution in the work here cited, and generally "wins" the "debate" with Narveson.

20. Stanley Fish, "Introduction" to his *Doing What Comes Naturally* (Durham, NC: Duke University Press, 1989), p. 30.

21. See the discussion in note 18 above.

22. Fish, "Introduction" to *Doing What Comes Naturally*, p. 29, emphasis added.

23. Fish, "Introduction" to his *There's No Such Thing as Free Speech*, p. 8.

24. Fish quotes Cheney in ibid., p. 7.

25. See Fish, "The Common Touch, or One Size Fits All," in *The Politics*

of Liberal Education, ed. Darryl J. Gless and Barbara Herrnstein Smith (Durham, NC: Duke University Press, 1992), pp. 250–251, for an example of the false dilemma just described.

26. Ibid., p. 251.

27. See chapter 1, section 3, of the present work for a detailed explanation of this point.

Chapter 3

THE ARGUMENT
FROM DISAGREEMENT

If relativism, subjectivism, and skepticism are as confused as I have been making them out to be, one might well wonder why they remain so popular. And yet, clearly they are popular, and not just among philosophers. For, while it is a widespread belief that the issues of primary interest to philosophers, especially in such abstract domains as ontology (the nature of reality) and epistemology (the nature and scope of knowledge), are of little concern to others, I find, quite radically to the contrary, that almost everyone has thought about these issues and has developed at least a tentative position with respect to them, together with supporting arguments. Moreover, a position that I find to be very frequently defended with explicit argumentation in popular culture is anti-realism, meaning either the doctrine that there is no such thing as "reality" (that is, there is no one way that "things are" or that "the world is"), or the more modest view that even if there is some way that "reality" or the world is, we cannot possibly know what this way is. The former thesis I will call "ontological anti-realism"; the latter I will term "epistemological anti-realism." And since I am concerned at present to deal with these strains of anti-realism as they occur in popular culture, I will refer to them as "pop anti-realism," whether ontological or epistemological, as the case may be.

Perhaps the argument most commonly used by the pop anti-realists might be called "the argument from disagreement." The first premise of this argument asserts that there is no consensus in some domain (that of values, perhaps, or of reality as a whole), but rather a great deal of controversy and disagreement. The second premise then asserts that if there really were a "way things are" (or "way the world is," or "objective values," or what have you), or at least if this "way things are" were really accessible to us, we would not have so much controversy about it. The conclusion is that some form of anti-realism must be "true." The argument is not always stated exactly this way, of course, but some version of the argument that the presence of disagreement is evidence of the absence of real facts and/or values is ubiquitous.[1]

I. ALLEN

Now, as a specimen of pop anti-realism, in this case of the epistemological variety, consider this observation of Steve Allen's, concerning his experience years ago after he had been given a nightly television program:

> The network people at once set up an almost endless series of press interviews. Half of the subsequently published accounts described me as witty, quick minded, a true humorist. The other half described me as deadly serious, humorless, dull, and inhibited. When I tell you that some of these stories were based on the same group interview, you'll perceive the point. The writers were describing their own reactions to me, not my essential reality, whatever that might be. This is true of all reality, of course. We're almost always describing our impressions, rarely the objective materiality.[2]

On what grounds do I object to Allen's reasoning? I will mention just six points.

(1) This idea that the pervasiveness of disagreement indicates that we are closed off within the sphere of our own impressions, closed off from "essential reality" or "objective materiality" (and note Allen's confidence that it does, as when he asserts that we have only to learn the details of the story to "perceive the point," a point which, moreover, he claims not only to be true in the case he is describing,

but also to be true of all reality, and to be so "*of course*"), rests in part on its own distortion of perception. We tend to notice the (vastly smaller) areas in which we disagree and to ignore the (vastly greater) areas in which we agree. Thus, while these observers may have disagreed among themselves as to the wittiness or seriousness of Steve Allen, certainly all of them agreed that he was a human being rather than a kangaroo, that he was not orange and purple striped, that he was less than ten feet tall, that he was located on or very near the surface of the Earth during these interviews, that at no time during the interviews did he undergo transformations from a solid to a liquid or gaseous state, etc., etc. If these writers were indeed closed off from Allen's "essential reality" and "objective materiality," how is this literally endless sphere of perfect agreement concerning him to be explained?

(2) Part of the answer becomes clear when we move beyond Allen's false dilemma. Our choices are not really between "our reactions" and "the essential reality," or between "our impressions" and "the objective materiality." Rather, and surely this is much closer to what actually *does* happen, we might react *to* an essential reality, and form impressions *of* an objective materiality, in such a way that both our own subjectivity in attending to an object and the objectivity of the object attended to make a contribution to our perception and thought. It is not an all-or-nothing either-or.

(3) Moreover, it is easy to see why the question of Allen's wittiness vs. seriousness would be one especially suited to generating disagreements, so that the disagreements that we do in fact find on this question do not lend strong support for a generalization to "all reality." (To make such a generalization cogently from just one example would require an *a fortiori* argument—that is, an argument from the stronger to the weaker. In other words, if Allen could show that disagreement is rampant even in the one case where conditions are optimal for agreement, then we might cautiously conclude that disagreement is to be had everywhere. But from the fact that disagreement arises precisely where we would expect it to, nothing follows about less troublesome cases, let alone about "all reality.") The reasons why this issue might be expected to provoke disagreement are at least twofold. First, wittiness is not a clear concept with clear boundaries. Nor is there any precise or algorithmic procedure for determining who is or is not witty. This is a matter of judgment, and

one about which there seems to be lots of room for differing criteria, standards, and taste. But lots of things are not like this, or are not so to the same degree. Second, the scenario that Allen describes seems to be one in which preconceptions would be likely to play an unusually distorting role in the perception of those called upon to observe and to write about Allen. For the context is this: Writers are being introduced to a young man who has just been given his own nightly television program, presumably because he is an unusually talented entertainer (which, given Allen's brand of entertaining, would include being "witty, quick minded, a true humorist"). Thus, these writers would not be observing Allen with no preconceptions about his wittiness. Rather, they would begin their observations with the idea that he is alleged to be extraordinarily witty. It is not surprising, then, that many people would see him that way, whether he was so or not. It is also not surprising that other observers might have harbored such strong expectations that no matter how witty Allen might have been, his actual performance would have paled in comparison to the expectation, making him seem "deadly serious, humorless, dull, and inhibited." (Moreover, given that Allen can be a far more serious person than many might expect of one who has earned a living as a comedian—he has, for example, written several nonfiction books on serious subjects—it is not surprising that some would be so surprised by his seriousness that they would be struck by only it, seeing it [falsely] as incompatible with wittiness.) When we encounter strong disagreements, we need not throw up our hands and invoke alternate universes, when more pedestrian explanations are so readily available and so plausible in the light of human experience.

(4) No one, including Allen, consistently believes these things. Earlier on the very page from which I have been quoting (p. 44), Allen lambastes Gail Rock's statement that some of Woody Allen's jokes are "terrible groaners," an opinion starkly at odds with his own opinion that Woody is "the best joke writer in the business." But does Steve Allen chalk this up to the idea that neither he nor Rock can penetrate to Woody's "essential reality" or "objective materiality"? No, he condemns Rock's judgment as "bullshit of the worst sort" and proceeds to heap scorn on her for four paragraphs before concluding that Woody "is constitutionally incapable of writing a 'groaner.'" And on page 64, Allen's response to a *Time* magazine criticism of Mel Brooks is equally uncompromising: "This is what we call, in simple terms, wrong."

(5) Allen, according to his own theory, must be understood as telling us not about the "essential reality" of the relationship between our own reactions and essential reality, but rather about his reaction to that relationship. But surely this undermines the force of his argument and is inconsistent with his intentions.

(6) Note also that he expects everyone to "perceive" the same point in connection with this story. Does that not undermine the story's own moral? If everyone is always seeing things differently than everyone else, because they are each enclosed within their own subjectivity and alienated from "essential reality" and "objective materiality," then how can he expect everyone to draw the same moral from his story?

II. Generic Objections to the Argument from Disagreement

From the six points just mentioned, I believe we can distill the three principal flaws that attach generically to attempts to support anti-realistic conclusions on the basis of some form of the argument from disagreement.

First, the premise of disagreement is, at best, a half-truth. I know of no area of human inquiry in which the sphere of disagreement (which typically attracts great interest, so that people are highly conscious of it) is not puny in size in comparison to the vast vistas of agreement (which are taken for granted and thus barely noticed) that the disagreements presuppose. Once attention is focused on the gigantic—indeed, I believe literally infinite—sphere of agreement, the argument begins to appear extremely unconvincing. For if the anti-realist conclusion is to be sustained, how are these billions of points of agreement (often background, unarticulated, previously unnoticed, never explicitly taught—such as that Steve Allen is not an iguana, that he weighs more than an ounce, that he has fewer than 679,023,467,985,124 nostrils, etc.) to be explained? In view of the nature of these points of agreement, the theory of education or socialization, for example, looks distinctly unpromising. Indeed, once one realizes that there is far more agreement than disagreement, the sheer size of the disparity makes it appear more plausible to attribute agreement to mutual confrontation with an external reality and to

seek a special explanation for disagreement than to attribute disagreement to the nonexistence or inaccessibility of such a reality and
seek a special explanation for agreement.

Second, the argument is self-referentially inconsistent. If it is
true that the objective truth of a judgment depends upon everyone's
accepting it, then that judgment is itself not true, since not everyone
accepts *it*. And if controversy and disagreement mean that we are
closed off from the reality of that over which we disagree, then we are
closed off from the reality of that statement itself, since there is controversy and disagreement over *it*. Finally, if disagreement in science,
say (or ethics, or perceptions of what is or is not funny, or what have
you), is supposed to establish the truth of ontological or epistemological anti-realism, what is to be done with the fact that there is no
agreement surrounding these anti-realisms? After all, ontology and
epistemology are at least as contentious as science (or ethics, or
humor, etc.).

Finally, it is difficult to understand why the mere fact of disagreement should ever be taken as evidence in support of anti-
realism. For as Dietrich Von Hildebrand points out, "[i]t is a great and
widespread error to assume that the objectivity and validity of a truth
depend upon the fact that everyone and anyone can grasp it or that
we can prove it in such a way that everyone must accept it. This
assumption itself is not . . . evident, nor has anyone ever attempted
to prove it."[3] And, as Edward H. Carr notes, "[i]t does not follow that,
because a mountain appears to take on different shapes from different angles of vision, it has objectively either no shape at all or an
infinity of shapes."[4]

III. EXPLAINING DISAGREEMENT

Defenders of the argument from disagreement might at this point
respond that, while it is indeed true that the fact of disagreement
does not by itself establish the truth of anti-realism, still, given the
extensive and pervasive nature of that disagreement, anti-realism
remains the best and most plausible explanation available for it.
While I think the points made above are already sufficient to refute
this claim, I will, both for reasons of completeness and because of the
intrinsic interest of the issue, now consider three alternative expla-

nations for the phenomenon of disagreement. While this list is by no means intended to be exhaustive, I submit that these three factors, pedestrian and commonplace as they may be, are more than sufficient to account for even the most intractable of controversies and thus to remove any need to invoke such an exotic thesis as anti-realism.

A. Difficulty of Issues

Aristotle remarks that "there are many ways of going wrong, but only one way which is right. . . . This . . . is also the reason why the one is easy and the other hard: it is easy to miss the target but hard to hit it."[5] To this I would only add (and surely Aristotle would agree) that the degree to which this is true varies considerably from case to case. Thus, to pursue his analogy, while it is easy to hit some targets if you only try (I have in mind big ones, fired upon at extremely close range, with good equipment, good lighting, and no wind, and when one is well-rested, well-fed, in good health, and well-practiced in hitting targets), others (small ones that are far away, when the weather is bad, etc.) are virtually impossible. Indeed, "there are many ways of going wrong": one could, for example, fall short of the mark, overshoot it, or go wide to the right or left. Surely it is obvious that many controversial issues are like such targets. The mere fact that we cannot hit these targets consistently is no reason to suppose that they do not exist, or that we are in principle and forever closed off from them (as if it were inconceivable that we might someday develop a better technique for aiming or firing, or a better technology for doing so), or that they are "social constructions," or anything of that sort.

Moreover, since controversial issues tend to be vastly more complex than targets, "hitting" the former properly is typically more difficult than hitting even rather remote and tiny bulls-eyes. Here again Aristotle's analysis of the virtues provides an apt analogy. He suggests that there is a virtuous way of experiencing fear, confidence, anger, and pity. However, the myriad ways of going wrong include not just experiencing them too little or too much (the point that Aristotle most often emphasizes), but also experiencing them at the wrong time, toward the wrong objects, toward the wrong people, for the wrong reason, and in the wrong manner.[6] Surely it is obvious that there are even more ways that one can go wrong in attempting to reach the best and most reasonable position on some difficult issue. Why, then, the leap to anti-realism?

B. Poor Reasoning

Moreover, even when an issue is not particularly difficult, disagreement can result when at least one party to the dispute reasons poorly. In the spirit of my Steve Allen discussion above, let me offer another example from popular culture. I once watched a Leo Buscaglia lecture on public television, in which he said something like the following (I am paraphrasing): "If you have met someone that you would like to get to know better, but you are afraid to make the first overture, for fear of being rejected, I say 'go ahead, make the first move,' because, look at it this way: the other person can only respond in one of two ways, either saying 'yes' or 'no.' Therefore, there is a fifty-fifty chance that he or she will say 'yes.'" Over the years I have often presented this bit of reasoning to my students, challenging them to find the fallacy in it. To my great surprise (because my students are often good at this sort of thing) only a tiny percentage of them seem to recognize that from the fact that there are only two options (and let us pretend that this premise of Buscaglia's is correct, and the other person cannot say "maybe" or nothing at all) it hardly follows that the two options are equal in likelihood. Indeed, one might as well argue that if I were to play Michael Jordan one-on-one in basketball, I would have a fifty-fifty chance of winning since, after all, there are only two possibilities: either I will win or I will lose.

Nor does this particular fallacy arise only in such silly examples as these. For example, when discussing arguments for the existence of God with my students, I have on several occasions encountered a variation on Pascal's wager, but with the added premise that since God either exists or does not, there is a fifty-fifty chance that He does!

Now, this is just one fallacy, illustrated with just three examples. But I submit that there are dozens (perhaps hundreds or thousands) of fallacies, that is, common mistakes in reasoning, and that one has only to pay attention to serious public discourse to encounter at least a few of them each day. Quite simply, as Philip Kitcher puts it, "[p]eople can make cognitive mistakes, perceiving badly, inferring hastily, failing to act to obtain inputs from nature that would guide them to improved cognitive states. . . . Some types of processes are conducive to cognitive progress; others are not."[7] Indeed, and this is another reason why disagreement should not be taken as entailing anti-realism.

C. *Ignorance and Evidential Relativity*

Another explanation for disagreement resides in the simple fact that frequently not all parties to a dispute have access to the same evidence. When this is so it is easy to understand how different people might arrive at conflicting answers, even on the supposition that there is one objectively correct answer to a given controversial question and that no party to the dispute in question is guilty of any cognitive shortcoming or epistemic vice.[8]

The problem, then, is that people confuse relativity of justified belief with relativity of truth. What you are justified in believing depends to a large extent upon what evidence you have access to, and this can vary from person to person, from situation to situation, from culture to culture, from time period to time period. It hardly follows that the truth itself does. The world has always been round, though there may have been times in which the most reasonable belief was that it is flat. Rationality is therefore relative in a way that truth is not. Note also that two different people within the same culture might be perfectly rational in believing mutually incompatible things, without this entailing that truth itself is relative. For example, if I have recently committed a crime, it would be rational for me, simply on the basis of the evidence of memory, to believe that I have. Now suppose that you, on the other hand, know of no evidence linking me to the crime and are even aware of extensive (though not conclusive) evidence suggesting that I did not do it. It would be rational for you to believe that, at least probably, I did not do it, and this would be so even if we do not invoke any special presumption of innocence with regard to the issue of criminal guilt. Still, the truth is not relative. There is only one truth as to the issue of whether or not I committed the crime: I did. Note, finally, that this relativism of rationality is an objective, not a subjective, relativism. Thinking that you are rational does not make you so—even though actually being right is, as we have seen, not required.

But, of course, people who make erroneous judgments on the basis of insufficient evidence are not always, or even usually, rational in doing so. Indeed, at the risk of appearing arrogant, I would suggest that many, perhaps most, debates that one witnesses in various public forums are best characterized not as disagreements between parties with access to the same evidence, nor as disputes between parties with access to different evidence, with the evidence in each case pointing in a different direction, but rather as arguments between those who have some idea what they are talking about and those who do not. What I am suggesting is that, with depressing frequency, one observes debates in which one side knows absolutely everything that the other side does, but also something more, with this something more including precisely what is needed to refute conclusively the position that the other side, on the basis of its inferior evidence, is attempting to uphold.

Let's look at some examples. In order to ease into this idea in an inoffensive way, I'll begin with an example from my favorite baseball scholar and writer, Bill James. By way of background for this example, let me point out that, as is widely known by students of baseball and even by many casual fans, most hitters tend to do better when facing a pitcher whose orientation as a right-hander or left-hander is opposite to their own. That is, left-handed batters tend to hit better against right-handed pitchers than against left-handers, with right-handed batters faring better against left-handed pitchers. Now, in the late 1970s and early 1980s the Detroit Tigers had many fine left-handed batters and relatively few good right-handed ones. Thus, one would expect them to be more vulnerable to left-handed pitching than to that of right-handers. And yet, in 1981 the Tigers hit about as well, and won about the same percentage of games, when facing left-handed pitchers as when facing righties. Therefore, many concluded that the Tigers of that year were just as good against lefties as they were against righties, and that this could be determined merely by "taking a look at the statistics."

But James considered, and then examined evidence concerning, a different hypothesis. Perhaps opposing teams were so eager to use left-handed pitchers against the Tigers that they scraped the bottom of the barrel to get them, using inferior lefties who would not otherwise be considered good enough to receive starting assignments; similarly, perhaps they were so reluctant to assign right-handed pitchers to the task of opposing the Tigers that they gave this job only to their very finest right-handed pitchers.

The evidence uncovered by James clearly shows that this is indeed what happened.[9] For one thing, the Tigers certainly did face more left-handed pitching than did other teams, accumulating 1,618 at bats against lefties, in comparison, for example, to 874 in the case of the Boston Red Sox, 954 for the Baltimore Orioles, and 800 for the Chicago White Sox. Next, in order to determine the quality of the left-handed and right-handed pitchers facing the Tigers, James looked at three simple and straightforward measures of quality: having twenty or more starts (on the theory that teams tend to give the better pitchers more work than their worse pitchers), giving up fewer runs (having a lower earned-run average) than the league average, and having more wins than losses. James designated pitchers as "Class A" if they met all three of these qualifications, "Class B" if they met two, "Class C" if they met one, and "Class D" if they met none. Now, while the Tigers did well against left-handed pitchers overall, compiling a 31-26 won-lost record in games started by them (and thus prompting people to say that they were good against lefties "if you look at the statistics"), James's hypothesis predicted that they would have accomplished this by facing, and beating, lots of bad lefties. Sure enough, the Tigers posted losing records against Class A lefties (6-8), Class B lefties (4-7), and even Class C lefties (5-7), but made up for it by facing Class D pitchers—and remember, to be a Class D pitcher one must be at least relatively rarely used, so we would normally expect a team to face them less often than they would pitchers from the other classes—a whopping 20 times and by posting a 16-4 record against them. Moreover, and again consistently with James's hypothesis, the Tigers faced inferior right-handed pitching far less often than they did lefties of similar quality—they opposed Class C right-handers only seven times, as opposed to twelve times for lefties, and Class D righties only eleven times, as opposed to twenty times for lefties—and did better against the righties (14-4 against Class C and D righties, as opposed to 21-11 against the lefties).

Well, that's good enough for me. I think James is right. The 1981 Detroit Tigers did about as well against left-handed pitchers as they did against right-handers not because they really were just as good against lefties (as you can tell by "taking a look at the statistics"), but rather because they faced a disproportionately large number of poor lefties and a disproportionately small number of poor righties. Now, in the debate between James and those he is here refuting, I submit that there is no equality of evidence. It is not the case that the two sides are looking at the same evidence and drawing different conclusions from it, nor that they are looking at different but roughly equally strong evidence pointing in different directions. Rather, James grasps every bit as fully as do his opponents all of the evidence supporting their conclusion; but he also grasps something of which they are not even aware—additional evidence that refutes their position. This, it seems to me, is the situation we find in many public debates.[10]

Incidentally, note that the different positions on this debate can be neatly arranged in the form of the following hierarchy. First, there are those extremely casual baseball fans, the sort of folk who enjoy the beauty and athleticism of the game without worrying about any arcane points of strategy, who have never heard of the idea of advantages and disadvantages based upon the right-handed or left-handed identity of the hitter and batter, and would never dream up such a notion themselves. Such persons would probably believe that the Tigers would be as good against lefties as against righties, because it would never occur to them to doubt this, presumably the default, position. Next would be those more knowledgeable fans who are aware of this point of strategy and also aware of the dominance of left-handed hitting on the Tigers. They would presumably believe (and correctly, as it turns out) that the Tigers would fare better against right-handed than against left-handed pitching. Third would be those even more sophisticated empiricists who would actually look at the statistics, note that the Tigers had hit about as well and won about as many games on a percentage basis against lefties as against righties, and conclude that the conventional strategic wisdom did not apply to these Tigers. Finally, we have the position of James, who has fully comprehended and surpassed these other positions and arrived at, dare I say it, the truth. Such a hierarchical structure accurately describes many public debates, including those devoted to more serious issues than that of baseball.

For example, Noam Chomsky points out that in late 1984

the World Court rejected the American contention that it had no jurisdiction with regard to the Nicaraguan complaint concerning U.S. aggression against Nicaragua. The issue arose [in April 1984], when Nicaragua brought to the Court its charge that the United

States was mining its harbors and attacking its territory. With exquisite timing, President Reagan chose that very day to issue a Presidential Proclamation designating May 1 as "Law Day 1984." He hailed our "200-year-old partnership between law and liberty," adding that without law, there can only be "chaos and disorder." The day before, as part of his tribute to the rule of law, he had announced that the United States would not recognize any decision of the World Court.

These events aroused much anger. In the *New York Times*, Anthony Lewis decried Reagan's "failure to understand what the rule of law has meant to this country." He observed that Senator Moynihan had "made the point with great power" in a law school address in which he criticized the Reagan administration for "forsaking our centuries-old commitment to the idea of law in the conduct of nations" and for its "mysterious collective amnesia," its "losing the memory that there once was such a commitment." Our U.N. delegation, Moynihan said, "does not know the history of our country."

Unfortunately it is Ronald Reagan and Jeanne Kirkpatrick who understand what the rule of law has meant to this country, and it is Anthony Lewis and Senator Moynihan who are suffering from a mysterious collective amnesia. The case they are discussing is a good example. It happened before, in almost exactly the same way.[11]

Chomsky proceeds to recount the relevant history: In 1907, a Central American Court of Justice was established, on the initiative of the United States, to adjudicate conflicts among nations in the region. But in 1912, and again in 1916, the United States refused to recognize court decisions that went against its interests in Nicaragua. This noncompliance on the part of the United States effectively destroyed the court.[12]

Notice that Chomsky's position here fully comprehends and surpasses those of Ronald Reagan and Jeanne Kirkpatrick, on the one hand, and of Anthony Lewis and Senator Moynihan, on the other (not to mention the position of those many who were oblivious to all of these events—in many cases through no fault of their own, as we shall soon see), in a manner quite analogous to that in which Bill James's position encompasses and transcends those of his rivals. Once again, I would suggest that this pattern applies to a good many public debates. But if that assertion is correct, it follows that anti-realism is not the best explanation for the persistent and widespread disagreement that we find in the public sphere.

IV. EXPLAINING POOR REASONING AND IGNORANCE

While I suspect that some of the factors that I have invoked in attempting to explain disagreement, such as the difficulty of issues and the fact that different people often do not have access to the same information, will elicit little controversy, others may not fare so well. In particular, my claim that many public debates result simply from poor reasoning and/or ignorance on one or more sides of a dispute may offend both some partisans of the Enlightenment (because of the claim's seeming denigration of reason) and many postmodernists (because of the claim's apparent arrogance and its real opposition to anti-realism).

In response, I will mention two factors which may account for much (though certainly not all) of the poor reasoning and ignorance that we find. Both of these factors tend to act as forces in opposition to reason, and thus their presence can help to explain why reason often fails to function properly without having to resort to the denial of the Enlightenment partisan's claims on behalf of the competence and relatively equal distribution of human reason. Whether or not the discussion of these factors helps to alleviate the charge of arrogance I will leave for the reader to decide.

A. The Contemporary Mass Media

Let us return to Chomsky's example concerning Nicaragua, the United States, and the World Court. Why were so many Americans ignorant of these events? Well, I recall that the paper I read regularly, the *Chicago Tribune*, failed to report on the World Court's condemnation of the United States. Could it be that vast amounts of (obviously newsworthy) information that is vital to the understanding of how the world works, and crucial for anyone who would participate knowledgeably in discussions of public policy matters, is routinely excluded from contemporary mass media journalism? Could it be, in short, that a major reason why most Americans are ignorant of their country's history is that the U.S. mass media generally fail to report on it?

Consider in this regard the sequence of events that unfolded after the World Court's decision. Chomsky, in another of his books,[13] provides the history. After the U.S. Congress defied the World Court by voting $100 million of military aid to the contras (the Court had called for termination of such aid),

> Nicaragua brought the matter to the U.N. Security Council, where the United States vetoed a resolution (11 to 1, 3 abstentions) calling on all states to observe international law. Nicaragua then turned to the General Assembly, which passed a resolution 94 to 3 calling for compliance with the World Court ruling. Two client states, Israel and El Salvador, joined the United States in opposition. The Security Council vote merited a brief note in the Newspaper of Record [Chomsky refers here to the *New York Times*], but the General Assembly endorsement passed unmentioned; the [*New York*] *Times* U.N. correspondent preferred a story that day on overly high U.N. salaries. . . . A year later, on November 12, 1987, the General Assembly again called for "full and immediate compliance" with the World Court decision. This time only Israel joined the United States in opposing adherence to international law. . . . The vote was not reported by the *New York Times*, the *Washington Post*, or the three TV networks. Subsequent World Court proceedings on the matter of reparations to Nicaragua for U.S. crimes have also rarely reached the threshold; thus the August 1988 World Court announcement that the United States had failed to meet the court's deadline on determining war reparations passed virtually without notice.[14]

Chomsky makes one more important observation in this connection. The press's failure to cover these United Nations votes in condemnation of the United States cannot be attributed to the press's lack of interest in comparable activities of the U.N. To the contrary, just one day prior to the unreported 1987 vote against the U.S., the *New York Times* ran a substantial story headlined "U.N. Urges Soviet to Pull Forces from Afghanistan" (11 November 1987).[15]

Thus, one large factor leading to ignorance—an ignorance which in turn stands as an obstacle in the way of the reaching of agreement—is the mass media's dismal performance in telling us what we need to know. That the media do routinely deprive us of vital information I will attempt to demonstrate more completely in chapter 6, where I shall also offer an attempt at an explanation as to why they behave this way. For now I will simply point out that, if I am right in making this charge, many Americans, who might otherwise be as intelligent and rational as you please, are, through no fault of their own save for an unwise over-reliance on the mass media for information, confronting the issues of public concern from a standpoint of appalling ignorance.

Moreover, in addition to the media's tendency to exclude important information, it is clear that at least two additional features of mass media treatments of serious public issues stand as obstacles to the intelligent resolution of disagreement. The features I have in mind—and here I do not fear that my remarks will be controversial—are the "both sides" model, and brevity. Let us look at each of these in turn.

1. The "Both Sides" Model

Part of the contemporary journalistic ethic of "objectivity" is that when controversial issues are to be addressed, the reader (or viewer or listener) must be presented with "both sides." Such an approach is deeply flawed, and for a good number of reasons.[16] For present purposes, I will concentrate only on those flaws which specifically render it harmful to the overcoming of disagreement in favor of the establishment of a rational consensus.

The first such flaw is revealed as soon as one considers that a rational consensus can only be reached if the focus of the discussion is centered on issues concerning the quality of the evidence and arguments supporting various positions on the issue at hand. But if that is the focus, it immediately follows that one will not automatically select two sides for consideration. Rather, on many issues, especially those of some complexity, the present state of human knowledge is such as to render more, and often *many* more, positions plausible and worthy of serious consideration. With regard to other issues (recall the examples of James and Chomsky above) it may be that one position is clearly correct, even if that position is not widely recognized as such. In the former kind of case, a consideration of only two issues illegitimately narrows and constricts the discussion, while in the latter kind of case an insistence on considering two views serves only to foist an unmerited plausibility on decisively refuted theses. Moreover, even in those relatively rare cases in which the rational procedure would indeed be to consider precisely two views, it is far from clear that the two views selected for inclusion in contemporary mass media discussions are the two which most merit this distinction in virtue of the strength of their supporting arguments and evidence. Rather, the two are selected by other criteria, such as entertainment value, or popularity, or, most notably, conformity to the spectrum of "mainstream" political opinion. Thus, both the insistence on presenting exactly two views and the criteria by which the two views are selected serve to distract us from the proper object of our attention (the strongest and most relevant evidence and arguments pertaining to the issue at hand), and often either deprive of us of a consideration of the positions most worthy of our attention or else dilute that consideration by juxtaposing it with unworthy competitors.[17]

But even more disastrous than the decision always to *start* with two positions is the insistence that one must also always *end* with two positions. Representatives of the two positions to be presented (I am thinking primarily of the broadcast media here) are chosen not for their knowledge, rationality, intellectual responsibility, fairness, willingness to consider carefully the merits of the other person's argument, openness to counterargument and counterevidence, and zeal to arrive at the truth, but rather for their entertainment value, which, in the context of pitting "both sides" against one another, usually translates to a lawyerly commitment to one's assigned side come what may, together with a readiness to engage in gratuitous name-calling and other varieties of specious argumentative strategies. As a result, viewers and listeners never have the experience of having "modeled" for them, to use some jargon from educational theory, a rational pursuit of truth resulting in the changing of minds and the reaching of consensus. It is little wonder that so many of those who saturate themselves in the mass media feel, perhaps even without ever thinking about it explicitly, that minds never are changed by rational arguments!

Indeed, what are the effects of repeated and unvarying exposure to this as the model of what a discussion of serious public issues is like? I suspect that the effects vary from person to person, but in just a few—I will mention three—standard ways, all of them bad. One likely effect is the reinforcement of dogmatism. Viewers and listeners who are most struck by the fact that the media experts never change their minds, never say something like, "Oh yes, I see; that's a good point; I overlooked that; perhaps I need to rethink my position," but rather stick to their guns no matter what, are most likely to be influenced in this way. On the other hand, another likely effect is the fostering of relativism or subjectivism. Audience members most likely to be influenced in this way would be those who are most taken with the "both sides" model's insinuation that there are always two equally credible sides to every question, and that no one can ever demonstrate that one is true and the other false. From there it is but a short step to believe that one may as well believe what one wants, or that such a belief will be "true for me," or that it is "all a matter of opinion." Finally, the "both sides" model may foster a centrist bias in some viewers and listeners. Some people are apparently quite easily persuaded that when two sides are locked in an intractable disagreement, the truth must lie "in the middle," somewhere "between" them. The fact that the participants in these media discussions are encouraged to be combative and stubborn may further encourage this belief by suggesting that the two sides are "extremes," even when, as is far too often the case, they represent a rather narrow range of opinion. What all three of these effects have in common is the discouraging of engaging in any effort to examine evidence and arguments in an attempt to arrive at the truth. Rather, one can simply stick with one's present position (the dogmatic reaction and one kind of relativist/subjectivist reaction), decide that there is no right or best position (another kind of relativist/subjectivist reaction), or else assume that the truth lies in between the two presented positions (the centrist bias reaction). In this way, the search for truth is killed and an intellectual quietism fostered.

2. Brevity

If this were not bad enough, on those extremely rare occasions in which someone attempts to use reason on television, there never seems to be enough time to present an argument, let alone reply thoughtfully to counterarguments and counterexamples, and the flow of argumentation that does manage to emerge, if any, is constantly interrupted by commercial messages. It is difficult to overcome disagreements by rational means under such constraints.[18]

B. *Confusions about Tolerance*

Another force acting in opposition to reason is the widespread idea that it is arrogant, oppressive, and intolerant to make truth claims. For example, Andrew Cutrofello asserts that "*truth claims and violence go hand in hand.* . . . [Our] sole 'truth' is the certainty that we do not possess truth. . . . So long as one claims to possess the truth, the will-to-violence is inevitable."[19]

But such an assertion is open to at least five objections:

(1) It seems to commit the *obscurum per obscurius* fallacy.[20] Is the (alleged) fact that we do not possess truth the most evident thing in the world? Is it more evident that we do not possess truth than that giraffes are taller than ants, that happiness is better than misery, or that colors are not shapes?

(2) If all we know is that we know nothing, then what is the status of the claim that truth claims and violence go hand in hand, with the former making the latter inevitable? Surely we do not know that and had best not make a truth claim concerning it, lest we be led to violence. What sort of terrain are we on here? How would one go about determining what sort of epistemic status this utterance has?

(3) Is there any way to investigate the claim empirically, perhaps by comparing those who make truth claims with those who do not, so as to see whether or not the former are more prone than the latter to engaging in acts of violence or to supporting such acts? Unfortunately, to perform this test we would have to find someone somewhere who does not make truth claims.

(4) Why can't one affirm, as truths, that giraffes are taller than ants, that happiness is better than misery, and that colors are not shapes without hauling off and punching someone? Couldn't one also affirm as a truth that violence is evil and to be avoided?

(5) Granted, dogmatism, imperviousness to reason, an unwillingness to entertain and consider other points of view than one's own, and general intolerance can lead to violence—though even here surely it is an exaggeration to say that this must happen "inevitably"—but this is not the same thing as merely making truth claims.

One reason why many people make such strange claims is that they apparently think that the only alternative to relativism or skepticism is to believe that "our" views (whatever that means) are better than those of another culture. For example, M. Leicester maintains that "[a]n absolutist assumes that her own cultural laws of thought and value judgments are *THE* only valid laws of thought and *THE* only valid value judgments and thus judges cultural alternatives from a perspective external to them. "[21] It is not uncommon for introductory discussions of relativism and objectivity to advance a similar claim.[22]

But realists need not be so ethnocentric or so arrogant. Rather, they can, and frequently do, believe that views prevailing in other cultures are right, and that those ascendant in their own are wrong[23] (or that both cultures are wrong, or that both of them are part right and part wrong). None of these options is open to the relativist or skeptic. Moreover, when realists believe that their own views are right (and how can this be avoided—what would it mean to believe x while not believing that such a belief is right?), they can do so while also holding a second-order belief that many of their first-order beliefs must be wrong.[24] Thus, the realists' main point is not that *they have* the right answer, but rather simply that *there is* a right answer.[25] It is the latter claim that relativists dispute; and when they hear realists make it they tend to conflate it with the former claim.

In any case, it is clear that many confused claims about tolerance stand as obstacles to the effective employment of reason, and that these confused claims, in turn, often spring from something like the argument from disagreement. In this case the variation on the argument goes something like this: Because we can't agree, it is arrogant, oppressive, and intolerant to claim to know the truth. So we'd better conclude that there is no (single, objective) truth. That way we can be tolerant of those who disagree with us.

That such an argument is confused and gives rise to multiple paradoxes can be seen by considering the following points (in addition to those made immediately above, and toward the end of chapter 1, part I). First, what is a defender of tolerance to do in the face of those who would treat others intolerantly? If one is tolerant of such intolerant individuals, then one fails to combat the intolerance that they inflict on others. Alternatively, if one refuses to tolerate this intolerance, then one acts intolerantly toward those who would inflict it. So which course of action is more consistent with a policy of tolerance? Can there be a general answer, or do we need a more nuanced position, one that is sensitive to, among other things, different kinds and different degrees of intolerance? And what does an explicit consideration of this dilemma tell us about the limitations of tolerance, about the relationships between tolerance and other values, about the rationale for tolerance, and about the incoherence of an attempted policy of pure tolerance? But notice that the argument in question tends to block off all of these urgently needed inquiries.

Second, notice that the paradoxes of tolerance are revealed whenever—and it happens with maddening and increasing frequency, both inside and outside of the academy—someone states, with great moral indignation, that it is morally wrong for anyone to make moral judgments about the actions of anyone else, and in so doing fails to notice the self-contradiction involved.

And the paradoxes are revealed yet again whenever a scholar claims that tolerance is morally mandated by our lack of moral knowledge, without noticing that this claim is itself a claim to moral knowledge. Finally, they are again revealed whenever someone asserts that tolerance is required, universally, by the "fact" that all knowledge is socially constructed and thus culture-specific, without noticing that, on its own terms, that claim itself would have to be understood as a social construct having only local validity, and as illegitimate in its claim to universality.

V. ETHICS

As this discussion of tolerance has now taken us in the direction of ethics, and since the argument from disagreement is perhaps most often appealed to in that domain,[26] it might prove useful to conclude this chapter by directly examining the argument in that context.

The argument is easy to state. The first premise is simply that we have a hard time achieving a consensus in ethics. Rather, we find a great deal of diversity and disagreement in the realm of ethics. The second premise is that such disagreement either implies, or at least is best explained by, the absence of real moral values and objective ethical truths. The conclusion is then that objectivity and realism should be rejected in ethics, in favor of some sort of relativism, subjectivism, or skepticism.

How might this reasoning be challenged? One possibility would be to attack the second premise, the one asserting that the presence of ethical disagreement tends to indicate the falsity of moral realism.

This premise is open to at least two objections. First, there are many nonmoral issues about which there is widespread and protracted disagreement, but about which it seems most implausible to assert that there is no objective truth. Thus, while there is great disagreement on the question of whether there is or is not a God, and on the question of whether or not there is intelligent life outside our solar system, it does appear that these questions, if formulated with adequate precision, must have objectively correct answers.[27]

Second, there is no mystery as to how moral disagreement might come about even on the assumption that there are objective moral truths. To put it another way, when people disagree in ethics, this need not be because ethics is not objective. People might disagree through ignorance, the distortion of violent emotions, commitment to an ideology learned at home or school, habit, a desire to conform, a desire to preserve one's self-image, or, quite simply, because of the complexity and difficulty of the moral question at hand.[28]

A more promising approach, however, might be to attack the first premise, the one asserting that the contemporary moral scene is indeed best characterized as exhibiting diversity, rather than consensus. Is there really so much disagreement? Such a claim is open to a wide variety of objections and counterarguments.

In this connection one might note, first, the argument, commonly found even in elementary textbook discussions of ethical relativism, that what is apparently ethical disagreement often proves on closer inspection to be more plausibly analyzed as ethical agreement applied either to different circumstances or to different non-ethical beliefs.

As an example of the former, consider the nature of the "disagreement" between, on the one hand, Inuit parents, who consider it right to dress one's children in many layers of warm clothing, and wrong to dress them in shorts, sandals, and light tops, and, on the other hand, Hawaiian parents, who assert the opposite valuations. Clearly this is not really an ethical disagreement, but rather an instance of the application of a single, agreed-upon ethical principle—something to the effect that children should be dressed in such a manner as is conducive to their optimum health and comfort—to widely divergent circumstances.

As an example of the latter, consider the disagreement between those who do and do not regard the eating of beef as immoral. Some, though of course not all, of the former take the position they do "because they believe that after death the souls of humans inhabit the bodies of animals, especially cows, so that a cow may be someone's grandmother."[29] Here the disagreement seems not to be ethical at all. Rather, as James Rachels puts it, "the difference lies elsewhere. The difference is in our belief systems, not in our values. We agree that we shouldn't eat Grandma; we simply disagree about whether the cow *is* (or could be) Grandma."[30] It should be pointed out, moreover, that the analysis of ethical disagreement suggested by these examples holds, not only for cross-cultural disagreements, but for disagreements within a single culture as well. For surely there too many seemingly ethical disputes are really attributable to disagreements concerning factual matters—the likely consequences of different policies or courses of action, for example.

Next, let us note that the impression that the extent of disagreement is greater in ethics than in such other domains of thought as, for example, science, may be attributable to what Alan Gewirth calls "the fallacy of disparateness—the fallacy of discussing one field on one level or in one respect and the other field on a quite different level or in a quite different respect."[31] Thus, the considerable disagreement surrounding *ultimate* principles in ethics is often unfairly compared to the considerable agreement to be found with regard to *intermediate level* questions in science—where the relevant matters of ultimate principle are simply assumed.[32] Similarly, comparisons between science and ethics with regard to the degree to which agreement is to be found within each domain are frequently rendered unfair by a failure to adjust for the fact that "science," unlike "ethics," is usually understood as implying certain normative restrictions. A belief or theory is not typically regarded as "scientific" unless it meets certain "value-criteria, such as logical consistency, empirical testability, [and] explanatory fruitfulness."[33] But no such restrictions are placed upon beliefs about ethical matters. Thus, the comparison between the agreement to be found in science and the disagreement running rampant in ethics is undone by the consideration that, for example, "philosophers do not regard both Christian Science and neurology as examples of 'science,' but they do regard the discourse of both Al Capone and Albert Schweitzer as examples of 'ethical' language."[34]

Finally, notice that we undoubtedly have a distorted view of the levels of agreement and disagreement prevailing in ethics simply because we tend to focus, for obvious reasons, on the disagreements. Abortion, euthanasia, and affirmative action occupy our attention precisely because they are controversial, while the consensus on the wrongness of slavery, murder, and rape goes unnoticed. But once we turn our focus explicitly to the domain of ethical agreement, we seem to encounter a rich and varied realm. It is difficult to imagine a greater degree of cross-cultural consensus to be found in any area of human thought than that regarding such value judgments as that "love is preferable to hate, peace to war, brotherhood to enmity, joy to sorrow, health to sickness, nourishment to hunger, life to death."[35] Thus, there appear to be ample grounds for challenging the claim that moral realism is rendered untenable by a lack of consensus with regard to moral beliefs.

NOTES

1. The widespread occurrence of this argument is by no means limited to the "popular" sphere, of course, but when philosophers and other scholars advance it they tend to do so in a more qualified and nuanced fashion than is characteristic of more popular presentations. Thus, to give just one famous example, J. L. Mackie's "argument from relativity" is an argument against the objectivity of ethics that takes as its premise "the well-known variation in moral codes from one society to another and from one period to another, and also the differences in moral beliefs between different groups and classes within a complex community" (*Ethics* [New York: Penguin, 1977], p. 36). But Mackie, in addition to confining his anti-realism to the domain of ethics, takes pains to insist that the premise supports ethical subjectivism only "indirectly," and that mere disagreement by itself is inconclusive. Thus, Mackie offers reasons for concluding that the argument from relativity, while cogent in the domain of ethics, is not in connection with science; and he addresses some likely objections to his position (see pp. 36–38). Nonetheless, it seems to me that the objections to pop anti-realism that I am about to present are also fatal to more sophisticated variants, such as Mackie's. Demonstrating this would be lengthy and tedious, however, so I will leave it as an exercise for the interested reader. In any case, focusing on simpler versions should help me to present the objections with maximum (by my standards, such as they are) economy and clarity.

2. Steve Allen, *Funny People* (New York: Stein and Day, 1984), p. 44.

3. Dietrich Von Hildebrand, *What Is Philosophy?* (New York: Routledge, 1991), p. 225, note 3.

4. Edward H. Carr, *What Is History?* (New York: Vintage, 1961), pp. 30–31.

5. Aristotle, *Nichomachean Ethics*, book two, section 6, 1106b28–33, trans. Martin Ostwald (Indianapolis: The Library of Liberal Arts, 1962), p. 43.

6. Ibid., 1106b18–23, p. 43.

7. Philip Kitcher, *The Advancement of Science* (New York: Oxford University Press, 1993), pp. 185–186.

8. As Nicholas Rescher puts it, "[a] view of this sort [that a lack of consensus undermines objectivity] fails to reckon satisfactorily with the reality of an *evidential* diversity that obtains (and must obtain) because different people are differently situated and accordingly have different bodies of evidence at their disposal. And this circumstance makes for a perfectly warranted—indeed rationally mandated—differentiation of belief." *Objectivity* (Notre Dame, IN: University of Notre Dame Press, 1997), pp. 46–47.

9. Bill James, *The Bill James Baseball Abstract 1982* (New York: Ballantine, 1982), pp. 44–45.

10. James himself provides many more examples of this sort of thing. For example, after showing that Milwaukee County Stadium, former home of the Milwaukee Brewers and, before that, the Milwaukee Braves, was (at least through 1984) a park favoring the pitcher and, in particular, a tough park in which to hit home runs (all of this relative to other major league baseball stadiums), gives in to exasperation in response to a correspondent who had inquired as to the reason why the opposite is so often believed: "[T]he 'dispute' isn't a disagreement about the evidence, but a disagreement between people who are looking at the evidence and people who aren't. It's like asking a naturalist why he doesn't do a complete, once-and-for-all study of the evidence on evolution and creationism. The evidence is already conclusive; it's just that there are people who don't intend to accept it unless the hand of God appears in the sky one afternoon and writes 'ALL RIGHT! I CONFESS! I DID IT BY EVOLUTION! IT TOOK ME YEARS! I'SE JUST KIDDING ABOUT THE SEVEN DAYS! AND BY THE WAY, MILWAUKEE COUNTY STADIUM IS A PITCHER'S PARK'" (Bill James, *The Bill James Baseball Abstract 1986* [New York: Ballantine, 1986], p. 147). For one more example, see James, *The Bill James Player Ratings Book 1993* (New York: Collier, 1993), pp. xviii–xix.

11. Noam Chomsky, "The Manufacture of Consent," in his *The Chomsky Reader*, ed. by James Peck (New York: Pantheon, 1987), pp. 124–125.

12. Other commentators have tended to take Moynihan at face value, not bothering to look up the historical record. For example, William Greider

in *Who Will Tell the People* (New York: Touchstone, 1993), p. 368, blandly asserts: "This was the first time in American history, Senator Moynihan noted, that an international tribunal had ever found the United States in violation of law."

13. Noam Chomsky, *Necessary Illusions* (Boston: South End Press, 1989), pp. 83–84.

14. In fairness to Greider, this time he gets it right: "[T]he World Court's decision received only brief, passing notice within the United States" (*Who Will Tell the People*, p. 368).

15. Chomsky, *Necessary Illusions*, p. 84.

16. For more on this, see chapter 6, section IV F, below.

17. I have presented these points abstractly here. For specific illustrative examples and further discussion, please see chapter 6, section IV F.

18. Chomsky points out an additional unfortunate effect of brevity in mass media discussions of serious issues:

> In the United States, if you do get on commercial radio or television you're allowed a minute or two, you can have a few words between commercials, that's what it comes down to. . . . There's a logic to this. In two minutes, between two commercials . . . you can say some conventional things. For example, if I'm given two minutes on the radio and I want to condemn the Russians for invading Afghanistan, that's easy. I don't need any evidence, I don't need any facts, I can make any claim that I want, anything goes because that's conventional thought, that's what everybody believes anyway, so if I say it it's not surprising, and I don't have to back it up.
>
> On the other hand, suppose I were to try in two minutes to condemn the U.S. invasion of South Vietnam, or the U.S. attack against Nicaragua. That sounds crazy. The U.S. isn't attacking people! So within two minutes between two commercials it sounds absurd, in fact any unconventional opinion sounds absurd. The reason is that if you say anything in the least way unconventional you naturally, and rightly, are expected to give a reason, to give evidence, to build up an argument, to say why you believe that unconventional thing. The very structure of the media in the United States prevents that, makes it impossible. The result is that what's expressible are conventional thoughts and conventional doctrine. That's a very effective technique for blocking thought and criticism. (*Chronicles of Dissent* [Monroe, ME: Common Courage Press, 1992], p. 131.)

This is the by now familiar problem of the seven-second soundbite, which dominates contemporary television news and public affairs programming.

19. Andrew Cutrofello, *The Owl at Dawn* (Albany: State University of New York Press, 1995), pp. 193, 195.

20. See chapter 1, part II.

21. M. Leicester, "Multicultural Curriculum or Anti-racist Education," *Multicultural Teaching to Combat Racism in School and Community* 4 (1986): 4–5.

22. One example is Michael Krausz and Jack W. Meiland, "Introduction" to a volume they edited, entitled *Relativism* (Notre Dame, IN: University of Notre Dame Press, 1982), pp. 1–3.

23. Max Hocutt, *First Philosophy* (Belmont, CA: Wadsworth, 1980), pp. 191–192, provides two examples:

> First, Europe uses the metric system whereas the United States uses the English units of measurement. Many people think that our system is better just because it is ours and we are familiar with it, but the metric system is vastly simpler and more orderly. Second, Americans eat many sweet and fatty foods with little natural fiber in them, but there is little doubt that we would be healthier if we ate more natural grains, as other peoples do. These two examples show that our own practices can be evaluated by using objective and impartial criteria.

And if ours can, why cannot those of other cultures (e.g., female circumcision, suttee, slavery, *tsujigiri* [the ancient Samurai practice of trying out one's new sword by bisecting an unsuspecting passerby], etc.)?

24. If this seems unclear, consider an example. Suppose I have to answer 100,000 arithmetic questions. Suppose further that they are all fairly easy problems well within my quite rudimentary mathematical competence. Suppose, finally, that I am quite careful in my work, and thus am confident with regard to any one of my answers that it is correct. Still, if I were asked if all 100,000 of my answers were right, I would feel an even greater confidence that the answer must be "no." Surely I must have made some mistakes. It's just that I don't know which ones they are, or I'd correct them! And I further realize that my beliefs on more difficult subjects are proportionately more likely to contain errors.

25. At the risk of trying the reader's patience, here is another simple example. If you and I are arguing about the height of a building that we are both observing from a distance, I will be far more confident that there is a single right answer to the question of whether it is or is not over one hundred feet tall than I will be that my own guess (that it is over one hundred feet tall) is the right one.

26. See, for example, the work by Mackie cited in note 1 above. Note

also that the argument from disagreement is used more often in ethics than in other domains primarily because it is widely believed that there is greater disagreement about ethical and other evaluative issues than there is about scientific or factual matters.

27. These examples come from Emmet Barcalow, *Moral Philosophy* (Belmont, CA: Wadsworth, 1994), p. 44.

28. A. C. Ewing explains this well. He suggests that differences of opinion in ethics

> may sometimes be explained by differences in people's experience of life. If I never experience A, I cannot realize the intrinsic goodness of A and may therefore wrongly subordinate it to something less good. . . . Even a long study of philosophical books would not qualify a person to pass a judgment on the intrinsic value of philosophy if he were hopelessly bad at the subject, because then, however many books he read, he would not have a genuinely philosophical experience. Two persons who differ as to the aesthetic value of a picture may really be judging about different things, their several experiences of it. Or at least their judgments will be based on different data. Other differences of view may be due to the misapplication of principles previously accepted, or to genuine intellectual confusions. . . . For instance a man may confuse badness and wrongness and conclude or assume, for example, that, because he really sees lying to be always bad (an evil), he sees it to be always wrong, while it may be a case of choosing the lesser evil rather than the greater. Often a man will think that he knows intuitively P to be R when he really sees it to be Q but confuses Q with R.
>
> Or the judgment that something is good or bad on the whole may have been due to concentrating attention on one side of it while ignoring or underestimating the other sides, as, for instance, militarists concentrate their attention on the unselfish heroism which war brings out in men and forget or underestimate war's evils. . . .
>
> The lack of attention I have mentioned is in some degree inevitable, but it is greatly enhanced by the influence of desire and prejudice. It is a commonplace that ethical mistakes are often due to non-intellectual factors. . . .
>
> So it may well be the case that all differences in people's judgments whether certain actions are right or wrong or certain things good or bad are due to factors other than an irreducible difference in ethical intuition. But, even if they should not be, we must remember that ethical intuition, like our other capacities, is presumably a developing factor and therefore may be capable of error.

But in any case we have said enough to show that great differences of opinion as to ethics are quite compatible with the objectivity of ethical judgments. (*The Definition of Good*, in *A Modern Introduction to Philosophy*, ed. Paul Edwards and Arthur Pap, 3d ed. [New York: Free Press, 1973], pp. 315–316; see also Ewing's *Ethics* [New York: Free Press, 1953], pp. 111–115.)

In a similar vein, John F. Post points out that "people frequently have powerful, self-interested motives for insisting that their position is the morally correct one—motives so strong as to compel them on occasion to deny even plain truth. . . . Little wonder, then, in light of the complexity of many moral issues and the partisan passions involved, that their history is one of widespread and continuing disagreement." *Metaphysics* (New York: Paragon House, 1991), p. 143.

29. James Rachels, *The Elements of Moral Philosophy*, 4th ed. (Boston: McGraw-Hill, 2003), p. 23. Ironically, despite our mutual fondness for this example, both Rachels and I condemn the eating of meat as immoral for reasons having nothing to do with a belief in reincarnation. Rachels's reasons can be found in his *Created from Animals* (New York: Oxford University Press, 1990). Mine are presented in "Of Pigs and Primitive Notions," *Between the Species* 8, no. 4 (fall 1992): 203–208.

30. Ibid. (emphasis added).

31. Alan Gewirth, "Positive 'Ethics' and Normative 'Science,'" in *Ethics*, ed. Julius R. Weinberg and Keith E. Yandell (New York: Holt, Rinehart and Winston, 1971), p. 54.

32. Ibid. Renford Bambrough expresses a similar disagreement with the argument from moral disagreement, noting that it

loses much of its plausibility as soon as we insist on comparing the comparable. We are usually invited to contrast our admirably close agreement that there is a glass of water on the table with the depth, vigour and tenacity of our disagreements about capital punishment, abortion, birth control and nuclear disarmament. But this game may be played by two or more players. A sufficient reply in kind is to contrast our general agreement that this child should have an anaesthetic with the strength and warmth of the disagreements between cosmologists and radio astronomers about the interpretation of certain radio-astronomical observations. If the moral sceptic then reminds us of Christian Science we can offer him in exchange the Flat Earth Society. (*Moral Scepticism and Moral Knowledge* [Atlantic Highlands, NJ: Humanities Press, 1979], p. 18.)

33. Gewirth, "Positive 'Ethics,'" p. 55.

34. Ibid.

35. Howard Zinn, *The Politics of History* (Boston: Beacon Press, 1971), p. 23. Education may also contribute to our distorted comparison of ethics and science. Quite simply, by the time we take a course in ethics we are sufficiently expert in ethics—we already know the obvious stuff that need not be discussed (that happiness is better than misery, that sadistic cruelty is wrong, etc.)—that we can dive right into the controversial material and use the knowledge and skills that we already have to make headway. But in science, by contrast, we have to learn the uncontroversial stuff in classes, and most of us, alas, quit taking science classes before we are ready to tackle anything controversial.

Chapter 4

SARTRE'S
DEFENSE OF TRUTH

L et me now attempt to be more positive. I will take a breather from advancing criticisms of those who reject objective truth and instead attempt to speak more directly in favor of that much-maligned concept. Unfortunately, my flesh is weak, and I fear that I will find myself renewing the attack on assorted postmodernists, relativists, and subjectivists as we move along. However, even then, I will at least attempt to lay off the self-referential inconsistency objection for a while and will mention it only a couple of times in this chapter, and briefly at that.

I. SARTRE ON THE ETHICS AND POLITICS OF TRUTH

In this chapter (and in the next two) my approach to the subject at hand will be by way of the work of Jean-Paul Sartre, who, implicitly in his discussions of authenticity and bad faith, and explicitly in his extensive discussion of epistemic responsibility in *Truth and Existence*,[1] advocates an "ethics of truth" every bit as severe and uncompromising as anything to be found in the writings of David Hume or William Kingdon Clifford. Like those thinkers, Sartre maintains that we have an ethical—and he would add a political—obligation to proportion our beliefs to the relevant evidence, and not to indulge in beliefs that are not warranted by a scrupulous examination of the relevant arguments. But what reasons can he offer in support of such strictures?

The first reason is simply that, in any undertaking, including that of political action, there is no substitute for having an accurate and truthful understanding of the relevant facts. For to be ignorant of intolerable political conditions is to be unaware of the need to change them; and to lack knowledge as to how these conditions might be changed for the better, or, what is worse, to have incorrect information—to mistake the false for the true—is to be unable to effect the positive changes that are called for (for the same reason that I am unable to perform a successful brain surgery). It is largely for these reasons that Sartre equates authenticity with "having a true and lucid consciousness of the situation," and with then "assuming the responsibilities and risks that it involves."[2] And this is also why, in *Truth and Existence*, he repeatedly associates the pursuit of truth with responsibility and identifies the courting of ignorance with irresponsibility. Here is just one representative passage:

> The will to ignore is . . . the refusal to face our responsibilities. Since indeed, Being appears, in principle, as that for which we have to assume responsibility without having wanted it, the For-itself can project the veiling of Being in order not to be obliged to assume it. As a bourgeois I want to ignore the proletariat's condition in order to ignore my responsibility for it. As a worker, I may want to ignore this condition because I am in solidarity with it and its unveiling obliges me to take sides. I am responsible for everything to myself and to everyone, and ignorance aims to limit my responsibility in the world. . . . Ignoring = denial of responsibilities.[3]

A second, though closely related, reason for regarding truth as essential to morality and to sound politics is this: Immoral policies are propped up by lies and sustained by ignorance. If a policy is indefensible, surely an accurate understanding of the facts relevant to it, coupled with an appreciation for the force of the arguments concerning it, will support those attempting to overturn it, and not those determined to keep it in force. For this reason, oppressors of all kinds have always sought to weaken in other people a sense of reality and an appreciation for truth. Ironically, it seems that they are lent considerable unwitting aid in this project by many contemporary postmodernists.

Eve Browning Cole explains this clearly in connection with feminism:

> There are . . . good reasons for caution about the relinquishing of the concept of objectivity as understood by Western science. Many of the most significant advances in women's political history have been achieved through successfully putting across the argument that barriers to women's freedom are based only on prejudice, a mistaken and subjective attitude. Appeals to fairness, justice, and dispassionate objectivity have been powerful elements in this argument. Most of us believe that sexism, racism, heterosexism, and other pernicious attitudes are not objectively defensible, are based in part on false beliefs and bad faith or moral inconsistency. If we no longer have a standpoint from which to make these claims, with what justification can we continue to decry the attitudes? We ought rather to seek to reconceive the notions of objectivity, justice, and truth than to discard them and leave ourselves rhetorically helpless.[4]

Or again, Douglas V. Porpora makes the point in connection with United States foreign policy:

> Intellectual reflection holds little interest for the majority of United States citizens, who tend to accept uncritically whatever beliefs have been handed down to them. . . . [S]uch lack of interest in critical reflection is one of the factors that make Holocaust-like events possible. Right actions require right beliefs, for if our beliefs are mistaken, our actions can be right only by accident. Often, the actions guided by mistaken beliefs will be mistaken as well. For example, if we are mistaken in our belief that communism is the ultimate evil to be countered in the world today, then we will be mistaken when we act to support our government in its promotion of anticommunist but genocidal regimes throughout the world. . . . Thus, particularly when our beliefs are socially consequential, we have a moral obligation to take responsibility for our beliefs, to constantly scrutinize them in light of new evidence, and if need be to refine them, modify them, or even outgrow them altogether. In the end, the quest for truth cannot be left to an intellectual elite in their ivory towers. It is a quest that each one of us is morally obliged to join. That may be the most important lesson of the Holocaust.[5]

Sartre makes similar points in many places. One need only recall, for example, his condemnation of "faith" in *Being and Nothingness*;[6]

his repeated appeal to writers to be "committed" to exposing the truth about injustices in the world, so as to facilitate their elimination;[7] his demand that the press, including the revolutionary press, tell the truth;[8] his insistence that "[w]e have to create a desire for the truth, in ourselves and in others";[9] and his numerous discussions of the ethics of truth in *Truth and Existence*.[10]

With these points in mind, I think it is remarkable, though, to my knowledge, it has never been noted, how existentialist—how Sartrean, in particular—is the famous position on the ethics of belief defended by William Kingdon Clifford. For example, Clifford tells of a ship-owner who, tempted by the profit to be made by sending an old ship of questionable sea-worthiness across the sea to deliver some cargo, but burdened by the thought that such a venture might endanger the crew, eventually

> succeeded in overcoming these melancholy reflections. He said to himself that [the ship] had gone safely through so many voyages and weathered so many storms that it was idle to suppose she would not come safely home from this trip also. He would put his trust in Providence. . . . He would dismiss from his mind all ungenerous suspicions about the honesty of builders and contractors. In such ways he acquired a sincere and comfortable conviction that his vessel was thoroughly safe and seaworthy; he watched her departure with a light heart, . . . and he got his insurance money when she went down in mid-ocean and told no tales.[11]

Or again:

> It is not only the leader of men, statesman, philosopher, or poet, that owes this bounden duty to mankind. Every rustic who delivers in the village alehouse his slow, infrequent sentences may help to kill or keep alive the fatal superstitions which clog his race. Every hard-worked wife of an artisan may transmit to her children beliefs which shall knit society together, or rend it in pieces. No simplicity of mind, no obscurity of station can escape the universal duty of questioning all that we believe.[12]

II. THE POLITICAL ECONOMY OF TRUTH-REJECTION

But why is such hortatory rhetoric, stirring though it might be, necessary? Why do we have so little desire for the truth? In answering this question, Sartre has contributed much to what might be called "the political economy of truth-rejection." For example, in *Saint Genet*, he refers to

> the bourgeois salons where the hostess knows how to avoid quarrels because she has the art of reducing objective value judgments [that play is *bad*, that political operation is *blameworthy*] to purely subjective opinions [I *don't like* that play, etc.]. If it is taken for granted that you are merely depicting yourself in condemning police repression of a miners' strike, you will not be disturbing anyone. "I disapprove of the death penalty," said Clemenceau. To which Barres, who was fond of the guillotine, replied: "Of course, Monsieur Clemenceau can't bear the sight of blood."[13]

The bad political implications of this are obvious, and are underscored even more sharply by Sartre in the first two paragraphs of his *Anti-Semite and Jew*:

> If a man attributes all or part of his own misfortunes and those of his country to the presence of Jewish elements in the community, if he proposes to remedy this state of affairs by depriving the Jews of certain of their rights, by keeping them out of certain economic and social activities, by expelling them from the country, by exterminating all of them, we say that he has anti-Semitic *opinions*.
>
> The word *opinion* makes us stop and think. It is the word a hostess uses to bring to an end a discussion that threatens to become acrimonious. It suggests that all points of view are equal; it reassures us, for it gives an inoffensive appearance to ideas by reducing them to the level of tastes. All tastes are natural; all opinions are permitted. Tastes, colors, and opinions are not open to discussion.[14]

Moreover, in *Truth and Existence* Sartre even goes so far as to say that the rejection of truth stems from a rejection of Being itself, and conversely, that "[t]he love of truth is the love of Being."[15] Alternatively, he sometimes says that to love the truth is to have "a taste for being,"[16] or "to enjoy Being."[17] And he makes remarks on a similarly deep ontological plane in connecting truth to freedom, as when he claims that "the fear of truth is fear of freedom"[18] or again that "truth appears only to free projects. . . . [A]ll free behavior is revelatory—unveiling"[19] or, finally: "no freedom without truth."[20]

His main point, however, is that the embracing of an anti-truth epistemology serves as a general foundation for a wide range of specific excuses—that is, in a global way, it serves to relieve us of our responsibilities (just as the acceptance of determinism does). Specifically, it relieves us of the responsibility to discover the truth, and to act accordingly. Rather, it always allows us to say, even in connection with an issue about which we have undertaken neither detailed research nor even a project of thinking, and even to an interlocutor whom we know to be very knowledgeable about it: "You have your opinion and I have mine, and who is to say which is right? They are both just opinions. Mine is as good as yours." Similarly, it entails that we need never fear having to change our way of life on the grounds that some aspect of it might be inconsistent with what is true. Here is perhaps Sartre's clearest statement of these matters, in which he explains how an *avoidance* of a *localized* and *specific* truth can lead, eventually, to the *denial* of *truth itself*:

> And, finally, I hide the very idea of truth. . . . Ultimately, truths are replaced by *opinion*. Opinion is no longer free and verifiable anticipation of Being. . . . It appears . . . as pure present or as pure contingency. We *have* an opinion, we do not know why. If we want to *explain*, we will seek the explanation contrary to the future one: the explanation by means of (past) causality. Opinion comes from heredity, our environment, education. . . . I am not *responsible* for my opinions. . . . Opinion being what it is, I feel no obligation at all to verify it. *Since* I am not responsible for it, why should I be obligated to find out if it is true? Ultimately, opinion is a pure *character trait*. In conclusion, to want a world of opinions, is to want a lesser *truth*, that is both a lesser Being, a lesser freedom and a looser relationship between unveiling freedom and the In-itself. If I say that this is my opinion, I mean that I cannot stop myself from thinking in this way but I admit that you cannot stop yourself from thinking the opposite. Yet I do not judge it possible that someone can possess the *truth* on this question. Otherwise my *opinion* would be in error. Therefore I figure quite simply that the truth is not possible. For this reason the sick person who does not want to know that she has

tuberculosis will say about doctors: Oh, what do they know! They
all have a pet theory, etc. Therefore, the will to ignore the truth
turns necessarily into the denial of truth.[21]

III. SARTRE VS. THE POSTMODERNISTS

At this point one might well wonder about the relevance of Sartre's
enthusiasm for truth in this postmodern age, in which that concept
has been cast under so much suspicion. After all, the postmodernists
have indeed mounted several powerful arguments against prevailing
positivist and naive realist understandings of truth, and it may appear
that Sartre's own position has failed to anticipate these arguments
and does not really make substantial contact with the postmodern
alternative. But I would argue, however, that even if we concede that
many of the postmodernists' arguments against some of the cruder
conceptions of objectivity, reality, and truth are indeed cogent and
convincing, it is premature to turn, as if by default, to the embracing
of a view in which all sense of reality and truth is lost, or else radically subjectivized or relativized. Rather, what is needed is first to
consider whether or not there might be available a subtler, more
nuanced understanding of objectivity, reality, and truth—one that
would be capable of reflecting our strong, experientially grounded
sense of their presence (to be discussed subsequently), but one
which would also be able to withstand the strong objections which
have motivated so many to renounce objectivity, reality, and truth
entirely. It seems to me that Sartre provides such an understanding.

A. Against the Positivist/Postmodernist False Dilemma: The Crag's Presence and Pierre's Absence

To see this, let us consider two of Sartre's famous examples from
Being and Nothingness. The first one[22] asks us to suppose that in
walking through the countryside I encounter a large crag, jutting up
out of the ground. As against the journalistic or positivistic "objectivist" position, Sartre argues that I cannot encounter the crag as a
neutral mass of data, but always, and from the very outset, as something that has a particular meaning which is at least in part
dependent upon my projects, interests, theories, etc. Thus, if I am a

farmer who is intent upon clearing the field, for purposes of planting crops, in which the crag is located, I am likely to see the crag *immediately* as an obstacle. If I am intent on getting high up in the air in order to view the countryside, I am likely to see the crag *immediately* as something to be climbed. If I am an enthusiast for natural landscapes, and engaged in no purely practical pursuits at present, I am likely to see the crag *immediately* in aesthetic terms—as beautiful or ugly, for example. These points—that observation is fundamentally *active*; that it requires of the observer *focusing* and *selective* attention; that perception is not something fully determined by the physical and physiological conditions of the external situation; that one does not "take in" brute, meaningless sense-data which are only subsequently fashioned into an interpretation which gives them meaning, but that observation, instead, always involves an interpretive dimension; and that value-judgments, far from being separate and additional to the data of perception, are present in them from the very outset, as when the crag is *immediately* perceived in such value-laden terms as "obstacle," "aid," or as "beautiful" or "ugly"—have been well made by assorted postmodernists. Why, then, should we not simply concur with their approach?

Here I think one should recall, following Sartre, the recalcitrant dimension of the "external," or the "real" in our perceptual experience—the dimension which distinguishes perception from imagination and fantasy. Thus, while the subjectivists are right to point out that the perception of something as an "obstacle" cannot arise apart from my subjective project of, say, trying to clear a field, they cannot account as easily for the fact that some crags are greater obstacles than others—some are easy to remove from the field, while others may prove impossible to budge. Similarly, my perception of a crag as an "aid to be climbed so as to view the countryside," while it undoubtedly rests substantially upon my desire to view the countryside, also rests upon the "climbability" of the crag—its height and the angle of its incline, for example. Are these last-named items to be understood as being "purely subjective"?

What needs to be underscored is the idea that there is never a pure datum or a pure constructum. What we find is never the object in its brute nudity, but rather always as it is illuminated by our focusing, questioning, valuing, etc. But these activities of ours, in turn, are always conditioned by, or in response to, what is given. The two phases of this dialectic are inextricably bound up with one another and cannot be intelligibly separated.

Moreover, insofar as it makes sense at all to distinguish "my" contribution to perception from that of "the object," my experience suggests that the degree to which the meaning inherent in a perception is determined by the former as opposed to the latter varies greatly from case to case. Thus, for example, while "the meaning" of a fable written for children might be so obvious that absolutely no one can mistake it, no matter how differently the individual readers might approach it, and no matter how diverse their interests, values, and expectations might be, a story by Kafka, contrastingly, is likely to admit of several different and incompatible interpretations, so that the influence of the reader's activity in reading the story on the ultimate determination of its meaning is likely to be much greater. And in a looser, more poetic and open-ended story than those composed by Kafka—one lacking the tight narrative structure characteristic of his works—the determining influence of the reader's activity is likely to increase still more, with the controlling influence of "the given" diminishing correspondingly.

A final moral of the crag story concerns the nature of realism. It shows that realism does not imply that there is one true description of the crag to the exclusion of all other true descriptions. Rather, there are an infinite number of true things that one can say about the crag, though the realism of this account means that they are made true by virtue of the nature of the crag, not by our opinion, taste, consensus or the like. Opinion-independence is not at all the same thing as being describable in only one correct way. Nor, for the same reason, does realism entail that there is some "final vocabulary" in terms of which the crag ought to be described. The question of whether or not there is such a final vocabulary is utterly different from the question of whether or not, relative to some vocabulary, statements are made true by the nature of things, as opposed to by cultural consensus or something of that kind.

The other famous example of Sartre's that I wish to consider runs roughly as follows.[23] Suppose I go to a café and immediately undertake an exhaustive search for my friend Pierre, whom I hope to find there. When my thorough and careful search for Pierre reveals only his absence, I reluctantly conclude that he is not in the café. The point of this story, for my present purpose, is that it too illustrates the inadequacy of the positivism/postmodernism dichotomy. For notice that it seems odd to deny that Pierre's absence in some sense depends upon my being engaged in the project of looking for him. (After all, billions of other people are also absent from the café—would we want to say that all of these billions of absences objectively exist in the café?) But notice as well that Pierre's absence is not "projected" upon the café by some subjective act of consciousness, or by some kind of "social construction." Rather, and in a very real sense, this absence is *found* or *discovered* in the café. Had Pierre *really been there* in the café, an exhaustive search for his presence would have rendered the discovery of his absence impossible. His real presence would have precluded any "social construction" of his absence, just as it would have falsified any individual "choice" affirming the same.

Sartre's view retains objectivity, then, in the sense that it is hostile to the notion that truth is simply a construction. Rather, he contends that our constructions often turn out to be flat-out wrong, with their wrongness being revealed through our contact with something external and alien to us, and to our constructions—hence the realism of Sartre's position. To put it another way, we encounter the "coefficient of adversity" of things just as much in our activity of constructing theories as we do in any of our other projects. Thus, while Sartre's disagreement with positivists and naive realists, and his agreement with postmodernists, is apparent in such claims as that "destruction is an essentially human thing and . . . *it is man* who destroys his cities through the agency of earthquakes or . . . who destroys his ships through the agency of cyclones . . . ,"[24] and that "my expectation has caused the absence of Pierre *to happen* as a real event concerning this café,"[25] his disagreement with postmodernists is equally apparent when he immediately goes on to explain that "destruction, although coming into being through man, is an *objective fact* and not a thought[;] [f]ragility has been impressed upon the very being of this vase, and its destruction would be an irreversible absolute event which I could only verify,"[26] and that "[i]t is an objective fact at present that I have *discovered* [Pierre's] absence, and it presents itself as a synthetic relation between Pierre and the setting in which I am looking for him."[27] Given these strong differences which distinguish Sartre's position—let's call it "phenomenological realism"—from both positivism and naive realism, on the one hand, and postmodernism, on the other, it follows that postmodernism cannot justify itself merely by refuting positivism and naive realism, and then presenting itself as the alternative. Rather, it must justify itself in comparison to Sartre's position as well. Can it do so?

B. *The Lived Experience of Truth*

The first point to be made here is that the presence of reality and of truth, in the senses described above, does appear powerfully as a datum of our experience, a fact which postmodernists implicitly acknowledge by admitting that the affirmation of this presence is the "obvious" or "commonsensical" position, and by always pitching their attacks instead against (some) theoretical accounts of this datum. This leaves the postmodernist position vulnerable on two fronts. First, as we have already seen, this argumentative strategy entails that the postmodernist position is plausible only insofar as the many different theoretical accounts supporting the "obvious" data of our experience have been *exhaustively* considered and dismissed. Second, and this is the point I wish to explore now, in their readiness to explain away the "givens" of experience as deceptive and illusory, the postmodernists tend not to explore these givens to any degree of detail adequate to determining their evidential value. Rather, the strategy is to point out, quite correctly, that some things that are taken as obvious are in fact unfounded cultural prejudices or other distortions, and then to proceed directly to arguments undermining *some theoretical accounts* of the data of experience. Thus, since I have already pointed out that postmodernists address only some of these theoretical accounts, not all, and specifically not Sartre's, now I want to underscore the point that they address *theoretical accounts* of the data of experience, and not the data themselves, by turning to Sartre's description of these data.

In *Truth and Existence*, Sartre writes:

> I live amid the true and the false. The beings that manifest themselves to me are given as true and subsequently they sometimes reveal themselves as false. The For-Itself lives in the truth like a fish in the water. . . . [28] The reality . . . is that the being that manifests truth is in the world, is of the world, and is in danger in the world. The reality is that the illuminator can be destroyed (or strengthened or overcome) by what it illuminates. This belonging to the world of truth, or Reality, can also be defined as the fact that truth is *experienced* or lived.[29]

What might he mean by this? Once in graduate school a friend of mine, in a conversation with me, passionately defended relativism and the thesis that the concept of "truth" should be rejected as outmoded, unintelligible, and pernicious. A few minutes later, after we had tired of this topic and turned instead to a consideration of recent developments in his personal life, he informed me that his former realtor was now claiming that he had had cats in his apartment, and thus that his deposit would not be returned. Then, in a deliciously unguarded moment, he angrily exclaimed that this "just is not true; it is totally false!"

Indeed, the defenders of postmodernism do not really want, *in their own lives*, the kind of relativism which would render equally valid the claims of the basest oppressors and those of their victims. Nor do they wish, *in their own lives*, to embrace a skepticism so sweeping as to render us incapable of knowing whether or not we have kept pets in our apartment, or of finding out the facts relevant to determining who is right in the dispute described above, or, once the facts have been found, so to determining. Thus, there is a dilemma for the postmodern truth-rejecters: Either they are guilty of robbing us of the capacity for acknowledging the simple truths that we recognize and need in the daily functioning of our lives, and for political purposes in denouncing gross and obvious injustices, or else they have to admit that some of our claims are simply true. We simply find that some things are the case, others not—think, for example, of painful acknowledgments.

What is needed, then, is an experientially grounded sense of reality and unreality, together with a recognition that the comforts of subjectivism (e.g., I can never be wrong) are bought at too high a price (e.g., no one else can ever be wrong, including evil realtors, Hitler, etc.). Also, the case shows that subjectivism is not always comforting. Consider, for example, how outraged, even violated, one can feel when an important remembered experience is misrepresented. From a Sartrean standpoint, or from an existential-phenomenological one more generally, moreover, I would argue that my graduate-school friend's problem stemmed from overvaluing theory at the expense of concrete and specific judgments formed in the richness of lived experience. That such a failing is ubiquitous among postmodernists is an irony, given postmodernism's obsession with contingency and particularity.

In any case, it seems to me that Sartre provides concrete, detailed descriptions which establish the ineliminable presence of truth, in some "hard," non-relativist sense, as a datum of our experience. I will mention just four of the many features of our experience to which he calls attention in this connection.

1. Transphenomenality

The first such feature Sartre calls "the transphenomenal being of the phenomenon" (this is a major theme of Sartre's "Introduction" to *Being and Nothingness*),[30] that is, the inexhaustible character of objects of experience, or the fact that there is always more, indeed, infinitely more, to be seen in any object than can be gleaned from any finite series of its appearances. The relevance of such transphenomenality becomes clear when we ask: Were I imprisoned within my own perspective, so that I saw only it and not the object in question, or if it were the case that I could see in the object only what had in some sense already been put there in it by some process of "social construction of meaning," how could it be that I can *always*, and with regard to *anything*, and *forever*, no matter how long I continue looking, ceaselessly find new features and aspects of the thing—features, moreover, some of which cannot plausibly be said to have been instilled in me by any kind of cultural conditioning? How can this be unless I do in fact have some sort of contact (albeit partial) with real things which infinitely overflow our constructions, societal and otherwise, concerning them? (Note the implications of this for humility and tolerance. Objectivity entails that there are always things that we do not know.)

2. Surprise

The second relevant feature of experience is the phenomenon of surprise.[31] For no matter how strongly I might have been conditioned to look at a given phenomenon in a certain way, the possibility always remains that my experience of the phenomenon will run counter to my, say, culturally induced expectations, with the resulting surprise motivating me to revise, or perhaps reject, the relevant culturally induced beliefs and attitudes. Such experiences suggest that it is possible to encounter things and meanings which are not cultural constructs and which transcend or overflow any constructions which may have been built up around them.

3. Coefficient of Adversity

Next, recall Sartre's many famous discussions of "the coefficient of adversity" of things, that is, the strong, experientially grounded sense that external objects and states of affairs frequently put up actual resistance to us in the undertaking of our projects—even including the projects of perceiving and conceptualization.[32] Quite simply, I cannot easily bend things to my will, even in thought. Rather, the objects of my experience tend to present themselves with a certain stubborn obtrusiveness, so that they resist my attempt to deny them or alter them, or even, though perhaps less so, to reconceptualize or redescribe them. Such experienced resistance strongly suggests, once again, that I am encountering something real, and something which is, moreover, external to and more than my perspectives of it and my conceptions concerning it.

4. Bad Faith

A related phenomenon is that of bad faith. For notice that if it were possible for us to alter the world at will, we would have no need to lie to ourselves about the world. In fact, however, the coefficient of adversity of things is such that frequently reality stubbornly insists upon pressing unpleasant, unalterable (or alterable only at great cost) truths to our attention, thus tempting us to pursue the active project of denying to ourselves the truths we cannot tolerate. This is a major theme of *Truth and Existence*, in which Sartre presents such memorable examples as that of the "distinguished carnivore" who "refuses to visit the slaughterhouses"[33] and the tubercular woman who refuses to see a doctor, for fear that he will verify that she does, indeed, have tuberculosis.[34] These examples make clear that at least this form of bad faith is motivated by an encounter with a recalcitrant reality. One can deny that one has tuberculosis, and a culture can redefine or reconceptualize it out of existence—but that will not stop "this cough, this spitting of blood, this fever."[35] Granted, reality leaves us considerable freedom to construct alternative taxonomies of diseases, but this does not render illness itself, or the miserable experience of it, a social construction of any kind. Were it otherwise, the force of the temptation to lie to oneself about the symptoms of tuberculosis would be greatly diminished.

C. *Self-Referential Inconsistency*

An additional objection of Sartre's to postmodern truth-rejection, though hardly original or unique to him, is that such a position tends to be self-referentially inconsistent. He makes the point in *Saint Genet*:

> A feeble fashion in keeping with present-day complacency . . . claim[s] that the novelist depicts himself in his characters and the critic in his criticism. If Blanchot writes about Mallarmé, we are told that he reveals much more about himself than about the author he is examining. This is the residue of nineteenth-century bourgeois idealism, that inane subjectivism which is responsible for a great deal of . . . nonsense. . . . See what it leads to: Blanchot has seen, in Mallarmé, only Blanchot; very well: then you see, in Blanchot, only yourself. In that case, how can you know whether Blanchot is talking about Mallarmé or about himself? That is the vicious circle of all skepticism. So let us drop this outmoded cleverness.[36]

D. *Reductionism and Simple-Mindedness*

Bearing these Sartrean points in mind, and noting especially Sartre's skill at handling complexity and nuance, one can also criticize postmodern truth-rejection on grounds of reductionism and simplemindedness. To see this, let us look at a specimen of such thinking.

Barry W. Sarchett, while endorsing what he calls "the postmodern turn," writes:

> The postmodern turn . . . requires that we pay as much attention to who is speaking and who is not authorized to speak as we do to what is being spoken. It requires a sense therefore that all knowledge and values depend on power differentials. . . . When people talk about what is true or false, good or bad, the postmodern response is to pose more questions: better or worse for whom? In what context? For what purposes? [37]

Now, before I get to the "reductionism and simple-mindedness" bit, please note the self-referential inconsistency problem. Insofar as Sarchett is claiming that these postmodern insights are true, or at least constitute a better way of looking at things than do their competitors, his own position forces him to concede that this truth or superiority depends upon "power differentials"; that postmodernism is a better way of looking at things (than would be, say, the idea that there are universal, timeless truths, accessible to everyone) only for *some* people, in *some* contexts, and for *some* purposes; and that in assessing these claims in support of the postmodern turn we must pay as much attention to the fact that it is Barry Sarchett who is issuing them (what exactly are we to do with this information?) as to the content of the assertions themselves. (Note also how well Sarchett's reasoning fits the pattern that Sartre rejects as "outmoded cleverness" in the passage from *Saint Genet* quoted above.)

Moving now to my central point for this section, note that postmodernists pride themselves on their sophistication, especially their appreciation of complexities and problems that the dimwitted positivists blithely ignore (postmodernists like to talk about "problematizing" issues, and about discovering "aporias" in what would seem to the more naive to be straightforward matters of commonsense reasoning), and on their love of diversity. But they constantly take positions just as simplistic and lacking in nuance and diversification as those they criticize. They imagine that their antagonists are never interested in who is speaking, as opposed to the content of what is being said. Their response is to insist that we should always take such an interest ("the postmodern turn *requires*" this, Sarchett tells us). Where is their vaunted love of context now? Would not a more sophisticated and complex position, as well as (infinitely more importantly) a more *valid* one, be that the taking of such an interest is sometimes called for and sometimes not, and, further, that when it is called for it is sometimes crucial and sometimes of lesser significance, and so forth, all depending, in large matter, upon context? (For example, such questions are crucial when someone is offering testimony, that is, telling us what he or she has witnessed that we have not, as opposed to presenting arguments, especially when these have the character of drawing inferences from information that is already accessible to the audience evaluating the arguments. These questions are also sometimes helpful in evaluating claims by experts, when we lack the knowledge or competence to assess their arguments on their merits.) Similarly, while it is doubtless often useful to ask Sarchett's "better or worse for whom, and in what context and for what purposes?" questions, should we *always* ask them, in *all* contexts? Here again we find a simplistic, absolutistic position that is insensitive of context and intolerant of diversity. (Please note that Sarchett says that these questions are to be asked "when people talk about what is true or false, good or bad.") Should we ask these questions when we are told that 2 + 2 = 4, that giraffes are taller than ants, that having a bullet shot through your heart at point-blank range will tend to injure or kill you, and that kindness is better than cruelty?[38]

E. The Communicative Adequacy of Language

Some postmodernists regard language as such a slippery and unstable medium as to foreclose the possibility of its use in saying anything clearly or in formulating valid truth-claims. Sartre's own view is about as far from this as one could possibly get, and he supports his position with the following powerful example: "[L]anguage is elliptical. If I want to let my neighbor know that a wasp has got in by the window, there is no need for a long speech. 'Look out!' or 'Hey!'—a word is enough, a gesture—as soon as he sees the wasp, everything is clear."[39]

F. History vs. Historicism

Recall Bridges's claim, quoted in the introductory section of chapter 1, that the historically situated character of our thought and of the contents of our thought is sufficient to close off for us the possibility of acquiring "objective knowledge of history." As against such reasoning, Sartre remarks in *Saint Genet*: "I believe in the existence of transhistorical truths. There is nothing sublime about these truths. But if I say, for example: 'Descartes wrote the *Discourse on Method*,' that is true for all ages. This truth is not 'eternal,' since its content is historical and dated. But it is transhistorical, for it does not depend on the economic, social or religious evolution of mankind. It will be as true in a hundred years as it is today."[40]

G. The Blindingly Obvious vs. The Culturally Familiar

In *Nausea*, Sartre writes: "They have proof, a hundred times a day, that everything happens mechanically, that the world obeys fixed, unchangeable laws. In a vacuum all bodies fall at the same rate of speed, the public park is closed at 4 P.M. in winter, at 6 P.M. in summer, lead melts at 335 degrees centigrade, the last streetcar leaves the Hotel de Ville at 11.05 P.M."[41] Indeed, "common sense" contains at least two things: the blindingly obvious and the culturally familiar. While the good citizens of Bouville are guilty of collapsing the latter into the former, contemporary postmodern relativists are just as guilty of collapsing the former into the latter. But, and surely this is Sartre's point, we must learn to distinguish them. We must not conflate the "laws" concerning the hours of the public park and the streetcar schedule with those regarding bodies in a vacuum and the melting temperature of lead. This is politically important. We need to know what we can change and what we cannot.

NOTES

1. Jean-Paul Sartre, *Truth and Existence*, trans. Adrian van den Hoven, ed. Ronald Aronson (Chicago: University of Chicago Press, 1992).

2. Sartre, *Anti-Semite and Jew*, trans. George J. Becker (New York: Schocken Books, 1974), p. 90.

3. Sartre, *Truth and Existence*, p. 52.

4. Eve Browning Cole, *Philosophy and Feminist Criticism* (New York: Paragon House, 1993), pp. 95–96.

5. Douglas V. Porpora, *How Holocausts Happen* (Philadelphia: Temple University Press, 1990), pp. 12–13.

6. Sartre, *Being and Nothingness*, trans. Hazel E. Barnes (New York: Washington Square Press, 1992), especially pp. 112–116.

7. See, for example, the following works of Sartre's: "What Is Literature?" trans. Bernard Frechtman, and "Introducing 'Les Temps Modernes,'" trans. Jeffrey Mehlman, both in Sartre's *"What Is Literature?" and Other Essays* (Cambridge, MA: Harvard University Press, 1988); and "The Responsibility of the Writer," trans. Betty Askwith, in *The Creative Vision*, ed. Haskell M. Block and Herman Salinger (New York: Grove Press, 1960).

8. Sartre, "A Friend of the People," in his *Between Existentialism and Marxism*, trans. John Mathews (New York: William Morrow and Company, 1976), pp. 296–297.

9. Ibid.

10. Sartre, *Truth and Existence*. See, for example, pp. 33, 38, and 52.

11. W. K. Clifford, "The Ethics of Belief," in his *The Ethics of Belief and Other Essays* (Amherst, NY: Prometheus Books, 1999), p. 70.

12. Ibid., pp. 74–75.

13. Sartre, *Saint Genet*, trans. Bernard Frechtman (New York: Mentor, 1964), p. 606.

14. Sartre, *Anti-Semite and Jew*, p. 7.

15. Sartre, *Truth and Existence*, p. 4.

16. Ibid., p. 28.

17. Ibid., p. 30.

18. Ibid., p. 34.

19. Ibid., p. 17.

20. Ibid., p. 16.

21. Ibid., pp. 41–42.

22. Sartre, *Being and Nothingness*, pp. 620ff.

23. Ibid., pp. 40ff.

24. Ibid., p. 40.

25. Ibid., p. 42.

26. Ibid., p. 40.

27. Ibid., p. 42.

28. Sartre, *Truth and Existence*, p. 3.

29. Ibid., p. 8.

30. Sartre, *Being and Nothingness*, pp. 3–30.

31. This is a major theme of chapter 1 of *Being and Nothingness*. See especially pp. 33–44.

32. I discuss this topic extensively in *Freedom as a Value: A Critique of the Ethical Theory of Jean-Paul Sartre* (La Salle, IL: Open Court, 1988). The relevant passages are indexed under the heading "Coefficient of adversity (resistance)."

33. Sartre, *Truth and Existence*, p. 34.

34. Ibid., pp. 33–41.

35. Ibid., p. 35.

36. Sartre, *Saint Genet*, p. 605.

37. Barry W. Sarchett, "What's All the Fuss about This Postmodernist Stuff?" in *Campus Wars*, ed. John Arthur and Amy Shapiro (Boulder, CO: Westview Press, 1995), p. 24.

38. For more on Sarchett, see chapter 7, section XIII, below.

39. Sartre, "What Is Literature?" p. 71.

40. Sartre, *Saint Genet*, p. 605.

41. Sartre, *Nausea*, trans. Lloyd Alexander (New York: New Directions, 1964), p. 158.

Chapter 5

TRUTH IN ETHICS AND POLITICS

SARTRE VS. RORTY

I t is well known that Richard Rorty has little use for the concept of truth, but it is always best to document one's central claims. Thus, I begin with a quotation from Rorty: "You can still find philosophy professors who will solemnly tell you that they are seeking *the truth*, not just a story or a consensus but an . . . accurate representation of the way the world is." Rorty immediately goes on to call such professors "[l]ovably old-fashioned prigs."[1]

What is not as well known is that Rorty occasionally names Sartre as a kindred spirit in his project of truth-rejection. I shall argue, however, that Rorty's interpretation of Sartre is defective, and that Sartre, having anticipated positions much like Rorty's, offers us compelling reasons for rejecting them.

I. RORTY'S INTERPRETATION OF SARTRE

While Sartre is certainly not one of Rorty's philosophical heroes, it is surprising, given their obvious differences,[2] how often Rorty turns to him in support of his views.[3] The explanation for this surprising fact is quite simple, however: Rorty simply misreads Sartre at every turn.

Here is a striking example. One of Rorty's favorite passages from Sartre—he has discussed it at least twice—is the following:

> Tomorrow, after my death, certain people may decide to establish fascism, and the others may be cowardly or miserable enough to let them get away with it. At that moment, fascism will be the truth of man, and so much the worse for us. In reality, things will be as much as man has decided they are.[4]

Rorty's comment on this passage is this:

> This hard saying brings out what ties Dewey and Foucault, James and Nietzsche, together—the sense that there is nothing deep down inside us except what we have put there ourselves, no criterion that we have not created in the course of creating a practice, no standard of rationality that is not an appeal to such a criterion, no rigorous argumentation that is not obedience to our own conventions.[5]

Perhaps I am being overly literal, but I cannot help noticing that the passage from Sartre does not mention any of the items that are featured in Rorty's interpretation. Sartre says nothing there about the creation of criteria or of practices, or about standards of rationality, rigorous argumentation, or obedience to conventions. Rather, as I read it, Sartre is making just two points in the passage in question: (1) that in the future people might make this world a fascist world; and (2) that this would be a bad thing.

What has happened here is quite simple: Rorty has taken Sartre's comment completely out of context. That comment occurs in the context of Sartre's discussion of "despair," which he defines as meaning "merely . . . that we limit ourselves to a reliance upon that which is within our wills, or within the sum of the probabilities which render our action feasible."[6] Sartre then points out that some Marxists to whom he has spoken of such matters have objected that his doctrine seems to preclude reliance upon the help of others. Sartre goes on to deny that his position has this implication, and to affirm the possibility, and indeed the moral necessity, of working with others in commitment to a common cause. But he also says this:

> I cannot count upon men whom I do not know, I cannot base my confidence upon human goodness or upon man's interest in the

good of society, seeing that man is free and that there is no human nature which I can take as foundational. I do not know whither the Russian revolution will lead. . . . I cannot affirm that [it] will necessarily lead to the triumph of the proletariat: I must confine myself to what I see. Nor can I be sure that comrades-in-arms will take up my work after my death and carry it to the maximum perfection, seeing that those men are free agents and will freely decide, tomorrow, what man is then to be.[7]

The passage quoted by Rorty then appears immediately after the passage that I have just quoted. Thus, there clearly is no basis whatsoever for Rorty's interpretation. Sartre simply does not take up in the passage in question any of the issues discussed in Rorty's interpretation, let alone adopt any of the positions that Rorty attributes to him.

The closest Rorty ever comes to connecting with anything that Sartre actually says is in his attributing to Sartre the claim that "there is nothing deep down inside us except what we have put there ourselves." This does indeed harmonize with Sartre's denials of human nature and of historical inevitability (in the passages I have just quoted), and of the existence of God.[8] But Sartre calls attention to these denials in order to make the point that nothing other than human freedom can determine what *will*, as opposed to *should* (as Rorty seems to think he means), happen in the future. To put it another way, Sartre is saying that it is entirely up to us whether or not we *will* become fascists; whereas Rorty, with his talk of no criteria or rationality outside of our own conventions, seems to read him as saying that it is up to us whether or not we *should* become fascists, as if, were we to choose fascism, this choice would thereby become rational and right (in the only senses of these terms that Rorty will allow). To be sure, Sartre does indeed think that what should happen depends upon human freedom, but in the sense that what should happen is, for Sartre (at least at this point in his intellectual itinerary), that which is consistent with, and enhances, human freedom, and certainly not in the sense that what is right is simply a matter of "obedience to our own conventions." Indeed, can a more profoundly un-Sartrean position even be imagined?[9]

II. RORTY VS. SARTRE ON THE COLD WAR

While most of Rorty's references to Sartre are approving, he does occasionally, especially in connection with explicitly political matters, express disagreement with him. Here is an example:

> Those of us who were, like myself, militantly anticommunist believe that the war against Stalin was as legitimate, and as needed, as the war against Hitler. Some of my contemporaries, like Fredric Jameson, still agree with Jean-Paul Sartre. Sartre said that he had always believed, and would always believe, that anticommunists are scum. Such people see the Cold War as nothing more than an American drive for world domination. They mock the idea that America could have prosecuted that war without propping up right-wing dictators. My anticommunist side of the argument gets a lot of support from leftists in central and eastern Europe. Jameson's side of the argument gets a lot of support among leftists in Latin America and Asia—people who have first-hand knowledge of what the CIA can do to a poor nation's hopes for social justice.[10]

By way of reply, I would point out the following.

(1) Note that Rorty does not defend his position, aside from appealing to the authority of leftists in central and eastern Europe—an appeal that he immediately cancels out by appealing, in support of the opposite conclusion, to the authority of leftists in Latin America and Asia.

(2) If one really wants to know what the motives of the U.S. government were (and are) in propping up right-wing dictators, there are good ways to investigate this. I will mention two. One is to read internal memoranda by State Department planners as these come to be released or leaked. I have in mind documents in which the formulators of U.S. foreign policy explain to one another, rather than to the general public, the nature of their motivations. The *Pentagon Papers*, leaked by Daniel Ellsberg, are perhaps the most famous example.[11] They establish, among other things, that the rationale offered to the U.S. public for the Vietnam War consisted of nothing but lies, and that the purpose of the war, largely, was to prevent a democratic election in Vietnam which would have had, from the planner's perspective, the wrong outcome. Or again, consider George Kennan's "Policy Planning Study 23" of 1948, which was for many

years a classified document, unavailable to the public, in which
Kennan explains quite clearly the rationale for maintaining a system
of "military client states":

> [W]e have about 50% of the world's wealth, but only 6.3% of its pop-
> ulation. . . . In this situation, we cannot fail to be the object of envy
> and resentment. Our real task in the coming period is to devise a
> pattern of relationships which will permit us to maintain this posi-
> tion of disparity. . . . To do so, we will have to dispense with all sen-
> timentality and day-dreaming; and our attention will have to be
> concentrated everywhere on our immediate national objectives. . . .
> We should cease to talk about vague and . . . unreal objectives such
> as human rights, the raising of living standards and democratiza-
> tion. The day is not far off when we are going to have to deal in
> straight power concepts. The less we are then hampered by ideal-
> istic slogans, the better.[12]

A second way to investigate the motives of U.S. planners is simply by
appealing to the principle of parsimony. For example, often the U.S.
gives aid and weapons to human rights abusers. Other times it ostra-
cizes them or aggresses against them, citing their human rights
records as the reason. So this leaves us with the question, what is its
position on human rights? How can we determine its true motives in
this regard? The official theory is that the U.S. is for human rights,
and only supports human rights abusers, and even then only reluctantly, when it thinks this will be a "constructive engagement" that
will encourage the abusers to do better in this area, or when the alternatives to the human rights abusing regime in question would be
even greater abusers. Another theory is that the U.S, government
does not give a damn about human rights, rewarding human rights
abusers not for that reason, but rather because they are helpful to
U.S. corporate interests (which often necessitates that they do abuse
human rights), and likewise punishing human rights abusers not for
that reason, but rather because they are harmful to U.S. corporate
interests. In the latter case, however, it is rhetorically effective to
point to the human rights abuses as the reason for the punishment.
How to determine which of these theories is more plausible? The
principles of consistency and parsimony, it seems to me, will do the
trick. Noam Chomsky makes the point in connection with the U.S.
government's nearly simultaneous actions of, on the one hand, selling

$300 million worth of communications and other high tech equipment to China, shortly after the Tiananmen Square massacre, and, on the other, invading Panama, ostensibly because of its miserable human rights record:

> [S]ome commentators in the United States noticed that there was something funny about invading Panama to save human rights while we on the same day announce that we're sending $300 million worth of high tech equipment to China, to leaders whose human rights record was a thousand times worse. So a couple of people said, "Gee, this seems kind of inconsistent, what's going on?" Nobody would point out the obvious—that it's not the least bit inconsistent, it's completely consistent. In both cases it's good for business, and that's the consistent feature.[13]

(3) While many leftists in central and eastern Europe, and, for that matter, leftists in the United States, have indeed been highly critical of the Soviet Union and of its satellites, I am unfamiliar with any who believe that the United States's motives in prosecuting the Cold War were altruistic, or who supported, as a necessary means in that war, the propping up of right-wing dictators. Perhaps I am simply ignorant here, but in fairness to myself I do note that Rorty fails to cite these leftists. On the other hand, perhaps the problem is merely one of definition, since Rorty makes a point in *Achieving Our Country* of defining as "leftists" such figures as Woodrow Wilson, Lyndon Johnson, Arthur Schlesinger, and Sidney Hook.[14] Indeed, Michael Albert argues that Rorty's "categorization would include Richard Nixon, Herbert Hoover, Newt Gingrich, Joseph Stalin, Saddam Hussein, and Adolf Hitler . . . in his 'reformist left.'"[15]

(4) Finally, how is the testimony of the leftists in central and eastern Europe vs. that of those in Latin America and Asia even *relevant* to Rorty's claims here? Rorty's point in distinguishing along geographical lines in this way is presumably that the former group of leftists has suffered (or at least seen) firsthand oppressions perpetrated by communist governments, while the latter group has similarly witnessed oppressions meted out by right-wing dictators. In what ways do such experiences give either group insight into the question of the United States's *motive* in prosecuting the Cold War, or of whether or not it could prosecute it without propping up right-wing dictators?

III. POLITICS AND RORTY'S ANTI-TRUTH EPISTEMOLOGY

Let us now return to Rorty's anti-truth epistemology and see how it connects with political issues of the sort we have been discussing. To focus the discussion, let us consider that epistemology in relation to one specific political claim of Rorty's:

> We should concede Francis Fukuyama's point . . . that if you still long for total revolution, for the Radically Other on a world-historical scale, the events of 1989 show that you are out of luck. Fukuyama suggested, and I agree, that no more romantic prospect stretches before the Left than an attempt to create bourgeois democratic welfare states and to equalize life chances among the citizens of those states by redistributing the surplus produced by market economies.[16]

By way of reply, I would point out the following.

(1) How can the events of 1989, in which *one* particular alternative to the "bourgeois democratic welfare state" fell under *one* particular set of historical circumstances, possibly demonstrate that *all* possible alternatives, including ones currently unimagined, must also fail—and must do so in *all* possible future circumstances, including ones currently unimagined? Once again, Rorty offers no argument, except for an appeal to the authority of Fukuyama.

(2) More importantly, given Rorty's relentless attacks on the notion of objective truth, his own remarks, such as the one just quoted, must be understood as not intended by him to be taken as objectively true. To see this, consider the following remark of Rorty's (he has made many others like it): "We think that there are many ways to talk about what is going on, and that none of them gets closer to the way things are in themselves than any other. . . . [W]e suggest that the appearance-reality distinction be dropped in favor of a distinction between less useful and more useful ways of talking."[17] So Rorty's claim that there are no possible viable alternatives to the "bourgeois democratic welfare state" does not, on his own theory, get us any closer to the way things really are than would the denial of this claim. It is, instead, simply a useful way of talking.

(3) How can Rorty rely on a distinction between less useful and

more useful ways of talking, given his oft-repeated claim that "anything [can] be made to look good or bad, important or unimportant, *useful or useless*, by being redescribed"?[18] One might attempt to defend Rorty by pointing out that even if it is true that anything can be made to *look* useful, this need not entail that anything can be made to *be* useful, since appearing useful and being useful are not identical. But this alternative is closed off to Rorty, since he repeatedly calls for the abolition of the appearance/reality distinction (as he does in the quotation in the immediately preceding paragraph).

(4) If taken literally, such an epistemology seems absurd. It entails that the claim that "giraffes are taller than ants" gets us no closer to the way things are in themselves than does the claim that "ants are taller than giraffes." The former is to be preferred, presumably, because it is "a more useful way of talking." But if one has enough intellectual curiosity as to continue the inquiry by asking *why* it is more useful, it seems, to me at any rate, that the answer has to do with the fact that giraffes are, indeed, taller than ants.

(5) Rorty's argument seems to depend upon the positivist/postmodernist false dilemma described in chapter 4. But as we saw there[19] Sartre has demonstrated that it is possible to raise questions about our ability to know how things are in themselves without thereby abandoning realism in favor of a Rortian reduction of truth claims to claims about useful ways of talking (or about group consensus—to be discussed subsequently).

(6) An additional objection to Rorty's epistemology is that it is self-referentially inconsistent. As we have seen, he offers what might be characterized as a crude pragmatist theory of (or alternative to) truth—a belief is true (or the equivalent, in Rorty's system) when its effects are good (in his version—these effects have to do with its utility as a way of talking). So A is a true belief (or the equivalent), since the consequences of belief in A are good; and B is a false belief, since the consequences of belief in B are bad. But notice that in order to make this determination, one must know what the effects of belief in A and B are (let alone the issue of having to have the ethical knowledge required to judge these effects good or bad). So suppose I say that the effects of belief in A are such-and-such, rather than so-and-so. What can this mean? If it means that the effects *really are* such-and-such, as opposed to meaning that the effects of *believing that they are* such-and-such are themselves *good*, then the theory con-

tradicts itself by relying on an objectivist, and non-pragmatist, account of truth. But if the theory is to remain consistent, then an infinite regress ensues: A is true because the effects of belief in A are good; and the belief that A does indeed have those good effects is itself true because the belief that it does has good effects; and the belief that that belief has those good effects is, in turn, true because this new belief—that the belief that belief in A has good effects—is itself a belief which has good effects, and so on ad infinitum.

Not surprisingly, Rorty is sophisticated enough to be aware of this problem and to attempt a way out. He wants to avoid the self-referential inconsistency involved in claiming that traditional epistemological claims are false. Thus, he instead announces merely that the project of making such claims is useless, or has not panned out.[20] But surely this is itself a truth claim of the sort he seems to be saying it is useless to make. (And of course, if this claim itself is offered as having only the credential that belief in it succeeds, or is beneficial, or what have you, then we have the problem we have been discussing: that of having to choose between the self-referentially inconsistent reading of such an offer as covertly entailing the claim that it is really true that belief in it succeeds, or else the reading which yields an infinite regress of appeals to the utility of belief—"the project of epistemology has not panned out" means that it is useful to believe that it has not panned out; that claim that it is useful to believe this means that this new claim about the utility of this belief is itself useful to believe; and this new claim is justified by the utility of believing *it*, and so forth.)[21]

Elsewhere Rorty defines objectivity and truth not in terms of usefulness, but rather in terms of intersubjective agreement. For example, Rorty writes: "[O]bjectivity is not a matter of corresponding to objects but a matter of getting together with other subjects. . . . [T]here is nothing to objectivity except intersubjectivity."[22] Or again, he states that truth can never be anything more than "conformity to the norms of the day."[23]

This faces at least six problems.

(1) The two definitions are not the same, a point that Rorty seems not to have noticed. There seems to be no reason to assume that the most useful way of talking will always be the one in agreement with which there is a cultural consensus.

(2) This new understanding of truth and objectivity is no more

plausible than is its predecessor. For example, it clearly entails that when we judge that giraffes are objectively taller than ants, or, if you prefer, that it is objectively true that giraffes are taller than ants, the truth and objectivity of this judgment result from our agreement, as opposed to our agreement flowing from a recognition of the way things are quite apart from what we think—namely, that giraffes are taller than ants. This flunks Socrates' *Euthyphro* test. Rorty's position entails that if "we" (one of Rorty's favorite terms) were to agree that ants are taller than giraffes, then they would be, and the statement reflecting this would thereby be objectively true. The natural rejoinder that we would never agree to this, since it is obvious that, in fact, giraffes are taller than ants, rather than the reverse, and that this observation constrains our judgment, is unavailable to Rorty.

Consider, in this regard, Piotr Gutowski's remark, issued immediately after offering an objection to Rorty's argument that we should dispense with the distinction between finding and making:

> As Professor Rorty ponders this objection of mine, I hope he will consider the big green giraffe, just behind him, that is trying to eat the violet leaves growing on his head. Is Professor Rorty able to see this giraffe? If not, can he make the giraffe be there, occupying part of what (probably) seems to be empty space? Rorty might say that he cannot do this as an individual, but that there might be some cultures where it is possible to do so. . . .
>
> Well, I cannot imagine any culture creating the picture I sketched, for the simple reason that nobody can find green giraffes here in this portion of space and time and because there really are no leaves growing on Rorty's head. There has to be a certain composition of molecules in any portion of space we find that enables us to make anything, and this is also an objective restriction for any nonhuman "making." Obviously, someone might say that there is a giraffe here, but he or she would simply be wrong.[24]

Here is Rorty's reply:

> Now about giraffes: I want to urge that if you have the distinction between the idiosyncratic and the intersubjective, or the relatively idiosyncratic and the relatively intersubjective, that is the only distinction you need to take care of real versus imaginary giraffes. You do not need a further distinction between the made and the found or the subjective and the objective. You do not need a distinction

between reality and appearance, or between inside and outside, but only one between what you can get a consensus about and what you cannot.[25]

My main objection to this is that the question of what distinctions you need depends upon what questions you are asking, a point that should be obvious to Rorty, a self-professed pragmatist. For example, suppose that, rather than resting content with the explanation that you can get a reasonable consensus that giraffes are tall but not that a green one is eating leaves growing out of Rorty's head, you have enough curiosity as to want to know *why* this is so. Gutowski offers an explanation (e.g., "there really are no leaves growing on Rorty's head," etc.), but Rorty wants to drop the distinctions that would allow us to explore this issue. Similarly, suppose we want to know whether or not a given consensus really reflects the truth. Again, on Rorty's terms, we should not ask such a question. If public relations people "can get a reasonable consensus about" their lies, then, perhaps, we can attempt to undo this consensus and establish an opposite consensus, but what would be our motive for doing so? After all, the established consensus would not be, on Rorty's view, "wrong" or "false." And even if our objection to this consensus were ethical, say, that it would lead to massive and needless suffering, rather than that it failed to correspond with reality, would not the cogency of this ethical objection itself depend upon an accurate correspondence with reality (e.g., that the consensus would indeed cause massive and needless suffering)? What if there were also a consensus that the consensus would not cause this harm? Would this consensus be wrong? How, on Rorty's terms, would we be able to find out?

Consider, in this connection, the following remarks of Robert W. McChesney. In

the commercial marketplace of ideas . . . [t]ruth, as such, loses its intrinsic meaning. It is less something to be respected and argued over than it is something to be auctioned off to the highest bidder; it is bought and sold. In the commercial marketplace of ideas, something becomes "true" if you can get people to believe it. And one attempts to get people to believe something to profit off them. For example, the notion that drinking a particular beer will make one more athletic, sexually attractive and have more friends is patently false. But if one "convinces" people of it and they purchase the beer, it becomes true and the creator of the message is duly rewarded. (Someone who actually told the truth would be fired.) This spirit permeates conventional political discourse as well, as much of campaign research is predicated upon finding which decontextualized facts, half-truths, and outright lies can be successfully deployed against an opponent. As this notion of "truth" is generalized, the sense of a moral common ground declines, and the function of communication becomes to advance narrowly defined self-interest. The implications of democracy are disastrous.[26]

Rorty's line, it seems to me, unwittingly feeds right into this disaster.

How might Rorty be defended against this criticism? I can think of two possibilities, both of which interpret Rorty as having been careless when, in his reply to Gutowski, he seemed to say, without qualification, that attaining truth was just a matter of being able to get a consensus. Rather (and this is the first of the two ways of trying to rescue Rorty), perhaps his intended, and more considered, meaning is, as he has expressed it elsewhere, that we should be "content to call 'true' whatever the upshot of [free and open] encounters turns out to be."[27]

Now, this does at first look promising. We now have a way to reject as false the evil manipulations of assorted politicians, advertisers, and public relations officers, even when they successfully manufacture a consensus, for we can argue that this consensus was achieved through distorted, rather than free and open, communication. But when we look more closely, all the old, familiar problems return. For notice that, on the view we are now considering, to call a statement "true" one would have to *know* whether or not the encounter from which it had arisen had been a free and open one. Either we do this in a realist way, in which case we get a self-referential inconsistency, or we look to see whether or not our conclusion that this had in fact been a free and open encounter was itself the upshot of a free and open encounter, in which case we get an infinite regress.

And there is an *obscurum per obscurius* problem as well. In order to know whether or not giraffes are taller than ants we must first know (a) whether or not there is a consensus that giraffes are taller than ants, and (b) if there is, whether or not the communication that produced that consensus was free, open, and undistorted. But isn't it obvious that it is easier to determine whether or not giraffes are taller than ants than it is to determine either (a) or (b)? Or, to put it another way, wouldn't any skeptical doubts about our ability to determine even something so obvious as that giraffes are taller than ants also be more than sufficient to wipe out any hope of being able to know about the outcome, and degree of openness, of any process of public communication? So what problem is solved by saying that what it means to know, or to hold as true, that giraffes are taller than ants is to know that there is a consensus, formed as a result of free and open communication, that giraffes are taller than ants? (And incidentally, if Rorty argues and loses—that is to say, he fails to get others to agree with him, fails to generate a consensus—does this show anything? Does it suggest that his position is wrong, or that the communication was distorted, or what?)

The other way to try to defend Rorty is to read his reduction of truth to social consensus not as entailing that whatever the group in question happens to believe is therefore automatically right or true, but rather that the epistemic norms according to which truth is established are themselves established only through group consensus. On this view it would be possible to criticize as false a consensus (first-order or particular) belief held in one's society, provided that one could show that the belief in question ran afoul of the (second-order or general) societal consensus regarding truth-establishing epistemic norms.

Once again, at first this seems promising. One is not simply stuck with odious or ludicrous claims (including, though not limited to, those promoted by the advertisers, politicians, and public relations officials of our earlier discussion) that one's group has happened, for whatever reason (e.g., manipulation, deception, or perhaps simple, morally blameless, confusion) to adopt. Rather, one can invoke standards and criteria for establishing truth that the group members themselves accept in order to try and convince them that they are wrong.

But this only pushes the problem back a step, moving it to a more abstract level. While we no longer have to accept without argument consensus first-order beliefs, we do have to accept the group consensus concerning the epistemic norms according to which the truth of first-order beliefs is to be determined. While we no longer have to say that reformers and radicals are by definition wrong (with regard to particular beliefs), we do have to say that reformers and radicals in epistemology are wrong by definition (which means that Rorty, an epistemological radical, is wrong, but I won't pursue that point here). And while we no longer have to say that our particular beliefs are arbitrary (having nothing more than a consensus of opinion to back them, with no question of the cogency of that opinion being admissible), we do have to say that our epistemic norms themselves are arbitrary and are based on nothing more than a consensus, which cannot itself be evaluated by any standard external to it. And many other questions and puzzles remain. Is it easier to know what our culture's epistemic norms are in terms of which it is to be determined whether or not giraffes are taller than ants than it is to know that giraffes are taller than ants? Is our knowledge concerning the identity of those norms to be construed on a realist model, or must we rather consult our culture's epistemic norms in order to use them to figure out the identity of those norms? If the former, why is it that we can have objective knowledge concerning the identity of our culture's epistemic norms when we can't have it with regard to the relative height of giraffes and ants? And if the latter, how is an infinite regress to be avoided?

Let's come at this another way. It is one thing to develop epistemic norms in an attempt to get at the way things really are—the objective truth. It is quite another to say, as Rorty does, that the epistemic norms are constitutive of truth. Why should we prefer the former to the latter?

Consider an example. Suppose there is a close election, leading to a hand re-counting of the ballots. While most of the ballots have been handled correctly by the voters and are easy to decipher, others contain errors and thus must be interpreted. For example, in some cases the chad has not been completely dislodged from the paper (voters are supposed to punch a hole in a designated place next to the name of their preferred candidate) and instead "hangs" next to the name of one of the candidates. In other cases voters fail even to make a hole, but instead leave a "dimple" in the place where a hole should be. In still other cases voters create two holes, as if they were attempting, illegally, to vote for two candidates. There are other possibilities as well.

Now there are likely to be rules in place which are to be consulted by election judges when they are trying to decipher these ballots. For example, the rules might state that hanging chads should be counted, but that dimpled chads should not (perhaps on the grounds that they are too subjective, that it is too easy for one's bias to lead one to think there is a dimple when really there is not), and that ballots containing votes for two candidates should be rejected.

But notice that there would be no rationale for these rules if they were ends in themselves. Rather, they can make sense and be justified (or be seen as unjustified and standing in need of revision) only if they are instruments to be used to achieve an end—that of determining the wishes of the voters. For example, consider the rule that ballots containing multiple votes for the same office should not be counted. This certainly seems like a sound rule. But what if we find that the ballot is confusing, so that it is not all that clear whether the hole to be punched belongs to the candidate to the left of the hole or the candidate to the right of the hole? And what if, further, we find when we examine the ballots by hand that many of the ones containing two punched holes are further marked, in pencil or pen, by a crossing out of one of the punched candidates and a circling of the other? Wouldn't that suggest, to any reasonable person with an average background knowledge of human psychology and behavior, that the voter had made a mistake, realized it, attempted to correct it, and had done so in such a manner as to make clear what his or her intent had been? If so, then a construal of the vote-judging norms as instrumental to the goal of recording accurately the intent of the voters would necessitate either counting those votes or, at the very least, changing the rules in subsequent elections so that such votes would be counted in the future. But if the norms and rules are held to be constitutive of the truth, rather than instruments to be used to help us achieve a goal, why change them? We cannot use failure to achieve a goal external to the rules themselves as a reason for reforming the rules when we view the goal as unattainable and the rules as ends in themselves.

The application of this analogy to Rorty's position is direct. If our aim is the objective truth, we can have a motivation and a reason for revising our epistemic norms whenever we have reason to think they aren't helping us optimally to reach that goal, and we can have a sound basis for criticizing others' claims that we should adhere to the norms. But how can we have any of these things if the truth just *is* whatever follows from our epistemic norms?

To be sure, Rorty might reply that we could still use pragmatist criteria for revising our norms. We might abandon or modify them if they are no longer "working." But how can we make sense of this without invoking objective knowledge—knowledge of how things really are? For in order to judge that something is not working, wouldn't we have to know what its effects really are? (And are we off on the regress again—we would have to know what the effects are of believing that the effects are such-and-such, etc.?) And surely some of our social practices cannot be judged to be "working" except by invoking the goal of objective truth. For example, to know whether or not the criminal justice system is working well, wouldn't we have to know something about the accuracy of its results—is it tending to find guilty those who are really guilty and to find not guilty those who really are not guilty?

Lastly, Rorty might respond simply by asserting the unattainability of the goal in terms of which I assert that our norms and rules should be judged. That is, he might claim that we can't know "the mind of the voter," or (apart from the rules and procedures of our criminal justice system) who "really" is guilty or not guilty, or, finally and most generally and importantly, what the objective truth is. But I think the examples I have given here show that he is wrong. Would he really want to say that we don't know the intent of a voter who crosses out one name and circles another, or that DNA evidence cannot subsequently establish the innocence of a person who had been convicted through our criminal justice system before such evidence became available? (And notice, in connection with this last example, that such occurrences can give us a rational reason for reforming the epistemic standards currently reigning in our court system. As DNA evidence repeatedly clears those who had been convicted, this ought to motivate us in future trials, even in cases in which there is no DNA evidence, to downgrade the sorts of evidence on the basis of which these innocents had been found guilty.) Indeed, these examples suggest that the central fallacy in asserting that our norms are constitutive of truth might be that such an approach requires us always to judge our particular beliefs in terms of our general principles and never to find that our principles are defective because they clash with some of the particular discoveries we make about the world.

(3) The new understanding of objectivity and truth is also just as self-referentially inconsistent as is its predecessor, for if what is true

is what the group takes to be true, the same results ensue. A is true because the group takes it to be true. But in order to say this, we must know that the group does, in fact, take A to be true. But if we affirm that it does, what is the status of this claim? If it is a claim to objective truth—that the group really does take A to be true, even if this fact about itself is not one that the group knows (and it seems that such a thing is possible—a majority of people might believe A, without a majority of them knowing enough about their neighbor's beliefs to know that a majority did so believe), then the theory contradicts itself by relying on objective truth, the very thing it is attempting to abolish. But if the theory remains consistent, an infinite regress results. A is true because the group takes it to be true. But the determination that the group does take A to be true is itself to be understood as true only in the sense that the group takes *it* to be true. But the truth that the group takes as true that the group takes A as true is itself, in turn, true only insofar as the group takes *it* to be true, and so on ad infinitum.

(4) There is another self-referential inconsistency problem. When Rorty claims that truth can never be anything more than "conformity to the norms of the day," or what our cultural peers will let us get away with, or other locutions of that sort, he seems to mean either one of two things, and both lead to trouble. If he is saying that this is how it *really* is—no matter what anyone, or any culture, might think about, no more objective or realistic or consensus-transcending kind of truth can ever be found—then he simply contradicts himself, because that claim itself is one which is explicitly set in opposition to what any possible culture or consensus might say. But if he is instead simply making the ethnocentric claim that this non-objectivist, non-realist understanding of truth is the one prevailing in our culture, our traditions, or something of that sort, then he seems to be mistaken, for our intellectual culture is shot through with distinctions between prejudice and reasoned conviction, between appearance and reality, between what is *thought* to be the case and what simply *is* the case, and so forth.[28] So to urge, as Rorty often seems to be doing, that we abandon the effort to grasp what is really the case, and instead settle for affirming as true merely what our culture takes to be true, is simply incoherent, since one of the things our culture takes to be true is that it is important not to settle merely for what it takes to be true.

Put another way, it is strange that Rorty, and so many others like him, complain that our culture holds on to the palpably false view that it can grasp what is really true, as opposed to what we contingently and culturally happen at this moment to believe. The complaint is strange because one either thinks that we in fact can grasp what is really true, in which case Rorty's complaint is unfounded (because we can do what he says we cannot), or else one thinks that we cannot, and thus must settle merely for what we contingently and culturally happen at this moment to believe—in which case the complaint is pointless, both because the fact that what is really true is in principle closed off to us cannot, on its own terms, possibly be known to be true by critics like Rorty (or anyone else), so that their complaint is groundless, and because if the upshot is that we are then simply left with what we happen to believe—well, we believe in real (non–culturally relative, not contingent on what we just happen to believe) truth, which we should therefore affirm.

(5) On Rorty's conception, on what basis would I attempt to build a consensus with others? On a realist view, if I believe, on the basis of evidence or arguments of some kind, that things are a certain way, and that others who see things differently are mistaken, then I have a basis and a reason for attempting to persuade them that they are mistaken—presumably by pointing out to them the same evidence and arguments that have convinced me. But if truth is simply a function of what people agree to, then I am powerless, always and in principle, to claim that the consensus is mistaken. In fact, such a claim would appear to be a simple contradiction, on Rorty's account, akin to saying "this truth is untrue." Thus, Rorty's position seems open to the objection, fatal to many other forms of relativism as well,[29] that it renders all reformers and revolutionaries wrong, always and in principle, and makes it unclear how and why one would engage in any form of inquiry, as opposed to engaging in consensus-building.[30]

(6) With which other subjects does one have to agree in order to achieve objectivity, as Rorty understands it? For it is noteworthy that Rorty constantly uses the terms "we," "us," "our peers," and the like, and seeks to replace objectivity (as traditionally conceived) with solidarity with this "we" or "us." Is it everyone? Or all Americans? All professional philosophers?[31] No, when Rorty uses these terms, it is clear that he is not referring to these groups, in part because, as he candidly admits, most members of them do not agree with him. The only interpretation that seems to make sense is that "we," "us," and

the like mean something along the lines of "those who agree with me—Richard Rorty." Thus, objectivity, for Rorty, turns out (though he does not point this out himself) not to be something hard-won, and something which could be lost. No, objectivity means being in agreement and solidarity with "us," where "us" is not some independent group with which I might, despite my best efforts, fail to achieve agreement and solidarity—no, it is simply those with whom I do feel solidarity and with whom I do agree!

Let us now apply all of this to Rorty's statements about the meaning of the events of 1989. Recall that they must be understood not as capturing how things really are, but rather either as more useful ways of talking than are any of their competitors, or else simply as statements of cultural consensus, which in turn must be understood as statements of what people like Richard Rorty happen to think. Rejecting the latter interpretation as of interest only to those engaged in the project of being like Rorty, we must address the former interpretation and ask, "useful to whom, and for what purpose?" For, after all, if indeed it were true that the best kind of political arrangement that human beings are capable of sustaining is an improved version of "the bourgeois democratic welfare state" with a market economy, it would be enormously useful to know this (so that we might not waste time and cause harm by pursuing futile alternatives), and to communicate it to others (so that they might be persuaded similarly not to waste time and to cause harm). But all of this would be true only if it were indeed true—not in the sense that "we" find it useful to say so, or in the sense that "we" believe it, but rather in some realist sense—that no superior alternatives are available. But on Rorty's position, why should we not simply solve the world's political problems by agreeing that everything is fine the way it is—no one is suffering; no one is oppressed; there is no injustice; all is bliss? Why, on his viewpoint, would this not be enormously useful? It would, after all, solve all political problems at once and would require no effort or bloodshed.

Is this unfair to Rorty? Well, he often says such things as, "for us 'rational' merely means 'persuasive' . . . ,"[32] and, as we have seen, he repeatedly insists "that anything can be made to look good or bad by being redescribed."[33] These are excellent mottoes for a public relations official or advertising executive! But what do they mean? How do you make the rape and murder of children look good by redescribing these acts? Can they be made to look good to everyone? As Rorty seems to disallow the question of whether anything really is good, as opposed to looking good, it seems to be his view that if it looks good it *is* good, albeit only contingently and perhaps temporarily, but in the only sense in which anything can be good. (In fairness to Rorty, it is indeed often easy to change people's perception of reality, and often much easier to do that than to change reality itself—a point all too well understood by advertisers and public relations persons. But on the other hand, this is clearly a philosophy for the comfortable, rather than the oppressed. If your country is dropping bombs on others, perhaps this can be made to look good to you. Those on whom the bombs are dropping are less likely to be convinced [or fooled.])

In a similar vein, Rorty claims that "[t]o see a common social practice as cruel and unjust . . . is a matter of redescription rather than discovery. It is a matter of changing vocabularies rather than of stripping away the veil of appearances from an objective reality, an experimentation with new ways of speaking rather than of overcoming 'false consciousness'."[34] This claim is open to multiple powerful objections. First, contrary to Rorty's claim, it is obviously the case that common social practices are sometimes discovered to be cruel, and that this discovery has nothing to do with changing vocabularies or experimentation with new ways of speaking. For example, we can learn that something is cruel because the pain that it produces is fruitless (e.g., spanking), or because the motive behind it, or rationale for it, is not what we thought it was or had been told it was (e.g., the Vietnam War). Or again, think of discovering that a given animal feels pain where it was previously supposed that it did not—we learn something about its nervous system, let us say—with the result that behavior toward it which we once thought harmless we now see to be cruel.

Second, I submit that it is morally problematic to call someone "cruel and unjust" when one has not discovered any basis for the charge but is instead merely engaging in "an experimentation with new ways of speaking."

Third, consider what results when we combine this point about cruelty with the previous one about making anything look good by redescribing it. Where what we now describe as cruelty is going on, why not get rid of the cruelty by redescribing it away? Notice that

Rorty cannot say that it is still "really" cruelty. On his view nothing is really anything. In any case, such an impression is buttressed by his many ethnocentric statements, as when, for example, he endorses a position which "makes it impossible to ask the question 'Is ours a moral society?'"[35] This seems to mean that had Rorty been born into a slave-holding faction of a society in which slavery is practiced, or if he had been born into a fascist state—had he been born a Nazi, let us say—then, had he access to the philosophy that he has in fact developed as a contemporary American, slavery and Nazism would find in it as ample a justification as any political order can ever receive. Everything, from Rorty's point of view, turns on whether you happen to like or dislike a given description, and whether you will or not depends upon historical contingencies and rhetoric, not reason. Happily, one can "refute" Rorty's own redescriptions, in the only sense of the word that he seems to recognize, simply by being repulsed by them.

On a realist view, by contrast, no matter how much we might regret it, the facts prevent us from redescribing the world as a place in which justice reigns, and these facts constrain us in the sense that they entail that anyone who thinks otherwise, no matter how many confederates in this delusion he or she may find, and no matter how useful such a belief might be, would be simply wrong, mistaken. But Rorty admits of no such constraints. Here again, Rorty flunks the *Euthyphro* test. "We" (to steal one of Rorty's favorite rhetorical devices) believe there is injustice because there is injustice; it is not the case that there is injustice because we believe there is.

IV. RORTY'S RELATIVISM

Rorty has repeatedly denied that he is a relativist. I will here present four of his formulations of this denial and explain why I find them unpersuasive. First, Rorty claims that "'[r]elativism' is the view that every belief on a certain topic, or perhaps about *any* topic, is as good as every other. No one holds this view. Except for the occasional cooperative freshman, one cannot find anybody who says that two incompatible opinions on an important topic are equally good."[36]

I begin my response by noting in passing that, even by this eccentric definition, way more than one or two people are relativists, and they are by no means all freshman (nor, for that matter, are they all precocious).

Moreover, in what sense is this affirmation of a doctrine that Rorty finds ridiculous supposed to be "cooperative"? And with whom are these freshman supposed to be cooperating? I suppose a student's announcement in class that any one idea is as good as any other would be helpful to a teacher who appreciates having the students be the ones to advance claims for discussion, and who is eager to spend class time discussing just this claim. But is it helpful to teachers to have their every effort to discuss arguments purporting to show that some idea *is* better than another one derailed, at least initially, by always having first to take up the question of whether or not such a thing is even possible in principle? How is it helpful to block investigations into substantive questions of science, ethics, history, or what have you by inserting into the discussion a preposterous epistemological claim which, were it to be accepted, would render all such investigations pointless from the outset? Rorty seems to be offering the insulting suggestion that critics of student relativism are secretly glad that a few freshmen can be found who will espouse this nonsense so we can—what, beat up on their ideas in class? Nothing could be further from the truth. In fact, many teachers go to elaborate lengths to try to figure out how they can go about the business of engaging students in the effort to think for themselves, to follow evidence and arguments wherever they might lead, and to try to discover on their own which positions on difficult and important subjects are wisest, most reasonable, or even, perhaps, true, without having every such effort in this direction preempted by the inevitable rearing of relativism's ugly head.

Finally, and most importantly, the definition offered does not capture what is ordinarily meant by "relativism." To see this, let us consider Rorty's remark that "[t]here is nothing to be said about either truth or rationality apart from descriptions of the familiar procedures of justification which a given society—*ours*—uses in one or another area of inquiry."[37] To be sure, this claim does not entail that "every belief is as good as every other," for our society's "familiar procedures of justification" are surely more discriminating than that. They will declare some ideas to be better than others. But the claim is still relativistic in that its analysis of truth and rationality reaches rock bottom when it hits the procedures that a given society happens to use. It thus countenances the idea that different societies might use different procedures of justification, and thereby arrive at quite different and indeed mutually incompatible "truths" and "rationalities," with no way left open for investigating which (if any) of these seemingly opposed "truths" and "rationalities" might be "really" and "truly" true or best or most reasonable. It would seem, then, that the view of truth and rationality endorsed by Rorty entails that it might very well by "true" for some other culture that the Earth is flat precisely in the same sense and way in which it is "true" for us that the Earth is (approximately) round. This is relativism, and its adherents number considerably more than one or two.

Such relativistic statements abound in Rorty's writings. Thus, in addition to those statements already cited elsewhere in this chapter, one might list such utterances as these:

[W]e . . . need something to distinguish the sort of individual conscience we respect from the sort we condemn as "fanatical." This can only be something relatively local and ethnocentric—the tradition of a particular community, the consensus of a particular culture. According to this view [which Rorty calls "pragmatism," and defends as his own position], what counts as rational and as fanatical is relative to the group to which we think it necessary to justify ourselves—to the body of shared belief that determines the reference of the word "we";[38]

Anti-anti-ethnocentrists [the group to which Rorty is here pledging allegiance] suggest that liberals should . . . simply drop the distinction between rational judgment and cultural bias;[39]

[T]here is no human dignity that is not derivative from the dignity of some specific community, and no appeal beyond the relative merits of various actual or proposed communities to impartial criteria which will help us weigh those merits;[40]

[J]ustification is relative to an audience.[41]

Rorty's denial that he is a relativist, and my insistence that he is, finds a parallel in Alexander Nehamas's statement about Nietzsche's "perspectivism," and A. C. Graham's rejoinder. To Nehamas's claim that "[p]erspectivism does not result in the relativism that holds that any view is as good as any other; it holds that one's own views are the best for oneself without implying that they need be good for anyone else,"[42] Graham replies: "But to affirm that the massacre of whole peoples is right for me as a Nazi although wrong for you as a Christian or a liberal is surely what is commonly understood by relativism."[43] In any case, we need not fight over terms. Even if there are few "relativists" according to the definition of that term offered by Rorty, there are millions who hold views similar to the one just described by Graham, and it is the nature of these views—the issue of their cogency (or lack thereof), and questions concerning their causes and consequences—that are of interest here, as opposed to the utterly trivial matter of what name we choose to affix to them.

Rorty's other denials that he is a relativist can be dealt with more quickly. In one passage he defends himself against the charge that he is a relativist by claiming that he "does not have a theory of truth, much less a relativistic one. As a partisan of solidarity, [my] account of the value of cooperative human inquiry has only an ethical base, not an epistemological or metaphysical one. Not having *any* epistemology, *a fortiori* [I do] not have a relativistic one."[44] But surely this is unconvincing. How can anyone, let alone someone with Rorty's background in philosophy, get through life without an epistemological outlook of some sort, however fragmentary and incoherent it might be? Indeed, Rorty's move here is more than a bit like the familiar gambit of claiming to have no politics: "Yes, I buy Nike shoes, even though Nike pays third-world child workers inadequate wages. But I take no political stand on this. You see, I have no politics whatsoever. I think we do better by dropping the politics/nonpolitics distinction. Thus, having *no* politics, *a fortiori* I do not have reactionary politics."

Another of Rorty's strategies, when dealing with the charge that he is a relativist, is simple evasion: "My strategy will be to try to make the vocabulary in which these objections are phrased look bad, thereby changing the subject."[45] But recall that he also says, repeatedly, and in the very same book, that "anything can be made to look good or bad by being redescribed,"[46] so what would such a making-look-bad in this case really accomplish?

Let us consider one final instance of Rorty's repeated insistence that he is not a relativist:

> [A] sense of moral obligation is a matter of conditioning rather than of insight. . . . We decent, liberal, humanitarian types (representatives of the moral community to which both my reviewers and I

belong) are just luckier, not more insightful, than the bullies with whom we struggle.

This view is often referred to dismissively as "cultural relativism." But it is not relativistic, if that means saying that every moral view is as good as every other. *Our* moral view is, I firmly believe, much better than any competing view.[47]

The quick way to deal with this is to point out, once again, that "relativism" rarely refers to such a crude view as that "every moral view is as good as every other." But let's look deeper. Note that Rorty admits in this passage that his first-order moral views have arisen as a result of his conditioning, rather than his insight. But what about his second-order views—that is to say, his views about his moral views—and in particular his claim that his (and "our") moral views are better than any competing views? Does that claim arise from genuine insight, or is it merely the product of Rorty's conditioning? On the former interpretation Rorty seems either to contradict himself or, at the very least, to be granting an arbitrary and undefended privilege to second-order moral views (why should these be exempt from Rorty's general line about the utterly contingent and socially contingent nature of our beliefs?). But on the latter interpretation, Rorty can claim no genuine insight into the superiority of his own views and would presumably have to grant that people who thought that their own (quite different) moral views were superior to his could claim an insight into their position that would be every bit the equal of his—a concession that leads naturally to relativism.

Consider, as a thought experiment, what Rorty might say had he been born a Nazi. Either he would say (in line with the actual Richard Rorty's general views about the causes of, and epistemological standing of, moral views), "It is just my good luck that I am a Nazi, but Nazism is better than anything else—I'm no relativist," or he would not. The former alternative, aside from being a moral and political disaster, is essentially an attack on thought—you can't improve on, by criticism and the use of intelligence, the political cards you are dealt. But if the latter alternative is the correct one, then Rorty's (actual) moral views are not just a matter of luck. In that case, he is no relativist, but he is also not one who really holds the views that Richard Rorty claims to hold.

V. RORTY'S SOCIAL CONSTRUCTIONISM

Rorty's difficulties are typical of those plaguing social constructionism generally. To bring this out, let's critically examine five of Rorty's most explicitly social constructionist statements.

(1) [E]verything, including giraffes and molecules, is socially constructed, for no vocabulary (e.g., that of zoology or physics) cuts reality at the joints. Reality has no joints. It just has descriptions—some more socially useful than others.[48]

Several questions fairly hurl themselves at this passage. First, how, consistent with his own philosophy, can Rorty possibly *know* that "reality has no joints"? Second, even if we could somehow rule out the cutting-reality-at-the-joints idea, why is social construction the only alternative? Why isn't Rorty's reasoning here either a false dilemma or a non sequitur? Finally, even if reality has no joints, why is social utility the only criterion by which to judge descriptions? Why not, for example, accuracy? Even if reality does not force us to divide the world up into elephants and ants, or use the words "bigger" and "smaller" as we do, given that we do so divide and use, ants would not be bigger than elephants even if, somehow, it would be socially useful to say and believe that they were.

(2) There is nothing to people except what has been socialized into them.[49]

Once again, there are problems. First, this seems to imply that people have hair, bones, skin, muscle, blood, and fat, and go through puberty, eat, grow, sleep, and get wrinkles and gray hair because of the way in which they have been socialized. I trust that I need provide no argument to show that this is not correct. But if Rorty's statement is not to be taken as entailing these preposterous consequences, then what does it mean?

Second, this entails (and, as we have seen, Rorty frequently states it explicitly) that our intuitions—all of them—are the result of socialization. But surely our intuition that a > b; b > c; therefore, a > c is more evident than is our intuition that we have this intuition only because of socialization. Moreover, either Rorty's judgment in this case transcends his socialization, in which case he contradicts himself, or else it merely reflects it, in which case those of us who have been socialized differently need not be troubled by it.

To put it another way, if socialization goes all the way down, as Rorty insists, if there is nothing to us beyond what we have been socialized to be, then we are *caused* by our socialization to believe this. That is, we are dealing here with a kind of determinism, according to which our beliefs are the results of causal antecedents, and thus it would be only a matter of our chance that our beliefs (including the belief that socialization goes all the way down) are true (if they are).

(3) Rorty endorses "a picture of human beings as children of their time and place, without any significant metaphysical or biological limits on their plasticity."[50]

Does this mean that we can learn to grow twenty heads, flap our wings and fly to the sun, or that we can learn to be in two places at one time, travel backward in time, and exist as colored beings who are not extended in space? Or does it mean merely that the reason why we cannot do things is that we are "children of our time and place," with the possibility being left open that people in other times and places can (or could or will) do all of these things? And if it doesn't mean any of these crazy things, what does it mean?

(4) As Nelson Goodman said about logic, all the logician can do is tell you what deductive arguments people usually accept as valid, she cannot correct their notions of deductive validity.[51]

Here are three comments: First, presumably this means that we should correct those logicians who want to correct other people's notions of deductive validity. But why is it OK to do that, when the other correction is ruled out of order?

Second, insofar as this conclusion of Goodman's is based upon reasoning, it must be that his canons are simply "what people usually accept as valid." But most people recognize that it is possible to err when reasoning, including when reasoning deductively, and that there are times when it is appropriate to correct them. Thus, while Goodman and Rorty appear to be affirming what most people believe, in fact, at another level, they are renouncing it.

Finally, how, on this view, are we to explain logical fallacies—that is, *common* mistakes in reasoning? Are we to believe that there are no such things?

> (5) [I]t is pointless to ask whether reality is independent of our ways of talking about it. Given that it pays to talk about mountains, as it certainly does, one of the obvious truths about mountains is that they were here before we talked about them. If you do not believe that, you probably do not know how to play the usual language-games which employ the word "mountain." But the utility of those language-games has nothing to do with the question of whether Reality as It Is In Itself, apart from the way it is handy for human beings to describe it, has mountains in it.[52]

Here Rorty seems to be defending, indeed, even calling it an "obvious truth," the idea that mountains existed before we talked about them, and thus that they have an independent existence. But notice that this is so, for Rorty, only because it is useful to play a language-game in which mountains are understood that way. Thus, the seemingly human-practice-independent status of mountains turns out, for Rorty, in the final analysis, to depend upon the utility of certain human linguistic practices.

But why, aside from the fact that there are mountains of evidence to indicate that it is simply true, a reason not available to Rorty, is it advantageous to suppose that mountains have independent existence? And what is the status of the claim that it has such utility? Surely for Rorty it is not an objective claim—the kind of thing that people could be simply wrong about. Rather, it must be that it is useful to think that such a conception is useful, and useful to think that it is useful to think it useful, and so on.

Moreover, Rorty seems to be conflating two distinct issues here: (a) does reality really divide itself up, or articulate itself, as in distinguishing mountains from nonmountains, apart from human linguistic descriptions? and (b), given that we do define "mountains" the way we do, is it really just a matter of convention, albeit a useful one, to conceive of them as antedating our thoughts about them? To see that these two questions are distinct, notice that one could easily agree with Rorty that the differentiation of mountains from the rest of being depends in some sense upon linguistic and conceptual systems, while disagreeing with him that their existence depends in any way upon our consent, or upon the utility of our system of beliefs about them.

VI. RORTY'S FALSE DILEMMAS

When Rorty offers arguments in support of his position they often take the following form: "Either you must take my position or else believe x; but look at all the problems there are with x; therefore, you should adopt my position." For example (and let me stress that these are only examples—he reasons this way constantly), he offers his view as the only alternative to (1) the belief that there are algorithms for resolving moral dilemmas, (2) the belief that there is a final vocabulary underlying all specific vocabularies, and (3) the arrogant and dogmatic conviction that one knows the correct standards of rationality, morality, and aesthetic taste.

But these are false dilemmas. One can reject beliefs (1), (2), and (3), without being forced to embrace Rorty's position. Or, to put it the other way around, one can reject Rorty's view without having to take on the odious beliefs that he presents as their alternative. To see this, let's critically examine Rorty's dilemmas.

(1) Rorty criticizes those who disagree with his claim that we must do without rational justifications for our moral values and for our resolutions of moral dilemmas by attributing to them the belief that there are "algorithms for resolving moral dilemmas."[53]

This is a false dilemma. One need not choose between Rorty's groundless "liberal ironism" and a belief in moral algorithms. In response, Frank B. Farrell correctly points out that "no good Aristotelian, and few moral philosophers at all, would hold that there are such algorithms, or that the adjustment of our ethical beliefs to the world would require that sort of outcome."[54]

Rorty's mistake is to assume that rationality and objectivity require exactitude or precision, together with a definite procedure for resolving dilemmas—a procedure that will yield agreement among all inquirers. He is right that such precision and such procedures are often lacking in ethics—indeed, many people make the same observation, and I suspect this is a major reason why so many are ethical relativists or subjectivists—but wrong to conclude that their absence precludes "rational justification." To see why, I offer an example from personal experience.

When I was about twelve years old I entered a children's golf tournament. A boy in my foursome held the lead going into the final hole. But he scored a disastrous triple-bogey on the final hole, causing him to finish second. He immediately proceeded to throw the most spectacular temper tantrum I have ever witnessed. He screamed, cursed, called the victor vicious names, cried, threw things, broke several of his golf clubs, and rudely dismissed all offers of congratulations for having finished second. But when the awards ceremony was held a few minutes later, he received, in addition to his prize for having finished second, a trophy for winning the "sportsmanship" award, signifying that, of all the assembled competitors, in the opinion of the adult judges he had best exemplified good sportsmanship! It was immediately clear to all of the golfers present what had happened. The judges had been too irresponsible to have undertaken any real investigation into who had or had not been a good sport during the proceedings. Rather, they had lazily awarded the sportsmanship award as a kind of consolation prize to the second place finisher.

What is the moral of the story? Well, notice that even though the concept of being a good sport is somewhat vague and inexact, and even though there is no algorithm for determining who is or is not the best exemplar of good sportsmanship, or sure-fire methods for reaching consensus on the matter, it is nonetheless an obviously objectively true and rationally justified statement that the judges made a mistake here—the winner of the sportsmanship award did not deserve it and should not have won it. Objectivity and rationality do not require exactitude, algorithmic decision procedures, or perfect agreement.

To be sure, many (indeed most) moral issues are not so clear-cut as this one is. But that does not justify Rorty's algorithmic exactitude/no rational justification false dilemma. For example, while I have very little skill at estimating crowd sizes, I might in a given case be able to claim legitimately to know that there are more than ten people in a room, but fewer than one million. This is not precise, makes no use of a decision procedure (there are far too many to count), and depends upon judgment. But that does not preclude its being rationally justified. I need not be a liberal ironist about crowd sizes.

(2) Rorty claims that his philosophical opponents are searching "for some final vocabulary, which can somehow be known in advance to be the common core, the truth of, all the other vocabularies which might be advanced in its place."[55]

This is another false dilemma. Between this position and Rorty's there are a million alternatives. Moreover, Rorty is attacking a straw man. Does *anyone* fit his description? In any case, one can easily be a realist without supposing that there is some "final vocabulary." Things have an infinity of different aspects, and many different vocabularies will be needed to describe them. Moreover, vocabularies, though not truths, are indeed relative to our purposes. The issue is, *given* a certain vocabulary, is a specific claim made within it made true or false by something outside of it or not.

The question of what is the right vocabulary to use is a pragmatic one. Some vocabularies will suit our purposes better than others will. The world cannot make our vocabularies right, nor can our vocabularies be true to the world. Still, some vocabularies will be better or worse suited to disclosing what reality is like. Suppose, for example, that we investigate reality only with the categories "round" and "not-round." Obviously we will not get very far. So, Rorty is once again right in what he rejects, but wrong in supposing that his opponents are committed to what he rightly rejects, and in claiming that his own position is the only viable alternative to it.

(3) Rorty asks us to "[i]magine . . . that a few years from now you open your copy of the *New York Times* and read that the philosophers, in convention assembled, have unanimously agreed that values are objective, science rational, truth a matter of correspondence to reality, and so on." But then, in order to show the ridiculousness of this, he writes (about five lines down on the page):

> By way of making amends for the intellectual confusion which the philosophical profession has recently caused, the philosophers have adopted a short, crisp set of standards of rationality and morality. Next year the convention is expected to adopt the report of the committee charged with formulating a standard of aesthetic taste.
>
> Surely the public reaction to this would not be "Saved!" but rather "Who on earth do these philosophers think they *are*?" It is one of the best things about the intellectual life we Western liberals lead that this *would* be our reaction.[56]

But notice that Rorty here shifts his target without pointing out that he has done so. It is one thing to agree that "values are objective, science rational, and truth a matter of correspondence to reality." It is quite another to claim to have discovered what these objective values and truths are, or to have determined what are the correct "standards of rationality and morality," or of aesthetic taste, let alone "a short, crisp set" of such standards. But Rorty seems to think that the ridiculousness of the latter sort of claim establishes also the ridiculousness of the former. It does not. He confuses the claim that there *are* objective truths with the quite different idea that we have *discovered* them.

Such confusions are quite common. People tend to confuse realism—the idea that reality and truth are in some important and powerful ways independent of our thoughts and theories—with the quite different idea that such truth is obvious and easily attained. Thus, since truth in fact often is not obvious or easily attained, people think that realism is thus refuted.

Similarly, many people confuse objectivity with consensus and certainty. They think that if something is objectively true, everyone ought to agree that it is, and we ought to know it with certainty. But these are simply different ideas. To say that something is objectively true is to say that there is a way things are independent of anyone's opinion or taste. In no way does it follow that even a single person knows what that way is, let alone that they know it with certainty, or that everyone knows it. I believe that the tree in my backyard has a definite height and that it has this height independent of anyone's opinion, even though, for all I know, no one in the world knows what that height is, and even though, given human fallibility, even careful measuring would not yield absolute certainty concerning its height. No one knows, not even me, what I ate for breakfast on 17 January 1973; yet, there obviously is some objective truth to this question.

Returning to Rorty, another problem with his argument is that it seems to rest on a confusion of two distinct issues, or perhaps levels of belief. On the one hand, or on the first level of analysis, to say that I regard a given belief of mine as objectively true is to say that everyone ought to, or would be right to, adopt it. If the belief is an important one, it might also be appropriate for me to try to convince others of its truth and to attempt to persuade them to accept it. But on the other hand, at a more general level of analysis, in response to the question "Do you think it would be a good thing if everyone came to hold as true all of the beliefs that you regard as objectively true?" my answer would be no, both because of my awareness of my own fallibility, and for Mill's reasons—the presence of wrong views provides a contrast which sharpens our understanding of true ones; the false ones may perhaps contain some kernel of truth which should not be extinguished; variety and diversity, including in the area of belief, is itself something which adds color and interest to life, etc.[57] For that matter, can anyone seriously entertain the idea that Rorty would be pleased if everyone came to accept his ironist views, and no one remained to carry on the search for objective truths? Thus, the fact that we would be horrified by universal acceptance even of the thesis that there is such a thing as objective truth hardly suffices to establish the ridiculousness of that thesis.

VII. SARTRE'S PREMONITORY WARNING AGAINST RORTY

Sartre saw Rorty coming and warned against such epistemologies of truth-rejection, most notably in *Truth and Existence*. Because many of his arguments are discussed in chapter 4, there is no need to go over all of them again to show how they apply to Rorty (an exercise I leave for the interested reader). Here I will content myself by recalling just one of Sartre's major points, namely, that the embracing of an anti-truth epistemology serves as a general foundation for a wide range of specific excuses—that is, in a global way, it serves to relieve us of our responsibilities (just as the acceptance of determinism does). Specifically, it relieves us of the responsibility to discover the truth, and to act accordingly. Similarly, it entails that we need never fear having to change our way of life on the grounds that some aspect of it might be inconsistent with what is true.[58]

To see the relevance of this to Rorty, consider the following four passages from his writings. In the first he urges us "simply [to] drop the distinction between rational judgment and cultural bias."[59] In the second he asserts that "we heirs of the Enlightenment think of enemies of liberal democracy like Nietzsche or Loyola as . . . 'mad.' . . . They are not crazy because they have mistaken the ahistorical nature of human beings. They are crazy because the limits of sanity are set by what *we* can take seriously. This, in turn, is determined by our upbringing, our historical situation."[60] In the third he endorses a position which "makes it impossible to ask the question 'Is ours a moral society?'"[61] Finally, in a brief discussion of the Vietnam War,

Rorty criticizes those who "attempted to rehabilitate Kantian notions in order to say, with Chomsky, that the War not merely betrayed America's hopes and interests and self-image, but was *immoral*, one which we had no *right* to engage in in the first place."[62] So the problem with the Vietnam War was not that what we did to the Vietnamese was *immoral*; rather, the problem was that it betrayed *our self-image*. Can anything more narcissistic be imagined?

Notice also that Rorty's view is politically quite conservative in its implications, for, as James Robert Brown notes, despite its philosophical radicalness,

> it implicitly defends the status quo. Rorty's historically embedded actors can tolerate some disagreement and still carry on "the conversation"; but on a solidarity view, such as his, they cannot abide deep criticisms. Revolutionary alternatives—about the adventure of space-time or the structure of society—cannot be taken seriously. "We Western liberal intellectuals", Rorty remarks, "should accept the fact that we have to start from where we are, and that this means that there are lots of views which we simply cannot take seriously." This attitude—so wrong, morally and historically—stems from Rorty's inherent conservatism. It is tempting to paraphrase it as "We white, middle-class, males are happy to stay put and to thumb our noses at other views."[63]

Indeed, the conservatism of Rorty's position is brought out by the simple observation that if truth is what my group believes, this blocks off the question of whether they ought to believe it.[64]

One would think that Rorty himself would be able to appreciate how maddening is his repeated insistence that we should affirm our own culture uncritically, with no need to offer a defense or consider alternatives seriously, given how vehemently he attacks the unexamined life when he doesn't like the beliefs that would go unexamined and undefended. For example, how does Rorty's defense of the unexamined life square with what he says here?

> The public sphere simply can't be served by people who say: "I'm not going to give you any argument for this but it's against my religion so I'm not about to tolerate it." . . . [T]o say it's against my religion isn't an argument. If you can give some reasons that don't have to do with relevation, then the question of whether or not your

belief is held because of your religion is irrelevant. You can just produce the arguments. If you say "It's just against my religion, and that's as far as I can go," then you're stepping outside of your responsibilities as a citizen.[65]

But why, then, is it not an abrogation of one's responsibilities to say, "It's just against my culture (or it's just not how we do things here), and that's as far as I go"? Why should the fact that something happens to be part of our tradition, or be our way of doing things, count as any kind of justification? Could not our practices/traditions be bad ones? In any case, Rorty's position leads either to anything-goes relativism (if we grant the same privileges to other people with other cultures and traditions), or else to a crude and thuggish ethnocentrism, in which no outrage visited upon outsiders can be condemned as unjust unless our own traditions and customs happen so to decree it (as Rorty explicitly admits, as we have seen, in connection with the Vietnam War).

When one goes the ethnocentric route, defining truth in terms of consensus, basic questions become insulated from critical examination, or even from thought itself. When everyone who counts agrees with your basic principles, you tend not even to be aware of those principles. They become as invisible as the air you breathe. When you encounter people who disagree with them, however, you are forced to defend them, which requires focusing on them and thematizing them. Such a focusing on and debating of fundamental principles, often taken for granted, is a fair characterization of philosophy, and one can readily see its importance to anyone who wants to engage others responsibly. In this connection, it is interesting to note that Rorty's endorsement of ethnocentrism goes hand-in-hand with his rejection of philosophy.

NOTES

1. Richard Rorty, "Deconstruction and Circumvention," in his *Essays on Heidegger and Others* (New York: Cambridge University Press, 1991), p. 86.
2. See chapter 4 for a discussion of Sartre's views on truth.
3. Incidentally, the only critical work on Rorty that I have noticed in which this point has been mentioned is Jeffrey Stout's *Ethics after Babel* (Boston: Beacon Press, 1988). There Stout remarks that it is usually "a sign

of backsliding or an invitation to misreading when favorable references to Sartre and existentialism appear in Rorty's work" (p. 260).

4. Jean-Paul Sartre, *L'Existentialisme est un humanisme* (Paris: Nagel, 1946), pp. 53–54, as quoted, apparently in Rorty's own translation, in the "Introduction" to Rorty's *Consequences of Pragmatism* (Minneapolis: University of Minnesota Press, 1982), p. xlii.

5. Rorty, "Introduction" to *Consequences of Pragmatism*, p. xlii.

6. Sartre, *Existentialism and Humanism*, trans. Philip Mairet (London: Methuen, 1973), p. 39.

7. Ibid., p. 40.

8. For example, see ibid., p. 39: "[T]here is no God and no prevenient design." There are many such passages in *Existentialism and Humanism*.

9. Incidentally, the other place in which Rorty quotes and discusses this passage from Sartre is in "Hilary Putnam and the Relativist Menace," in Rorty's *Truth and Progress* (New York: Cambridge University Press, 1998), p. 53. While still citing the passage approvingly, Rorty does here issue a criticism, along with what he takes to be a clarification. The criticism is that "Sartre should not have said that Fascism will be 'the truth of man.' There is no such thing." The clarification is this: "'Us' here does not mean 'us humans.' . . . It means something like 'us tolerant wet liberals.'"

10. Rorty, *Achieving Our Country* (Cambridge, MA: Harvard University Press, 1998), p. 57.

11. The Senator Gravel Edition, *The Pentagon Papers: The Defense Department History of United States Decisionmaking on Vietnam*, 5 vols. (Boston: Beacon Press, 1972).

12. P.P.S. 23, "Review of Current Trends; U.S. Foreign Policy," 24 February 1948, *Foreign Relations of the United States, 1948*, vol. 1, part 2 (Washington, D.C: U.S. Government Printing Office, 1976), pp. 524–525.

13. Noam Chomsky, *Terrorizing the Neighborhood* (San Francisco: Pressure Drop Press, 1991), p. 58.

14. Rorty, *Achieving Our Country*, pp. 43–44, 56, 70–71.

15. Michael Albert, "Rorty the Politico," *Z* 11, no. 10 (October 1998): 50.

16. Rorty, "The End of Leninism, Havel, and Social Hope," in *Truth and Progress*, p. 229.

17. Rorty, "Introduction" to *Truth and Progress*, p. 1.

18. Rorty, *Contingency, Irony, and Solidarity* (New York: Cambridge University Press, 1989), p. 7, emphasis added. (Rorty makes the identical claim in almost exactly the same words on p. 73 of that book, and then again on p. 113.) Notice that this assertion is self-referentially inconsistent. If "anything can be made to look good or bad by being redescribed," then this thesis itself can be made to look bad, and its denial good, by being redescribed. And what does this claim mean? That anyone can be made,

through redescription, to think that anything is good? That most people can be made to think that anything is good? That there exists somewhere some credulous dunce who can be persuaded to believe anything? And how would we test these claims?

19. See chapter 4, especially section III A.

20. For example, Rorty suggests, in "Solidarity or Objectivity?" in his *Objectivity, Relativism, and Truth* (New York: Cambridge University Press, 1991), p. 33, that "[t]he best argument we . . . have against the realistic partisans of objectivity is Nietzsche's argument that the traditional Western metaphysico-epistemological way of firming up our habits simply isn't working anymore. It isn't doing its job. . . . [T]he Enlightenment's search for objectivity has often gone sour." But what is the status of this claim? Is it itself objectively true? If so, then it is self-referentially inconsistent. But if not, then what is it its status? For another example of the many such passages in Rorty's writings, see *Contingency, Irony, and Solidarity*, p. 8.

21. This pattern of issuing incoherent statements and then attempting unsuccessfully to explain away the incoherence appears regularly in Rorty's writings. Consider, for example, the following remark (from Rorty's "Pragmatism, Relativism, and Irrationalism," in *Consequences of Pragmatism*, pp. 165–166): "There is no method for knowing *when* one has reached the truth, or when one is closer to it than before." But how, consistently with his own philosophy, can Rorty possibly know *that*? Rorty cannot claim to have a method whereby he could know it to be true that "there is no method for knowing," or even that this claim is any closer to the truth than would be the claim that there are methods for determining when we have reached, or come closer to reaching, the truth. But Rorty is, of course, aware of this problem and attempts to answer it in several places. The following (from *Contingency, Irony, and Solidarity*, p. 8) is typical:

> To say that there is no such thing as intrinsic nature is not to say that the intrinsic nature of reality has turned out to be extrinsic. It is to say that the term "intrinsic nature" is one which it would pay us not to use, an expression which has caused more trouble than it has been worth. To say that we should drop the idea of truth as out there waiting to be discovered is not to say that we have discovered, out there, there is no truth. It is to say that our purposes would be served best by ceasing to see truth as a deep matter, as a topic of philosophical interest, or "true" as a term which repays "analysis."

But then, what is the status of such claims as that "'intrinsic nature' is an expression which has caused more trouble than it has been worth"? Is this claim intended to capture the way things really are, or what it would be useful for us to say, or what? If the first, we have an inconsistency; if the second, we set up an infinite regress; and if the third, what is this third alternative?

22. Rorty, "John Searle on Realism and Relativism," in *Truth and Progress*, pp. 71–72.

23. Rorty, *Philosophy and the Mirror of Nature* (Princeton, NJ: Princeton University Press, 1980), p. 367.

24. Piotr Gutowski, "Comments on Richard Rorty, 'Relativism: Finding and Making,'" in *Debating the State of Philosophy*, ed. Józef Niznik and John T. Sanders (Westport, CT: Praeger, 1996), p. 111.

25. Ibid., pp. 114–115.

26. Robert W. McChesney, *Corporate Media and the Threat to Democracy* (New York: Seven Stories Press, 1997), pp. 48–49.

27. Rorty, *Contingency, Irony, and Solidarity*, p. 52.

28. Rorty himself acknowledges this in the "Introduction" to *Consequences of Pragmatism*, pp. xxix–xxx.

29. Rorty insists that he is not a relativist. I will assess this claim in section IV below.

30. There are interpretations of Rorty according to which he is not vulnerable to this objection. On this point see the discussion above in the present section, item (2).

31. For example, should Rorty support creationism or evolution? The former is favored by more Americans than is the latter, so should Rorty, in solidarity with them, do so as well? Or does he get to pick and choose which group he is going to be in solidarity with, perhaps varying it from question to question, so that here he would be in alignment with scientists? Is he ever at risk of being wrong?

32. Rorty, "Cosmopolitanism without Emancipation," in *Objectivity, Relativism, and Truth*, p. 220.

33. Rorty, *Contingency, Irony, and Solidarity*, pp. 7, 73, 113.

34. Rorty, "The Contingency of Community," *London Review of Books* 8 (24 July 1986): 14.

35. Rorty, *Contingency, Irony, and Solidarity*, p. 59.

36. Rorty, "Pragmatism, Relativism, and Irrationalism," in *Consequences of Pragmatism*, p. 166.

37. Rorty, "Solidarity or Objectivity?" in *Objectivity, Relativism, and Truth*, p. 23.

38. Rorty, "The Priority of Democracy to Philosophy," in *Objectivity, Relativism, and Truth*, pp. 176–177.

39. Rorty, "On Ethnocentrism," in *Objectivity, Relativism, and Truth*, pp. 207–208.

40. Rorty, "Postmodernist Bourgeois Liberalism," in *Objectivity, Relativism, and Truth*, p. 197.

41. Rorty, "Is Truth a Goal of Inquiry? Donald Davidson versus Crispin Wright," in *Truth and Progress*, p. 22.

42. Alexander Nehamas, *Nietzsche: Life as Literature* (Cambridge, MA: Harvard University Press, 1985), p. 72.

43. A. C. Graham, *Unreason within Reason* (La Salle, IL: Open Court, 1992), p. 29.

44. Rorty, "Solidarity or Objectivity?" in *Objectivity, Relativism, and Truth*, p. 24. (Note: I have changed Rorty's pronouns here. He refers to himself in the third person, calling himself "the pragmatist.") Similarly, in response to John Searle's charge that Rorty is guilty of systematically confusing epistemology with ontology, Rorty replies that "pragmatists have neither an epistemology nor an ontology. So we can't confuse them." Richard Rorty and John Searle, "Rorty v. Searle, at Last: A Debate," *Logos* 2, no. 3 (summer 1999): 50.

45. Rorty, *Contingency, Irony, and Solidarity*, p. 44.

46. Ibid., pp. 7, 73, 113.

47. Rorty, "Trotsky and the Wild Orchids," in his *Philosophy and Social Hope* (New York: Penguin, 1999), p. 15. Rorty is, indeed, quite consistent in defending this ethnocentric form of relativism, as opposed to the "anything goes," "any culture is as good as another," ultra-tolerant variety.

48. Rorty, "John Searle on Realism and Relativism," in *Truth and Progress*, p. 83.

49. Rorty, *Contingency, Irony, and Solidarity*, p. 177.

50. Rorty, "Trotsky and the Wild Orchids," in *Philosophy and Social Hope*, pp. 14–15.

51. Rorty, "John Searle on Realism and Relativism," in *Truth and Progress*, p. 71.

52. Ibid., p. 72.

53. Rorty, *Contingency, Irony, and Solidarity*, p. xv.

54. Frank B. Farrell, *Subjectivity, Realism, and Postmodernism* (New York: Cambridge University Press, 1994), p. 119.

55. Rorty, "Introduction" to *Consequences of Pragmatism*, p. xlii.

56. Rorty, "Science as Solidarity," in *Objectivity, Relativism, and Truth*, pp. 43–44.

57. John Stuart Mill, *On Liberty* (Indianapolis: Hackett, 1978).

58. Rorty (in "John Searle on Realism and Relativism," in *Truth and Progress*, p. 67) declares himself to be "nostalgic for the days when leftist professors concerned themselves with issues in real politics (such as the availability of health care to the poor, or the need for strong labor unions) rather than with academic politics." Part of the context for this remark is Rorty's disagreement with John Searle's assertion that the abandonment of traditional standards of objectivity, truth, and rationality is likely to lead to

dire political consequences. Rorty seems to think that "real" political issues swing clear of such epistemological debates. The problem, however—and Rorty fails to address it—is that when you try to talk to people about the real political issues that Rorty names here, a sizable number of them will tell you that it is just an opinion or a story, and not the truth, that there is not enough health care for the poor or that strong labor unions are needed. They will tell you that the opposite opinion or story is every bit as sound, that the whole issue is "undecidable," etc. Epistemological anti-realism has political consequences.

59. Rorty, "On Ethnocentrism," in *Objectivity, Relativism, and Truth*, pp. 207–208.

60. Rorty, "The Priority of Democracy to Philosophy," in *Objectivity, Relativism, and Truth*, pp. 187–188. Note that the claim that what we can take seriously is determined by our upbringing is itself, apparently, determined by our upbringing. Note also the reductionism of Rorty's view, and that it leaves the prospects for openness to what is alien to us quite poor indeed.

61. Rorty, *Contingency, Irony, and Solidarity*, p. 59.

62. Rorty, "Postmodernist Bourgeois Liberalism," in *Objectivity, Relativism, and Truth*, p. 201.

63. James Robert Brown, *Smoke and Mirrors* (New York: Routledge, 1994), p. 31. The Rorty quotation is from "Solidarity or Objectivity?" in *Objectivity, Relativism, and Truth*, p. 29.

64. In fairness to Rorty I should add that when I say that his view is politically conservative, I am referring to the political implications of his epistemology and not to the positions he has adopted on specific political issues, some of which are quite progressive.

On the other hand, when it comes to philosophy, and more specifically, epistemology, at times Rorty appears much more conservative than I've made him out to be. Indeed, sometimes he claims that truth is not merely a matter of obtaining a consensus or engaging in useful ways of talking, but rather has to do with arriving at beliefs that are well justified by relevant arguments and evidence. For example, Rorty suggests that we should "think of truth as the sort of belief which is attained by the usual methods of patient argument and discussion among informed persons, the sort of method characteristic of our universities" ("Rorty v. Searle, at Last: A Debate," p. 26), and urges us to understand "true" as "simply the word that we use to commend the beliefs which we find justified[.] We go through a long process of argument, listening to opposing words in the jury box, listening to opposing scientists argue for their respective theories, and then decide that the weight of argument favors one side or the other. Thereafter we call the statements made by that side of the argument true" (ibid., p. 41). Does any of this rescue Rorty from the criticisms I have been pressing against him?

By way of reply I note first that it is highly doubtful that Rorty intends any of this as inconsistent with, or in any way a modification of, the more radical-sounding ethnocentrist, pragmatist, and consensus-based formulations that I have been criticizing. That is to say, when Rorty here speaks of justification in terms of "the weight of argument" as it emerges from "the usual methods of patient discussion," the criteria by which I think he still intends to urge us to evaluate evidence and to assess where the weight of argument lies are thoroughly ethnocentric and pragmatist, and these, I have argued, generate fallacies and paradoxes.

But leaving that aside, reducing truth to justification, or even to *rational* justification, is objectionable in its own right because it runs together two things that seem to be quite different. To say that a claim is true is to say that matters *are* as the claim says they are; to say that our belief in that claim is justified is to say that we have good reason to *think* that matters are as the claim says they are, or that in this case we've properly followed all of the procedures that we think are conducive to arriving at an accurate belief. To reduce the former to the latter is therefore to conflate a target with good reasons for thinking we've hit the target, or with good procedures for hitting targets. But, just as we can follow all of the right procedures and still miss the target, so can a rationally justified belief miss the mark and be false, not true.

Now Rorty admits that a belief can be perfectly justified and yet be untrue. Indeed, he claims that the purpose of what he calls the "cautionary" use of "truth" is precisely to remind us of this (see, for example, "Pragmatism, Davidson, and Truth," in *Objectivity, Relativism, and Truth*, p. 128; and "Universality and Truth," in Robert B. Brandom, ed., *Rorty and His Critics* [Malden, MA: Blackwell, 2000], p. 4). However, as he makes clear in the passages just cited, his interpretation of this cautionary use of "truth" is always either pragmatist (e.g., though we are rationally justified in believing x, it may turn out that things won't go well if we base our actions on x) or ethnocentric (e.g., though we are rationally justified in believing x, it may be that we will later decide that x is not warranted by our criteria and standards—indeed, those criteria and standards might themselves change in such a way as to rule x out). So we are still blocked from considering that our standards might simply be the wrong ones, and not because they don't work or because we might later decide that they are wrong, but rather because they are not conducive to holding accurate beliefs about the world (as when, for example, our criminal justice procedures lead to massive errors in deciding who is or is not guilty of a crime). And the paradoxes remain. For example, if Rorty's objection to distinguishing between justification and truth in a realist manner is that we cannot know what the world is really like, than how are we to know such things as the consequences of our beliefs, whether or not they are working, what our neighbors are thinking, what are the intellectual standards prevailing in our society, and so forth—all of the facts about the world that we would have to know in order to get Rorty's alternative program off the ground?

Finally, just as many of our justified beliefs are untrue (as Rorty concedes), so is it the case that there are many truths that we will never be justified in believing (think, for example, of all of the historical events concerning which no evidence remains, or all of the empirical matters that lie outside of our perceptual range, or the conceptual matters the understanding of which is beyond our intellectual capacity). This is yet another reason to reject Rorty's suggestion that we reduce truth to justification.

65. Rorty, in "Towards a Liberal Utopia: An Interview with Richard Rorty," *Times Literary Supplement*, 24 June 1994, 14.

Chapter 6

WHAT IS OBJECTIVITY?
Sartre vs. the Journalists

One of the main reasons why contemporary postmodernists and social constructionists reject the idea of objectivity is that they often have a defective conception of this idea in mind—the conception promulgated by U.S. mass media journalists. Accordingly, in this chapter I will offer, based in part upon insights drawn from Sartre, an alternative understanding of objectivity—an understanding which would not only better serve the practice of journalism, but also be able to withstand the critical onslaught of the postmodernists.

The issue is extremely important because democracies cannot function without an effective system of political communication. If citizens are not aware of the policies that are carried out in their name, they are powerless to oppose them. Consequently, one of the chief responsibilities of journalists in a democracy is to provide their readers (or viewers or listeners) with news accounts that are accurate, reasonably comprehensive, and free from subordination to governmental or corporate power (or to that of other "special interests").

Certainly, most mass media journalists in the United States[1] accept such a characterization of their responsibility, which they interpret as entailing an obligation on their part to present news "objectively." But what does this mean? As these journalists understand the term, to present the news "objectively" is to present it in a "nonpartisan," "unbiased," "balanced," "nonideological," and "neutral" manner. This is to be done, so the story goes, not so much by finding and presenting "the truth"—that would require drawing conclusions and making judgments, often about controversial matters—as by simply reporting "the facts," leaving the job of synthesizing and evaluating these facts to its audience. To be sure, the press does publish commentaries and editorials, and in this way participates in the clash of competing theories and values. Still, these commentaries and editorials are always (in theory) clearly labeled as such and are distinguished sharply from "straight news," the gathering and presenting of which is, on the view we are now considering, the press's primary function.

Sartre, in quite radical contrast, consistently advocated an "engaged" journalism, a "committed" journalism—a journalism that would be dedicated to finding and telling the truth, and to doing so explicitly and self-consciously in the service of such fundamental values as freedom, justice, and human rights.[2] This conception of journalism calls for selective attention—one is to focus more on those truths which concern these fundamental values than on those which do not.[3] It calls for interpretation, theorizing, and the testing of interpretations and theories—for only in this way can we determine, insofar as human beings can do so at all, what *is* true or false.[4] And it calls for partisanship—one is to stand for truth and those who promote it, while opposing falsehood and those who promote *it*.[5] Similarly, the fundamental values mentioned a moment ago are to be vigorously and unapologetically defended against whomever and whatever stands in their way.

Which of these two conceptions of journalism is more defensible? I will argue that Sartre's theory is clearly the superior one. In order to support this judgment I will attempt to show that mainstream U.S. journalism in fact fails miserably to realize its idea of "objectivity." It does so not because of the limitations of individual journalists, but rather as a result of the inherent incoherence of the journalistic notion of objectivity—an incoherence which precludes this "ideal" from being realized, or even approximated, in practice. Moreover, the presently practiced "objective" journalism suffers, paradoxically, far more from "subjectivism," "partisanship," and "bias," in the objectionable senses of these terms, than would the Sartrean kind of journalism I am calling for; and this is so in large part because of the different and conflicting understandings of "objectivity" operating within these opposed theories of journalism.

I. THE U.S. MASS MEDIA'S COVERAGE OF INTERNATIONAL AFFAIRS: THE NATURE OF THE PROBLEM

One of the benefits of the U.S. mass media's understanding of objectivity and general approach to journalism, according to its defenders, is that it provides an effective counterweight to the often biased and self-serving accounts of events issued by representatives of, and spokespersons for, the U.S. government. Indeed, such a counterweight seems especially needed in the area of international affairs, for at least three reasons. First, while Americans presumably have ample resources for detecting errors and bias with regard to coverage of what takes place right in front of their own noses, this is manifestly not the case in connection with events in distant lands. Second, the resulting susceptibility of the American people to ignorance and error in connection with foreign affairs might well tempt government figures to inculcate and to exploit such ignorance and error for their own gain. Third, the stakes are very high: U.S. foreign policy often results, as even its most ardent defenders must admit, in death and destruction on a grand scale. American citizens therefore have a great need for accurate, undistorted information about foreign affairs, so that they might be able to make their own informed and competent judgment as to whether their government's foreign policy initiatives are justified and deserving of their support. This is a matter of no small practical significance, since the American people's support or opposition to their government's foreign policy initiatives can serve either to facilitate their continuance or to hasten their abandonment.

But how well is this need for accurate, independent information met? Do the U.S. media indeed tend to act as an effective counterweight to the government? Do U.S. citizens receive from their mass media what they require in order to arrive at informed opinions concerning the foreign policy initiatives of their government? In this chapter I will attempt to demonstrate that these questions must be answered clearly and resoundingly in the negative. Moreover, I will suggest that the major shortcomings of this coverage have to do not primarily with the transmission of outright errors and falsehoods, but much more frequently with problems of omission and emphasis: Information that is vitally important to any adequate understanding of the issue at hand is routinely excluded, while distortions are introduced by emphasizing information which, when stripped of its proper background and context, creates a misleading impression. I will attempt to show, moreover, that these omissions and distortions, far from contributing to a counterweight to government pronouncements, invariably lend them undeserved support. Finally, drawing inspiration from Sartre and focusing extensively on the idea of "objectivity," I will offer a diagnosis of the causes of these media failings and offer suggestions for change.

II. DOCUMENTING THE PROBLEM

In attempting to assess the quality of the U.S. mass media's coverage of foreign nations, it seems reasonable to begin with Iran. For while the press obviously cannot report on everything, and thus might be forgiven for inadequate coverage of, say, a tiny nation of little interest to American audiences, such a description obviously does not apply to Iran. Rather, as William A. Dorman points out,

> Iran by 1978 and the coming of the revolution had become the most important client state in United States history. More arms had been delivered by the United States to Iran than had ever been sold by any country in history. The United States had entered into a bilateral trade agreement with Iran that was larger in dollar amount than the total amount of money it took to reconstruct Europe under the Marshall Plan following World War II. Iranians comprised the largest group of foreign students in the United States. The United States had trained Iran's secret police and Army. American advisors and technocrats comprised one of the largest national minorities in Iran by 1978.[6]

Thus, we might be excused for assuming that the U.S. mass media must surely have kept Americans well-informed of events in Iran in the 1970s. And yet, Dorman continues, "Americans knew little if anything about Iran under the Shah Reza Pahlavi, and the revolution of 1978 came as a complete surprise to policymakers as well as the general public."[7]

Still, if the U.S. mass media performance had indeed been poor prior to the 1978 revolution, surely that dramatic event, coupled with a related and long-running affair of special interest to Americans—the seizing and holding of several Americans as hostages in Iran—must have aroused the intense interest of both the mass media and the public, resulting in vastly improved coverage of Iran and a greatly more informed American citizenry. And, to be sure, the *quantity* of coverage did increase immensely—the ABC news program *Nightline*, for example, began life as a nightly update on the plight of the hostages. Indeed, the coverage achieved such a level of intensity as to move Neil Postman to remark: "I don't suppose there has been a story in years that received more continuous attention from television."[8] And yet, Postman goes on to pose these provocative questions:

> Would it be an exaggeration to say that not one American in a hundred knows what language the Iranians speak? Or what the word "Ayatollah" means or implies? Or knows any details of the tenets of Iranian religious beliefs? Or the main outlines of their political history? Or knows who the Shah was, and where he came from?[9]

Thus, just as Americans had lacked the information needed to *foresee* the Iranian revolution, so did they subsequently lack the information that would have enabled them to *understand* it, let alone sympathize with the motives of the Iranians who had brought it about. It is perhaps understandable, then, that Americans tended to view the Iranian revolutionaries through an ignorant and thoroughly ethnocentric lens, regarding them as "religious fanatics" and "Muslim extremists," and attributing their anti-Americanism to simple barbarism and unreasonable, naked malevolence.

While it cannot be assumed that access to a greater quantity of accurate and relevant information about Iran would have made Americans sympathetic to hostage-takers, it seems possible that such access would at least have generated a better understanding of the plight of the Iranians under the shah, and thus rendered clear their reasons for revolution. It might even have persuaded some Americans of the legitimacy of Iranian grievances against the U.S. government.

But what is this "accurate and relevant information" of which I speak? What, specifically, has been left out of U.S. mass media coverage of Iran?

Consider the treatment of the shah's Iran, prior to his 1978 ouster. For if Americans failed to anticipate, or subsequently to comprehend, the Iranian revolution, it may well be because the mass media news accounts on which they relied for their understanding of the shah's reign conveyed little of its brutal and dictatorial character. To be sure, this information was available in non–mass media sources. Indeed, that the shah's record of human rights abuses was one of the worst in the world had, by the early 1970s, been well documented by such diverse organizations as Amnesty International, International Association of Democratic Lawyers, International Federation of Human Rights, International League for the Rights of Man, International Commission of Jurists, Writers and Scholars International, and the International Red Cross.[10] But the reports of these organizations reached a relatively small audience and thus exerted a minuscule influence in comparison to that of the mass media, in which the shah was portrayed quite differently. There his strengths, primarily as assessed from the standpoint of U.S. strategic interests, were emphasized, while the despotic, repressive aspects of his regime were de-emphasized when they were not ignored outright. Thus, for example, a study by William A. Dorman and Mansour Farhang of U.S. mass media news coverage of Iran over a twenty-five-year period found only four uses of the word "dictator" to describe the shah,[11] including just one in 1978, the crucial year of revolution.[12] Similarly, in 1975, the high point both of human rights violations in Iran and of U.S.-Iran economic and foreign relations, Dorman and Farhang found only three items in the *New York Times* on Iran's human rights abuses. By way of comparison, they discovered 150 articles in the *Times* on such violations in the Soviet Union.[13] Perhaps more to the point, it should be noted that the U.S. mass media had shown no similar reticence to focus on human rights violations in Iran during the administration of the shah's predecessor, Mohammad Mossadeq, and even exhibited a robust willingness to use the term "dictator" liberally in describing him, albeit with much less justification than they would have had in applying that label to the shah.[14]

Similarly, the incredulity and outrage with which Americans reacted to the anti-Americanism of Iranian revolutionaries can be attributed in part to the Americans' ignorance of the essential information—regularly excluded from U.S. mass media news accounts—which, by revealing the role of the United States government in sustaining the shah and his atrocities, would have rendered that attitude comprehensible. For example, while the *New York Times* had learned by 1954 of the U.S. Central Intelligence Agency's major role in engineering the coup of 1953 (in which the popular, democratically selected Mossadeq was overthrown and the shah returned to power), it did not report this to its readers (and then only in passing) until 1971.[15] Nor did the U.S. mass media inform Americans that the shah's secret police force, known as SAVAK—which tortured, mutilated, and/or killed thousands of Iranians who opposed the shah politically—had been trained in large part by the Central Intelligence Agency.[16]

Regrettably, we find no noticeable improvement in the mass media's coverage of Iran, especially with regard to achieving a greater independence from official U.S. government perspectives, when we turn to more recent events, such as the July 1988 shootdown of an Iranian civilian airliner by an American warship, the USS *Vincennes*. Mass media treatments of this event consisted of little more than the utterly uncritical passing along of the official U.S. government explanation of the tragedy: that the *Vincennes* was in international waters at the time of the incident; that the airliner was not within the commercial air corridor at the time (thus partially explaining the failure of the *Vincennes* personnel to recognize it as a civilian airliner); and that the Iranian plane was heading at a high rate of speed directly for the *Vincennes* when it drew the *Vincennes*'s fire.

We now know that all of these claims are false: the *Vincennes* was in *Iranian* waters at the time of the shooting; the Iranian plane was well within the commercial air corridor; and it was moving *away* from the *Vincennes* when it was shot down. Indeed, it must in all fairness be pointed out that the demolition of the U.S. government cover story concerning the *Vincennes* incident was eventually—in 1992—presented in ample detail by two mass media organizations working in cooperation with one another: *Newsweek*[17] and *Nightline*.[18] Still, praiseworthy though these 1992 reports may be, both *Newsweek* and *Nightline* also merit criticism for having uncritically parroted the U.S. government's false cover story in 1988,[19] and for failing to correct the public record for four years—by which time the opportunity for appropriate public action had passed, and even the capacity for moral outrage had been greatly diminished.

Notice, once again, that the most objectionable feature of the mass media's coverage of the *Vincennes* incident is not inaccuracy, for, as a result of the mass media's use of attribution, the great bulk of that coverage was, in the strictest sense, accurate. For example, while it is not true that the *Vincennes* was in international waters at the time of the shootdown, it is indeed true that government officials *claimed* that it was, and it is this *claim*, duly noted as such, that the mass media tended to pass along, albeit without adequately emphasizing its unsubstantiated status, and without ever deviating from a news "frame" in which the government's story was (implicitly) accepted as true. The biggest problem, then, was the failure to present any information that would *undermine* the government's story, or at least to suggest that it was dubitable.

But what, specifically, was left out? Let us concede that it would be unfair to expect the mass media to have debunked the government's story immediately. Perhaps the facts needed for such debunking simply were not available in 1988 (though, given the paucity of evidence that the media searched for such facts with sufficient vigor, such a concession may be unreasonably generous). Still, at least three kinds of information were left out which might, had they been included, have led to a significantly different public perception of the *Vincennes* incident.

First, the media should have presented more, and a greater variety of, background information on the political situation of the region, so as to provide a context in which to understand the shootdown, and in particular to make possible the consideration of explanations for it which would conflict with the self-serving one provided by the U.S. government. To give just one obvious example, the media could have brought together the facts, many of which were available at the time, suggesting that the U.S. government was secretly engaged in a war against Iran. Indeed, according to former Marine lieutenant colonel Roger Charles, interviewed in the 1992 *Nightline* special, keeping this engagement secret was the main purpose of the government's *Vincennes* cover story: "The full disclosure of what happened with the *Vincennes* would have brought about the disclosure of a secret war, the United States as an active military participant on the side of the Iraqis, fighting the Iranians."[20]

Second, the media might have reviewed other shootdowns of civilian airliners in recent history, searching for, and ultimately presenting, information pertaining to their causes, so as to generate insights into the possible causes of the *Vincennes* case. Such a review would also have had the virtue of helping to guide the media in searching for new evidence on the *Vincennes* shootdown. Moreover, in researching their own past performances in covering shootdowns, and more specifically those in which the perpetrators were official "enemies" of the U.S. government, the mass media might have learned something about the possibilities of being aggressive in challenging official misconduct, as well as the lies and rationalizations offered by authorities to cover up such misconduct. All of this could have then been usefully applied to coverage of the *Vincennes* case. Similarly, in contrasting this aggressiveness with the passivity they would have found in reviewing their past coverage of shootdowns by "friendly" governments,[21] the mass media might have learned something about fairness and the need for independence from official U.S. government perspectives in covering such events. This too could then have been usefully applied to coverage of the *Vincennes* shootdown.

Finally, the mass media should have been willing to point out in 1988 what they so willingly conceded in 1992, that, in Ted Koppel's words, "[g]overnments lie; they do it all the time. And, much as we'd like to believe otherwise, the U.S. government is no exception."[22] *Newsweek* made the point even more strongly: "The U.S. Navy did what all navies do after terrible blunders at sea: it told lies and handed out medals."[23] But if governments, including that of the United States, lie "*all the time*," and if *all* navies tell lies "after terrible blunders at sea," what possible justification could there have been for failing to make these highly relevant and utterly elementary points in 1988? Doing so would have given news audiences an alternative framework for making sense of the *Vincennes* incident and provided journalists with a promising avenue for further investigation into the shootdown. The massive scale of this failure to learn from history is underscored by the fact that on 18 January 1988, the *New York Times* had concluded, in an editorial entitled "The Lie That Wasn't Shot Down," that the U.S. government had lied about a previous shootdown of a civilian airliner—the Soviet Union's attack on a Korean plane in 1983.[24] And yet, just six months later, when the U.S. government issued new pronouncements on a new shootdown, no information disputing these pronouncements would appear in the mass media, nor would the possibility of U.S. government lying be given any serious consideration.

The story is very much the same when we turn to Iraq. For

example, Jeff Cohen makes the point that, prior to the buildup of tensions that led to the Gulf War, during the period in which Saddam Hussein was a U.S. ally,

> there was no [media] coverage of his human rights abuses. There was almost nil. After the crisis began, when the invasion of Kuwait occurred, all of a sudden he was the greatest human rights abuser in the world. All of a sudden, Amnesty International reports on Iraq mattered. Those reports were released all through the 1980s, when Iraq was an ally of the United States, when the Reagan administration took Iraq off the terrorist list so they could give them billions of dollars in agricultural credits, when the Reagan-Bush administration was getting guns to Iraq through third-party states, including Jordan and Kuwait. During that whole period when the United States was helping build up the military and economic might of Saddam Hussein in Iraq, the issue of his human rights abuses was off the media agenda. There was this classic in the *New York Post*, a tabloid in New York. After the crisis began they had a picture of Saddam Hussein patting the British kid on the head and their banner headline was "Child abuser." That was . . . very ironic, because Amnesty International and other human rights groups had released studies in 1984 and 1985 which showed that Saddam Hussein's regime regularly tortured children to get information about their parents, their parents' views. That just didn't get the coverage. It shows . . . that when a foreign government is in favor with the United States, with the White House, its human rights record is basically off the mainstream media agenda, and when they do something that puts them out of favor with the U.S. government, the foreign government's human rights abuses are, all of a sudden, major news.[25]

One might add that had the press called attention to Hussein's child abusing activities at a time when he was receiving U.S. support, such coverage might have made a difference.

The same point might well be made about press coverage of Turkey's program of ethnic cleansing of their own Kurds during the 1990s. For just as the mass media neglected to cover Saddam Hussein's genocidal campaign against Iraqi Kurds during the period in which he was a U.S. ally, despite the fact that he even went so far as to use chemical weapons against them, and, even more significantly, despite the fact that such human rights abuses somehow became newsworthy once Hussein fell out of favor with the U.S. government, so should we expect the same inattention to Turkey's comparable abuses, since it is currently a U.S. ally. Indeed, this is what we do find. A Nexus database search of the *Los Angeles Times*, the *New York Times*, the *Washington Post*, *Newsweek*, and *Time* for the years 1990–1999 revealed that the word "genocide" was used more than nine times as often (132 to 14) in reference to the Iraqi treatment of the Kurds as it was in connection with Turkey's treatment of its Kurds. The disparity grows to a margin of twenty-four to one when we focus exclusively on front-page coverage.[26]

As an additional illustration of the U.S. mass media's coverage of Iraq, consider the following. When the U.S. was found guilty in the International Court of Justice of "unlawful use of force" against Nicaragua and ordered to pay damages, the U.S. refused to pay.[27] But when President Bush invoked international law in demanding that Iraq pay reparations for having unlawfully attacked Kuwait, the U.S.'s own recent refusal to abide by international law or to pay damages for having failed to do so were not mentioned by the national mass media, which uncritically parroted Bush's demands concerning Iraq.

Let's turn next to the mainstream media's coverage of censorship of the press when it is practiced in foreign countries. Since freedom of the press is obviously a value of great importance to journalists and to news organizations, and since press censorship presumably is "newsworthy," and of interest to readers and viewers of journalism, one would expect the press to be ever ready to focus on it. Obviously, this is not to say that it would be reasonable to expect the press to cover *all*, or even most, instances of censorship—there are too many such instances, and there is a finite amount of space in newspapers and time in news broadcasts available for such coverage. Thus, we might well expect even the most responsible of news media to ignore instances of censorship which are small in scale, minor in effect, or which occur in places that are otherwise of little current interest to their readers or viewers. But we would not expect a *responsible* press to highlight censorship activities of our "enemies," as defined by those who wield political power in our country, while ignoring much more serious instances of censorship perpetrated by those officially designated our "friends."

One good test of the responsibility of mainstream U.S. journalism in its coverage of freedom of the press, then, would be to compare its coverage of censorship as practiced in the 1980s by the governments of Nicaragua and El Salvador. These two countries are geographically proximate to each other and to the U.S. and were in the 1980s of interest to the U.S. news audience. (Or at least, there was at that time a great deal of news coverage of these two countries, in comparison to most foreign nations.) Thus, to the extent that the U.S. press is unbiased and nonpartisan, we should expect its relative coverage of censorship in the two countries to vary in accordance with such factors as the relative scale and severity of effects of the censorship in the two nations. On the other hand, since El Salvador was officially our "friend" and a "fledgling democracy," while Nicaragua under the Sandinistas was officially our "enemy" and a "totalitarian dungeon," we should expect a more partisan press, a less responsible one, to play up censorship in Nicaragua while ignoring it as much as possible in El Salvador. What, then, do we find?

Censorship in Nicaragua did indeed receive extensive coverage during the period in question. For example, one study of 104 articles from the *Boston Globe*, *New York Times*, and *Washington Post* dealing with the 1984 Nicaraguan elections found that 65 mentioned press censorship.[28] Another study, conducted in 1988, found 263 references in the *New York Times* to the difficulties of the Nicaraguan newspaper *La Prensa* over a period of four years.[29]

Coverage of censorship in El Salvador, on the other hand, was so scanty that I cannot assume my readers to know of the existence of such censorship, let alone be familiar with its details. Thus, I quote the following from the September 1985 Americas Watch Report on El Salvador:

> Any discussion of press freedom in El Salvador must begin by pointing out the elimination of the country's two main opposition newspapers. *La Crónica del Pueblo* was closed in 1980 when members of the security forces raided a San Salvador coffee shop where the paper's editor and one of its photographers were meeting. Editor Jaime Suarez, a 31-year-old prize-winning poet, and Cesar Najarro, were disemboweled by machete and then shot. In 1981 *El Independiente* was closed when army tanks surrounded its offices. This was the culmination of a long series of attacks, which included the machinegunning of a 14-year-old newsboy, bombing and assassination attempts against editor Jorge Pinto. The Archdiocese's radio station, WMAX, spent several years out of commission after its offices were repeatedly bombed. Since 1981 the Salvadoran press

has either supported the government or criticized it from a right-wing perspective. Daily newspapers do not publish criticism . . . from a leftist perspective, nor do they print stories critical of government forces from a human rights standpoint.[30]

In contrast to the extensive coverage in the *New York Times* of censorship in Nicaragua, these far more serious abuses of press freedoms in El Salvador have gone unmentioned in that publication. The newspaper which claims to publish "all the news that's fit to print" has not seen fit to report the use of terrorism by the government of El Salvador against the press of that nation.[31] The story (or lack thereof) is very much the same when we turn to abuses of press freedoms in other "pro-U.S." nations. Thus, when security forces of the Guatemalan government in June 1988 succeeded in "persuading" the editor of *La Epoca* to shut down that weekly newspaper by fire-bombing its offices, stealing its valuable equipment, kidnapping its night watchman, and threatening to murder its "traitor journalists"— not a threat to be taken lightly in view of the fact that dozens of journalists in Guatemala already had been murdered in recent years—no report of these events was to be found in the *New York Times* or *Washington Post.*[32] Two months prior to these events, and one month following them, there were many articles in those two newspapers about lesser abuses of the press in Nicaragua.

In September 1988 Israeli security forces raided the offices of *Al-Fajr*, a leading daily newspaper in Jerusalem, arrested its managing editor, Hatem Abdel-Qader, and jailed him for six months without trial on unspecified grounds. This story was not covered in the *New York Times* or *Washington Post.*[33] In this noncoverage the two papers followed the precedent which they had set in 1986 when, during the height of their coverage of the suspension of publication of *La Prensa* in Nicaragua, they failed to inform their readers that the government of Israel had closed two newspapers, *Al-Mithaq* and *Al-Ahd*, on the grounds that their publication was "harmful to the state of Israel."[34]

Similarly, Martin A. Lee points out that

during the 90-day period following the signing of the Central American peace plan on August 7, 1987 FAIR [Fairness and Accuracy in Reporting] tallied the column inches of 215 articles in the *[New York] Times* and found a clear pattern. The *Times* devoted 3.6 times more column inches to Nicaragua than to three of its neighbors combined. The ratio of Nicaragua coverage to that of El Salvador was 5 to 1; Honduras 22 to 1; and Guatemala 26 to 1. This was a period of assassination and human rights reversals in El Salvador, rejection of the peace accord in Honduras and intensified warfare in Guatemala. Consider the coverage in a single week: the brief detentions of oppositionists in Nicaragua were reported far more prominently in the *Times* (1-16 through 1-20-88) than the murder of human rights monitors in Honduras.[35]

For more evidence of the even-handedness and objectivity of the press, let's examine another matched set of examples. In May 1986 the prison memoirs of released Cuban prisoner Armando Valladares were published in book form. The book accused the Castro government of imprisoning political opponents and of making routine use of torture in its penal system. The Valladares memoirs received widespread coverage in the mainstream U.S. press. Substantial articles about the book's revelations appeared in the *New York Times*, the *Washington Post, Time* magazine, and many other major newspapers and magazines. In addition, the book was widely reviewed in publications that feature book reviews. Even President Reagan took notice, singling out Valladares for praise during a White House ceremony marking Human Rights Day in December.[36]

Meanwhile, also in May 1986, most of the members of the nongovernmental human rights commission of El Salvador (CDHES) were arrested and tortured, including the commission's director, Herbert Anaya. While in prison the commission compiled a 160-page report of sworn testimony of 430 political prisoners, who testified in precise and explicit detail about their torture by the U.S.-backed security forces. This report, along with a videotape of some of its sworn testimony, was smuggled out of prison and distributed to the U.S. media right in the midst of extensive coverage of the Valladares memoirs. But not a word about the report was printed in the *New York Times*, the *Washington Post, Time* magazine, or indeed in any major U.S. publication other than the *San Francisco Examiner*.[37] When Anaya was released from prison he was, predictably, immediately assassinated.

With regard to the U.S. mass media's coverage of U.S.-Cuba relations, it would be difficult to improve upon Noam Chomsky and Edward S. Herman's analysis which, despite having originally been presented during the Carter administration, is not in the least dated:

Suppose that Fidel Castro had organized or participated in at least eight assassination attempts against the various presidents of the United States since 1959. It is safe to conclude that the *New York Times*, CBS News, and the mass media in general would have portrayed him as an international gangster and assassin, who must be excluded from the community of civilized nations. But when it is revealed that the United States has made or participated in that many attempts on Castro's life, it's just "one of those things that governments do." . . .

Suppose further that Fidel Castro had arranged for his agents in the United States to disperse various disease carriers in agricultural regions in an attempt to poison and destroy livestock and crops. Can one imagine the hysteria of the *Wall Street Journal* and the *Times* on the depths to which barbarian evil can sink under Communism? The United States actually did carry out such acts against Cuba, reported in the press in early 1977 as minor news items—500,000 pigs had to be destroyed in Cuba as a result of a deliberately spread viral disease. And according to a recent statement of a Canadian adviser to the Cuban government, as early as 1962 he was paid $5,000 by a Defense Intelligence Agency representative to infect Cuban poultry with a viral disease. Editorial outrage has been modest, to say the least.

President Carter has kindly offered to move toward normalizing relations with Cuba, but under conditions that are worth presenting in his own words:

> If I can be convinced that Cuba wants to remove their aggravating influence from other countries in this hemisphere, will not participate in violence in nations across the oceans, will recommit [*sic*] the former relationship that existed in Cuba toward human rights—then I would be willing to move toward normalizing relations with Cuba, as well.

It is Cuba that must cease its "aggravating influence" in this hemisphere and refrain from the use of force in international affairs if normal relations are to be established, not the superpower that has instituted subfascist regimes throughout the hemisphere. . . . But even put that aside. Eight admitted attempts on Castro's life, a sponsored invasion, innumerable acts of sabotage—and still Carter can talk about Cuban external violence *and not be challenged or ridiculed by anyone whose voice can be heard.* Carter's reference to the state of civil rights in Cuba under the Batista dictatorship, to which he urges that Cuba should "recommit" itself, also elicited neither criticism nor satire. Where such hypocrisy and distortion can pass without comment, it is evident that the mass media are maintaining a system of thought control which can establish and nourish the Big Lie as effectively as any system of state censorship.[38]

The significance of these media shortcomings has become all the clearer in the aftermath of the horrific events of September 11, 2001, in which terrorists hijacked four commercial planes and deliberately crashed two of them into the two towers of the World Trade Center in New York City and one into the Pentagon in Washington, D.C. The remaining plane crashed in rural Pennsylvania when passengers, having learned of the fate of the other planes, fought the hijackers and prevented them from hitting yet another major target (perhaps the White House). More than three thousand innocent people, who were simply going about their daily business at the time of the attacks, were suddenly murdered on that terrible day. In the aftermath of this tragedy, the U.S. has attacked Afghanistan, successfully toppling its government (which had harbored the alleged mastermind behind the crimes), but in the process killing thousands more innocent people who had no connection with terrorism or the murderous assault of September 11.[39] The U.S. has also announced that its attack on Afghanistan is part of an expanding "war on terrorism," to be carried out all over the world, with no end in sight. Indeed, as I write (May 2003), the U.S. has just completed a war toppling Saddam Hussein's regime from power in Iraq, having offered as part of its justification for doing so the need to combat international terrorism. Meanwhile, on the domestic scene, "homeland security" and the war on terrorism have been cited as justifying a great relaxing of civil liberties, so we are now becoming accustomed to an environment of secret detentions, secret trials, and increased governmental eavesdropping on interpersonal communications of all sort. We are living in tense times.

What has any of this to do with the mass media? Well, I would suggest that the media's dismal performance has left many Americans—those who rely on mainstream journalism as their principal source of information about the world—ignorant of the history underlying the terrorist attacks of September 11, and thus unable to understand them except at the level at which one understands a cartoon aimed at young children. And this ignorance also extends, and for the same reason, to the nature of the regimes and of the world leaders with whom the U.S. is currently allying itself in its "war on terrorism." As a result, a significant number of Americans find themselves ill positioned to evaluate their government's policies rationally.

To begin to see this, let's consider the concept of "blowback," the subject of a prophetic book published in 2000, well before the terrorist attacks of September 11.[40] The author, Chalmers Johnson, notes that the term was coined by officials of the Central Intelligence Agency for internal use, and that it "refers to the unintended consequences of policies that were kept secret from the American people." He points out, furthermore, that "[w]hat the daily press reports as the malign acts of 'terrorists' or 'drug lords' or 'rogue states' or 'illegal arms merchants' often turn out to be blowback from earlier American operations."[41]

As a case in point, Johnson discusses the U.S. reaction to the 7 August 1998 bombings of American embassy buildings in Nairobi and Dar es Salaam, in which twelve Americans and 212 Kenyans and Tanzanians were killed. The U.S. blamed Osama bin Laden (the same man whom it would later accuse of masterminding the September 11 attacks) and retaliated by firing nearly eighty cruise missiles into a pharmaceutical plant in Khartoum, Sudan, and an old camp site in Afghanistan. Though U.S. intelligence had identified both targets as being associated with bin Laden or his followers, it was later admitted that this intelligence had been erroneous. The pharmaceutical plant in Khartoum had been entirely legitimate and had made medicines, not nerve gas.[42] Its bombing has proved an utter disaster for the people of Sudan, as it had provided 50 percent of Sudan's medicines, and its destruction left the country with no supplies of chloroquine, the standard treatment for malaria. It had also been the only Sudanese manufacturer of drugs for the treatment of tuberculosis, which it provided inexpensively to about 100,000 Sudanese. As Sudan is a poor country, most of its citizens cannot afford costly foreign drugs. As a direct consequence of the U.S. bombing, it is estimated that several tens of thousands of Sudanese, many of them children, have died from malaria, tuberculosis, and other treatable diseases.[43] As Johnson points out, "[i]n this way, future blowback possibilities are seeded into the world."[44]

Moreover, it is important to understand that bin Laden, the alleged mastermind both of the embassy bombings and of the terrorist attacks of September 11, is a former protégé of the United States. Johnson explains: "When America was organizing Afghan rebels against the USSR in the 1980s, he played an important role in driving the Soviet Union from Afghanistan and only turned against the United States in 1992 because he regarded the stationing of American troops in his native Saudi Arabia during and after the Persian Gulf War as a violation of his religious beliefs."[45] It is difficult, then, to dispute Johnson's conclusion that "the attacks on our embassies in Africa, if they were indeed his work, are an instance of blowback rather than unprovoked terrorism. Instead of bombing sites in Sudan and Afghanistan in response, the United States might better have considered reducing or removing our large-scale and provocative military presence in Saudi Arabia."[46]

The U.S. mass media, despite the enormous volume of its coverage of September 11 and its aftermath, has said very little about these matters. The term "blowback" is seldom used and has not become part of the vocabulary of the average consumer of mass media news. Nor has there been much discussion of the fact that the mujahideen, the militant Islamic warriors, including bin Laden, who had fought against the Soviet-backed government in Afghanistan, had been trained and funded by the U.S. (in concert with Pakistan and Saudi Arabia, among others). Nor has much ink or air time been expended in pointing out that these mujahideen, whom President Reagan had likened to our "founding fathers," were (and were known by the U.S to be even as they chose to arm, finance, and train them) religious fanatics who had no loyalty to their American sponsors, and still less to such values as democracy, religious tolerance, and gender equality.[47] As a result, in the extensive media discussion of the causes of terrorism and of the ways in which we should try to prevent or combat it, there is no room for the elementary observation that it might be a good idea not to arm, organize, finance, encourage, and in other ways assist, the likes of Osama bin Laden (not to mention Saddam Hussein[48] and Manuel Noriega, among the other thugs, murderers, and drug dealers[49] whom the U.S. government has made a habit of befriending). Instead, there is a strange, Orwellian quality to the mass media's coverage of these characters. When they are U.S. allies, they are portrayed positively. When they fall out of favor, they are depicted not only as evil, but as having always been evil. The fact that they had once been highly praised U.S. allies goes unmentioned.

As Johnson suggests, however, blowback is seeded not only by arming and backing terrorist murderers, but also by the commission of such outrageous actions as the bombing of the Sudanese pharmaceutical camp. This, too, is ignored in the U.S. mass media. Indeed, in what little commentary on these elementary points as one can find in "respectable" political circles, there is the suggestion that to focus on evil (or perhaps merely misguided) actions of the U.S. government as part of the explanation for acts of terrorism against the U.S. is to justify these terroristic actions, and to say that their victims "had it coming."[50] But this is nonsense. It confuses understanding with approval, and explanation with excuse. To point out that some terrorists have legitimate grievances against the U.S. government, and that the addressing of these grievances would remove much of the motivation for, and consequently the incidence of, terrorist actions, is hardly the same thing as saying that these terrorist acts are morally defensible. If you harm me wrongly and outrageously it does not follow that I have the right to react violently, especially if I have available to me other, more peaceful, ways of stopping your aggression. Still less does it follow that any particular magnitude of violence would be justified. If you slap me, I have no right to respond by killing you. Finally, I am on even shakier ground if my response is to attack not you, but rather your family, or your neighbors, or others of your country, religion, or ethnicity. So the terrorists don't have a leg to stand on. Their actions are every bit as immoral and unjustified (or, if you will, evil) as is constantly asserted in mainstream circles. But that is fully consistent with recognizing that their actions are to be explained partly as a reaction, albeit an excessive and unjustified one, to American misdeeds. Similarly, to return to my analogy, while my act of killing your neighbors is indeed evil, we would misunderstand it if we regarded it as unprovoked, and we would be foolish not to recognize that its occurrence would have been rendered less likely had you not first harmed me wrongfully and outrageously. So to say that claiming that wrongful U.S. conduct has increased the likelihood of terrorist attacks against Americans (and that part of the solution might reside in our government's ceasing to support terrorists and murderers and ceasing to aggress against other nations[51] and flouting international law) is to excuse the actions of the terrorists is like saying that the observation that there are social and economic factors that tend to lead to an increase in homicides, and that the homicide rate might be diminished by addressing these (improving educational opportunities, for example) is to excuse or justify acts of homicide! In any case, in evaluating the current U.S. "war on terrorism" one would think it might be relevant to examine the last one. It began on 28 January 1981 when then Secretary of State Alexander Haig of the newly elected Reagan administration announced that "terrorism" was going to replace "human rights" as a central concern of U.S. foreign policy. What was the result? While the U.S. did indeed oppose the terrorism of Libya, the PLO, the IRA, the African National Congress (though Dick Cheney and the U.S. State Department may now be embarrassed at having denounced Nelson Mandela, then the leader of the ANC, but now a highly regarded statesman and South Africa's president emeritus, as a terrorist), the Soviet Union, and a few others, it also supported the military government of Argentina (which kidnapped, tortured, and assassinated thousands), the government of El Salvador (the "deranged killing machine" of Argentinian novelist Juan Corradi's description, which murdered about eight hundred civilians a month in the year leading up to the election of March 1982), the military government of Guatemala (which murdered over 100,000 civilians between 1978 and 1985, and also practiced mutilation on a grand scale), the apartheid government of South Africa (which, in addition to its abysmal treatment of its black population, funded the terrorist organizations UNITA in Angola and RENAMO in Mozambique, which were, in turn, directly supported by the U.S.), Israeli Prime Minister Ariel Sharon (who bears significant responsibility for the 1982 massacre of about 1800 innocent persons—mainly women, children, and older men—at the Sabra and Shatila refugee camps in Lebanon), the Nicaraguan contras (whose modus operandi in pursuit of "freedom" in Nicaragua consisted largely of murdering civilians, torturing, mutilating, raping, and killing prisoners, and destroying schools, hospitals, and other public institutions), and various Cuban refugee terrorists (including Luis Posada Carriles, the world-class terrorist who had helped organize the destruction of a Cuban civilian airliner in 1976), not to mention Saddam Hussein and Osama bin Laden, among others.[52] None of this has ever been adequately covered by the mass media. Nor is it recalled now, when it is clearly relevant to the issue of whether or to what extent we should support the present "war on terrorism." (Of course, that issue itself isn't discussed, it being assumed in mainstream journalism that we should all support our president's policies on this matter. I will discuss this point shortly.)

Is history repeating itself? Who are the current allies of the U.S. in its "war on terrorism"? They include dictator Musharaff's Pakistan, with its dismal human rights record, Uzbekistan, with its repressive dictator Karimov, and Afghanistan's drug-dealing Northern Alliance, which had previously carried out a program of such destruction and terror that much of the population of Afghanistan welcomed the horrific Taliban as a relatively peaceful alternative. And if the aim is to fight terrorism, why does the U.S. selectively target Afghanistan (and there is talk that Somalia or Syria might be next), but not Turkey or Saudi Arabia, which also harbor terrorists? How one wishes that a U.S. journalist would ask President Bush this question, suggested by Martin A. Lee:

> By making counter-terrorism the top priority in bilateral relations, aren't you signaling to abusive governments in Sudan, Indonesia, Turkey, and elsewhere that they need not worry much about their human rights performance as long as they join America's anti-terrorist crusade? Will you barter human rights violations like corporations' trade pollution credits? Will you condone, for example, the brutalization of Chechnya in exchange for Russian participation in the "war against terrorism?" Or will you send a message loud and clear to America's allies that they must not use the fight against terrorism as a cover for waging repressive campaigns that smother democratic aspirations in their own countries?[53]

But no such questions are ever asked by U.S. mass media journalists. Instead, their performance in connection with the "war on terrorism" is typified by the anchorman of the *CBS Evening News*, Dan Rather's, declaration that "George Bush is the president, he makes the decisions, and, you know, as just one American, he wants me to line up, just tell me where. And he'll make the call."[54] As Howard Zinn points out, "[t]his is the language you might hear in a totalitarian state, not in a democracy: If the president says get in line, we get in line. The first rule of journalism is to be an independent voice, an independent critic, not a hand-maiden of government."[55] But, as I have attempted to document in this section, the U.S. mass media does not have an independent voice; it is, indeed, a hand-maiden of government.

As a final, and quite spectacular, illustration of this point, consider the U.S. mass media's performance in covering the just-completed U.S. war against Saddam Hussein's Iraq. I'll limit myself to ten points.

(1) When Iraq delivered to the United Nations a 12,000-page report on its weapons supply, the U.N. obeyed the U.S. demand that the report be censored, prior to distribution to members of the Security Council, so as to conceal the suppliers of those weapons. But the Berlin newspaper *Tageszeitung* managed to obtain an uncensored copy, and the revelations it contained were treated as a major news story in the European press. It seems that several U.S., British, and German corporations had supplied Iraq with nuclear, chemical, biological, and missile technology prior to 1991, even though such shipments were at the time illegal under the terms of various international treaties and laws. Among the U.S. corporations involved were Honeywell, SpectraPhysics, Rockwell, Hewlett Packard, Dupont, Eastman Kodak, and Bechtel, among others. The U.S. mass media ignored the story.[56] It is not hard to understand why the U.S. government would want to suppress this information. But it is remarkable that a supposedly free and independent U.S. press should be so willing to oblige the government in this regard.

(2) The U.S. mass media also downplayed (at best) or ignored (at worst) a major piece of evidence concerning the question of whether or not Iraq, prior to the U.S. attack, was, as the U.S. claimed in the face of Iraqi denials, stockpiling chemical and biological weapons and banned missiles. The issue is a significant one, since the U.S. cited Iraq's alleged illegal stockpiling of such weapons as a major justification for its war effort. The evidence in question was a transcript of Iraqi General Hussein Kamel's debriefing by officials from the International Atomic Energy Agency and the U.N. inspections team (UNSCOM). In this transcript, obtained by *Newsweek's* John Barry, Kamel claims that "after the Gulf War, Iraq destroyed all its chemical and biological weapons stocks and the missiles to deliver them. . . . All weapons—biological, chemical, missile, nuclear, were destroyed."

While *Newsweek* devoted a small article to Kamel's claims (in its 3 March 2003 issue), the rest of the U.S. mass media failed to pick up the story. To see why they should have pursued it, it is necessary to consider some background information about Kamel. He was an Iraqi defector, a son-in-law of Saddam Hussein, and he had been the head of Iraq's military industries. When he defected he took with him crates of secret documents on Iraq's past weapons programs and exposed many of the claims issued by his father-in-law's government as self-serving lies. And Kamel's claims consistently checked out, making his testimony invaluable to U.N. weapons inspectors. Indeed, in a 25 January 1999 letter to the U.N. Security Council, UNSCOM reported that its entire eight years of disarmament work "must be divided into two parts, separated by the events following the departure from Iraq, in August 1995, of Lt. General Hussein Kamel." Similarly, President George W. Bush (in a 7 October 2002 speech), Secretary of State Colin Powell (in his 5 February 2003 presentation to the U.N. Security Council), Vice President Dick Cheney (in a 27 August 2002 speech), and Deputy National Security Advisor Stephen Hadley (in the *Chicago Tribune*, 16 February 2003), all specifically and explicitly cited Kamel, praising his information as accurate, reliable, and invaluable. And yet all of these U.S. government officials omitted (and continue to omit) the part of his testimony that hurts their cause. Clearly they are withholding relevant, indeed critical, evidence.[57] It is understandable that they would want to do so. But it is also remarkable that U.S. mass media outlets, for the most part, let them get away with it.

(3) Consistent with its practice during the Gulf War of 1991, the U.S. mass media again generally refrained from pointing out that Saddam Hussein had once been, despite his dismal human rights record, a major recipient of U.S. military, economic, and diplomatic aid. For example, amidst all the talk about chemical weapons and U.N. resolutions, the U.S, mass media failed to provide some helpful historical perspective by reminding their readers, viewers, and listeners (or, more likely, informing them for the first time) of the statement of the U.N. Security Council President on 21 March 1986 on Saddam Hussein's use of chemical weapons. The president declared that the Council members were "profoundly concerned by the unanimous conclusion of the specialists that chemical weapons on many occasions have been used by Iraqi forces against Iranian forces . . . [and] the members of the Council strongly condemn this continued use of chemical weapons in clear violation of the Geneva Protocol of 1925 which prohibits the use in war of chemical weapons." The United States voted against the issuance of this statement.[58]

(4) Despite the fact that the Bush administration has repeatedly

cited Saddam Hussein's horrific human rights record as part of its rationale for going to war against Iraq, there has been very little mass media discussion of the U.S.'s continued support for many regimes around the world with similarly terrible records. To be sure, occasionally one does encounter the observation that it seems arbitrary to single out Iraq for its human rights record, but this, more often then not, only leads to the retort that we have to start somewhere— we shouldn't refrain from bringing freedom and democracy to Iraq just because we can't get to all of the other repressive regimes at the same time. The point is never made, nor, apparently, would it be comprehensible to many, that if we are concerned about human rights we might at least refrain from supporting, militarily, economically, and diplomatically, nations with abysmal human rights records.

(5) Despite the fact that the Bush administration has repeatedly cited Iraq's violations of U.N. Security Council resolutions as a justification for war, the U.S. mass media almost never makes the elementary point that the U.S. not only refrains from going to war against, but rather actively supports, other nations, most notably Israel, who also have a disturbing record of noncompliance with such resolutions.[59] To be sure, there might be legitimate reasons for finding some violations of Security Council resolutions tolerable and others intolerable. The problem, however, is that the issue is never confronted, and thus there is no debate. Indeed, one can't help but suspect that the suppression of this issue signifies that the double standard is in fact unjustifiable.

(6) Perhaps even more significantly, I have never heard, read, or seen, in the U.S. mass media discussions of the Bush administration's argument that Iraq's violations of U.N. Security Council resolutions constitute grounds for war, the elementary point that no country has the right unilaterally to enforce U.N. resolutions. Articles 41 and 42 of the U.N. Charter proscribe such unilateral action.[60] Thus, the U.S.'s action of attacking Iraq for violating U.N. resolutions appears itself to be a violation of the U.N. Charter. Of course I could be wrong—I'm no expert on international law. But isn't it disappointing that the issue is not even discussed?

(7) Officials in the Bush administration have often claimed to have access to special "intelligence" establishing the truth of their claims. Thus, it is critical to consider the credibility of these officials with respect to such matters. Accordingly, the question of a history

of official lying at the outset of wars is not without relevance. Nonetheless, the U.S. mass media has not focused attention on the previous Bush administration's record of lying in setting up its justification for the earlier Gulf War. Officials in that administration apparently had felt that Saddam Hussein's actual record of barbarism and aggression wasn't quite bad enough, so they decided to embellish it. One of their lies was a claim that Iraqi soldiers had taken more than 300 babies from incubators in Kuwait and tossed them on the cold hospital floor to die. The media played the story up and then, as so often happens, showed far less enthusiasm in publishing or broadcasting retractions once the story was revealed to be a hoax. It turned out that the whole incubator atrocity story had been concocted by the U.S. public relations firm of Hill and Knowlton, and that its main witness (she testified before Congress) was the daughter of the Kuwaiti ambassador to Washington.[61]

The other big lie was the claim that the U.S. had classified satellite photos showing the Iraqi army mobilizing and massing on the Saudi border. Every major broadcasting outlet and newspaper in the U.S., save one, swallowed the story and relayed it uncritically. One newspaper, the *St. Petersburg* (Florida) *Times*, bothered to investigate. The newspaper purchased commercial satellite photos of the Iraq-Saudi border and then hired former government image analysts to examine them. Their verdict, of course, was that the claim was fictional.[62] Now when the current administration, with many of the old crowd still around in positions of prominence, issues its many statements about what their intelligence reveals, do any mainstream journalists, in any forum, ever remind us (let alone confront them) with the facts of their previous prevarications?

(8) The U.S. mass media currently parrots the claim by the U.S. government that Saddam Hussein had kicked the U.N. weapons inspectors out of Iraq in 1998. But this claim is not true. Iraq did not expel the inspectors. UNSCOM head Richard Butler withdrew them, on advice from the U.S., in December 1998—one day before the U.S. engaged in its bombing campaign known as "Operation Desert Fox."[63] Similarly, the U.S. mass media consistently calls the claim that American spies had engaged in illegal espionage against Iraq under the cover of arms inspection a mere "allegation" by Saddam Hussein, in spite of the fact that these same media outlets (including the *New York Times*, the *Washington Post*, the *Boston*

Globe, and *USA Today*) had in 1999 reported those same allegations as established facts.[64]

(9) Another failure of the U.S. mass media with regard to facilitating debate about the war on Iraq was revealed in a study conducted by Fairness and Accuracy in Reporting of the 393 on-camera sources who appeared on the nightly news broadcasts on the ABC, CBS, NBC, and PBS networks over a two-week period (late January and early February 2003). The findings? While 76 percent of all sources were current or former U.S. government officials, fewer than 1 percent were affiliated with antiwar activism, and only 6 percent of those appearing could be described as skeptics regarding the need for war.[65]

(10) Finally, the U.S. mass media uncritically endorsed and appropriated the U.S. government's Orwellian terminology concerning the war, repeatedly referring to the war as "Operation Iraqi Freedom" (as if there were no room to question the administration's claims about its motives in going to war) and the soldiers as "coalition forces" (when in fact it was a U.S. war with help from the British). It is hard to argue with journalist Robert Fisk's characterization of mainstream American journalism as increasingly "vapid, hopeless, gutless, unchallenging" since September 11, 2001.[66]

III. Methodological Points and Responses to Criticisms

An appropriately skeptical reader might object at this point that perhaps my examples are unfair. Of course it is easy, such a reader might argue, to find examples in which the U.S. mass media irresponsibly ignores press censorship and other human rights abuses perpetrated by nations regarded as "friendly" by U.S. political elites, while simultaneously, and hypocritically, trumpeting comparable or much lesser abuses carried out by "our enemies." The problem, to conclude my imaginary reader's argument, is that there may be other cases in which the media exhibit the opposite bias, or even no bias at all, in which case I would be guilty of making my case by means of a highly selective presentation of evidence.[67]

My response to this objection is that there is no need to be selective in marshalling the evidence for the simple reason that there is *no* counterevidence. To be sure, one can find a different "slant" in non-mainstream journals of opinion, such as the *Nation*, *Z* magazine, or the *Progressive*, and an occasional isolated article of this sort sometimes finds its way into mass media publications as well. But one can never find a case in which, on balance, the *New York Times*, the *Washington Post*, *Time* magazine, *Newsweek*, or ABC, CBS, or NBC news deal evenhandedly with the transgressions of "our friends" and "our enemies." Rather, these media always adopt the perspective of the U.S. government, and never—literally never—develop an alternative, independent framework of their own.

Readers with a little time, energy, access to a good library, and eagerness to understand the world in which they live can easily verify this for themselves. Let me suggest one way of doing so. Many highly respected organizations are devoted to the task of investigating and documenting human rights abuses around the world. Their diversity is suggested by the following partial list: Amnesty International, Americas Watch, the International Association of Democratic Lawyers, the International Federation of Human Rights, the International League for the Rights of Man, the International Commission of Jurists, Writers and Scholars International, and the International Red Cross. I suggest that you pick any human rights issue that interests you—the use of torture, the imprisonment of political dissidents, press censorship, the staging of fraudulent elections, you name it. Now go through the reports of these organizations and find examples of comparable abuses carried out by two nations, one of which establishes policies and practices conducive to the financial interests of large U.S.-based corporations (and which receives lots of U.S. aid, in terms of both cash and weapons), and the other of which is readily condemned by U.S. governmental officials as an enemy (or "communist" or "terrorist") state. Obviously, it is in the U.S. corporate and governmental interest to play down the abuses in the former nation and to play up the ones occurring in the latter nation. And, in every case, that is how the U.S. mass media, on balance, plays it.[68] You, dear reader, can refute me by finding a single counterexample. Good luck![69]

A final methodological point about the selection of examples is this. If you wish to prove that you're an excellent golfer, it won't do simply to put together a list of people you can beat, for a skeptic could always wonder about your list of conquests—perhaps they were selected precisely on the basis of being bad golfers. But if you show that you can consistently beat Tiger Woods, you'll have made your point.

Similarly, if you wish to show that the media have a procorporate bias, the most convincing way to demonstrate this is by examining those media which are alleged to have a liberal, anticorporate bias. Moreover, it proves little to criticize the worst, or the most right-wing, of the mass media. That would only prove that there is a range of quality and of political slant in the mass media. It is far more effective to pick on what are thought to be the best and the most liberal of the mass media. If it can be shown (as indeed it can) that even these media uncritically parrot the governmental and corporate line at every turn, then the point is made. If one gets a certain result even when examining those examples wherein one would least expect to obtain that result, then there can be no complaint about the selection of examples.[70]

But there are always complaints. Let's look at a few representative criticisms of the sorts of claims that I (following Herman, Chomsky, and others) am making about U.S. mass media coverage of international affairs.

Here's an example of such criticism. Herman and Chomsky point out that the murder of one priest in Poland, Father Popieluszko, by the communist bad guys, received more media coverage in the United States than did the murders of one hundred religious martyrs in Latin America, including Archbishop Romero, at the hands of U.S. allies. Herman and Chomsky cite this as evidence in support of their claim that the U.S. mass media serve a progovernmental and procorporate propaganda function. But, as Chomsky, points out,

> In this case, there is an alternative that's been proposed. In one of the critical reviews of our book . . . by Nicholas Lemann, who is the political correspondent of the *Atlantic Monthly*, he suggests an alternative theory. He says the problem isn't that Popieluszko was more important than, say, Archbishop Romero, it's that the press focuses only on one thing at a time. . . . He says the murder of Popieluszko took place at a time when the focus of the press was on Poland, but the murder of Romero—somehow the other 99 disappeared—took place before the press had begun to focus on El Salvador [his words, in a letter to the *New Republic*, March 6, 1989, are these: "As for Father Popieluszko, he was killed when the U.S. press was most focused on Poland. Archbishop Romero was killed before the press had really focused on El Salvador. Popieluszko's murder wasn't more important; the discrepancy can be explained by saying the press tends to focus on only a few things at a time"].

Apart from lots of other problems with that theory [for example, the qualitative differences—differences in tone, in compassion for the victims, and so forth—as opposed to the quantitative], the obvious thing to do is to check the facts. So I did, and it turns out that *New York Times* coverage of El Salvador during the relevant period was slightly higher than *New York Times* coverage of Poland. So by his criterion we understand the bias of the case in this example. Notice, this is typical. People who defend the traditional view don't need any evidence. They can just make things up as they go along. The five minutes of research that it would take to discover this in the index of the *New York Times* is too much and considered irrelevant. That's typical of such criticism as there is.[71]

Similarly, Lemann criticizes Herman and Chomsky for dismissing "the standard sources on the countries they write about," and for instead relying, as in their discussion of the Nicaraguan election of 1984, on reports of human rights organizations, delegations of observers sent by various nations around the world (including many composed primarily of center-right parties), and the professional association of Latin American scholars, all of whom had, in radical contrast to the mainstream U.S. media, declared the election, won by the Sandinistas, to be free and fair. When asked which sources Herman and Chomsky should have used, he replied: "[b]y standard sources, I mean the American press, which usually weighs the government handouts against other sources." Chomsky replies:

What he is saying, then, is that in investigating how the media dealt with the Nicaraguan election, we must rely on the media that are under investigation and not make use of independent material to assess their performance. Following this ingenious procedure, we will naturally conclude that the media are performing superbly: what they produce corresponds exactly to what they produce.[72]

Here is another example. Chomsky had published a study of all eighty-five opinion columns devoted to the debate over U.S. policy toward Nicaragua that were carried in the *New York Times* and the *Washington Post* during the first three months of 1986, when attention was heavily focused on that issue. The results of the study: while there was substantial disagreement over aid to the contras, all eighty-five columns were anti-Sandinista, the overwhelming majority harshly so. Tom Wicker then attacked the study in the *New York Times* (31 December 1987), on two grounds. First, he saw "no reason why I have to praise the Sandinistas"; second, "criticism by foot-rule and calculator is often as simplistic as the reportage it purports to measure." In Chomsky's response he concedes that Wicker's first point is "quite true," but immediately adds that it is also

> entirely irrelevant. As was clear and explicit, the individual contributions were not at issue but rather the range of permitted views; the question is not whether Wicker should be granted the opportunity to express his opinion that a "regional arrangement" must be imposed on Nicaragua alone and enforced by the U.S. terror states, but whether, in a free press, the spectrum of opinion should be bounded by this position, as the extreme of permissible dissent from government policy.[73]

In response to Wicker's second criticism, Chomsky writes: "Curious to learn whether Wicker had some methodological or other critique to support his judgment, I wrote him a series of letters of inquiry, eliciting no response."[74] This second criticism, the astonishingly lazy one, is defective because, while Wicker is undoubtedly right that statistical arguments are often simplistic, surely they need not be and often are not. (Suppose one of my students objected to receiving a poor grade that was given on the basis of answering only, say, 4 percent of the test questions correctly, by arguing that "criticism by calculator is often simplistic"?) Thus, it is incumbent upon Wicker to specify in what way this particular criticism involving statistics is defective—and note also how reductionistic it is to call the study "criticism by foot-rule and calculator," as if there were nothing to the critique other than statistical information, and as if no methodological thinking went into the use of the statistics as a measure.

Similarly, in response to studies conducted by David Croteau and William Hoynes,[75] in which they document the near monopoly of conservative white males with ties to the federal government and/or to corporations as guests on such news programs as *Nightline* and the *Mac-Neil-Lehrer NewsHour*, *Nightline* executive producer Richard Kaplan told reporters, "[M]y basic objection is that they take *Nightline* and reduce it to a bunch of numbers."[76] And Robert MacNeil added that the criticism of his show "went wrong in a number of ways. One is, like a lot of sociologists, they think that everything can be quantified and that you can analyze by quantity . . . and not qualitative analysis."[77]

By way of response, at least three points should be made. First, the studies by Croteau and Hoynes contain considerable qualitative analysis, and not merely quantitative data. Thus, it is not true that they "take *Nightline* and reduce it to a bunch of numbers"; rather, it is Kaplan who is guilty of reductionism—that of reducing Croteau and Hoyne's critique to its purely quantitative component. Similarly, MacNeil's quite literally irresponsible charge that the authors "think that everything can be quantified" is demonstrably false. Second, these critics content themselves with generic complaints about the use of quantitative analyses, failing to note in what specific ways these in particularly are allegedly defective. Finally, is it not obvious that quantitative evidence has its legitimate uses? If, for example, one were to do a study of mass media coverage of the debate over slavery in the United States prior to its abolition, and determine that, say, 62 percent of the arguments or opinions presented were in favor of unregulated slavery, with 37.9 percent being devoted to the advocacy of regulated slavery, and the remaining .1 percent going to the abolitionist position, would this not tell us something valid and instructive?

Finally, let's consider the objection that the U.S. mass media consistently exhibits a "liberal" bias, rather than the progovernment, procorporate one I've been describing. This view of the media is widely known, in part because it is much discussed in the media. There the debate is, "Do the media have a liberal bias, or are they 'straight' and objective?"[78] No notice is ever taken of the sorts of criticisms I've been advancing here.

Perhaps the most recent, and the most attention-getting, attempt to make the case that the media are excessively "liberal" is Bernard Goldberg's *New York Times* number-one best-selling book, *Bias*.[79] Does his work cast doubt on the analysis of the media presented above? The question must be answered negatively, both because Goldberg fails to establish that there is a "liberal" bias in the mass media and because the existence of such a bias, even if it were real, would not be inconsistent with the sort of bias I've been describing.

Goldberg's failure to establish his case stems primarily from his faulty methodology. It is almost entirely anecdotal. He simply presents a few examples of allegedly slanted news coverage and considers the case clinched. But he never discusses the principles (if any) underlying his selection, examines any counterexamples, or entertains any alternative hypotheses concerning the examples he does present.

Moreover, many of his prime examples are ill suited for the job of establishing his thesis. His first example, which he discusses extensively in the book and which had been the centerpiece of his first op-ed piece on the subject, concerns a one-sided *CBS Evening News* segment criticizing presidential candidate Steve Forbes's flat-tax proposal.[80] Goldberg seems to be on sound ground in saying that the piece, by the mass media's self-professed standards, was slanted and unfair. The report ridiculed Forbes and his proposal, used loaded language in describing it, and presented expert testimony only of critics of the flat tax, passing over the many experts, including Nobel laureates in economics, who supported it. While this may be bad reporting, is it necessarily evidence of liberal bias? If one were to draw up a list of issues dividing "liberals" from "conservatives" (as these terms are understood in mainstream U.S. political circles), I doubt that the flat-tax proposal would make an appearance. Indeed, as even Goldberg grudgingly admits, "a number of conservative politicians came out against it."[81] Moreover, though Goldberg does not himself mention it, it was primarily these conservative voices that were heard in the CBS piece. The flat-tax critics featured in the segment included then House Speaker Newt Gingrich, an advisor to the elder President George Bush, and a former Nixon-era IRS commissioner.[82] "Liberal" voices were excluded. (Is this a case of antiliberal bias?) One must therefore conclude, with Steve Rendall and Peter Hart, that "[a] single segment featuring mostly right-of-center sources criticizing one Republican's tax proposal is hardly smoking-gun evidence of a left-wing media tilt."[83]

In many of Goldberg's other examples it is even harder to see why the bias on display should be described as "liberal." For example, he makes the case convincingly that the major television networks are extremely reluctant to feature blacks on their "magazine" shows, such as *20/20*, *48 Hours*, and *Dateline*.[84] But what has this to do with "*liberal*" bias? The closest Goldberg comes to answering is this: "The Liberals of Convenience don't dislike blacks. Or Hispanics. Or poor people. Quite the opposite. They like them very much—*in theory*. They just don't want too many of them on their TV shows."[85] Goldberg's tortured logic seems to be something like the following: "The people who determine the content of these television programs are liberals; therefore, any bias they exhibit is liberal bias." That's nonsense. What Goldberg's findings really suggest is that these network bigwigs are hypocrites and not true liberals at all, because their performance deviates not only from the standards of journalism which they profess to honor, but also from liberalism. The issue, quite obviously, is not the moral character of the journalists and network news executives, but rather the content of their work.

The same point holds for Goldberg's otherwise cogent criticism of NBC anchorman Tom Brokaw's failure to do a story on a defective airplane engine made by General Electric, which owns NBC.[86] As Goldberg points out, other news organizations considered it a significant story, and it received wide coverage, suggesting that Brokaw was placing the interests of his bosses (and perhaps of himself—they could fire him, if they so chose) above those of his viewers. But how, exactly, is this evidence of "liberal" bias, as opposed to the kind of procorporate bias about which leftists have been complaining for years? Perhaps Goldberg's point is simply that Tom Brokaw is a liberal, and therefore all of his biases are liberal ones. That's senseless, of course, but I can't come up with another explanation.

More important than the problems with Goldberg's individual examples, however, is the fact that he fails to address the issue of the selection of his examples. It seems that he has simply picked the examples that he thinks will best support his case, without inquiring as to whether or not they are typical or representative. He also ignores counterexamples. As we saw in our discussion of the CBS story on the flat tax, Goldberg is quick to object when he detects liberal bias in the selection of guests to appear in a news story. But he never discusses such things as a Fairness and Accuracy in Reporting study revealing that on *Nightline* shows devoted to debating economic issues, seven representatives of corporations appeared for every one representative of a labor union.[87] Thus, Goldberg's complaints about one-sidedness are themselves one-sided.

An even more telling example concerns Goldberg's claim to have noticed one day that the media "pointedly identified conservatives as conservatives, . . . but for some crazy reason didn't bother to identify liberals as liberals."[88] The reason for this alleged tendency, according to Goldberg, is that "[i]n the world of the Jenningses and Brokaws and Rathers, conservatives are out of the mainstream and need to be identified. Liberals, on the other hand, *are* the mainstream and don't need to be identified."[89]

The problem here is that, as usual, Goldberg is content to rely entirely on his impressions, buttressed by a few examples, most notably, in this case, a broadcast of U.S Senate proceedings (the Clinton impeachment trial of 1999) during which Peter Jennings allegedly referred to almost all conservative senators as "conservative" while scrupulously refraining from labeling the liberal senators.[90] But a critical reader will immediately ask whether or not this example is really typical. Might not there be many other broadcasts and news articles with the opposite labeling bias, or no bias at all? What seems to be needed, in order to verify or refute Goldberg's claim, is some sort of careful, systematic study of the issue.

Fortunately, one has been done. Its author, Geoffrey Nunberg, describes it:

> I went to a Dialog Corporation database that has the contents of more than 20 major US dailies, including the *New York Times*, the *Los Angeles Times*, the *Washington Post*, the *Boston Globe*, the *Miami Herald*, *Newsday*, and the *San Francisco Chronicle*. I took the names of 10 well-known politicians, five liberals, and five conservatives. On the liberal side were Senators Barbara Boxer, Paul Wellstone, Tom Harkin, and Ted Kennedy, and Representative Barney Frank, all with lifetime Americans for Democratic Action (ADA) ratings greater than 90 percent. On the conservative side were Senators Trent Lott and Jesse Helms, Attorney General John Ashcroft, and Representatives Dick Armey and Tom DeLay, all with lifetime ADA averages less than 15 percent. Then I looked to see how often each of those names occurred within seven words of "liberal" or "conservative," whichever was appropriate. . . .
>
> And indeed, there was a discrepancy in the frequency of labeling, but not in the way Goldberg . . . assumed. On the contrary, the average liberal legislator has a better than 30 percent *greater* likelihood of being given a political label than the average conservative does. The press describes Frank as a liberal two-and-a-half times as frequently as it describes Armey as a conservative. It labels Boxer almost twice as often as it labels Lott and labels Wellstone more often than Helms. . . .
>
> The tendency isn't limited to legislators. For example, Goldberg writes that "it's not unusual to identify certain actors, like Tom Sel-

leck or Bruce Willis, as conservatives. But Barbra Streisand or Rob Reiner . . . are just Barbra Streisand and Rob Reiner." But that turns out to be dead wrong, too: The press labels Streisand and Reiner more than four times as frequently as Selleck and Willis. . . . Warren Beatty is labeled more often than Arnold Schwarzenegger, and Norman Lear is labeled more often than Charlton Heston.

It goes on. Goldberg claims that former Circuit Judge Robert Bork is always called a conservative whereas Laurence Tribe is identified merely as a Harvard law professor. But it turns out that Bork is labeled only a bit more frequently than Tribe is. And columnist Michael Kinsley gets a partisan label more often than either William Bennett or Jerry Falwell.[91]

It is also significant that Nunberg, in quite radical contrast to Goldberg, exhibits some methodological sophistication. He thus inquires into some of the ways in which his study might be faulty, and then checks them out. For example, he considers the possibility that Goldberg's claim might hold if the study were confined so as to include only the most liberal of the major daily newspapers. It doesn't. It also occurs to him that his study might have been skewed by its inclusion of opinion columns and letters to the editors. But when these are excluded, the results are virtually the same. Next, he worries over whether or not there might be a problem with his choice of which individuals to include in the study. For example, the labeling of Rob Reiner as a liberal might often occur in references to his portrayal of "Archie Bunker's liberal son-in-law," so Nunberg carefully excluded these. Similarly, he wonders whether the figures for Lott, DeLay, and Armey might be skewed by their having leadership titles that could take the place of partisan labels. So he made appropriate substitutions and got the same results. He concludes: "The fact is . . . that however you cherry-pick the groups, there's no way to make the survey come out as Goldberg claims it should, where conservatives are systematically labeled more than liberals are."[92] True, Nunberg studied newspapers, while Goldberg was primarily discussing television broadcasts. Still, it's hard to see why the practices of the television networks would differ from those of the newspapers in this regard and, in any case, as Nunberg notes, "given the way the labels are used in the 'liberal' press, the burden of proof is on Goldberg and other critics of liberal bias to do the studies that should have been done before making the claim."[93]

Nor do things go better for Goldberg on those few occasions when he does report actual studies, as opposed to anecdotes. For example, he makes much of two studies of the political attitudes and preferences of journalists. These studies suggest that journalists are much more likely to vote for Democratic candidates, and to see themselves as "Democrats" and "liberals," than are members of the public at large. Similarly, in comparison to the public, journalists are shown to be significantly more likely to favor abortion rights, affirmative action, and tougher gun controls, and significantly less likely to favor prayer in public schools and the death penalty.[94]

While this information is both relevant and revealing, it is far from conclusive, for the simple reason that the beliefs and attitudes of reporters are not the only factors entering into the slanting of the news. For example, without even leaving the terrain of beliefs and attitudes, what if those of editors and of the corporate bosses who own the media outlets turn out to be as conservative as the journalists' are liberal? In this regard it is significant that Republicans have received a majority of newspaper endorsements in all but two presidential elections since 1932.[95] How is this to be explained if the opinions of the journalists, a substantial majority of whom are, allegedly, Democrats, constitute the controlling factor in the slanting of media coverage?

Moreover, even if reporters tend to be more liberal than the general public on the issues Goldberg mentions, perhaps they are more conservative than the public on others. Indeed, this is precisely what a 1998 Fairness and Accuracy in Reporting survey of the opinions of the Washington press corps found. In that study the journalists were found to be "more conservative—not more liberal—than the general public on major economic issues such as trade, taxes, Social Security, health care and corporate power."[96]

This brings me to my final, and most important, point about Goldberg's thesis. Even if it were true, it wouldn't contradict the analysis of the U.S mass media that I've been offering above. The reason is that Goldberg is charging that there is a systematic bias in the mass media with regard to its slant *within* the spectrum of mainstream U.S. political opinion. That is, he assumes that it is perfectly legitimate for the media to proceed as if all serious political and social thought is confined within a boundary established, on the one side, by the most liberal of the Democrats (Ted Kennedy, perhaps) and, on the other, by the most conservative of the Republicans (someone like Jesse Helms).

Goldberg's complaint, then, is simply that the media allegedly have a strong tendency to tilt toward the Kennedy end of this spectrum. My claim, on the other hand, is that the media exhibit a massive and systematic bias in favor of mainstream U.S. political opinion and against all opinion lying outside of it. For example, when liberal Democrats and conservative Republicans agree on certain fundamentals, such as the identity of the good guys and the bad guys around the world, disagreeing with one another only on points of emphasis, rhetoric, tactics, and priorities, the media always assume that these agreed-upon fundamentals are correct, even when the rest of the world disagrees, and even when independent human rights organizations and independent scholars tend to agree with the rest of the world. Goldberg is talking about an alleged bias in favor of one side of U.S. mainstream political opinion with regard to the issues, chiefly social and cultural, on which the two sides disagree. I'm talking about a massive and exceptionless bias in favor of U.S. mainstream political opinion, and against all those who oppose it, with regard to the issues, chiefly concerning economics and foreign affairs, on which U.S. mainstream political opinion has achieved a consensus on fundamentals. Thus, even if Goldberg were right that the media tilt left within the mainstream spectrum, this would not conflict with my claim that they tilt vastly more heavily in favor of that spectrum itself, and that, in so doing, they deviate from fairness and accuracy to a degree undreamt of in Goldberg's complaints about the "liberal" media. Goldberg is talking about an ant, which he may or may not actually be seeing. I'm talking about Godzilla.

IV. Explaining the Problem

Why do the mass media behave so irresponsibly? Must we conclude that they, together with the U.S. government, are engaged in a gigantic conspiracy to keep information that would cast U.S. foreign policy in an unflattering light from being published or broadcast?

As no evidence of such a conspiracy exists, to my knowledge, it is fortunate that one need not be invoked in order to explain the media's disastrous performance. While an adequate analysis would have to include many factors and deal with numerous subtleties and complexities, we can go a long way toward understanding the phenomena in question on the basis of six fairly simple and straightforward principles of news gathering and presentation. The first two are economic; the other four, having to do with the media's understanding of the idea of "objectivity," are ideological.

A. The Economics of News-Gathering

Investigative reporting is expensive. It also takes time, and its results are uncertain—the reporter may or may not succeed in digging up a usable story. (All three of these negative features of investigative reporting are exacerbated, moreover, when the investigation in question concerns events taking place overseas.) Consequently, the vast majority of news stories involve no significant investigative effort on the part of reporters. Rather, such news is either gathered through established "beats"—places, such as the White House, Congress, city hall, and so on, where news is regularly generated—or else handed to reporters through press conferences and press releases. Notice that these methods of gathering news suffer from none of the defects of investigative reporting noted above.

This economic factor alone goes a long way toward explaining why the news is tilted so heavily in one direction. For notice that only two sectors of society have the resources to provide the media with canned news regularly: the government and corporations, with their big public relations budgets. Thus, when a foreign nation acts against U.S. governmental and corporate interests, these two powerful sectors of society have a strong motive to mobilize public opinion against that nation, and to lay the groundwork for intervention against it. One way to do so is to publicize its faults, both real and alleged, by bringing these to the attention of journalists. But when a foreign nation behaves in a manner that is favorable to U.S. governmental and corporate interests, there is no motive to publicize its transgressions (quite the contrary), leaving journalists with the task of discovering these themselves. It is not advisable to hold one's breath, however, while waiting for this to happen.

B. The Economics of Maximizing Audience Size

To maximize profit, a media outlet must not only find quick, reliable, and inexpensive methods of gathering news, but must also manage to sell that news to the largest possible audience (so that it can then sell its advertising at the highest possible price). This necessity entails certain consequences with regard to the content of the news. One of these is that the news should entertain, and above all not bore, the audience. As Calvin F. Exoo puts it, this translates into the imperative: "Avoid the arcana of social issues. Instead, hit [the audience's] pleasure buttons: laughter, sex, violence, and so on."[97] Now let's apply this imperative to the media's discussion of Iran. While it certainly explains why the mass media do not discuss the high points of Iranian culture, or present the details of Iranian political history, or examine the basic tenets of Iranian religious beliefs, it does not explain why the media would not call attention to the shah's human rights abuses or attempt to dig up the true facts pertaining to the *Vincennes* incident. But the attempt to garner, and retain, the largest possible audience for one's news yields more than one implication concerning the content of the news. In particular, just as purveyors of news should avoid boring their audience, so should they, and for the same reasons, refrain from offending them. Thus, insofar as news stories suggesting that the United States is responsible for nefarious policies or actions resulting in innocent deaths on a large scale tend to offend a substantial portion of potential news consumers, the imperative to maximize the size of the news audience argues strongly against the inclusion of such stories. Moreover, it must be remembered that these factors do not operate in isolation from one another, but rather are mutually reinforcing. Thus, insofar as the facts pointing to U.S. culpability with respect to events in Iran would require investigatory effort and expense to uncover (or at least a willingness to gather news from sources other than those official ones which, for economic reasons described above, the mass media tend to rely on almost exclusively), the economic factors would also militate against their presentation in U.S. mass media news accounts.

C. Objectivity: The Mind as Tabula Rasa

Perhaps the most significant ideological factor underlying the mass media's almost uniformly wretched performance is its radically defective concept of objectivity. This issue is also of great significance to the overall concerns of this book, since the postmodern attack on objectivity is directed primarily against the confused understanding of this concept currently prevailing in mainstream journalistic theory. This understanding of objectivity, in turn, is then confused with the more defensible version that one finds in the sciences and in philosophy, leading to the false impression that objectivity as such has been successfully debunked. In this section, and in the following three, I'll present criticisms of four aspects of the journalistic theory of objectivity. These criticisms are fully consonant with postmodern critiques of objectivity. But I will also present, in the concluding section of this chapter, an alternative account of objectivity that is not vulnerable to these postmodern criticisms.

I once saw a television panel discussion in which several leading television journalists (including Walter Cronkite and Ted Koppel) discussed the principles underlying their craft. They all agreed that a reporter's mind, when approaching a news story, should be a *tabula rasa*, or blank slate, because otherwise his or her preconceptions and biases would surely lead to distorted and slanted reporting. These journalists cheerfully conceded that it can be frightfully difficult at first to achieve this blank slate state of mind, but they nonetheless all agreed that, with diligence, one can learn to leave his or her "opinions" at the door, and instead observe and report only "the facts." In this way one can succeed at one's proper journalistic goal: to be an *objective* reporter.

This understanding of objectivity seems to imply at least three claims: (1) Observation is, or at least can be, passive, in the sense that observers can observe competently without *acting*, that is, without doing anything other than opening their eyes and ears and generally being alert. (2) Not only is it the case that observers *need* not make any contribution of their own in their observing, since passivity is sufficient for competent observing, but they also *should* not make any such contribution, since doing so would "bias" the observation by introducing into it the subjectivity of the observer. (3) Since observers need not and should not make an active contribution of their own in their acts of observing, it follows that they need no special knowledge as a prerequisite to competent observation of any given phenomenon. Anyone can passively take in "what is there to be seen."

We have already seen (in our discussion of Sartre's crag—chapter 4, section III A) what is wrong with this idea: observation is *active*, not passive; it requires of the observer *focusing* and *selective* attention. As the Gestalt psychologists have shown with their ingenious drawings,[98] "the 'having of objects' is not something fully determined by the physical and physiological conditions of the external situation within which consciousness operates; an 'object' is not anything fully fixed independently of the operations of consciousness."[99] Seeing is always seeing-as. It is interpretive and takes place within the framework of a conceptual background in terms of which it emerges as meaningful.

All of this suggests, moreover, the need for the observer to be knowledgeable in order to understand what is being seen. Granted, nearly everyone has the background knowledge needed to observe a crag competently—to recognize it as a natural rather than an artificial object, for example—but such knowledge is nonetheless *necessary*. Here Sartre is recognizing a rather unremarkable point, long acknowledged by sociologists and anthropologists, but, strangely, denied by journalists, namely, that observation is of *necessity* theory-laden, and thus, the better the observer's theory—the more knowledgeable he or she is—the better the observation is likely to be. The ideal observer is not ignorant.

Consider Gilbert Harman's illustration of this:

> You see some children pour gasoline on a cat and ignite it. To really see that, you have to possess a great deal of knowledge, know about a considerable number of objects, know about people: that people pass through the life stages infant, baby, child, adolescent, adult. You must know what flesh and blood animals are, and in particular, cats. You must have some idea of life. You must know what gasoline is, what burning is, and much more. In one sense what you "see" is a pattern of light on your retina, a shifting array of splotches, although even that is a theory, and you could never adequately describe what you see in that sense. In another sense, you see what you do because of the theories you hold. Change those theories and you would see something else, given the same pattern of light.[100]

Thus, the "mind as *tabula rasa*" theory of objectivity collapses in multiple ways. And yet, reporters attempt to follow this doctrine in their reporting. What is the result of this attempt? Since knowledge supposedly is not needed for accurate observing and reporting, reporters are often asked to cover subjects about which they are massively ignorant. For example, reporters who do not speak Farsi, and who are ignorant of Iranian culture and history, are sent to cover events in Iran. Naturally, they misunderstand what they see.[101] Not knowing what to focus on, and not realizing that they are focusing, they focus on the wrong things. Not knowing that they are theorizing and interpreting, they theorize and interpret from their standpoint as Westerners, and undoubtedly from the standpoint of background information that they will have obtained from U.S. government officials. No conspiracy theory is needed to understand why U.S. reporters report the rest of the world incompetently, and with a fiercely pro-U.S. bias.

D. Objectivity: Just the Facts

Most mass media journalists subscribe to a theory of "objectivity," according to which reporters should present only "the facts" (which are said to be objective), while scrupulously omitting from their stories their opinions, interpretations, conclusions, theories, and value judgments (all of which are said to be "personal" and "subjective").

Such a conception of objectivity fosters journalistic irresponsibility of the sort described above in at least two ways. First, it discourages investigative journalism, since reporters who do their own investigations are pretty much obliged to draw their own conclusions, and this, according to the principle in question, is to inject their own "bias" and "personal opinions" into the news. Moreover, if a journalist were to investigate a foreign leader, favored by U.S. governmental and corporate interests, and find that he is a brutal dictator, such a journalist would be constrained from saying so by "objectivity's" ban on value judgments.[102] Thus, it is infinitely safer to present only those conclusions and value judgments that can be attributed to others— and we have already seen who these others will be, and why.

Second, since the journalistic theory of objectivity demands the impossible (that judgments and conclusions be rigorously separated from facts, when in fact these things are inextricably connected to one another in all thinking and writing), it encourages journalists to finesse the issue by presenting only those judgments and conclusions that neither they themselves nor the bulk of their audience will recognize as such. For, with regard to facts, typically one has to *reason*, on the basis of evidence of some kind, to the *conclusion* that something is a fact. Facts are often not self-evident. It requires theorizing, selective (intelligently guided) looking, and (sometimes) special knowledge to discover them. Thus, since concluding, theorizing, and the like are banned as supposedly inconsistent with "objectivity," what we tend to get in mainstream journalism are "obvious" facts—meaning those emerging from the consensus of mainstream political opinion, where no evidence is needed.

And as for value judgments, people think they are being neutral and objective when their value commitments, like the air they breathe, are invisible to them—and that only happens when they are of the assumed consensus mainstream variety.[103] Radical, nonestablishment, or otherwise nonconsensus values, by contrast, stand out, are noticed as values, and are thus excluded from mainstream journalism as nonobjective.[104]

And in any case, it's just not true that value judgments are normally *added on* to, and thus can fairly easily be left out of, pure observations, rather than being a dimension of our experience which is present even at the most primitive level of observation. For one thing, values guide our observations from the outset since the very focusing which allows objects to emerge as meaningful depends to a large extent upon our interests and preferences in the realm of values. And for another thing, the meanings which then immediately emerge in our perception of objects are value-laden, as can be noticed in Sartre's claim that we immediately see the crag as an "obstacle," as an "aid," or as "beautiful or ugly."

And there is worse to follow. Even if, as is not the case, it *were* possible to observe and to report pure facts, divorced from all interpretations, theories, opinions, conclusions, and values, this would not tell us which, of the infinite number of facts available, to report, and which not to report. Sartre commented on this problem in an attempt to report on the United States to a French audience: "'Stick to facts!' some tell us. But what facts? The length of a certain shipyard, or the electric blue of the oxyhydrogen blowpipe in the pale light of a shed? In choosing, I am already making a decision as to what America is."[105]

As if this were not enough, it should be noted that all of the decisions of inclusion and exclusion in journalism—decisions concerning which stories to cover, which facts to include within a story, which stories to give the most prominence, and so forth—inevitably involve value judgments. And news accounts are never presented as random collections of facts. Rather, the facts are ordered so as to tell a story—a story which will inevitably reflect and express some sort of theory or interpretation of the issue at hand, just as the gathering of facts to be included will necessarily have been guided by such theorizing and interpreting. So the problem is not merely that "objectivity" in the journalistic sense can never be fully achieved, as even many of the fiercest defenders of the theory of objectivity freely concede. The point, rather, is that what journalists call "objectivity" is always and necessarily (and thus not because of some personal failing of this or that journalist) shot through with what journalists call "subjectivity." Journalism is, and must be, saturated with "subjectivity," from start to finish.

E. *Objectivity: Neutrality or Centrism*

It is easy to confuse the following three distinct notions: objectivity, neutrality, and centrism. And many journalists, convinced that they should be objective, misinterpret that as entailing either that they should be neutral or that they should take a centrist, or "middle of the road," position.

Let's begin by distinguishing neutrality from taking a "middle of the road" position. To be neutral is to take no position, to be partial to no side. But it is quite another thing to take a middle of the road position, for it is, after all, *a position*. For if one is in the middle of the road, then one is rejecting the positions of "the extremists," on the left or the right side of the road. But then one is obliged to *defend* the middle of the road position, to show *why* it is more reasonable than its competitors. After all, to use an example from American history, there was a time in which the defense of regulated slavery, or of a situation in which some states would be allowed to have slaves and others would not, constituted a "middle of the road position," in contrast not only to those who would allow unregulated slavery everywhere, but also to those who would abolish slavery entirely. It is simply a prejudice, albeit a popular one, that "middle of the road" positions are automatically more reasonable than "extremist" positions, a prejudice which, in turn, seems to arise from a confusion of a middle of the road position with the quite different notions of neutrality and objectivity.

Jeff Cohen observes:

> When you've talked to journalists for years in the mainstream, they always tell you, "We have no biases. We're dead center. We're not

left nor right." I think there is a commonly believed myth in the mainstream media that if you are a centrist you have no ideology. You issue no propaganda. You just issue straight news. The only people that are propagandists are propagandists for the right wing or the left wing. . . . [But] if you're in the center, your ideology is centrism, which is every bit as much an ideology as leftism or rightism. I've talked to journalists and they say, "We ward off propaganda from both left and right." And my question is always, "Well, who's warding off propaganda from the center? . . . " They don't have a response.[106]

Similarly, David Eakins notes: "The most serious criticism of this whole effort [to play it down the middle] is that it is wholly independent of evidence—hence of objectivity. The decision to maintain balance or neutrality, in this sense, is an a priori decision that has nothing whatever to do with facts or the weighing of facts. The balancer is as committed as any ideologue."[107]

One might add that if objectivity in practice amounts to a bias in favor of the mainstream or the status quo, then it is genuinely hostile to objectivity in the sense of drawing conclusions based upon a scrupulous assessment of the relevant evidence. That is, one who is not "objective" in the former sense is ready to reject the status quo when the evidence warrants doing so, whereas one who is "objective" is not.

The press claims as proof that it is objective the fact that it is criticized by both left and right, but this could just as well be taken as evidence of centrist bias. For example, PBS spokesperson Karen Doyne remarks, "We take it from both ends of the spectrum and the truth is exactly in between."[108] But this is like claiming that you must be right in adding two and two and getting five, since you draw fire both from those who think it is four and from those who think it six. It also sets up a paradox: Does the truth lie in the middle of the spectrum of opinion in which, on one end, some think that the truth lies in between the ends of a spectrum, and, on the other end, those who think that it does not? This would entail that the truth does not lie in the middle. Why can't one side or another sometimes be right? Or why can't the whole debate be misconceived, so that the truth can emerge only when the assumptions uniting both sides are overturned? And what of those ignored because they are outside of the spectrum under consideration? Can they never be right?[109]

F. Objectivity: "Both Sides"

Journalists claim that, while they do not present their own opinions at all, they do present the opinions of others and achieve "objectivity," "balance," and "evenhandedness" in doing so, simply by being careful to give "both sides" of every issue.

The central fallacy of this doctrine is exposed, of course, when we realize that there is nothing magical about the number two. Some issues are many-sided, so that several perspectives concerning them would have to be considered before one could reasonably expect to be able to form an intelligent, informed judgment about them. On the other hand, human knowledge may have advanced sufficiently on some other issues (e.g., "Is the earth flat?" "Is smoking unhealthy?") as to render only one conclusion concerning them at all reasonable. Where this is the case, the insistence that there is always "the other side" to consider may have the pernicious consequence of encouraging an indecisiveness, or worse, a feeling that all issues are at bottom subjective, on the part of the news audience.[110]

A further problem with the "both sides" doctrine is that the two sides to be heard from are rarely selected on the basis of their being most worthy of consideration in the light of the relevant evidence. Rather, they are selected on the basis of the economic and ideological principles discussed above, with the result that mass media "debates" in the United States almost always stick well within the narrow range of opinion to be found within the mainstreams of the two major political parties.

With regard to international affairs, this leads to a paltry debate indeed, since the two parties, despite their differences in connection with priorities, tactics, symbolism, and rhetoric, rarely disagree on fundamentals. They do not disagree, for example, on the identities of the "good guys" and "bad guys" around the world. Thus, when both the Democrats and the Republicans trumpet the human rights abuses of country A, while neither ever mentions the equal or greater abuses of country B, the idea that A is a totalitarian dungeon and B a land of freedom, democracy, and human rights begins to look not like a highly suspect conclusion or value judgment, but rather like an objective fact, no matter how vehemently Amnesty International, the International Red Cross, the United Nations, the foreign press, world opinion, and the judgments of scholars might disagree.[111]

V. SUGGESTIONS FOR IMPROVEMENT

What, then, is to be done? Is there another conception of journalism to which we might turn? Is there another way of understanding the notion of "objectivity"?

In Sartre's lecture on "The Responsibility of the Writer" he asks:

> If . . . a writer has chosen to be silent on one aspect of the world, we have the right to ask him: why have you spoken of this rather than that? And since you speak in order to make a change, since there is no other way you can speak, why do you want to change this rather than that? Why do you want to alter the way in which postage stamps are made rather than the way in which Jews are treated in an antisemitic country? And the other way around. He must therefore always answer the following questions: What do you want to change? Why this rather than that?[112]

It seems to me that Sartre's statement suggests many of the elements that are needed for the construction of a better theory of journalism. Sartre suggests that since journalists must be selective in their focusing and in their choices of subject matter—a point that is neglected by the traditional theory of objectivity—there is a need for them to be explicitly aware of their selecting, so that it can be guided by sound principles. He suggests, further, that since selectivity is inherently evaluative—another point that escapes the mainstream objectivity doctrine—there is a need to be clear about one's value choices, and to be prepared to answer for them. Finally, Sartre insists that writers (and thus journalists) take *responsibility* for their writing. Journalists have an obligation to seek, and ultimately to report, the *truth*. It is a sheer breach of this responsibility to let themselves serve, instead, as the passive mouthpiece of powerful political elites.[113]

Mainstream journalists might object at this point that all of this selecting, evaluating, and drawing of conclusions concerning what is true would surely only result in rampant "subjectivity." We would cease to be told about the real world and would instead be treated to the world of the journalist's personal interests, values, and conclusions.

But why need this follow? For while it is true that the crag, recalling Sartre's example discussed earlier, emerges only through human subjectivity, perhaps only through one individual's idiosyncratic project, whether or not it is climbable depends to a large extent on the nature of the crag. Focusing and asking selected questions are ways of letting the object focused on and asked about to emerge. Granted, only part of it will emerge, and only in a certain way, but that is part of the human condition, and not the result of a defect in some particular theory of news gathering.

It should be pointed out, moreover, that we are more likely to be able to *correct* any distortions resulting from our subjectivity if we at least *recognize* that our subjectivity is operating, rather than assuming falsely that we are observing the "pure" object. Furthermore, even if all perception occurs within a theoretical and interpretive framework, it hardly follows that we are doomed to vicious, solipsistic subjectivity! Rather, there are rational criteria for criticizing theories and interpretations, and for judging some of them to be better, or at least more suitable for a given project or purpose, than others. In short, while selection, theorizing, and interpretation are necessary for the initiating and conducting of any investigation, they do not fully determine its outcome; nor are they immune from criticism, revision, or rejection. But they *do* tend to remain immune from criticism when it is not recognized that they are present.

Consider the example of medicine. Medical research and medical practice are surely not "objective" in the journalistic sense. Both are full of theories and interpretations. Both are guided by explicit norms: most obviously, that health is good and sickness evil. And these norms, equally obviously, guide the focusing and selective attention of researchers and doctors at every stage. Does this make medicine "subjective" in any objectionable sense?

What makes modern mainstream journalism "subjectivistic" in the worst sense of that term is not that it is guided by values, but that it is guided, without even being aware of it, by *narrow, parochial* values—values which are often inconsistent with deeper, more fundamental, and more universal values. Thus, as I have tried to show, when the values of human rights and basic human needs, or of democracy and freedom, come into conflict with the values of a consensus of mainstream U.S. political opinion, the U.S. press tends to side with the latter, not because of a sinister conspiracy, but because of a confused and indefensible notion of objectivity, together with the distorting mechanisms of news gathering which result from it.

This notion of objectivity can and should be replaced. But "objectivity" need not refer to the (impossible) flight from interpretation, theory, and value. Rather, it can refer to the demand that theories, interpretations, and value judgments be adequately supported by argument and evidence, and be able to stand up to criticism. And it can refer to the insistence that the values guiding inquiry and reporting be fundamental and universal, as in the example of medicine discussed above, rather than narrow and parochial, as is so often the case in contemporary journalism. Such a conception of objectivity, with its simple demand that its adherents seek to discover, and to report, important truths, has always guided the finest writers and scholars, including Jean-Paul Sartre. Perhaps it is time that it guided journalists as well.

If the analysis presented above is cogent, there are at least five steps that journalists might take that would immediately enable them to do a much better job of meeting their fundamental ethical responsibilities.

First, journalists should engage in much more investigative reporting and rely much less on handouts from authority figures, since, in addition to the defects of such reliance already noted, "in the nature of public relations most authority figures issue a high quotient of imprecise and self-serving declarations."[114] To be sure, such a change might harm the media outfit's bottom line, but if journalism is correct in viewing itself as a genuinely honorable profession, it cannot allow its concern for profit to overwhelm its ethical responsibilities.

Second, insofar as it is necessary for journalists to rely on others to gather evidence for them, they should dramatically enlarge the pool of authorities from which they draw their information. Thus, with regard to international affairs, journalists would do well to engage in some library research, consulting the reports of the major human rights organizations mentioned above, as well as taking advantage of the findings of academics and foreign journalists. Similarly, they might take advantage of the information that is readily available at such "beats" as the United Nations and the World Court. Finally, in consulting all of these alternative sources, there should be a concerted effort to find and to present to news audiences perspectives other than those of U.S. corporate and governmental elites, so that these audiences might be better equipped to evaluate critically both mainstream perspectives and their competitors.

Third, journalists should not allow U.S. corporate and governmental spokespersons to "set the agenda" for media coverage of international affairs. Rather, the media should assert their own independence in this regard, as part of their professional responsibility. Thus, rather than remaining content to report the mainstream elite consensus, handed to reporters, that country A's elections are fraudulent because of factor X, while country B's are legitimate because of factor Y, the media would better serve us by drawing up a comprehensive list of the factors that tend to push an election in the direction of legitimacy or illegitimacy, and then check, preferably by direct investigation, but alternatively by a scrupulous assessment of a variety of independent sources, how different countries fare with regard to these factors.

Fourth, journalists should abandon the confused and irresponsible doctrine of objectivity that currently guides the profession, and replace it with a more scientific or scholarly conception of objectivity. The difference between the two is this. While the former requires the (impossible) avoidance of opinions, conclusions, and theories, the latter allows, indeed insists upon, these, while demanding that they be well grounded in evidence, logic, and reasoning, and that they hold up under the pressure of counterargument and counterevidence. Objectivity in this scholarly sense is not undermined by taking a strong position, displaying emotion, or anything of that sort. To the contrary, a strong position might be warranted, or even required, by a scrupulous examination of the relevant facts and arguments, and strong feelings might be utterly fitting and appropriate. Moreover, to think that objectivity requires a "balanced," "play it down the middle" result is just a confusion. To be committed to drawing conclusions based solely on the evidence is to be committed to letting the conclusions fall where they may. Thus, the fact that a person arrives at a "one-sided" conclusion is no more evidence of a lack of objectivity on his or her part than would the fact that a referee in a basketball game called thirty fouls on one team and only twelve on another. Perhaps the one team simply committed way more fouls. Indeed, for all we know, the referee might have been biased the other way, so that a more appropriate job of officiating would have resulted in a margin of forty fouls to two. In any case, I think it is clear that one of the factors driving the contemporary postmodern rejection of "objectivity" is that the opponents of "objectivity" often have in mind the radically defective and indefensible journalistic understanding of that notion.[115]

Fifth, journalists should also abandon the "both sides" approach to the presentation of opinion. To be sure, there is something to be said for airing more than one view when considering difficult or controversial issues, but no special magic should be accorded to the number two. On many issues, several different perspectives, as opposed to merely two, are worthy of consideration. Moreover, when multiple perspectives are aired, there is less chance that fundamental convictions held in common by the two sides usually heard from will go unchallenged. On the other hand, some issues, such as the question of whether or not cigarette smoking is harmful to health, are sufficiently well established as to make it a waste of time to consider "the other side." Such an insistence on always presenting "both sides" even when the currently available evidence is adequate to show that one is correct has the unfortunate consequence of suggesting that no issues ever are decidable on the basis of evidence, and that all issues are ultimately "subjective." Thus, journalists would be well advised to be guided by evidence in determining which views to include, as opposed to insisting on precisely two views (and two mainstream ones sharing most of the important contestable principles in common, at that).

It should be noted that these reforms, necessary though they may be if journalism is to meet its responsibilities in a democracy, are extremely unlikely to be undertaken. It is to be hoped that some journalists will attempt them, but this will require considerable courage on their part, since it is quite likely that any editor or reporter who behaved in the manner here recommended would quite quickly lose his or her job. Until these reforms are enacted, however, those U.S. citizens who would like to understand the world in which they live would be well advised to turn to other sources—the foreign press, scholarly books and articles, and the "alternative" or non-mass media—to supplement their careful and critical use of mainstream journalism.

In any case, we are now in a position to see why debates between mainstream political thinkers and their leftist postmodern critics are so impoverished and so frustrating. The former claim that their views are "objective" or "factual," when in fact they rest on a massive distortion of evidence facilitated by a confused and indefensible notion of objectivity; and the latter undermine their own efforts by renouncing objectivity outright, and by insisting that "truth" is nothing but a rhetorical or ideological construct, thus leaving themselves without any ground from which to denounce as such the simple untruths promulgated by politicians, journalists, advertisers, and public relations personnel. We need a better understanding of objectivity, and we desperately need a better debate.

NOTES

1. By "mainstream" journalism in the United States, I refer to the journalism of such newspapers as the *New York Times* and *Washington Post*, such newsmagazines as *Time* and *Newsweek*, and the news broadcasts of such major television networks as ABC, CBS, and NBC. I should also point out that in this discussion I will be using the terms "journalism," "press," and "media" more or less interchangeably.

2. See, for example, Jean-Paul Sartre, "The Responsibility of the Writer," trans. Betty Askwith, in *The Creative Vision*, ed. Haskell M. Block and Herman Salinger (New York: Grove Press, 1960); and Sartre, "Introducing 'Les Temps Modernes,'" trans. Jeffrey Mehlman, and "What Is Literature?" trans. Bernard Frechtman, both in Sartre, *"What Is Literature?" and Other Essays* (Cambridge, MA: Harvard University Press, 1988).

3. Sartre, "The Responsibility of the Writer," p. 170.

4. Ibid., p. 185.

5. Sartre, "A Friend of the People," in his *Between Existentialism and Marxism*, trans. John Mathews (New York: William Morrow and Company, 1976), pp. 296–297. There he writes:

> [A]s I see it, the revolutionary press should give a true account not only of successful actions, but of unsuccessful ones too. . . . There are certain well-tried techniques of lying that I do not like. What needs to be said, on the contrary, is the truth. . . . It's always more valuable to report the truth; the truth is revolutionary and the masses have a right to it. This is what has never been done. . . . What is even more serious is the fact that the bourgeois papers lie less. They lie more skillfully. They manage to discredit, but they stick to the facts. It's terrible to think that the revolutionary papers, far from being more truthful than the bourgeois papers, are less so. But what is also necessary is that we—who are also the masses—learn to live with the truth. Revolutionaries don't want to know the truth; they have been brainwashed. They live in a sort of dream-world. We have to create a desire for the truth, in ourselves and in others.

6. William A. Dorman, "Mass Media and International Conflict," in *Selected Issues in Logic and Communication*, ed. Trudy Govier (Belmont, CA: Wadsworth, 1988), p. 66.

7. Ibid.

8. Neil Postman, *Amusing Ourselves to Death* (New York: Penguin Books, 1986), p. 107.

9. Ibid.

10. William A. Dorman and Mansour Farhang, *The U.S. Press and Iran* (Berkeley: University of California Press, 1987), pp. 145–146; and Dorman, "Mass Media," p. 67.

11. Dorman and Farhang, *U.S. Press*, p. 99.

12. Ibid., p. 164.

13. Ibid., p. 145; and Dorman, "Mass Media," p. 67.

14. William A. Dorman, "Peripheral Vision: U.S. Journalism and the Third World," *World Policy* (summer 1986): 432; Richard W. Cottam, *Nationalism in Iran* (Pittsburgh: University of Pittsburgh Press, 1979), p. 2; James A. Bill, *The Eagle and the Lion* (New Haven, CT: Yale University Press, 1988), pp. 55–56; and Noam Chomsky, *Necessary Illusions* (Boston: South End Press, 1989), pp. 283–285.

15. Dorman and Farhang, *U.S. Press*, pp. 54, 119–120.

16. Ibid., pp. 69–70.

17. John Barry and Roger Charles, "Sea of Lies," *Newsweek*, 13 July 1992, pp. 29–33, 36–39.

18. Jay LaMonica and Leroy Sievers (producers), Tony Barrett (director), and Carolyn Curiel (writer), *Nightline* (ABC Television news program) (1 July 1992).

19. Jeff Cohen and Norman Solomon, *Adventures in Medialand* (Monroe, ME: Common Courage Press, 1993), pp. 123–124; Nancy Cooper and John Barry, "Seven Minutes to Death," *Newsweek*, 18 July 1988, pp. 18–22, 24; and Noam Chomsky, *Letters from Lexington* (Monroe, ME: Common Courage Press, 1993), pp. 123–124.

20. LaMonica, Sievers, Barrett, and Curiel, *Nightline*.

21. Edward S. Herman and Gerry O'Sullivan, *The "Terrorism" Industry* (New York: Pantheon, 1989), pp. 197–198; and Cohen and Solomon, *Adventures in Medialand*, pp. 73–74.

22. Lamonica, Sievers, Barrett, and Curiel, *Nightline*.

23. Barry and Charles, "Sea of Lies," p. 29.

24. Herman and O'Sullivan, *"Terrorism" Industry*, p. 291.

25. Jeff Cohen, "Stenographers to Power," an interview with David Barsamian in Barsamian's *Stenographers to Power* (Monroe, ME: Common Courage Press, 1992), p. 142.

26. Edward S. Herman and Noam Chomsky, *Manufacturing Consent* (New York: Pantheon, 2002), pp. xx–xxii.

27. See chapter 3, section III, C.

28. Jack Spence, "The U.S. Media: Covering (Over) Nicaragua," in

Reagan versus the Sandinistas, ed. Thomas W. Walker (Boulder, CO: Westview Press, 1987), p. 192.

29. Francisco Goldman, "Sad Tales of La Libertad de Prensa," *Harper's* (August 1988), cited in Noam Chomsky, *Necessary Illusions*, p. 42.

30. Americas Watch, *The Continuing Terror: Seventh Supplement to the Report on Human Rights in El Salvador* (September 1985), cited in Spence, "U.S. Media," p. 192.

31. Spence, "U.S. Media," p. 192; and Chomsky, *Necessary Illusions*, p. 41.

32. Chomsky, *Necessary Illusions*, p. 125, and sources cited in that work, p. 378, note 46. Note, in this connection, the justice of Dorman and Farhang's remark that whereas

> a pronouncement by the Philippines' Ferdinand Marcos in 1983 that antigovernment agitators and publishers who engaged in "propaganda" could be executed received only passing mention in the national news[, i]t is not difficult to imagine the tone and scope of press coverage if a similar statement had been made by the Sandinista government in Nicaragua. (*U.S. Press*, p. 211)

33. Chomsky, *Necessary Illusions*, p. 125; and *Boston Globe*, 5 September 1988.

34. Chomsky, *Necessary Illusions*, pp. 127–128; *Al-Hamishmar*, 25 July 1986 and 13 August 1986; *Jerusalem Post*, 12 August and 24 August 1986.

35. Martin A. Lee, "Human Rights and the Media: An Overview," *Extra!* 2, no. 7/8 (summer 1989): 5–6. Nor did television perform better on this issue than did the print media, as the following revealing study by David Croteau and William Hoynes makes clear:

> In our study period [1 January 1985–30 April 1988], *Nightline* presented 27 shows . . . focusing on Central America. Of these programs, almost all dealt exclusively with Nicaragua. . . . Nicaragua was typically covered as if the rest of Central America did not exist. The focus was on the government the U.S. opposes, its human rights record and alleged abuses of democracy. The same criteria of newsworthiness were not applied to the governments of Honduras, El Salvador and Guatemala, all of whom are closely allied with the U.S. and receive large sums of money from the U.S. government. These three governments had been condemned by independent human rights organizations for committing far worse abuses than Nicaragua, yet *Nightline* largely ignored Nicaragua's neighbors. . . .
> No one would deny that the Nicaraguan government committed

abuses; certainly it did. But Nicaragua's abuses paled in comparison to El Salvador, Honduras, and Guatemala. . . . This fundamental point was obscured by *Nightline*'s isolated and fragmented picture of the region. While 22 *Nightline* programs dealt principally with Nicaragua, not one focused principally on El Salvador, Honduras or Guatemala.

Debate about Nicaragua was almost always framed in terms of how the U.S. should deal with the Sandinistas. Should it try to overthrow the government overtly or covertly? Should it put pressure on them militarily, politically, or economically? *Nightline*'s coverage of the late-1980's peace process assumed that Nicaragua was the primary obstacle to peace in the region and that it did not plan to abide by any agreement and therefore needed to be pressured. These assumptions greatly limit the terms of the discussion. The fact that Nicaragua is an impoverished country of three million people defending itself against military intervention by the most powerful country in the world was seemingly irrelevant. Condemnation of U.S. policy by the World Court and by most of the countries of Latin America also seemed to be irrelevant. (*By Invitation Only* [Monroe, ME: Common Courage Press, 1994], pp. 88–89.)

36. Chomsky, *Necessary Illusions*, p. 138, and sources cited in that work, p. 380, note 3.

37. Ibid., pp. 138–139, and p. 380, note 4.

38. Noam Chomsky and Edward S. Herman, *The Political Economy of Human Rights, Vol. I: The Washington Connection and Third World Fascism* (Boston: South End Press, 1979), pp. 69–70. (Note: I have omitted the documentation provided by Chomsky and Herman in support of these assertions. This documentation may be found on page 379 of their book.)

39. See, for example, Marc Herold, "Who Will Count the Dead? Civilian Casualties in Afghanistan," in *September 11 and the U.S. War*, ed. Roger Burbach and Ben Clarke (San Francisco: City Lights Books, 2002), pp. 116–122.

40. Chalmers Johnson, *Blowback* (New York: Metropolitan Books, 2000).

41. Ibid., p. 8.

42. Ibid., p. 10.

43. Chomsky, *9–11* (New York: Seven Stories Press, 2001), pp. 47–49. His documentation is also presented on those pages.

44. Johnson, *Blowback*, p. 10.

45. Ibid., pp. 10–11.

46. Ibid., p. 11.

47. Roger Burbach, "September 11, Day of Infamy in the United States and Chile," in Burbach and Clarke, *September 11*, pp. 56–57.

48. John Tirman points out that "[a]t about the same time the Afghan resistance was being organized with U.S. aid, the Iraq regime of Saddam Hussein launched an attack on Iran to gain the oil fields on the gulf. This unprovoked act of war followed a period of quiet rapprochement with Washington . . . and throughout the ensuing eight years of carnage—in which one million people died—the U.S. government increasingly helped Iraq, supplying it with more than $5 billion in financial credits, intelligence data, heavy equipment and political respectability." "U.S. Policy on Iran and Southwest Asia," in Burbach and Clarke, *September 11*, p. 38.

49. In addition to the notorious Noriega, whose drug dealing was ignored by the U.S. mass media while he was on the CIA payroll, despite the fact that it had been well documented in non–mass media sources for years (though the mass media would publicize it extensively when the U.S. government later cited it as its reason for invading Panama), it should be pointed out that the mujahideen supplemented their CIA income by becoming one of the world's top heroin producers, supplying 60 percent of U.S. demand in the early and middle part of the 1980s. See Michel Chossudovsky, "Who Is Osama bin Laden?" in Burbach and Clarke, *September 11*, pp. 19–20.

50. Paul Street, in "Towards a 'Decent Left'?" *Z* 15, no. 7/8 (July/August 2002): 61–68, cites and skillfully criticizes several articles in which this ridiculous suggestion is propounded.

51. The following is a partial list of countries in which the U.S. has attempted (often successfully) to overthrow governments since the 1950s: Guatemala, Iran, Brazil, the Congo, Cuba, the Dominican Republic, Ghana, Indonesia, Chile, Jamaica, Afghanistan, Angola, Cambodia, Ethiopia, Granada, Nicaragua, and Panama. These interventions have caused countless deaths of innocent persons and the establishment of several brutal, dictatorial regimes which, in turn, have engaged in a great deal of additional killing of the innocent.

And here is a list of the countries the U.S. has bombed since World War II: China, Korea, Guatemala, Indonesia, Cuba, the Congo, Peru, Laos, Vietnam, Cambodia, Grenada, Libya, El Salvador, Nicaragua, Panama, Iraq, Bosnia, Sudan, Yugoslavia, and Afghanistan. See, for example, Arundhati Roy, "War Is Peace," in Burbach and Clarke, *September 11*, p. 102.

52. See, for example, Edward S. Herman, "The World Confronts the U.S. Wars of Terrorism," *Z* 15, no. 7/8 (July/August 2002): 43–47; Tirman, "U.S. Policy," p. 38; and Martin A. Lee, "Questions about America's Anti-Terrorism Crusade," in Burbach and Clarke, *September 11*, p. 149.

53. Lee, "Questions about America's Anti-Terrorism Crusade," p. 148. See also Herman, "World Confronts," pp. 45–47; Chomsky, *9–11*, p. 43; and Howard Zinn, *Terrorism and War* (New York: Seven Stories Press, 2002), p. 28.

54. Rather made these remarks as a guest on the *Late Show with David*

Letterman. He also appeared on *Larry King Live* and said, "[W]hatever arguments one may or may not have had with George Bush the younger before September Eleventh, he is our commander in chief, he's the man now. And we need unity, we need steadiness. I'm not preaching about it. We all know this." Both quotations may be found in Zinn, *Terrorism and War*, p. 58, though Zinn cuts off the first quotation just before its last sentence. A version of the quotation in which that last sentence does appear may be found in Norman Solomon, "Media War Without End," in Burbach and Clarke, *September 11*, p. 90.

55. Zinn, *Terrorism and War*, pp. 58–59. Zinn also points out that "[w]e have a long tradition in this country of stifling dissent exactly at those moments when dissent is badly needed. Exactly when you need free speech—when the lives of the young people in the armed forces, the lives of people overseas who may be the victims of our armed actions, are at stake—that's when they say you should shut up. Exactly when you need debate and free expression most. So you have free speech for trivial issues, and not for life-and-death issues, and that's called democracy. No, we can't accept that" (ibid., pp. 65–66).

56. Alexander Cockburn, "The Incubator Returns!" *Nation* 276, no. 2 (13/20 January 2003), p. 8.

57. Fairness and Accuracy in Reporting, "Star Witness on Iraq Said Weapons Were Destroyed," accessed online on 7 May 2003, at http://www.fair.org/press-releases/kamel.html.

58. U.N. Security Council Resolution 582, "The Situation Between Iran and Iraq" (1986), accessed online on May 8, 2003, at http://ods-dds-ny.un.org/doc/RESOLUTION/GEN/NRO/729/06/IMG/NRO72906.pdf?OpenElement.

59. On those extremely rare occasions when this elementary point is raised in the U.S. mass media, it is usually a foreign head of state who raises it. Thus, for example, CNN quoted Lebanese President Emile Lahoud as saying that any military action against Iraq for disobeying U.N. resolutions would be hypocritical so long as Israel goes unpunished for the same offense. See "Chirac: Iraq Force a Last Resort," accessed online on 8 May 2003, at http://www.cnn.com/2002/WORLD/europe/10/18/france.iraq/index.html.

60. See Articles 41 and 42 of the U.N. Charter, accessed online on 8 May 2003, at http://www.un.org/aboutun/charter/.

61. See Cockburn, "The Incubator Returns!"

62. Jean Heller, "The Army That Wasn't There," *St. Petersburg Times*, 6 January 1991.

63. Norman Solomon, "The Media's War," in *Target Iraq*, ed. Norman Solomon and Reese Erlich (New York: Context Books, 2003), pp. 29–31.

64. Ibid. See also Solomon, "Unilateral by Any Other Name," in Solomon and Erlich, *Target Iraq*, pp. 75–76; and Seth Ackerman, "A Scoop

They'd Rather Forget: U.N. Spying Scandal Goes from Fact to Allegation," in Solomon and Erlich, *Target Iraq*, pp. 123–125.

65. Fairness and Accuracy in Reporting, "In Iraq Crisis, Networks are Megaphones for Official Views," accessd online on 9 May 2003, at http://www.fair.org/reports/iraq-sources.html.

66. Robert Fisk, quoted in Robert Jensen, "The Military's Media," in *Progressive* 67, no. 5 (May 2003), p. 25.

67. See, for example, Charles T. Salmon's claim, in his review of Herman and Chomsky's *Manufacturing Consent* (New York: Pantheon Books, 1988), in *Journalism Quarterly* 66, no. 2 (Summer 1989), that "selection of examples necessarily reflect[s] researchers' filters and frames" (p. 495). Salmon offers no argument in support of this claim. Nor does he explain what, in particular, is wrong with Herman and Chomsky's selection.

68. I should note one other protocol for this experiment. To make the comparison between the two nations fair, some care should be taken to note the overall amount of coverage, as well as the favorable coverage, they each receive. Otherwise, one might claim to refute me by, for example, noting that the U.S. pays more attention to political corruption in Canada than in some tiny "hostile" African nation of little interest to U.S. political elites. Such a claim would be absurd, since U.S. audiences are obviously much more interested in Canadian affairs than in those of this African nation, so that the greater attention to corruption in the former nation is clearly to be attributed to this, rather than an anti-Canadian bias, a point that is also indicated by the comparatively vastly grater favorable coverage Canada receives. On this point see Chomsky, *Necessary Illusions*, pp. 151–152.

Also, though one would hope that this would be an obvious point, it is important, when comparing media coverage of abuses carried out by two different countries, to choose countries in which both the scale and the character of the abuses (as measured by reputable independent watchdog organizations, rather than by U.S. governmental spokespersons) are indeed comparable. Thus, in response to one observer's (L. Brent Bozell III) complaint that the mass media had given more coverage in 1984 to government death squads in El Salvador than to government death squads in Nicaragua, Peter Hart and Steve Rendall justly comment that this is "a bit like complaining that the basketball talents of Michael Jordan get more coverage than those of Woody Allen." "Meet the Myth Makers," *Extra!* 11, no. 4 (July/August 1998): 26.

69. Herman and Chomsky have made extensive and excellent use of this "matched pair" method, and the attentive reader will already have noticed how extensive is my debt to their work. See especially their *Manufacturing Consent*; Herman's *The Real Terror Network* (Boston: South End Press, 1982); and Chomsky's *Necessary Illusions*.

Herman, in particular, makes very effective use of quantitative measures in connection with the "matched pair" method. For example, he provides in *Real Terror Network* (p. 197) an eye-opening chart showing the frequency of mention in the *New York Times* of prominent persons who suffered from serious abuse at the hands of their own government. The result: those who were abused by the Soviet Union or by its satellites received extensive coverage; those of equal or greater prominence who were abused by U.S. client states received little or no coverage. For example, Luis Silva, trade union leader in Brazil, received three mentions over five years in the *New York Times*, as compared to eighty-one mentions over the same time period for Lech Walesa, trade union leader in Poland, despite Silva's comparable importance and despite the fact that he suffered even greater abuse (see page 15).

Moreover, in addition to such quantitative data, there is also a consistent qualitative difference in the media's coverage of abuse by our "friends" and by our "enemies," as Herman notes:

> A systematic dichotomous treatment can be found across the board, whereby huge crimes by state terrorists within the U.S. sphere of influence are either suppressed or given brief and muted treatment, abuses attributable to enemies are attended to repeatedly and with indignation and sarcasm. When enemy abuses are serious, as in the case of Pol Pot's Cambodia, the mass media follow events on a daily basis, accept or freely disseminate claims without the slightest attempt at critical evaluation, and wax hysterical with humanistic concern. Devotion to the victims knows no bounds. . . . But lesser enemy abuses . . . also attract steady mass media attention and deep concern. In contrast, the reign of terror in Latin America is being treated only occasionally, with antiseptic brevity, without context, and devoid of human detail and touches that might be conducive to sympathetic feeling. (*Real Terror Network*, p. 16.)

70. The best media critics understand these principles well. For example, Herman and Chomsky often adopt the strategy of letting their opponents pick their examples for them. That is, rather than looking for cases in which the press might be expected to be overly subservient to U.S. governmental perspectives, they instead turn to examine cases in which the media have been harshly criticized for being excessively critical. Thus, since it is a widely held view that media coverage of the Vietnam War was unfairly and severely adversary, and that this was especially manifest in media reporting of the Tet offensive, Herman and Chomsky devote more than ninety pages to an analysis of just this coverage (*Manufacturing Consent*, pp. 169–252, 368–380). Similarly, they devote very little attention to reporting found in conservative publications, or in those which are poorly

regarded. Instead, they critique the *New York Times* (the "newspaper of record," which is often criticized for having a liberal slant) and focus much of their attention on its most "liberal" columnists, such as Anthony Lewis and Tom Wicker.

With regard to broadcast media, Alexander Cockburn follows much the same practice. When he attempted, in one particularly brilliant satirical piece, to demonstrate the deficiencies of television news broadcasts, he focused on the *MacNeill-Lehrer News Hour* on PBS, which was at the time the longest, most serious, and most highly regarded of all television news programs. "The Tedium Twins," in *Selected Issues in Logic and Communication*, ed. Trudy Govier (Belmont, CA: Wadsworth, 1988).

71. Chomsky, *Noam Chomsky Meets the Press* (Westfield, NJ: Open Magazine Pamphlet Series, 1989), p. 4.

72. Chomsky, *Necessary Illusions*, pp. 147–148.

73. Ibid., p. 65.

74. Ibid.

75. Croteau and Hoynes, *By Invitation Only*.

76. Richard Kaplan, as quoted in Joseph Kahn, "Nightline Guest List Called Biased," *Boston Globe*, 6 February 1989.

77. Robert MacNeil, as quoted on *The Eleventh Hour*, 21 May 1990.

78. For example, when Bernard Goldberg pitched to his superiors at CBS News an idea for a segment about bias in television news, he spoke as follows: "I told Heyward I would put in requests to interview Rather and Brokaw and Jennings. I'd put responsible critics on, too. People who believed there was a leftward tilt to the news. The report I envisioned would be fair and balanced, just the way the news was supposed to be at CBS." *Bias* (Washington, DC: Regnery, 2002), p. 41. Notice that Goldberg apparently thinks that the only responsible critics are those who think there is a leftward tilt to the news, and that a report on bias in the news can be "fair and balanced" even when it excludes discussion of the possibility that there might be a conservative, or a progovernment, or a procorporate, tilt to the news. This is an excellent example of the "both sides fallacy," discussed in chapter 3, section IV A 1, above, and, in the present chapter, section IV F, below.

79. Ibid.

80. Ibid., pp. 15–20.

81. Ibid., p. 18.

82. Steve Rendall and Peter Hart, " 'Bias' Isn't Supported—Because It's Not True," accessed online on 17 August 2002, at http://www.fair.org/articles/bias-op-ed.html, p. 1.

83 Ibid., p. 2.

84. Goldberg, *Bias*, pp. 152–161.

85. Ibid., p. 161.

86. Ibid., pp. 34–35.

87. Rendall and Hart, "Bias," p. 1.

88. Goldberg, *Bias*, p. 56.

89. Ibid., p. 59.

90. Ibid., pp. 57–59.

91. Geoffrey Nunberg, "Media: Label Whores," *American Prospect* 13, no. 8 (6 May 2002), accessed online on 17 August 2002, at http://www.prospect.org/print/V13/8/nunberg-g.html, p. 2.

92. Ibid., p. 3.

93. Ibid.

94. Goldberg, *Bias*, pp. 123–126.

95. Rendall and Hart, "Bias," p. 1.

96. Ibid., p. 2. It is significant in this connection that, despite the impression created by his leading off with the example of the flat-tax proposal, Goldberg exhibits little interest in economic issues. Rather, he states that the problem of liberal bias manifests itself in "the big social and cultural issues" (*Bias*, p. 22), such as "abortion, gun control, feminism, gay rights, the environment, school prayer" (p. 24). Note that none of these issues, with the exception of the environment, poses any threat to corporate interests. Profits are not likely to be affected significantly no matter which way the fights over these issues eventually turn out. It is therefore not surprising that corporate bosses might tolerate "liberal" reporting in these areas. We should not expect this attitude to carry over to economic matters or foreign affairs, however.

97. Calvin F. Exoo, *The Politics of the Mass Media* (St. Paul: West, 1994), p. 50.

98. See, for example, T. R. Miles, "Gestalt Theory," in *The Encyclopedia of Philosophy*, vol. 3, ed. Paul Edwards (New York: Macmillan, 1967), pp. 318–319.

99. James M. Edie, *Edmund Husserl's Phenomenology* (Bloomington: Indiana University Press, 1987), p. 13.

100. Gilbert Harman, *The Nature of Morality* (New York: Oxford University Press, 1977), pp. 4–5.

101. John Dewey, in a manner similar to that of Harman, explains why:

Foreign languages that we do not understand always seem jabberings, babblings, in which it is impossible to fix a definite, clear-cut individualized group of sounds. The countryman in the crowded street, the landlubber at sea, the ignoramus in sport at a contest between experts in a complicated game, are further instances. Put an inexperienced man in a factory, and at first the work seems to him a meaningless medley. All strangers of another race proverbially look alike to the visiting foreigner. Only gross differences of size or color are perceived by an outsider in a flock of sheep, each of which is perfectly individualized to the shepherd. A diffusive blur and an indiscriminately shifting suction characterize what we do not understand. (*How We Think* [Amherst, N.Y.: Prometheus Books, 1991], pp. 121–122.)

102. Explaining his reluctance to use the word "lie" in an article about the untruths of Ronald Reagan, James N. Miller writes: "My avoidance of the word 'lie' was in deference to the rule of journalistic objectivity that says its use implies bias on the reporter's part, even when the objective facts warrant its use." "Lies," *Columbia Journalism Review* (May–June 1985), p. 72.

103. This invisibility is invaluable to propagandists, as Chomsky explains: "A principle familiar to propagandists is that the doctrines to be instilled in the target audience should not be articulated: that would only expose them to reflection, inquiry, and, very likely, ridicule. The proper procedure is to drill them home by constantly presupposing them, so that they become the very condition for discourse." (Chomsky, "Third World, First Threat," in his *Letters from Lexington*, p. 29). For example, the media do not say things like: "The U.S. always supports democracy, and does not aggress against other sovereign nations." Rather, this is the unstated presupposition of all mass media discussions of U.S. foreign policy.

104. Accordingly, those who favor pursuing corporate interests in U.S. foreign policy are presented as experts, while those with other views—environmentalists, feminists, people who favor the self-determination of foreign nations, etc.—can be dismissed as partisans, pursuing an "agenda," and representing "special interests."

It is also worth noting that while journalists might indeed, with practice, become skilled at bracketing their "personal opinions" and "biases" when it comes to controversial domestic issues—ones about which there is disagreement within the mainstream spectrum of U.S. political opinion—they obviously do not do so when it comes to international issues, where there is usually an elite consensus. When the U.S. government declares another nation to be "our" friend or enemy, the media never—that is, literally never—provide the slightest dissent or critical perspective. Biases shared by all respectable members of one's own society are not so easily bracketed.

105. Sartre, "Individualism and Conformism in the United States," in his *Literary and Philosophical Essays*, trans. Annette Michelson (New York: Collier Books, 1962), p. 104.

106. Jeff Cohen, "From *MacNeil-Lehrer* to *Nightline*: Experts Enforce the Party Line," an interview with David Barsamian in Barsamian, *Stenographers to Power*, p. 101.

107. David Eakins, "Objectivity and Commitment," *Studies on the Left* 1 (fall 1959): 52.

108. Karen Doyne, as quoted in Tracey Wong Briggs, "PBS 'bias' Missing in Programs," *USA Today*, 23 August 1993.

109. Robert W. McChesney also notes that "mainstream journalists usually proclaim, 'See, we're being shot at from both sides, so we must be doing it right.'" But, as McChesney goes on to point out,

> [t]he "shot at from both sides" thesis is absurd. All media systems generate criticism from different parts of the political spectrum. Even the Nazi media probably had critics who thought it was insufficiently nationalistic or too soft on Jews and communists. Does this mean that the Nazis were "doing it right?" Of course not. The way to analyze media accurately is through hard examination based on evidence. (*Corporate Media and the Threat to Democracy* [New York: Seven Stories Press, 1997], pp. 59–60.)

110. For further discussion of this point, see above, chapter 3, section IV A 1.

111. Daniel C. Hallin offers a useful imaginative device with which to capture the logic of the media's "two sides" doctrine, not as it is articulated in textbooks, but as it is implemented in actual journalistic practice:

> Imagine the journalist's world as divided into three regions, each of which is governed by different journalistic standards. . . . The province of objectivity is the . . . region which can be called the Sphere of Legitimate Controversy. This is the region of electoral contests and legislative debates, of issues recognized as such by the major established actors of the American political process. The limits of this sphere are defined primarily by the two-party system— by the parameters of debate between and within the Democratic and Republican parties—as well as by the decision-making process in the bureaucracies of the executive branch. Within this region, objectivity and balance reign as the supreme journalistic virtues.
>
> Bounding the Sphere of Legitimate Controversy on one side is what can be called the Sphere of Consensus. This is the region of "motherhood and apple pie"; it encompasses those social objects not regarded by the journalists and most of society as controversial. Within this region journalists do not feel compelled either to present opposing views or to remain disinterested observers. On the contrary, the journalist's role is to serve as an advocate or celebrant of consensus values.

And beyond the Sphere of Legitimate Controversy lies the Sphere of Deviance, the realm of those political actors and views which journalists and the political mainstream of the society reject as unworthy of being heard. (*The "Uncensored War": The Media and Vietnam* [New York: Oxford University Press, 1986], pp. 116–117.)

Similarly, J. Herbert Altschull notes that

under the code [of objectivity], fundamental institutions may not be attacked. Nor may the symbols of those fundamental institutions: the flag, for example, or "democracy". . . . Enemies of the system may not be applauded, nor symbolic representation of those enemies. Atheism may not be endorsed; freedom of religion does not extend that far. Nor may any symbol of animosity to "family" be supported. Homosexuality may be tolerated, but it may not be advocated. Motherhood may not be condemned. Communism may not be defended. Nor, for that matter, is it acceptable within the parameters of the system to attack the code of objectivity.

Moreover, the code of objectivity appears to be operative only within the geographical limits of the United States. When the United States is in collision with another nation, it is not necessary to give "both sides" to the dispute equal attention; to do so is to be unpatriotic. It is exceedingly rare to find the views of Fidel Castro given equal weight with those of his enemies, and when Castro's stance is presented, it is usually reported in such a way as to illustrate clearly the wrongheadedness of his views. The situation is similar with regard to the views of Soviet and Chinese leaders. And one would have sought long and hard to find the position of the Ayatollah Khomeini presented in a balanced fashion in the American press during (and after) the holding of the American hostages in Iran. (*Agents of Power* [New York: Longman, 1984], p. 132.)

112. Sartre, "The Responsibility of the Writer," p. 170.

113. Here is an example of the media's tendency to report only what the powerful call to their attention. In January 1996 the World Trade Organization, which had only recently been brought into existence by the GATT trade pact of 1994, ruled that the United States's Clean Air Act placed unacceptably tight environmental restrictions on imported gasolines. Prior to the passing of GATT and NAFTA, the U.S. had enjoyed autonomy in connection with setting environmental standards that all gasolines, whether domestic or imported, would have to meet. But these trade agreements removed such

authority from the United States government and placed it in the hands of the WTO. The result is that the United States now tolerates higher levels of toxic auto emissions than it did previously.

Why did this important story receive so little coverage? The reason is that no one important in mainstream U.S. political circles wanted to call it to the attention of journalists. President Clinton, who had pushed GATT through Congress, certainly had no motive to point out to the American people the poisonous consequences of his folly. But 1996 was an election year, so, one might think, surely his opponents would wish to do so! But no, Bob Dole, Clinton's eventual Republican challenger in the general election, had also supported GATT, and with it, the creation of the WTO. So had all the other major Republican candidates who initially ran during the primary phase of the election, with the single exception of Pat Buchanan, who was, nonetheless, ill positioned to criticize its weakening of the Clean Air Act, since he opposed federal regulations that protect the environment! So none of the major players brought this issue to the attention of journalists, and the journalists, in turn, bound by their peculiar notion of objectivity, refrained from alerting their audiences. See Norman Solomon and Jeff Cohen, "Shrugging Off an Attack on the Clean Air Act," in their *Wizards of Media Oz* (Monroe, ME: Common Courage Press, 1997), pp. 85–87.

114. Ben H. Bagdikian, *The Media Monopoly*, 4th ed. (Boston: Beacon, 1992), p. 180.

115. One way to see this is to look back at the quotations from postmodernists appearing in chapter 2, section II A. Consider this one: "[T]he consensus of most of the dominant theories is that all thought does, indeed, develop from particular standpoints, perspectives, interests. . . . As the most powerful modern philosophies and theories have been demonstrating, claims of disinterest, objectivity, and universality are not to be trusted and themselves tend to reflect local historical conditions." George Levine et al., *Speaking for the Humanities* (n.p.: American Council of Learned Societies, 1989), pp. 10, 18. Now, if "objectivity" here refers to the idea that there is a way things are, irrespective of our opinion about it, and that our best chance of holding views that are consonant with this way things are rests in our rigorously and critically examining the relevant arguments and evidence concerning them, this passage is absurd, as I have tried to show above. But if it refers to some region of pure, value-free facts, accessible to a passive, empty mind, and/or to the idea that the truth lies in the middle of some mainstream consensus, then the quotation makes considerably more sense. Claims of "objectivity" issued by mainstream politicians and journalists are not to be trusted, and do indeed tend to reflect their own narrow interests. And a similar analysis holds for other passages cited in that section (the verification of this I leave as an exercise for the reader). They attack "positivism," and the

idea of a mind unaffected by contingencies of race, class, and gender, but in so doing, they seem to think, erroneously, that they are effectively undermining the notion of objective truth itself. Another case in point is Barbara Herrnstein Smith, whose views are discussed in chapter 7, section XIV below. She seems to think, for example, that objectivity "in the classic sense" excludes a need for interpretation and judgment, when in fact this exclusion is a modern journalistic corruption of the classic sense of "objectivity." *Belief and Resistance* (Cambridge, MA: Harvard University Press, 1997), p. 78.

Chapter 7

THE ANTI-TRUTH SQUAD

According to Ronald Dworkin, "the very possibility of objective truth is now itself under challenge from an anti-truth squad of relativists, subjectivists, neo-pragmatists, postmodernists, and similar critics now powerful in the unconfident departments of American universities."[1] He's right, and he's far from alone in noticing this trend.[2] In this chapter, I propose to examine critically some of the clearest and most representative statements of the views of this anti-truth squad.

I. ANDERSON

Walter Truett Anderson tells the story of a battle that took place in "Lolo, Montana, a small rural community near the Idaho border." According to Anderson, this was a battle about epistemology, with "objectivists" squaring off against "constructivists." Here, Anderson tells us,

> people divided into opposed camps and engaged in a bitter and long-lasting battle about what was being taught in the local schools. Some

parents feared that their children were getting "global perspectives" instead of patriotism, "moral reasoning" and "values clarification" instead of traditional Christian and American principles. They considered such ideas to be subversive, and the people advancing them to be enemies of society. . . .

What some parents found subversive was the proposition that values are *not* based on any utter certainty about what is true and right, and have to be worked out by fallible human beings in the midst of daily life. This is a fairly common theme in public-school texts. A home economics book that drew heavy fire in one such dispute had the following statement: "Values are subjective. They vary from person to person. You will be able to understand and get along with other people better if you keep an open mind about the value judgments they make". . . .

A handbook for values clarification activities told teachers that such learning could not even be graded: "The teacher may, and is encouraged to, evaluate how well a particular activity is going, but this can never be translated into an evaluation of students. . . . There are no wrong answers, and grading would only serve to stifle trust, honesty and a willingness to self-disclose."

This sort of stuff, which to most of us might seem to suffer from no vice other than blandness, enrages fundamentalist critics, who say it comes perilously close to teaching that there is no right and wrong.[3]

Comments:

(1) Here Anderson conflates a number of distinct issues. Specifically, he collapses these three issues into one another, as if they were the same thing: (a) the question of the epistemological status of moral judgments (e.g., are some moral judgments objectively true, so that those who disagree with them are simply mistaken, or is it the case, rather, that all moral judgments are matters of taste, so that no one is ever mistaken?); (b) the normative question of which things are good and which bad (e.g., should we, to take an example suggested from this particular case, be patriotic, and show a partiality toward people of our own nation, or is it better to take a more cosmopolitan attitude, and show an equal concern for all people?); and (c) the question of whether it is possible to achieve certainty in our moral judgments, or whether they should all rather be regarded as fallible. Anderson seems to think that if one takes the position that some moral judgments are objectively true (issue a), then he or she must be in favor of traditional Christian and American patriotic

values (issue b), and must believe that these can be known with certainty to be the best values (issue c). But this is obviously false.

(2) Is tolerance really fostered by "keeping an open mind about the value judgments" of, say, Adolf Hitler, or by regarding them as subjective? And what does it mean to say that one should "keep an open mind about" other people's value judgments? If this means merely that I should maintain a willingness to consider these value judgments and their supporting arguments carefully and critically, while taking seriously the possibility that in any given case the other might be right and I might be wrong, then this advice is unassailable. But if it means that I should permanently put off forming even a tentative judgment of my own concerning these value judgments, it is difficult to see how such a strategy can lend support to any important human value, let alone such an important one as tolerance.

(3) To say that values "have to be worked out by fallible human beings" is precisely not to say that they are subjective. But Anderson seems to want to say both things. If values are subjective, it is unclear why they would have to be "worked out," a notion which usually suggests some sort of struggle away from error or inadequacy and toward something better. But if all values, including the ones you hold prior to any struggle, are subjective, and are to be tolerated by others, since "there are no wrong answers," why bother to struggle? This sense that "working out" values is incompatible with value subjectivism is further strengthened by Anderson's reference to "fallible human beings." To say that we are fallible means that we can make mistakes—we *can* get it wrong.

(4) To say that value judgments have to be worked out does not imply, as Anderson seems to think it does, that we cannot achieve certainty in our value judgments. If certainty can be attained at all, it is not clear why its attainment would always have to arise without effort; nor is it clear why the fact that one might have to expend effort in order to achieve certainty should be taken as proving that the certainty cannot be attained.

(5) Note that while Anderson ridicules fundamentalists for thinking that values clarification teaches "that there is no right and wrong," he does so in the sentence immediately following a quoted sentence from a values clarification textbook in which it is frankly declared that "there are no wrong answers"! Anderson says of "this sort of stuff" that it seems "to suffer from no vice other than bland-

ness." So does Anderson agree that there are no wrong answers? (Note here an asymmetry between right and wrong answers. To many ethical questions, such as "what is the best way to live?" it is quite implausible to say that there is one right answer. But it is equally implausible to deny that many proposed answers to such questions are wrong. For example, "the best way to live is to devote your life to torturing the innocent.")

Elsewhere Anderson informs us that "[i]n small towns all across America, . . . neighbor turns against neighbor in bitter disputes about whether children should be taught skills of 'moral reasoning'—a very postmodern concept—or should instead be taught to accept unquestioningly some rock-solid American values and beliefs."[4] Kant, Bentham, Mill, and Aristotle, among countless other decidedly nonpostmodernist thinkers would find it news indeed that moral reasoning is "a very postmodern concept." Each of these ethicists holds that we must reason about our moral obligations rather than accept traditional pieties unquestioningly. For Bentham and Mill, such reasoning takes the form of calculating the consequences, in terms of happiness and unhappiness, of various courses of action available to us. For Aristotle, it involves carefully steering a virtuous middle course between extremes, namely, the vices of deficiency and excess—with the identification of this virtuous mean not a simple manner of memorizing truths handed down by others, but rather the development, which requires much practice and education, of *phronesis* (practical wisdom). For Kant, who explicitly identified reason as the means by which we arrive at moral truths, moral reasoning involves the categorical imperative, a principle that demands of us consistency in our dealings with ourselves and others. In calling moral reasoning "a very postmodern concept," however, Anderson seems (in the light of his other remarks quoted above) to mean by it the social construction of values, which are understood to be subjective. Thus, he sets up another false dilemma: unquestioning, smug acceptance of patriotic pieties vs. social construction of values. This leaves out the entire tradition of rationalistic ethics. And Anderson is, once again, building claims to certainty, together with a smug conservatism, into the very definition of "objectivity."

A related confusion is to run together "judgment" in the sense of having to estimate the truth without being able to prove it (but where there clearly is an objective truth) with "judgment" in the sense that the matter is subjective and one's judgment is constitutive of truth. These confusions in Anderson come out here:

> An old joke about three umpires summarizes the range of viewpoints. They are sitting around over a beer, and one says, "There's balls and there's strikes, and I call 'em the way they are." Another says, "There's balls and there's strikes, and I call 'em the way I see 'em." The third says, "There's balls and there's strikes, and they ain't *nothin'* until I call 'em." Here we have an objectivist and two kinds of constructivists. The second ump is what I would call a mainstream constructivist, the third a postmodern radical.[5]

Here Anderson smuggles a dogmatic claim to certainty into the definition of objectivism. An objectivist umpire could perfectly well say, "There's balls and there's strikes, and I *try* to call 'em the way they are" (or "I try to call 'em right"). The second umpire could also be an objectivist, if "judgment" is understood in the nonconstitutive sense. If so, "I call 'em the way I see 'em" would mean "I try to call them right," not "whatever I call them is right, because it is my call that makes them be what they are." (Incidentally, the third umpire's statement is ambiguous as well. If the umpire is simply reminding us that umpires are the ones empowered by the rules of baseball to judge and to declare what is a ball and what is a strike, so that, officially, nothing is determined to be a ball or a strike until the umpire rules on the issue, then the statement is unassailable. If, on the other hand, the umpire means that reality antecedent to the umpire's call is utterly indeterminate on the question of whether a given pitch should be called a ball or strike—so that the umpire could never be wrong, even if he or she were to call a pitch that failed to come within one hundred feet of home plate [and that the batter did not swing at] a strike, then this is postmodern radicalism indeed. It is also a preposterous position.)

In any case, the same confusions recur in Anderson's argument that what is "critical to the prospects for peace in the world, and to the emergence of a global civilization," is "the competition between different stories about stories—between absolutist/objectivist and relativist/constructivist ideas about the nature of human truth. A pluralistic civilization can only be built with a great amount of tolerance, and the kind of tolerance that comes from people who believe in the cosmic certainty of their truth (and theirs alone) is both limited and patronizing."[6] Here he conflates objectivism with absolutism, and both with certainty. And there are problems with his claims about tolerance. If we all have our own stories, and none is really true, then why shouldn't we tolerate the Nazis' truth? If one is an objectivist, but also a fallibilist (not one who is certain), that can be a foundation for tolerance (but a critical, selective, and coherent one, not an incoherent, indiscriminate, uncritical one). Also, even where one is certain, one can see, in many cases, that disagreements are not worth fighting about, because of the objective value of peace, and of not injuring or murdering others. But Anderson thinks that tolerance can only be grounded in his constructivist epistemology. Indeed, he defines developing tolerance in terms of developing such an epistemological stance.[7] Similarly, he claims that "wherever a person who believes one thing lives with peace and respect near a person who believes something entirely different—a constructivist worldview, by whatever name, is present."[8] But many non-constructivists live with peace and respect near people who believe something entirely different. Moreover, Anderson is here confusing tolerance itself with what he believes (falsely, in my view, but that is not to my present point) to be its necessary precondition.

In another of Anderson's false dilemmas he says that "a constructivist world-view is present" whenever, among other things, "a person chooses to live within a belief system for the simple comfort it brings and not because he or she considers it the last word."[9] The real contrast is between believing something because it is comforting and believing it because you think it true (or likely to be true, or some such thing). Many people confuse the belief that there are objective truths with the quite different belief that I am in possession of them, or with the still different belief that I am certain of them, or with the still different belief that they constitute the last word. Anderson consistently conflates these things.

It should also be noted that while Anderson is quite right to condemn the mischief that is often produced by those who consider their beliefs to be "the last word," he seems utterly oblivious to all the social damage that comes from believing things because they are comforting.[10] And, as we have seen, he fails to consider any alternatives to these disastrous options, which he seems to regard as exhaustive.

On the other hand, Anderson does show an awareness of the self-referential inconsistency problem that tends to plague views like his, and he attempts to ward it off by declaring, at the very conclusion of a book defending social constructivism, that "[t]he idea of the social construction of reality is itself an SCR [social construction of reality], and this book is a story. . . . The constructivist worldview is a story about stories, and it is also a story. It is a belief, and in some ways an arbitrary one."[11]

Comments:

(1) This move is often made at the last minute, which is when Anderson makes it, in order to stave off the self-referential inconsistency objection. But one must then go back over the entire book and read each of the claims that have been issued in support of social constructivism (often in a cocksure manner, as if anyone who did not agree with such obvious truths is some sort of dullard) as mere stories, and in some ways (what ways, specifically, one wonders? And in what ways are they not?) arbitrary ones. (I am not committing the fallacy of division here. Anderson explicitly concedes not only that the whole account is a story, but also that it is a "story about stories.")

(2) The way would thus seem wide open for telling other, quite different stories, and Anderson acknowledges this: "There are other stories, stories that there is no objective cosmos at all, or that it is what we create. And yet other stories will probably come along."[12] Notice that the only alternative stories that Anderson mentions are either even more radical versions of constructivism than is his, or else future, currently undreamt-of stories. Thus, he does not seem to allow that one might legitimately tell a non-relativist, non-constructivist story. How can this be? Is the falsity of all such stories an objective one, and not just another story? If so, we have a self-referential inconsistency. If not, how can these stories be excluded?

(3) Notice that here, as everywhere, the attempt to dismiss statements attempting to capture how things are objectively fails. Anderson's attempt goes as follows. (a) One says that all claims of objective truth are really constructions—stories, and somewhat arbitrary ones at that. (b) But since this claim itself sounds like a statement of how things really are, and not just a story, in order to get rid of the self-referential inconsistency objection one must say that no, this claim too is just a story. (c) While Anderson drops the matter there, the logic of it entails either a legitimate self-referential inconsistency charge or else an infinite regress. Thus, either the statement that Anderson's claim that all claims of objective truth are really sto-

ries is itself intended as objectively true (in which case we have the self-referential inconsistency problem), or else it too is just a story (and then this just-made claim that it is a story is itself just a story, as is the claim just *now* made, as is *that* claim, and so on ad infinitum—the infinite regress). The only way to stop the regress is at some point to issue a statement intended to capture how things really are, but at that point one will have landed oneself in a self-referential inconsistency.

Next let's see what happens when Anderson turns his attention to science:

> It's quite possible . . . to go from seeing science as absolute and final truth to seeing it as an ever-changing body of ideas—a bigtime shift, any philosopher will tell you—without feeling that anything special has happened, without losing all confidence in scientific facts: For all practical purposes the speed of light remains 186,000 miles per second [and] gravity still makes water run downhill. . . . It's equally possible to move from seeing a religion as timeless truth to seeing it as the product of a certain culture—and still happily worship at your church or temple.[13]

Comments:

(1) This analogy obscures more than it illuminates. The shift that Anderson describes in connection with science is a shift to *fallibilism*; the shift that he describes in connection with religion is a shift to *relativism*.

(2) The reason that one can remain confident of science is that it can still be understood, consistently with what Anderson says here, as striving for, and as achieving to a very high degree, indeed to a degree sufficient "for all practical purposes," as Anderson puts it, *objective truth*. This point is obscured by Anderson's use of the vague phrase "an ever-changing body of ideas," which can mean anything from frequent, wild, unpredictable flip-flops, to occasional improvements in precision and scope within frameworks which retain a remarkable degree of stability. If it were the former, we would lose confidence in scientific claims. Since it is the latter we do not. (Consider Newtonian and Einsteinian physics, for example. Newton's insights still hold good "for all practical purposes." Einstein's comprehends these, and explains more—the behavior of bodies at extremely high speeds or low temperatures, for example.) As for

Anderson's contention that a shift from seeing one's religious views as timeless truths to regarding them as cultural products need not make any difference with regard to the content or intensity of one's religious belief or practice, this makes no sense to me. If, having once believed that I would really go to Hell and burn for eternity, I now come to see this as just a story that my culture tells—I recognize that people in other cultures do not believe this, and they are not wrong not to—I should think that this would have an effect on me.

(3) Anderson's discussion of science exhibits a widespread misunderstanding. The hallmark of modern science is, and always has been, evidentialism and fallibilism—the idea that scientific truths are always to be regarded as tentative, and thus subject to revision or rejection in the light of further evidence. It was never intended to be regarded "as absolute and final truth." Indeed, it was as against beliefs in "absolute and final truths" that modern science arose. But when people like Anderson, operating under the mistaken assumption that science is (or once was) supposed to be a system of "absolute and final truths," learn that it is in fact no such thing, they seem to think (as Anderson's comparison to, and remarks about, religion seem to indicate) that it is just another cultural product, rather than a (fallible, though remarkably successful) attempt to discover and to articulate objective truths that are binding on all cultures—truths of the sort that, if they are denied by any culture, that culture is (or at least in principle might be) simply mistaken.

This fallibilism/relativism (or subjectivism) ambiguity is also revealed, incidentally, in the common phrase "it's just an opinion," or the like. This phrase can mean either the modest, fallibilistic idea that "it's not something I can prove—I might be wrong," or the relativistic/subjectivistic imperative that "you should stop criticizing me, because I *can't* be wrong—this is the sort of thing that is outside of the *domain* of right and wrong." Again, the first interpretation implies both that there is some objective truth about the matter and that I may have failed to attain it—I'm not sure; whereas the latter interpretation implies that there is no objective truth about the matter and that I am thus excused from having to try to attain it. It is easy to slide confusedly back and forth between these two quite distinct ideas. The ambiguity is also helpful when one wishes to appear modest when not actually being so.

In any case, neither modesty nor anything else constrains

Anderson from issuing portentous statements about the cultural import of the ideas he favors. Here is an example: "There is something about postmodern ideas with their talk of socially constructed reality that can have a dizzying, vertiginous effect—a feeling of having no place left to stand, nothing in which to believe in. And, indeed, a deep *and probably permanent* change is taking place in our time."[14] There is something strange about this passage—and I am not talking about the gratuitous preposition thrown in at the end of its penultimate sentence. If reality is socially constructed, and if truth is therefore contingent, as postmodernists like Anderson ceaselessly argue, so that universal and timeless truths are rendered inaccessible to us (if the very idea is not simply rejected as incoherent), then how can we know that a change that is currently going on is probably a permanent one?

Leaving aside the question of permanence, what evidence does Anderson have that the change is justified? One source of justification to which Anderson appeals is the Sapir-Whorf hypothesis in linguistics, about which he remarks: "That idea is now part of the common understanding. I don't know how many times I have been informed that Eskimos have many words for snow, and that this linguistic richness enables them to see and understand snow variations that would be invisible to the rest of us."[15]

Comments:

(1) Too bad for Anderson that both the Sapir-Whorf hypothesis and the idea that Eskimos have a spectacularly rich snow vocabulary have been decisively debunked.[16]

(2) Rich vocabularies make it easier to see things; poorer vocabularies make it harder—you have to combine words and have a good, creative imagination, and perhaps an independence of mind. But if there is no word in your language for "a light, nonsticking snow, blowing from the north," you can always, if you want to, just *say*, "a light, nonsticking snow, blowing from the north."[17] There is no basis, either in fact or in logic, for Anderson's claim that there are snow variations that are "invisible" to non-Eskimos.

But Anderson's enthusiasm for drawing large epistemological conclusions from anthropological research is not confined to the issue of Eskimo snow vocabulary. Rather, it is quite general: "[Anthropologists] created a new profession out of the study of otherness, and their findings have made it impossible for any literate person to believe that there is only one way of seeing the world."[18]

Comments:

(1) Note the vagueness of this claim. What is meant by a "way of seeing the world"? If it is to refer to all of the details and nuances of a person's beliefs about anything and everything, and to the numerous ways in which these connect with one another, then surely long before the advent of anthropology every literate person already knew not only that there is more than one way of seeing the world, but also that everyone sees the world, to some degree, differently. But if Anderson means, for example, that not all peoples see the most fundamental color contrast as that between light and dark;[19] or that some peoples see ants as being larger than elephants; or that some think misery is better than happiness—in short, if he means that there are not a substantial number of fundamental ways in which everyone sees the world the same way, the evidence indicates that he is wrong.

(2) There is a self-referential inconsistency problem: In the very context of claiming that all literate persons have been shown that there is not only one way of seeing the world, he claims that all literate people, on this one important issue, at least, see the world the same way.

(3) Note the descriptive-prescriptive issue here. Even if it is true that people see the world in different ways (descriptive thesis), it does not follow that all of these different ways are equally valid, correct, justified, true (prescriptive thesis).

(4) There is one more self-referential inconsistency problem (and this one is noted by Anderson): Anthropologists are supposed to have shown, by making accurate, objective observations and statements about other cultures, that no understanding or observation is ever objective, since all of our seeing is thoroughly conditioned by cultural factors. This leads to a dilemma: Either the anthropologists have accurately understood these alien cultures, in which case cultural barriers can be transcended, or they have not, in which case they have not uncovered the data they need to establish their conclusions.

Finally, let's turn to some of the political implications of Anderson's views. According to Anderson, a self-proclaimed postmodernist, a good example in politics of a constructivist and a postmodernist is Ronald Reagan, since he did not ever "develop any concept of truth."[20] Anderson goes on to remark: "People who agree with my assessment of him will no doubt feel that if this is what postmodernism looks like in politics, we are in big trouble. I think that concern is well founded."[21]

Comments:

(1) Anderson gets himself into the horrible mess of having to put Reagan on his side of the fence because he embraces a series of false dilemmas. Because he thinks (perhaps rightly) that we have no access to the truth of things in themselves, and cannot attain a God's-eye-view, absolute, certain objectivity, he seems to think that we must embrace, as if by default, an "anything-goes" relativism, which countenances even Reaganesque whoppers.[22] But surely this over-looks other alternatives. If we cannot have a truth of things in them-selves, then why not at least a phenomenological truth—a truth of things as they appear in experience—as opposed to settling for cyni-cally making things up for political gain, or passively accepting as true (or at least as true as anything can be) such lies when they are presented to us? And if we can never get things exactly right, or know that we have so gotten them, surely we can at least know that lots of things are wrong. There is an asymmetry here, and we can exploit it to reject Reagan's howlers. Moreover, even if perfect certainty is unat-tainable, why should the only alternative be anything-goes rela-tivism? Aren't some claims at least more evident than others, even if none are (allegedly) perfectly evident?

(2) How can a constructivist make sense of lying, especially if the lies are not discovered, and persuade a large majority? Are they then true? That Anderson's social constructivist view deprives him of the resources to deal with this problem adequately is made evident by these remarks of his:

> We can also see an increasing theatricality of politics, in which events are scripted and stage-managed for mass consumption, and in which individuals and groups struggle for starring roles (or at least bit parts) in the dramas of life. This theatricality is a natural—and inevitable—feature of our time. It is what happens when a lot of people begin to understand that reality is a social construction. The more enterprising among us see that there is much to be gained by constructing—and selling to the public—a certain reality, and so reality making becomes a new art and business. And a very big busi-ness, if you consider how much money is spent (and made) in fields such as advertising and public relations and political campaigning.[23]

Note that Anderson's claim that a lot of people now "understand"—they do not merely believe—that reality is a social construction, must, on its own terms, be understood as a social construction. Anderson himself calls it a "story."[24] He further lists as "some of the givens of life in the early postmodern era" that "[w]e regard the collective beliefs of individuals (rather than the mind of God or the laws of history) as the ultimate repository of social reality (what is true is defined by what we all believe). . . . Consequently, all sectors of society are deeply interested in finding out what people believe (public opinion) and modifying those beliefs (advertising, propaganda, brainwashing, public relations, and so forth)."[25] There you have it. In the postmodern world of social construction, which Anderson so vigorously advocates, if you can successfully brainwash people into believing that war is peace, freedom is slavery, and ignorance is strength, they thereby become true. We have arrived at Orwell's nightmare.

II. BENEDICT

Ruth Benedict makes this analogy:

> Just as there are great numbers of possible phonetic articulations, and the possibility of language depends on a selection and standardization of a few of these in order that speech communication may be possible at all, so the possibility of organized behavior of every sort, from the fashions of local dress and houses to the dicta of a people's ethics and religion, depends upon a similar selection among the possible behavior traits. In the field of recognized economic obligations or sex tabus this selection is as nonrational and subconscious a process as it is in the field of phonetics.[26]

Comments:

(1) Notice that this analysis, contrary to its framer's explicit intent, would not seem to warrant the conclusion that *every* socially approved habit is good. For if the justification of the selection and standardization of just a few of the possible phonetic articulations at the expense of all the others is that this is required "in order that speech communication may be possible at all," then, by analogy, such selection and standardization in the field of conduct would also be justified only insofar as it facilitates communal living (or something of that sort). This seems to introduce an objective standard pre-

cisely where Benedict wants to deny that any are available. For example, to pursue her analogy further, just as selections and standardizations in phonetics would be bad if they failed to make communication possible (or, presumably, if they made it unreasonably difficult—imagine a language in which every word is 212 syllables long, 211 of which are identical, with each word being differentiated from each other in its 93rd syllable), so would moral principles which resulted in everyone dying of thirst, or killing each other, or mistrusting each other. In other words, just as successful speech communication is an objective and universal good, the interference with which is bad, so are there objective and universal goods the frustrating of which by a moral code renders that moral code bad.

(2) With regard to selection and standardization, Benedict is certainly right to note that they are indispensable to both language and ethics, and that they are often arbitrary. But she fails to observe that even where they are arbitrary, they often are put to the service of an underlying principle that is not arbitrary. For example, I submit that it is often immoral to drive on the left side of the street in the United States, and that a complete explanation of why it is immoral would have to include a reference to the fact that there is an arbitrary rule in accordance with it is expected that everyone will drive on the right. This rule is arbitrary in the sense that there is nothing special about the right-hand side of the road; the rule could just as well be that everyone should drive on the left, as is done in England. But it is not arbitrary in the sense that we could just as well get by with no rule at all. Rather, we need a convention by means of which we can all observe the nonarbitrary underlying rule that everyone driving in the same direction should drive on the same side of the road. In this way we can avoid accidents, with their resulting injuries and deaths, and such avoidance is a nonarbitrary good.

(3) Not everything is like the issue of which side of the road we drive on. With some issues, there is only one way to do it that will work (e.g., it is necessary to have rules requiring truth-telling and forbidding murder—having rules forbidding truth-telling and requiring murder would not work as well), and with others, it does not matter how people do it (e.g., how people wear their hair). Benedict's account is objectionable, in part, because it fails to make these distinctions and seems to deny that there is any legitimate way in which they could be made. On her account, there seems to be no difference

in principle between those who violate their society's moral code by committing murders and those who wear clothes that are not currently in fashion.

(4) If the formation and revision of a moral code indeed tends to be "nonrational and subconscious," why should we acquiesce in this? Is it not high time that we approached these issues consciously and rationally? Indeed, in this regard there seems to be an important asymmetry between language and ethics, as Thomas Nagel points out: "We want to write and speak well within the language of our place and time, but there is no *right* language. By contrast, merely to act well by the standards of some morality is not enough: one would have to be very morally lazy to be unconcerned with the possibility that the prevailing morality of one's culture had something fundamentally wrong with it."[27]

III. BÉRUBÉ

Many social constructionists maintain either that it makes no sense to speak of "what really happened" in the past, or else, more modestly, that this "real" sequence of events is in any case inaccessible to us now. Such historical skepticism seems to entail the impossibility of retributive and compensatory justice, since these forms of justice, insofar as they are concerned with rectifying wrongs done in the past, cannot even get off the ground if we cannot achieve a reasonably accurate knowledge of what did, in fact, happen in the past. Moreover, such skepticism also threatens to undermine any claim that it is important to learn history and to discern lessons from it, for the obvious reason that we cannot possibly learn of or from that which is in principle utterly closed off to us.

But many social constructionists reject these apparent implications of their doctrine and argue that social constructionism, far from undermining historical research, memory, and education, in fact provides a renewed and uniquely strong support for the worthiness of these enterprises. Michael Bérubé, for example, makes such an argument in connection with the Holocaust:

[B]ecause few thinking persons believe that human history exists wholly independently of human understanding, few are willing to maintain that the details of the Holocaust's occurrence and meaning are fixed forever and beyond challenge. Surely, it is precisely because people know that "history" is constructed and maintained by humans that we know we must never forget the Holocaust. To believe that the Holocaust, or any historical occurrence, is immune to challenge by revisionists is to believe that there is no need to remind our fellow men and women that the Holocaust did indeed occur.[28]

Given the popularity of social constructionism in many academic fields today, coupled with the seriousness of the charge that this doctrine has disabling consequences concerning the very possibility of learning of and from history, I trust that the reader will agree that it is a matter of some importance whether arguments like Bérubé's can be sustained. I shall make four points in response to Bérubé's claims in arguing that they cannot.

(1) While there are at least two senses in which, indeed, human history does not exist wholly independently of human understanding, there is at least one sense in which it does (and, incidentally, in that sense more than just a few "thinking persons" believe it does). One sense in which human history is not independent of human understanding is that any accurate description and explanation of human events is unintelligible without the inclusion of some account of the role(s) that human understanding played in those events. For example, to use Bérubé's Holocaust example, the Holocaust included killing—an idea that makes essential reference to human intentions. Moreover, the killing was done for reasons, the understanding of which is important for understanding the historical event itself, and so on, and so forth. Another sense in which human history is not independent of human understanding emerges when we understand by the word "history" written or spoken accounts of past events (as opposed to understanding the word as referring to the past events themselves). For any account involves interpretation, emphasis, omission, the ordering of details, and so on, all of which would be largely determined by the historian's understanding of the meaning, importance, causes and effects (among other things) of the event in question.

But there is another sense in which history is independent of human understanding. If we intend by the term past events themselves, it is clear history has happened the way it has happened, and that none of our current efforts at understanding it can change this fact. If, for example, a full-scale nuclear war were to wipe out all but a dozen or so human beings, and it so happened that these dozen had no knowledge of the Holocaust, and all historical records were likewise obliterated, so that none of the descendents of these twelve would ever know that the Holocaust had taken place, it would still be true (though a truth that no one would know) that the Holocaust had taken place. More realistically, there are millions of trivial things that happen to individuals in private that they later misremember and report on falsely to others, which are then repeated by those others and believed by them to be true, which are not true, in spite of the fact that everyone who has beliefs about them believes them to be so. Moreover, there are countless things that have happened that no one knows about, much less understands. Such events are examples of historical events that "exist wholly independently of human understanding."

(2) It is far from "surely" the case that the reason we must never forget the Holocaust is that "people know that 'history' is constructed and maintained by humans." First of all, lots of people do not believe that history is constructed, and therefore do not know it. Second, as just discussed, history is decidedly not constructed if we mean by "history" past events, as opposed to later accounts of them. Third, there is no mystery as to why people would be well advised not to forget the Holocaust even on the assumption that history is not constructed. Millions of people were killed, an event of some significance and interest for its own sake, and one which we would wish not to repeat. Thus, we would want to remember what had happened so that we might learn lessons from this debacle pertaining to how to prevent it from happening again. All of this makes perfect sense on the assumption that the Holocaust, though carried out by humans, and thus a human construct in that sense, and though communicated to present-day people through narrative descriptions, and thus a human construct in that sense, was a real human event, which would remain precisely what it was even if everyone were to forget about it or remember it falsely, and thus is not a human construct in that sense.

(3) Bérubé sets up a straw man and a false dilemma when he speaks of the belief "that the Holocaust, or any historical occurrence, is immune to challenge by revisionists." No sensible person holds this belief, and Bérubé does not cite anyone who does. Obviously our choice is not limited to that between the idea that the Holocaust is a human construction, on the one hand, and that it is immune to chal-

lenge by revisionists, on the other. Here is a third possibility. The Holocaust was a real human event, rather than a construct (in the relevant sense, distinguished above). But we know of historical events by means of evidence of various kinds, and it is always possible that our knowledge of such events might be improved by encountering new evidence, or by correcting mistakes in our prior evaluations of old evidence, or by noticing previously neglected connections between existing pieces of evidence hitherto thought to be disparate, or by understanding existing evidence in the light of recently won insights, etc., etc.

(4) Bérubé's final inference is a complete non sequitur. Suppose, simply for the sake of argument, and otherwise contrary to all good sense, that the belief of Bérubé's phantom, that is, the belief that the Holocaust is immune to challenge by revisionists, were true. Would it follow that there would therefore be "no need to remind our fellow men and women that the Holocaust did indeed occur"? Obviously not. Knowledge that is so well established that it cannot possibly be shaken still might be simply forgotten. Thus, if it is worth remembering, and if the possibility of forgetting is a real one, then reminding is needed.

Bérubé also declares that "human knowledge, like all things human, is historically conditioned and socially constructed," and that "things have only the merit that we ascribe to them." He then goes on to comment as follows:

People like Dinesh D'Souza have claimed that [this] position undermines all possibility for ethical judgment; but my guess is that stamp collectors, spin doctors, stockbrokers, writers, and other working folk won't be surprised or upset by the suggestion that "merit" and "value" are human inventions.

In other words, antifoundationalism is not a relativism; it doesn't say that every interpretation, every historical epoch, every value system or every form of government is "equal." On the contrary, it says we don't have access to the kind of historical omniscience that would enable us to equalize or rank everything in the first place. We can look back and say we're grateful that we now conduct trials by jury instead of trials by ordeal, but we shouldn't conclude from this that our current beliefs are the culmination and fulfillment of all human history.[29]

Comments:

(1) If "all things human" are "socially constructed," then opposable thumbs are socially constructed.

(2) If nothing has intrinsic merit, having instead "only the merit that we ascribe to it," then Michael Jordan is not intrinsically a better basketball player than I am; rather we merely ascribe to him—and why, if not on the basis of the fact that he really *is* much better?—greater value as a basketball player. Similar remarks apply to the merits and values of happiness, friendship, intelligence, and health, both absolutely and in comparison to those of misery, war, stupidity, and sickness.

(3) It is true that "people like Dinesh D'Souza" reject views like Bérubé's, but then, so do people like Plato, Aristotle, Descartes, Kant, and Husserl, together with such contemporary leftists as Noam Chomsky, Barbara Ehrenreich, and Michael Albert. Bérubé's rhetorical intent in characterizing his opposition in terms of "people like Dinesh D'Souza" is as transparent as it is unfair.

(4) Bérubé's "guess" about "stamp collectors . . . and other working folk" is seriously overstated. The debate over the objectivity or subjectivity of value judgments is ancient, and is one in which each side has throughout history attracted many adherents, both among philosophers and among the various kinds of "working folk" that Bérubé mentions. Bérubé is right to claim that few will be surprised by the suggestion that merit and value (or "merit" and "value," as he would have it) are human inventions; but he is wrong to think that there are not quite a few who are upset by it (at least in the sense that they strongly disagree with it).

(5) Bérubé's claim that "antifoundationalism is not a relativism" depends upon a highly idiosyncratic definition of "relativism," like that of Rorty.[30]

(6) In claiming that his position does not "say that every interpretation, every historical epoch, every value system or every form of government is 'equal,'" Bérubé gives as his reason that "we don't have access to the kind of historical omniscience that would enable us to equalize or rank everything in the first place." But why do we need *omniscience*, whether historical or of any other kind, to know that an interpretation of Orwell's *1984* as, among other things, a political allegory is superior to one that sees it *exclusively* as an egg-salad recipe; or that a value system that declares knowledge to be better than ignorance is superior to one which reverses these valuations; or that the form of

government found in contemporary Sweden is superior to that found in Nazi Germany? This looks like a false dilemma of the "all or nothing" variety: Either we have all knowledge (omniscience) or we have nothing and must refrain from ranking things. (In fairness to Bérubé, his claim is that we cannot rank *everything*, and in this claim he is surely right; as he also is in his assertion that to do so we would need omniscience. But these points are of little interest, since no one could be found who would claim otherwise, and thus Bérubé appears to be attacking a straw man. Even those relativists who do attempt, in a sense, to equalize everything do so not on the basis of a claim to omniscience, but precisely on the opposite basis—that we know nothing, or at least nothing about "other" cultures. If this is the position that Bérubé means to attack here he is, therefore, begging the question.)

(7) Bérubé also attacks a straw man, or, at the very least, makes an irrelevant point when he says, in connection with his point about trials by jury and by ordeal, that "we shouldn't conclude from this that our current beliefs are the culmination and fulfillment of all human history." Can Bérubé point to anyone who would so conclude, or who, for any reason, actually does believe that our current beliefs are the culmination and fulfillment of all human history? He does not cite any, not even "people like Dinesh D'Souza." All one can say with confidence about this remark is that it is irrelevant to the issues at hand. Why, then, has Bérubé included it? Perhaps he has confused the claim that some beliefs are objectively true and others objectively false, or that some things are intrinsically better than others, with the quite different claim that all, or even most, of our current beliefs are objectively true, or that all (or most) of our value judgments accurately reflect the intrinsic merits of things. But it is quite possible to endorse the former claim while rejecting the latter, a possibility that Bérubé does not discuss. Indeed, the impression one gets from his consideration of these issues is that there are just two possibilities (leaving aside the idiosyncratic version of relativism that he quickly dismisses): either one is an arrogant jerk who believes that he—such a jerk would surely have to be male—is omniscient and competent to recognize infallibly the intrinsic value of anything and everything, or else one is more modest and more realistic, and (therefore?) realizes that "merit" and "value" are human inventions. Ignored is the possibility of believing that there are intrinsic values that one fails to recognize, or evaluates erroneously.[31]

IV. CALHOUN

According to Laurie Calhoun, we never believe anything on the basis of rational considerations of arguments. Rather, we are seduced, by non-rational means, into believing what we are predisposed to believe.[32] On her view, there are no facts. When I had occasion to ask her whether or not it was a fact that giraffes are taller than ants, she replied that it was not a fact, but rather an article of religious faith in our culture.[33]

Here are some objections:

(1) This position faces the self-referential inconsistency/arbitrary/no bite trilemma. If Calhoun holds her position to be true, a fact, and demonstrable by rational considerations, then she contradicts herself. If she modifies her claim that there are no facts so as to allow that this, alone, indeed is a fact, then the contradiction is perhaps removed, but only at the cost of arbitrariness and implausibility. Is this difficult and counterintuitive epistemological claim a fact, but not that giraffes are taller than ants, or that Topeka is the capital of Kansas? This is especially hard to swallow when one realizes that, even under this modification of Calhoun's position, it would have to be read as holding that none of her supporting reasons are themselves true or factual. Finally, if she acknowledges that her strange doctrine is not true or factual, and is not one which a person can be led to believe on the basis of a rational consideration of arguments, but is rather something which she has been seduced, based upon her peculiar predispositions, into believing, why should we take it seriously?

(2) Related to the second item of the above trilemma, Calhoun's position faces the *obscurum per obscurius* objection. What reasons could Calhoun possibly have in support of her contention that are not less certain than the ones she would overturn?

(3) It is ridiculous to claim that "giraffes are taller than ants" is a religious belief of our culture. Is there a culture that denies it or holds any beliefs inconsistent with it? Have you ever heard any other person even remark on the relative heights of giraffes and ants? What kind of a religious belief is it that no one disagrees with and no one articulates?

(4) The claim that no one is ever persuaded by a rational argument to believe something that he or she was not already predisposed to believe is a disguised tautology. When I inquired of Calhoun as to

what, in principle, would count as a counterexample to this claim, she responded that nothing would, since, whenever someone was persuaded, it would always be the case that the person in question would have been persuaded to believe something that he or she was predisposed to believe.[34] But I can explain what would count as a counterexample to my claim that giraffes are taller than ants, even though I am confident that all giraffes are, indeed, taller than ants.

Leaving these criticisms aside for the time being, let's ask what reasons Calhoun offers in support of her views. Here is an example of her argumentation:

> In my view, belief is *essentially* religious, because no argument could ever, in principle, compel any belief. . . . How do I know this? Because . . . "Non-things have no properties. Non-things have no price. You cannot go shopping for non-things. Who would pay something for nothing?" In other words, no one can claim to have come to believe a thesis because of its utility, because only existent *things* have properties, so until one first believes in some *thing*, one cannot have any interest in determining its properties, such as its utility or its putative fruitfulness. . . . And those who really think that arguments "brought them" . . . to belief must be self-deceived, as my own "argument" reveals.[35]

Comments:

(1) If Calhoun is correct, then no one could possibly be compelled to accept her conclusion on the basis of her argument.

(2) But the argument is a non sequitur. Even if we accept the claim that a thesis or proposition must first "exist," whatever that might mean in this context, before it can have epistemic properties, it hardly follows that the only manner in which it can be brought into existence is by belief. Surely it is enough merely to entertain a thesis in order for it to become possible, in principle, for its epistemic properties to emerge. Suppose I want to buy a carton of orange juice. I have a favorite brand, and plenty of room in my refrigerator, so, let us say, I am only concerned about price. The orange juice comes in different sizes, and I choose one based upon my calculation of the price per ounce. My shopping companion points out that I have made a mathematical error: another size is, in fact, cheaper by the ounce. I recheck my math and discover that my companion is right. I choose the other size. Now, perhaps I had to *consider* the idea that I might

be better off buying the other-sized juice in order to bother about the argument that it is in fact the cheaper one, but I obviously did not have first to *believe* that it is cheaper before the mathematical argument could persuade me that it was.

Similar logical problems emerge when we turn to Calhoun's answer to the self-referential inconsistency problem:

> According to perspectivism, that perspectivism is true is only one possible perspective or interpretation among an infinity of others. But a perspectivist can easily sanction some world version according to which paradox is innocuous or irrelevant to judgments about what sorts of views are reasonable to accept. The perspectivist is not even constrained by the ordinary (commonsense) minimal rational constraints of consistency and nonhypocrisy. . . . Perspectivism is divine.[36]

This is great, but why stop there? Why not say both that all beliefs are equally valid perspectives and that all others but your own are wrong? When it is pointed out that this is inconsistent, just point out that consistency is not part of your perspective, and you are home free!

On the other hand, she does state that "the fundamental, indeed the only, constraint on philosophical theories is inconsistency."[37] Comments: (1) If so, then she is not entitled to the way out, just discussed, of the self-referential inconsistency problem. (2) What is the status of this claim? Is it just her perspective that holds that inconsistency is the only constraint on philosophical theories, or is this a non-perspectival truth? (3) Either way, it is highly implausible. Why are not plausibility, consistency with other relevant facts, explanatory power, parsimony, etc., also constraints?

But there is worse to follow. Calhoun writes: "[A]ny reader who finds my story implausible or riddled with contradiction or oblivious of certain indismissible data, may be justified in rejecting my theory on those grounds."[38] Comments: (1) Done. (2) Look what happens when we juxtapose these last three Calhoun quotations with one another. First she denies that one's philosophical theory need be consistent. Then she asserts that it must be, but denies that it must face any other constraints. Now we are informed of several other constraints. Calhoun is inconsistent on the subject of consistency.

Furthermore, Calhoun claims that "no one can fail to be 'rational,' when 'rationality' is appropriately relativized to the individual's world,"[39] adding that "relative to his own private world, the individual is the absolute, so his belief is necessarily veridical."[40] It follows that it is not irrational to deny these claims in their entirety. After all, I do believe them to be false, and my belief "is necessarily veridical."

Finally, let us turn to the political implications of Calhoun's views:

> "Vulgar relativism" asserts both that normative theories are relative to communities (the limiting case being a society of one) and that it is wrong to judge "outsiders," that is, those who are not members of the relevant community, by the standards of theories which they do not affirm. Under one interpretation, this thesis is self-contradictory, since it assumes an absolute value of tolerance, while simultaneously denying absolutism. A more charitable manner in which to interpret this position is as asserting that it is a linguistic impropriety to apply the standards of one community to outsiders, since it constitutes a sort of category mistake. If normative constructs are relative to a given community, then they can only be applied with linguistic propriety to members of that community. Outsiders are not "persons," in the relevant sense, since they are not located within the insider's sphere of morality. To illustrate the point in a simple case, judging outsiders would be to commit the same sort of mistake which one commits in morally reprimanding a dog for having harmed a person. . . . But outsiders, such as dogs, may be treated in any manner in which one wishes (in the absence of other proscriptive beliefs to the contrary). They may be destroyed if they cause harm to the relevant community, in just the manner in which noxious weeds may be extirpated from a garden.[41]

Comments:

(1) This does not look good for tolerance. An outsider, indeed a "nonperson," is simply anyone who does not accept the same standards that I accept.[42] Should such an entity harm me, I am entitled to destroy it—that is, someone who does not accept the same standards that I accept—as if it were a noxious weed.

(2) It is preposterous to claim that an entity must accept the same standards that I accept in order to be entitled to decent treatment from me. Dogs, and for that matter, babies, cannot even understand the standards that I accept. It hardly follows that I am entitled, say, to inflict upon them gratuitous pain.

(3) The reason that it is inappropriate to reprimand a dog morally

is that it cannot understand me. Surely it is possible to engage in meaningful moral discussion, including the issuing and receiving (with understanding) of moral reprimands, with at least some of those who do not accept the same standards that I accept. I can, for example, explain why I accept those standards and give reasons why they should too. They, in turn, might well reject my arguments and might supply reasons that I would recognize as cogent for doing so, in which case I might retract my moral criticism. It is not the same thing as dealing with dogs.

(4) What is the status of Calhoun's reasoning here? Notice that in the passage quoted above she engages in reasoning, drawing conclusions from premises, and marking these moves with such terms as "since" and "then." Are her inferences valid only relative to her perspective, or are they supposed to be valid for everyone? If the former, then why should we care, especially as this would, apparently, mark us as nonpersons fit for slaughter? But if the latter, how is this self-consistent? What is to be said for perspectives that would deny these inferences? Are they simply wrong?[43]

V. CAMPBELL

Richard Campbell remarks that "so long as we hanker after timeless truth we are doomed to scepticism, because *that* sort of truth is not attainable by historically relative mortals."[44] The phrase "so long as" suggests the irrelevance of time here—no matter how far into the future we go, we will always be doomed to skepticism if we seek timeless truths. And to say that such truth is "not attainable," without qualifying it by adding "yet," or "for now," or something of that sort, again is to suggest that the author of this statement regards his claim as one which transcends temporality and historicity. But this contradicts the main thrust of the claim—that temporality and historicity cannot be transcended. The claim contradicts itself.

VI. FISH

Stanley Fish claims that "the mechanisms of persuasion, like everything else, are context-specific."[45] Is this dictum itself context-specific? Note also the reductionism—everything is the same in this regard. There is, furthermore, an *obscurum per obscurius* problem. Is the velocity of light context-specific? Is 2 + 2 = 4 context-specific? Is the law of gravity context-specific? The fact that giraffes are taller than ants? The value-judgment that happiness is better than misery?

In any case, it is instructive to follow Fish's reasoning as he applies his version of postmodernism to the task of understanding the events of September 11, 2001:

> The basis for condemning what was done on September 11 is not some abstract vocabulary of justice, truth, and virtue . . . but the historical reality of the way of life, our way of life, that was the target of a massive assault.
>
> At times like these, all nations fall back on, and are right to fall back on, the record of aspiration and accomplishment that makes up their citizens' understanding of what they live by and live for. That understanding is sufficient, and far from undermining its sufficiency, postmodern thought underwrites it by sending us back to the justificatory grounds we rely on in ordinary life after having turned us away from the illusory justification of universal absolutes . . . [46]

It is unclear whether Fish's preferred alternative to such "universal attributes" as "justice, truth, and virtue" is a straightforward ethnocentrism or rather an incoherent universal relativism. The former alternative is suggested by his Rortian appeal to "our way of life." But the latter is implied by his claim that "*all* nations . . . are right to fall back on the record of aspiration and accomplishment that makes up their citizens' understanding of what they live by and live for."

Any attempt to turn away from what is really true, just, virtuous, etc., in favor of an ethnocentric claim that our convictions are adequately founded in "our way of life" or "our understanding of what we live for" faces *Euthyphro* objections. One would think that "our way of life" would be defensible, and worth holding onto and defending, only to the extent that it is true, just, and virtuous. But if one simply *defines* truth, justice, and virtue in terms of our way of life, it becomes impossible then to ask whether or not our way of life really *is* true, just, and virtuous. Indeed, it renders the claim that our way of life is true, just, and virtuous trivially true—a miserable tautology.

Joshua Cohen, commenting on this very passage of Fish's, makes a similar objection: "[N]early 20 years ago, I recall Alasdair MacIntyre saying to Richard Rorty: 'In your view, the worst thing someone can say about the Soviet Union is that it is un-American.' With a shrug of his shoulders, Rorty replied: 'What could be worse?' Fish is on Rorty's side."[47] In Fish's reply to Cohen he concedes that he would, indeed, be on Rorty's side. He adds the following explanation: "I would be hearing in his typically laconic and deadpan throwaway line a thicker statement and a serious question. The statement would be a rehearsal of the interlocking values, investments, and social commitments that are the content of the institutions—legal, political, educational, financial—we implicitly refer to when we say 'America.' The serious question would be, 'What could be worse than a state and an ideology opposed in every way to everything we cherish and believe in?'"[48]

Fish recognizes that this leaves him vulnerable to *Euthyphro*-type objections, and he attempts to address them. But his response creates new difficulties: "Someone like Cohen might respond by accusing Rorty (and me) of falling in with the Eichmann position ('I was just part of the system and I went along with its agenda') and leaving himself with no basis for criticizing anything America does. But Rorty embraces America because its history and practices (not every one of them, but most of them) display the values to which he is committed. . . . [I]f some piece of American practice were in his view subversive of [these values] he would have no trouble criticizing it."[49] But at this point Fish seems to be going in circles (and dragging poor Rorty along with him). First we are told that we should give up on referring to abstractions like justice, truth, and virtue and should instead be content to justify our beliefs and practices simply by appealing to our way of life. But now, in order to avoid "the Eichmann position," Fish concedes that we owe no allegiance to "our way of life" if it fails to conform to certain values. Which is it: Should we embrace certain beliefs and values because they are American—they constitute our history and practices—or rather should we embrace America's history and practices because (and only insofar as) they embody certain beliefs and values? It may be that Rorty is more consistent on this issue. Recall that he supports a position which "makes it impossible to ask the question 'Is ours a moral society?'"[50]

Fish might reply by saying that "Americanism" (and remember, he's on record as agreeing with Rorty that to call something "un-

American" is to say the worst thing that could possibly be said about it) has a core or essence to which one might appeal in order to judge particular American practices "un-American," and therefore wrong. It seems unlikely that he would do so, since postmodernists tend not to like the word "essence," but let's put that aside. Such a move would still leave us with the *Euthyphro*/Eichmann problem, but at a more abstract level. We would still have to say either that this essence or core is true and just by definition, no matter what its content (e.g., torture, genocide, slavery) might happen to be, or else that this content must meet certain standards in order to pass muster, in which case the game is up—we aren't really trying to justify anything just by pointing out that it is American.

Moreover, such a move underscores another problem with Fish's position. "America" is hardly monolithic. It contains liberals and fundamentalists, patriots and cosmopolitans, pacifists and warmongers, feminists and misogynists, etc., etc. So what is "our way of life"? What is our understanding of what we "live by and live for"? In short, how is this appeal to Americanism any less abstract and contentious than is an appeal to truth, justice, and virtue?

In rejecting appeals to objective truth and value, Fish (like Rorty) is always quick to emphasize that we are finite beings, conditioned by our contingencies. "We must start from where we are" is a common refrain. But why should we pick just one of these contingencies, the fact that we are Americans, and confer on it alone the power to serve as the (dare I say it?) foundation of our beliefs and values? I am an American, but I am many other things as well. I am a man, a human being, a sentient being, a philosopher, a teacher, and a father. I am one who has lived at a particular time and in particular places; I have had certain experiences and entertained certain thoughts; I've reached a particular age; I might be described as belonging to a certain race and to a certain socioeconomic class, etc., etc. So why, when trying to figure out what to think about the events of September 11 (or anything else for that matter) should I place such special, indeed such exclusive, emphasis on the fact that I'm an American? Why can't I make use of insights gleaned through some other contingencies of mine (things I've learned from being, for example, a father, a sentient being, and a philosopher) in criticizing values and beliefs that would otherwise be foisted on me by another of my contingencies (being an American)? And why can't I exploit some of the resources I share with non-Americans (e.g., the capacity to feel pain, the ability to take in information by using my senses, and the ability to evaluate claims by consulting principles of consistency, parsimony, clarity, and plausibility) in order to criticize certain "American" beliefs and practices? Why is socialization at a national level everything, and socialization at all other levels, in concert with biology and reason, nothing?

In any case, Fish cannot be correct in his claim that "our way of life" provides the "basis" for condemning the massacre of innocents on September 11, 2001, for if that were the case, then, as Cohen points out,

> Only Americans—or only admirers of our way of life—would be in a position to condemn the attack, or get "the basis" of the condemnation right. But the attack was, of course, widely condemned by people who neither share in our way of life nor admire our "record of aspiration and accomplishment." For example, in a *fatwa* issued in early October, Sheik Qaradawi—an advisor to the Muslim Brotherhood and sharp critic of U.S. policy in Israel—condemned the attack for taking "the lives of innocents." That strikes me as a very compelling "basis" for condemning what happened on September 11: that it was an *intentional slaughter of innocents*. Whatever your affections for America, and whether you are a traditionalist or hedonist, a Muslim or Jew or Christian or Hindu or Buddhist or secular Kantian, you cannot reasonably condone the intentional slaughter of innocents. So the condemnation need not be founded on the American way of life, democracy, individualism, or open societies and pluralism. Rather, and simply, it follows from an elementary and widely accepted abstract principle of human conduct.[51]

One might add that adherence to the abstract principle that it is wrong to slaughter innocent people gives an American a straightforward and reliable basis to condemn American foreign policy. Adherence to the idea that nothing can be worse than to be "un-American" (or that we should strive to make it impossible to ask whether ours is an immoral society) does not.[52]

VII. FitzGerald

Frances FitzGerald refers to "the lingering hope that there is, somewhere out there, an objective truth" and immediately goes on to comment: "The hope is, of course, foolish. All of us children of the twentieth century know, or should know, that there are no absolutes in human affairs, and thus there can be no such thing as perfect objectivity."[53]

Comments:

(1) The desperate search to find, somewhere out there, some objective truths, might yield the following as candidates: "Giraffes are taller than ants." "Some human beings can make sounds come out of an oboe." "There is a city in Illinois called 'Chicago.'" "It is possible for a round thing to be red, but it is not necessary that it be red." "There are no living human beings who weigh more than a billion pounds." If these, and trillions more statements like them, are not objective truths, then what, in principle (even if, in fact, none exist), would one look like. What definition of "objective truth" are we using here?

(2) The statement that there are no objective truths (and that there are none *of course*, for that matter) must, if inconsistency is to be avoided, not be construed as itself objectively true. But what is its status, then?

(3) What are "absolutes," and how does the (alleged) fact that there are none in human affairs—not even "absolutely no man has ever been married simultaneously to a clarinet, a raisin, and twenty-seven mandrill baboons," and billions of others of this sort?—entail that there can be no such thing as perfect objectivity?

(4) What is "perfect objectivity," how does it differ from plain old "objectivity," and why, above all, does the alleged nonexistence of the former entail the nonexistence of the latter? None of this is explained.

VIII. Giroux

Henry Giroux urges us to "reject as totalitarian and terroristic" "[g]eneral abstractions that deny the specificity and particularity of everyday life, that generalize out of existence the particular and the local, that smother difference under the banner of universalizing categories."[54]

Comments:

(1) Note that this sentence contradicts itself. It implicitly exemplifies the very thing it explicitly condemns. That is, its sweeping rejection of all general abstractions that deny specificity and particularity is itself a general abstraction that denies specificity and particularity. For Giroux does not reject some abstractions that deny specificity and particularity while embracing others, depending upon the specifics and particulars of the different specificity and particularity-denying general abstractions in question, or upon the particular and specific ways in which, or circumstances in which, they are used. Accordingly, Giroux's context-insensitive and difference-denying wielding of universalizing categories must, on its own terms, be rejected as totalitarian and terroristic.

(2) Sometimes particulars are relevant, but often they are not. 2 + 2 *never* = 172,396.7; Green is *always* a color; *All* human beings die, etc. These truths do not vary with circumstances.

(3) These are not cheap, showy, picky logical points, but vital existential ones. The educational consequences of Giroux's claim are disastrous. I am to disavow abstract, general claims, such as that hot things can burn me, or even that stoves are hot, and instead must investigate whether this, and this, and this particular stove will burn me? This is likely to be painful—and so on with the billions and billions of other bits of general and abstract knowledge that I, Giroux, and everyone else uses to get through life. We are not totalitarians or terrorists for doing so.

(4) That the world's evils are best attributed to foundationalism, enlightenment thought, science, and abstract reasoning, rather than to, say, greed, cruelty, and ignorance, though fashionable, might justly be regarded as crackpot.

IX. HAWKESWORTH

Mary E. Hawkesworth claims that

> [o]bjectivity . . . promises to free us from distortion, bias, and error in intellectual inquiry and from arbitrariness, self-interest, and caprice in ethical, legal, and administrative decisions. Feminist critiques of objectivity have been triggered by breach of promise. Fem-

inist scholars have argued that observations, beliefs, theories, methods of inquiry, and institutional practices routinely labeled "objective" fall short of the norm. A significant proportion of feminist scholarship involves detailed refutations of erroneous claims about women produced in conformity with prevailing disciplinary standards of objectivity. The pervasiveness of the mistakes about the nature of women and their roles in history and society, as well as the imperviousness of mistaken views to refutation, have led some feminist scholars to examine the nature of objectivity *per se*.[55]

Comments:

(1) I fear there may be a straw man fallacy here. Who has ever, in the name of objectivity or anything else for that matter, "promised to free us from distortion, bias, and error in intellectual inquiry," etc.?

(2) There is here a confusion of the issue of the status of a claim—is it an attempt to state how things really are, quite apart from what people may believe about it?—with the quite different issue of one's degree of confidence that the claim is indeed true (that is, if it is an attempt to state how things really are, how certain are we that the attempt is successful?). Remember that defenders of objectivity can be, and typically, as in the case of scientists are, fallibilists. Thus, objectivity does not make the promises that Hawkesworth claims it makes. There has been no breach of promise.

(3) It is true that many defenders of objectivity think there are methods that are useful in moving us away from distortion, bias, and error, but no one thinks that they are even close to infallible or even foolproof. And is not the record of science one of considerable achievement in this regard? Granted, many biased, distorted, and erroneous claims have been made on the basis of science, but is not our record on this score better with science than it would have been without it, especially if we focus on the entirety of scientific activity, and not merely its legacy of error?

(4) While it is undoubtedly true that "erroneous claims about women produced in conformity with prevailing disciplinary standards of objectivity" have been "pervasive," it hardly follows that this is due to some problem with the nature of objectivity. Three other plausible possibilities are: (a) that the entire culture is so saturated with sexism that even the use of very good "disciplinary standards of objectivity" are insufficient, by themselves, to overcome them; (b) that such standards are not consistently adhered to, again, no doubt

in part because of pervasive sexism; and (c) that these disciplinary standards of objectivity might not be very good standards—that is, they might not be standards that are well-suited to the achievement of objectivity. For example, suppose that a scientist does a study exclusively of male subjects, and then generalizes the results to all of humanity. Does this show that there is something wrong with objectivity per se, or does it show, rather, either that this scientist failed to follow "disciplinary standards of objectivity," or, if he did, that those standards themselves are, objectively speaking, lousy?

(5) Are those areas of life, such as science, in which some standards of objectivity are at least sometimes aimed at, more, or rather less, infected with sexism and other similarly objectionable beliefs? Are you more likely to encounter sexism in a scientific study (or scientific laboratory, for that matter) than you are at the local tavern, public park, or grocery store? If not, this further suggests that the problem may not lie primarily with science or with objectivity as such, but rather with somewhat intractable beliefs and ways of life which antedate science, and against which it is making (admittedly slow and meager) inroads.

(6) When Hawkesworth calls scientific claims about women "erroneous," surely this claim itself aims at objectivity, and achieves it.

X. HUBBARD

Ruth Hubbard asserts that

> facts aren't just out there. Every fact has a factor, a maker. . . .
> One thing is clear: making facts is a social enterprise. Individuals cannot just go off by themselves and come up with their own brand of facts. When people do that and the rest of us do not agree to accept or share the facts they offer us as descriptions of the world, they are considered schizophrenic, crazy. If we do agree, either because their facts sufficiently resemble ours or because they have the power to force us to accept their facts as real or true—to make us see the emperor's new clothes—then the new facts become part of our shared reality and their making, part of the fact-making enterprise.[56]

Comments:

(1) The claim that every fact has a maker is either trivially true or else false. If we define fact in such a way that something cannot be

a fact until someone thinks it, or formulates it in words, then it is trivially true that every fact has a maker—a person who thinks or formulates the fact in question. But if one defines a fact as my dictionary does, namely, as "[s]omething having existence supported by evidence; an actuality,"[57] then the statement can only be true if the idealistic thesis that actualities depend upon minds for their existence is true. Hubbard's claim would seem, on this construal, to yield the implausible result that it was not a fact that the Earth was round until someone thought so (and, to anticipate what she goes on to say, persuaded others to agree).

(2) Perhaps it is reductionistic, at least in some instances, to say that facts are "found." But is it not equally reductionistic to say that they are "made"? If I measure my son's height, and then measure it again three months later, finding that he has grown two inches, is this fact something I simply *make*?

(3) What is meant by the locution *"brand* of facts"? Perhaps I cannot come up with my own "brand of facts," whatever that might mean, but this does not establish that the determining of facts is always "a social enterprise," though it undoubtedly often is. Can I not, by making the appropriate measurements, determine all by myself the facts concerning my son's growth over a period of time—and a million other things of this sort as well?

(4) When "the rest of us" do not agree with the fact-claims of others, it is far from true that we always consider them "schizophrenic, crazy." Frequently we consider them simply to be mistaken. (I might note, parenthetically, that in another essay appearing in the same collection containing Hubbard's piece, Kenneth J. Gergen defends an orientation toward knowledge that "would view knowledge claims as discursive commitments, fundamentally unconstrained by observation."[58] I will concede to Hubbard that we do tend to call "crazy" people whose knowledge claims are "fundamentally unconstrained by observation.")

(5) Note the cynical and impoverished view of discussion, argumentation, and persuasion that Hubbard presents. On her account, we agree with others only when either (a) what they are saying is close to what we already believe, or (b) when they "have the power to force us" to agree (and even then Hubbard implies, through her "emperor's new clothes" reference, that the other's views must be wrong). Why cannot I be persuaded of views quite dissimilar to my

present ones by means of rational arguments?

(6) Note the self-referential inconsistency problem—if these really are the only alternatives in the context of argumentation, then we should only accept what Hubbard is saying if we already (almost) believe it, or else if she "has the power to force us" to accept what would have to be, on her own analysis, "emperor's new clothes"-style snake oil.

XI. McEvilley

Thomas McEvilley informs us that "all judgments, in fact, are relative (to claim otherwise is to claim divine revelation)."[59]

Comments:

(1) The idea that the denial that all judgments are relative entails a claim to divine revelation is just a non sequitur. Perhaps McEvilley means that such a denial entails a claim to certainty, and that this latter claim could only be justified by an appeal to divine revelation. But I claim that I know certainly that if A is taller than B, and B is taller than C, then A must be taller than C, and I cannot see what divine revelation, or even the existence of any divinity, has to do with it.

(2) In any case, the denial that all judgments are relative entails merely that some are non-relative, not that any are certain. Objectivity and certainty are not the same thing, and fallibilism is not relativism.

(3) If all judgments are relative—indeed, if they are so *in fact*— then so is this judgment itself relative. Presumably, then, the way is left clear for it to be the case that, at least in some context, culture, or contingency, not all judgments are relative.

XII. Pickard

According to Dean Pickard,

[t]o speak generally of necessity and contingency, of absolute and relative, is to already have bought into dichotomous thinking that has gone beyond the bounds of its contextual utility. What is the context of such claims and divisions? We cannot achieve an absolute orientation to everything else. We create the orientation.

Accepting rules of reason and the notion of universality is an orientation that attempts to step outside itself and proclaim itself "objective." But we can never outrun our orientation, our perspective, and can never achieve the objectivity of a view from everywhere (which is nowhere). . . . To universalize any rule is to ignore the context of particularity that gives rise to the desire to universalize in the first place. There is in fact always already a context of meaning in which we are operating. That context is inescapable if we are to be discussing anything at all. It is this obvious fact that is overlooked in the rush toward the fixity of universals.[60]

Comments:

(1) The first sentence quoted, in which Pickard sweepingly condemns speaking generally of necessity and contingency, of absolute and relative, is itself an excellent example of speaking generally of necessity and contingency, of absolute and relative. The same holds for most of his other statements.

(2) Pickard's repeated claim that everything is contextual and perspectival and rooted in an orientation that "we create" is itself contextual, perspectival, and rooted in an orientation that we create, or else it is not. If the latter (which seems to be Pickard's intent), he contradicts himself. If the former, then, for all Pickard knows, there may well be many contexts in which, and perspectives from which, claims of objectivity, universal reason and the like make perfect sense, are socially useful, and are in every respect appropriate and faultless.

(3) For someone who is so ardent in defending contextualism and attacking claims to universal validity, Pickard makes a rather large number of grand claims which seem rather incompatible with such a stance. Note that he tells us what "we can never do" (What?—not in *any* context, or from *any* perspective? Do you mean that this is a universal truth, transcending all such particularities?), tells us that all attempts "to universalize any rule" commit the same mistake (so there are no contextual differences here, either), that "there is in fact"—and remember that it is an "obvious fact"—"always already a context of meaning in which we are operating" (Oh, to be as cocksure about these difficult epistemological issues as are these scrupulous thinkers, with their skepticism regarding even the most modest claims to know a few noncontextual truths!).

Pickard further informs us that "[t]he law of non-contradiction is itself part of a way of seeing things. Not something prior to and governing of that seeing. A way of seeing things is what is primary."[61] My response: Let's consider Pickard's own "way of seeing things," as articulated here. If it is not governed by the law of contradiction, then it does not rule out the following: "The law of non-contradiction is *not* itself part of a way of seeing things. It is, rather, something prior to and governing of that seeing. A way of seeming is *not* what is primary." (Should Pickard claim that this is not an implication of his views, my reply would be that, in the absence of the law of non-contradiction, that is perfectly consistent with its *being* such an implication.) Can anyone make sense of such a conjunction of contradictory assertions? So in what sense does the law of non-contradiction not govern, and in what sense is it a dispensable option, as Pickard's use of the indefinite article—part of *a way* of seeing things—suggests it is?

Pickard holds predictably similar views on truth: "From a postmodern perspective, [which Pickard is defending,] . . . [t]he notion of truth has been jettisoned altogether, relative or absolute. The notion of a 'truth' itself has traditionally implied closure. If one has the truth, any further movement could only be a deviation from it."[62] So we must avoid being enclosed in such "truths" as that elephants are bigger than ants, that racism is wrong, or that if A is greater than B, and B is greater than C, therefore, A is greater than C.

XIII. Sarchett

According to Barry W. Sarchett, "[o]ne of the primary lessons of poststructuralism is to be *extremely* wary of speaking for others—something only those possessed of Truth or Universal Reason can do. So I don't pretend to be speaking for a we of any kind here."[63] But to be consistent here, Sarchett would have to admit that he cannot be speaking for others even in claiming that "one of the primary lessons of poststructuralism is to be extremely wary of speaking for others." If Sarchett were a fallibilist—if his meaning, that is, were simply that he is acknowledging that he is a fallible human being who might be mistaken in his attribution of views to others—then his caveat, though understandable, would seem excessive. What is wrong with making claims about what other people believe, or about what is true, so long as it is understood that such claims might be erroneous, and thus should not be uncritically accepted without scrutiny of the relevant evidence and arguments concerning them? Indeed, why not offer tentative, provisional, fallible, probabilistic statements about what is true, not only for oneself, but generally (and thus for others), being ready to listen to their disagreements and their reasons for doing so, and being ready to revise one's convictions in the light of those reasons? But if Sarchett's (unwitting) claim is that there is some generally true insight of poststructuralism which validly implies (for everyone) that they should be wary of speaking for others, then his position is incoherent. Similarly, what is the status of Sarchett's claim that "only those possessed of Truth or Universal Reason" can speak for others? This sounds like a sweeping claim about everybody, a statement, intended to have general validity, which is justified by the (universally valid) insights of poststructuralism. Indeed, it appears that here Sarchett speaks for others—that it is wrong for anyone to speak for others unless they have Absolute Truth on their side. But why does Sarchett get to lay down this law? Does he possess some sort of Absolute Truth concerning these matters? On the other hand, if this is just another confession of Sarchett's private obsessions, why should we not lose interest? For communication to get off the ground at all, at least something you are saying has to have some claim to general validity, and not just be true for you. ("Look, there's a beautiful blue jay on that branch! Wait, you don't understand. It is not really, objectively there, accessible equally to you, me, and any other competent observer. It is just there for me." Why bother to look?)

Notice also that, while Sarchett's attempt to be modest and tolerant is commendable, there is an ambiguity in the phrase "I am only speaking for myself." It could mean either "there is an objective truth, but I am only presenting what the objective truth appears to me to be," or "there is no objective truth, and thus all that is left is my individual perspective." The former interpretation presents a commonplace insight, not something new from poststructuralism, and is quite consistent with the idea of objectivity (that stuff about "Truth"—with a capital "T"—and Universal Reason is a red herring about claims to certainty). But the latter alternative is incoherent.

Let's now turn to one of the other primary lessons of poststructuralism, according to Sarchett: "From a Saussurian viewpoint 'tree' does not convey meaning because it has some innate connection to a 'real' thing like 'treeness' (some languages, for example, don't distinguish between 'trees' and what we might call a 'bush'), but because it exists in a system of different sounds and written marks. This of course leads to the disconcerting possibility that language is a self-enclosed system which can have only a very murky relationship to a 'real' world without words."[64] This conclusion, which Sarchett even marks with an "of course" (though remember, he disavows any access to "Truth" or "Universal Reason"), is a non sequitur, which arises from his confusion of meaning with reference. Even if we concede that the meaning of a term depends upon its (somewhat arbitrary and conventional) differences from other terms (so that, to pursue Sarchett's example, the word "tree" means something different in a linguistic system in which it is contrasted with "bush" than it does in a system in which it is not), this does nothing to make the referential relationship between words and things murky or in any way difficult. In the former system, a sequoia will be a "tree," while the little leafy plant in my front yard will not; in the latter system they will both be "trees"; and in both systems furry animals, the structure in which I live, and the vehicle I drive will not be "trees."

Here's another point about the unavoidability of reference, and its irreducibility to meaning. Suppose you are in a bus that has just gone over a mountain ledge and you are hurtling toward the ground and almost certain death. Changing your vocabulary, and thus changing the relations of meanings of words (and thus changing the meanings themselves) will do nothing to prevent the violent fate that awaits.

Nor is this the end of the valuable insights to be gleaned from poststructuralism, according to Sarchett:

> I had been taught that only certain select texts were full of the "complexity" and "ambiguity" which mark the truly worthwhile literary work. But then I realized that an insightful and probing reader can make any text dance with possibility because reading itself puts into play so many diverse and complicated acts. . . . I began to suspect that what made something great might depend more on what texts particular sets of readers value than on any intrinsic literary merits of the texts themselves.[65]

Comments:

(1) Sarchett celebrates poststructuralism's sophisticated attention to context and appreciation of difference. But note that his current view, according to which all texts are complex and ambiguous,

seems to be simpler and more homogenous—not to mention less nuanced, less contextually sensitive, and less complicated—than one in which some texts are seen to be full of complexity and ambiguity in a way that others are not.

(2) Despite the explicit subjectivism of the last sentence of the just-quoted passage, it does not seem to occur to Sarchett that his failure to find intrinsic qualities in different texts by which they might be differentiated both in terms of literary merit and with regard to such qualities as complexity and ambiguity might stem from his employment of a literary theory that obliterates any such intrinsic differences as might be there to find. After all, if it were my practice to marinate everything I eat in vinegar (or cover it in hot peppers, or pour ketchup all over it), I might find that everything I eat tastes pretty much the same, as well.

(3) Finally, the position offered here is highly implausible. Is there really any more reason to think that all texts are richly complex and ambiguous than to suppose that all basketball players are multitalented, that all bridges are well constructed, or that all people are friendly and trustworthy? And are the distinctions that we all make in these and countless other areas really subjective and unmotivated by real differences to be found in the objects about which we judge? For what it's worth, it seems to me just as senseless to claim that the differences we note between a Dostoyevsky novel and the work of a tenth-rate hack's novelization of a bad Hollywood film are subjective and flow more from us than they do from the texts themselves as it would be to make the analogous claim about the differences we would all agree on concerning the relative merits of Michael Jordan and Woody Allen as basketball players.

In any case, let's see what happens when Sarchett applies these poststructuralist lessons to classroom teaching:

> To treat literary works as timeless and universal statements seems to me the most boring, reductive method of teaching and reading imaginable. As the critic Myra Jehlen says, if we present students an Othello who embodies the general human condition, the complexities of human difference are submerged. Instead Jehlen argues for "explicating the particular." . . . [W]e [should] insert Shakespeare back into the messiness of political and cultural *life* not into the cloudy realms of "enduring truth."[66]

Comments:

(1) Yes, it is reductive to focus only on the timeless and universal, and to ignore the particular. But then again—and it is truly staggering that Sarchett does not even discuss this—so is it reductive to focus only on the particular, and to ignore not only the timeless and the universal, but also the complex ways in which particulars are related to universals.

(2) While Sarchett decries reductionism, the reductionism of his own approach is apparent on every page of his essay. For example, he claims that what he finds "most exciting about life inside and outside the classroom" is "the endless proliferation of difference."[67] If such proliferation is indeed endless, I should think it would eventually become tedious, rather than exciting. Indeed, would it not be more interesting, less "boring and reductive," to use Sarchett's phrase, to mix things up a bit, to discuss some of the interesting and surprising ways in which seemingly disparate things are in some sense *similar* or even the *same*, as when, for example, they embody the same principle? Similar remarks apply to Sarchett's own contribution to classroom discussions, which seems to consist mainly of "repeated demonstrations of interpretive undecidability."[68] (How, exactly, is such a thing demonstrated? If some students reject Sarchett's demonstrations, is this "difference" one to be celebrated?) This apparent celebration of difference is really the reductive suppression of difference, which is accomplished by covering up all of the works of literature considered with the same (not different) epistemological and political convictions, so that they all, like different foods that have all been drenched in ketchup, end up tasting the same.

(3) To ignore what is universal in literature, what is common in the experiences of different people in different times and places, is to render literature unintelligible. We have not lived in the times and places of the characters; we have not had exactly the same experiences as they have endured; millions of particularities separate us from them. So how are we to understand them without recourse to common general structures which unite otherwise disparate experiences?[69]

(4) If understanding and appreciating are truly confined to the realm of the contingent and the particular, and fail to achieve timeless and universal validity, then Sarchett's own pronouncements must be understood as products of his own contingent circumstances, and as failing to achieve such validity. The way is left fully

clear for others, differently situated, to rub up against the timeless and the universal. (Remember, the denial that one can do so either is itself timeless and universal, in which case it contradicts itself, or else it itself can achieve only a contingent and contextual validity).

(5) It is odd that someone who insists that we cannot make valid claims which transcend our own sociohistorical context would want us to "explicate the particular" with regard to works of literature written in, and set in, vastly different sociohistorical contexts than our own. For if the reason that we cannot have access to the universal and timeless is precisely that we cannot transcend our own context, then neither can we transcend it so as to rub up against the particularities to which Sarchett would have us direct our attention.

In fairness to Sarchett, he does offer something of a rebuttal to point (2) above, the charge that he reductively makes everything equal and the same. Here is what he says on this point:

> Notice I [do] *not* say that everything is as true or good as everything else; I am however implying that everything is *contingently* good or bad or true or false, and that judgments are *differently* validated. Thus I am quite willing to believe that for Allan Bloom and people more or less like him, given their personal economies, rock music would indeed harm their souls. Bloom's problem is that he takes his soul as some kind of universal soul.[70]

Here are my comments by way of reply.

(1) What does it mean to say that "everything is contingently good or bad or true or false," and that "judgments are differently validated"? This claim could mean any number of things, and Sarchett gives us only this one example, and no other kind of explanation, to help sort them out. This is not enough. It might mean (a) the descriptive thesis that different people differ in their judgments of what is good or bad or true or false, and that they arrive at these different judgments by different means; (b) the relativist thesis that the goodness or badness or truth or falsity of things or statements depends upon the judgments that one makes on these matters (e.g., thinking makes it so, and people think differently, so truth, etc., is contingent in this way), or on the criteria by which one does so (there being no one correct set of criteria); or (c) that judgments concerning what is good or bad or true or false always must, if they are to be valid, take into due account objective matters of context, circumstances, or sit-

uation; among other possibilities. (a) is a truism, accepted by all parties to the debates we are considering, and thus holds little interest. (b) is unlikely to be Sarchett's meaning, since he is eager to distance himself from the view that "everything is as true or good as everything else." Still, I hold it out as a possible interpretation, since one might construe (b) as saying just this, in the sense that not everything is as true or good as everything else *relative to the judgments of different person, or to the different validity criteria that different people actually employ.* In any case, if this is his position, it is clearly a relativistic one in the sense we are considering. (c) seems to me the most plausible interpretation of Sarchett's intended meaning, especially in the light of his example. I will reserve my remaining comments for it.

(2) The idea that the soundness of truth claims and value judgments often depends upon circumstantial or contextual considerations is uncontroversial. But the idea that they always are so dependent is. For consider: Under what circumstances is it true that a square is round? In what context is it the case that our highest duty is to torture the innocent? And in what situation is *modus ponens* not a valid argument form?

(3) Note here the self-referential inconsistency problem. If "everything is contingently good or bad or true or false, and judgments are differently validated" then the claim that everything is contingently good or bad or true or false, and that judgments are differently validated, is itself only contingently good or true and is differently validated (a problem on any interpretation).

(4) Note also the taking of a less contextually sensitive position than might be taken. To say that some judgments depend for their truth upon context and that some do not is itself a more "contingent" and contextually sensitive statement than is the "absolutist" claim that *every* judgment is in this category.

(5) Why does not Sarchett simply say of Bloom, who seems to think that rock music is bad for everyone's soul, that he is wrong? If Sarchett were to say this, I would agree with him completely. Instead, he trots out this vague "differently validated" language and says that Bloom's claim is probably true if its scope is restricted to applying to Bloom and others like him. If this is what Sarchett means generally by his "contingently true" and "differently validated" concept—and the Bloom example is all he gives us by way of characterization—

then there is little to say on its behalf. Suppose I were to claim that "cellos are musical instruments." Is this supposed to mean that cellos are musical instruments for me and for people more or less like me, but not for other people? Are squares excluded from being round only for me and for people like me? Or, to take a more pertinent example, suppose I make claims about all human beings: that they are all under one hundred feet tall, less than one thousand years old, lighter than one million pounds, and so forth. Is that supposed to be true just of me and people like me, but not for other human beings? Who are these huge and old people?

(6) And then there is the self-referential question again. Is the claim that rock music harms Bloom's soul and those of people like him, but not those of other people, itself true absolutely, or is it true only for Sarchett and people like *him*?

Let me point out one more of Sarchett's errors, because it is pervasive and because its pervasiveness partially explains why relativistic positions are currently so popular. I refer to the confusion of the formal meaning of a term with its material meaning. For example, "tomorrow" means (formally) "the day after today"; materially it means (since I write on a Wednesday) "Thursday." Similarly, while everyone agrees with the formal principle that happiness is better than misery, they often disagree as to what materially gives rise to happiness. Focusing on the latter point while ignoring or failing to understand the former gives undeserved credence to relativism.

Enter Sarchett. In attempting to debunk the idea that there are "enduring," "transcendental," or "timeless" truths, Sarchett remarks: "After all, a timeless truth must be very clear or how could it be true?" He then proceeds to show how certain terms are materially unclear, especially since their material meanings change over time. But he fails to recognize that this does not affect their formal meaning. He does a number on the word "love," pointing out that our understanding of what is or is not love changes over time. But stripped of the formal-material distinction, he winds up saying that the idea that child molestation is not love is nothing more than "a specific cultural agreement to limit the possible significations of the word,"[71] as if there were no formal idea of love which we could discover to be inconsistent with child molestation! I mean, surely we have good reasons for declaring child molestation not to be love. Must the final analysis of this really reside simply in the (arbitrary? unmotivated?) *fact* of agreement?[72]

XIV. SMITH

Barbara Herrnstein Smith defends "the programmatic effort by certain revisionist theorists—notably, constructivist sociologists and historians of science—to maintain 'symmetry' in their analyses and accounts of scientific and other beliefs, those beliefs currently seen as absurd or wrong as well as those now generally accepted as true." This certainly looks like "anything-goes" relativism, but Smith disagrees:

> Contrary to widespread misunderstanding, this commitment to methodological symmetry is not equivalent to maintaining that all *beliefs* are equally *valid*. . . . That commitment is equivalent, however, to maintaining that the *credibility* of all beliefs, including those currently regarded as true, reasonable, self-evident, and so forth, is equally *contingent*: equally the product, in other words, of conditions (experiential, contextual, institutional, and so forth) that are fundamentally variable and always to some extent unpredictable and uncontrollable. So understood, epistemic symmetry, whether as an idea or a method, constitutes a strong challenge to familiar Whiggish history of science, to the normative project of rationalist philosophy of science, and to rationalist epistemology more generally.[73]

So why is this not relativism? Surely everyone would agree that the credibility of a given belief to a given person might well depend to some extent (I realize that Smith's claim is stronger than this, but that will only strengthen the point I am about to make) on that person's history and context, but this is not relativism, precisely because it does not entail that each belief is equally valid—perhaps some experiences and contexts are more beneficial to enabling a person to see a given truth than are others; or perhaps one person sees and another fails to see a given truth, even when their experiences and contexts are relevantly similar, simply because one has reasoned carefully and cogently about the evidence equally available to both of them, and the other has failed to do this. But Smith cannot avail herself of these options, since she rejects the idea of validity entirely, pointing out that constructivism, which she defends, "rejects classic ideas of *objective* validity," and recognizes that "to say all beliefs are equally *subjectively* valid is just to say that people really believe what they believe." Immediately after making these remarks,

Smith goes on to affirm her belief in the equally contingent credibility of all beliefs, already quoted. Thus, whereas from Smith's claim that she rejects the relativistic notion that all beliefs are equally valid, the reader might suppose that she is endorsing the non-relativistic claim that some are valid and others invalid, or at least that some ideas are more valid than others, she, instead, simply dismisses validity claims altogether, claiming that "they would have to be, from a constructivist perspective, either vacuous . . . or tautologous." Validity, on this account, simply collapses into "credibility," and a credibility which, moreover, is not merely *often influenced, and to varying degrees*, by such things as a person's circumstances and experiential history, which, as I suggested, would be a commonplace, but rather is *always* and "*equally* the *product*" of them. So everyone's beliefs, about anything and everything, turn out to be in exactly the same boat: not a whit valid (except in a tautological subjectivist sense), but all equally contingently credible. That, I submit, is relativism.[74]

In any case, she defends it in part on the grounds that, in comparison with more traditional approaches, it allegedly leads to greater tolerance in dealing with those with whom one disagrees. Accordingly, she objects to what she calls "[t]he two favored solutions" to the puzzle of why other people might disagree with oneself. The two solutions are those of

demonology and, so to speak, dementology: that is, the comforting and sometimes automatic conclusion that the other fellow . . . is either a devil or a fool—or, in more (officially) enlightened terms, that he or she suffers from defects or deficiencies of character and/or intellect: ignorance, innate capacity, delusion, poor training, captivity to false doctrine, and so on. Both solutions reflect a more general tendency of some significance here, namely, "epistemic self-privileging" or "epistemic asymmetry": that is, our inclination to believe that we believe the true and sensible things we do because they are true and sensible, while other people believe the foolish and outrageous things they do because there is something the matter with those people.[75]

Smith's proposed alternative solution, as we have seen, is to maintain "that the credibility of all beliefs . . . is equally contingent."

Comments:

(1) Smith seems to be conflating the issue of the objective or non-

objective status of a given belief with the rather different issue of whether that belief is true (let alone known with certainty to be true).

(2) There is also a levels confusion. If I genuinely believe x, then I must believe, on the first level, that those who disagree with x are mistaken. For example, if I genuinely believe that giraffes are taller than ants, that no human being weighs more than 10,000 pounds, and that happiness is better than misery, then I must think that anyone who believes that ants are taller than giraffes, that there are human beings who weigh more than 10,000 pounds, or that misery is as good as or better than happiness, is mistaken. This is part of what it means to believe something. To believe that something is one way is to believe that it is not any way that is inconsistent with its being that way. But I also know about myself (and surely most other people realize it about themselves) that I sometimes make mistakes in my beliefs and believe things that turn out not to be true, and do so even sometimes in regard to things that seem to me very evident and obvious indeed. Thus, even when I hold the first-level belief that x, and consequently that those who believe not-x are wrong, I can still at the same time hold the second-level belief that this might be one of those many times when I am wrong and they are right—and thus that if intellectual or other deficiencies are responsible for the erroneous belief, then these deficiencies are mine and not theirs.

(3) Even if I do often feel that those who disagree with me are wrong (and I do, since I do hold beliefs, and since this is a consequence of doing so, as I have just argued), it hardly follows that I regard this as stemming always or typically from any cognitive or moral shortcomings on their part, except in the trivial and noninvidious sense that any failing of any kind can be attributed to shortcomings of the one who failed (e.g., if I were a lot stronger I could just jump over the Washington monument). Whenever anyone fails at anything, the explanation can be sought by looking at two different factors, at the very least: some lack of ability on the part of the person in question to succeed at the activity at issue would be one, to be sure, but the other would be the difficulty to achieve such success. Many activities prove difficult for human beings, given their abilities and disabilities, to succeed at consistently. Arriving at the truth on difficult questions appears to be one of these. Thus, why would not a defender of objective truth attribute the failings of others to the difficulty of the enterprise, more so than to the stupidity or

malevolence of people? Smith provides no evidence that they do so, still less that there is anything in the belief in objective truth which would force them, or even strongly incline them, to do so.

(4) Having said this, it must be added that not all issues are difficult, and it is a palpable datum of experience that other people, and ourselves as well, are not infrequently guilty of failing to observe obvious truths—truths staring us right in the face—precisely because of carelessness, stupidity, self-deception, laziness in thinking, or any other number of intellectual or moral failings. Smith's refusal to acknowledge this, and her insistence instead to see all beliefs as equally credible products of the experiences and circumstances of the persons holding them, is thus objectionable on multiple grounds. First, as already mentioned, it constitutes the denial of something that is clearly and inescapably part of our experience, both of ourselves and of others. Second, if in fact it is true (as it obviously is), that thinking cogently requires effort and scruples, any doctrine which concludes a priori that anything I might happen to believe is every bit as credible as any other belief I might have held instead, that no belief can ever be valid, and that I am not even responsible for my beliefs (since they are the "products," as Smith says, of my history and circumstances) may well encourage me to forego the effort needed to arrive at a cogently reasoned conclusion. Why should I not simply believe whatever appeals to me, or what I am in the habit of thinking, or something of that sort? Finally, many evils in the world flow from faulty thinking, in such a way that correcting the faulty thinking might ameliorate, or even be necessary for ameliorating, the evils. Thus, we need to face the possibility that some thinking is faulty.

(5) Note the reductionism and simplicity of Smith's account. Postmodern constructivists always claim great sophistication for their views and see in them a great sensitivity to nuance, difference, and context. Frequently, however, as here, what we actually get is a sledgehammer doctrine which is insensitive to all of these things. Remember, Smith's view is not that some views are more credible than others (to varying degrees, depending upon context, so that they might differ from one another in this respect); nor is it her claim that our views are influenced by our experiences and circumstances to different degrees. No, everything is the same in these regards, as in so many others.

(6) It is unclear why the best approach to matters of intellectual tolerance should be to declare that all beliefs are equally and contingently credible. Nor is it clear why this approach should lead to greater "flexibility and responsiveness," as Smith claims.[76] For why cannot a defender of objectivity, especially one sensitive to the distinction between levels discussed above, acknowledge that his or her own position might very well be the one that is mistaken? What is needed here is a willingness to take up and to consider fairly evidence which runs counter to one's own views, as well as a (selective and critical) recognition of the independent value, both ultimate and instrumental, of tolerance. Moreover, if, as is the case on Smith's claim, my views are already as credible and valid as they are ever going to be, what would my motive be to listen to your arguments that they are not the best? If, on the other hand, I take seriously the possibility that I might be *wrong*, really, objectively wrong—a notion that Smith cannot countenance—I would have such motivation.

(7) Next, let us examine Smith's rhetoric, to see the extent to which her approach allows her to avoid "'epistemic self-privileging' or 'epistemic asymmetry.'" If I am right in saying that to believe x, we must believe that the deniers of x are wrong, and in also asserting that it is a palpable and common datum of experience that people often make mistakes because of intellectual errors, and not merely as a result of their conditions and circumstances, then we should expect to find evidence of this in Smith's discussions as well. I think we do. In Smith's critique of Robin West, for example, we read that West "misses the central point of the critique of objectivist claims," prompting Smith to clarify the matter so as "[t]o prevent other misunderstandings."[77] Three pages later she complains of matters that "continue to elude quite a few . . . people, even after some determined efforts at exposure and demonstration." Is there really no hint of the suggestion, to use Smith's own phrase for the attitude she so much deplores, that "these people believe the foolish and outrageous things they do because there is something the matter with those people?" Similarly, Smith accuses West of "obscur[ing] important issues" with "tendentious language."[78] And we are further told that "West equivocates significantly,"[79] and so on and so forth, throughout the entire book. Is this not the attribution of mistakes—of cognitive errors—on the part of her intellectual adversaries, and is this not inconsistent with her critique of "epistemic self-privileging" and

"epistemic asymmetry"? I will leave the matter up to you, after quoting one more of her statements of that critique: "I do not think that we should understand the differences of our views and their views as reflections of our enlightenment and their benightedness. Rather, as just described, I think we should understand those differences as products of our and their more or less different personal histories (familial, social education, and so on) and current positions in the relevant society."[80] In general, is it not clear from her initial statement that she considers the demonizers and dementizers to be wrong, and that her explanation of their wrongness is either demonization or dementization? In any case, to avoid this charge, she would have to take a symmetrical view of her views and those of her opponents: they are both equally credible, depending on the contingencies of the experiences of these different believers, and blah, blah, blah. Note also that other constructivists do not even try to refrain from "demonizing or dementizing" their intellectual opponents.[81]

(8) Smith's position involves collapsing the following two seemingly distinct issues: (a) why does so-and-so *believe* such-and-such?; and (b) is such-and-such *true* (or likely to be true, or plausible, or evident, or some such thing)?

(9) Finally, on the social causes of belief: how does she know that beliefs are caused—the products of experiential and circumstantial conditions—rather than reasoned to? It would be interesting to test the specifics of this. Can she predict, to a degree significantly higher than chance, what experiences a person has had in life merely from knowing his or her beliefs? Alternatively, from knowing what someone's history has been, and what his or her circumstances are now, can she predict what beliefs he or she holds? It is easy to say, in a sweeping, undetailed way, that people's beliefs are products in this way. Why isn't this metaphysics of the sort that she is trying to avoid?

But she persists in it, arguing that while it is not remarkable that philosophers, logicians, and classicists sometimes experience their thoughts and beliefs as self-evident or intuitively right, "[w]hat is worth remarking . . . is the move from *experiencing* one's own cognitive activities and their conceptual and discursive products . . . as self-evident or intuitively right to *positing and claiming* them as . . . autonomous, transcendentally presupposed, and properly universal." "On the contrary," she continues, "it is possible to believe that such concepts . . . are, rather, the products and effects of rigorous instruction and routine participation in a particular conceptual tradition and its related idiom," and "that instruction . . . in some other conceptual tradition" would yield quite different conceptions and understandings.[82]

Comments:

(1) Experience is one of the better warrants we have for making claims. Compare: "It is not remarkable to report having *seen* a bear outside, but it is remarkable that one would move from that to *positing and claiming* that there really was a bear outside. Perhaps such positing is a product of your training; others with other training would have seen something else."

(2) To be sure, you might very well refrain from such positing and claiming, especially if you have some specific reason to suppose that your experience was illusory—say, you know that you were drunk when you saw the bear, and that you live in an area where no bears live. But this is far different from following a general policy of refraining to posit and claim as true the data of one's own direct experience. Why would one want to do that?

(3) Notice also that here one does not simply refuse to make a claim based upon what one sees. Rather, one denies one thing that one sees on the basis of something else that one "sees," in the extended sense of "grasps" or "understands."

(4) If the worry is simply that, in any situation, you might be wrong, then making fallibilistic claims (as opposed to refusing to make any claims at all) would seem to be the appropriate response. Such a stance seems especially warranted here, since we undoubtedly often do confuse the essential and necessary with the contingent and culturally familiar.

(5) Note, once again, the reductionism and simplicity of this view. Instead of the complex and messy view that our beliefs are sometimes warranted by evidence and at other times merely caused by experience, we get the view that the latter is always the case. Ketchup is poured over everything, and all food tastes the same.

(6) Notice here the self-referential inconsistency of claiming that one is not positing based upon one's seeing. Smith thinks she sees something about beliefs being produced by disciplinary training, and makes claims accordingly. There is nothing remarkable about her moving from understanding things this way to claiming that they are this way.

(7) And notice that her explanation of why philosophers, logicians, and classicists believe in self-evidence, universal truths, and

the like—namely, that these beliefs result from their disciplinary training—must itself be seen as stemming from her disciplinary training. And it is not just that her alternative view of self-evidence must, on its own terms, have so resulted, but also that her belief that such beliefs have so resulted must itself have so resulted. She tells us that "philosophers, logicians, and classicists" believe what they do because of the ways in which they have been "formally educated and professionally disciplined."[83] But this belief itself is evidently held by Smith because of the ways in which she has been formally educated and professionally disciplined. So how can we know what is really true? If we cannot, this is skepticism. If her claim that my beliefs are due to my having been disciplined and my belief that they are not are both equally and contingently "credible," then we have relativism.

(8) While Smith is quick to claim that that those with whom she disagrees, such as philosophers, hold the views they do because of the way they have been trained, disciplined, and instructed,[84] she is much less quick to concede, despite her official allegiance to the symmetry principle, to offer a similar explanation for her own views. One gets the distinct impression that she regards philosophical training as a cause of errors that she, with her different education, is able to avoid. Part of my disagreement with constructivists like Smith is that I think it is more respectful to tell those with whom I disagree that I think they are wrong, and to give my reasons, and to engage in discussion if it is desired, than to attribute their views to causal factors such as disciplinary instruction. Thus, I want to be very clear in saying that I regard it in general (I will overlook a few exceptions as not relevant here) as indefensible to attempt to reject other persons' views by making causal claims pertaining to how they may have come to hold them (after all, the issue is not why they believe it, but rather whether or not it is true), or, to mention the flip side, to attempt to defend your own views by a similar analysis—typically the claim, an appeal to authority on one's own behalf, that one has achieved a special competence in making judgments in the area in question because of one's education in it. And yet, I find it ironic that so many people whose education is in some field other than philosophy (Smith is a professor of comparative literature and English) should be so comfortable in rejecting the views of philosophers, on philosophical questions, mind you, and in blithely attributing their errors to their having received instruction in philosophy! It would be

one thing if Smith were prepared to argue that philosophers are objectively wrong. But she rejects any such notion, holding instead that all beliefs—both hers and those with whom she disagrees—are equally the products of historical, cultural, and circumstantial conditions. So if my beliefs about philosophy are the result of my having received instruction in philosophy, and hers the result of her having received instruction in comparative literature and English, then why would she think that the products of the latter instruction should be affirmed over those of the former, given that the subject matter in question is philosophy?

(9) Most people, as she admits, subscribe to an asymmetry thesis and think that scientific facts are about an external world, rather than socially constructed, etc. So she thinks most people are wrong! How extraordinary!

(10) Most importantly, here we have the *obscurum per obscurius* fallacy. I claim to grasp the necessity of *modus ponens* and the disjunctive syllogism; Smith would say that this is due to my disciplinary training. But surely these elementary logical principles are more evident than are her sociological theories of belief formation.

In any case, let's have a look at Smith's symmetry thesis in action. She quotes Philip Kitcher as saying:

> The behavior of creation scientists indicates a kind of inflexibility, deafness, or blindness. They make an objection to some facet of evolutionary biology. Darwin's defenders respond by suggesting that the objection is misformulated, that it does not attack what Darwinists claim, that it rests on false assumptions, or that it is logically fallacious. How do creationists reply? Typically, *by reiterating the argument.* Anyone who has followed exchanges in this controversy . . . sees that there is no adaptation to any of the principal criticisms.[85]

But Smith, with her a priori commitment to symmetry, will not stand for such an asymmetrical treatment of evolution and creationism. She responds to Kitcher as follows:

> He means, of course, that there is no adaptation by creationists to the criticisms of their views by Darwinists. But the "anyone" who sees this could not be quite anyone, since creationists could observe that, as far as adapting to criticism goes, Darwinists—blind, deaf,

and inflexible as anyone can see they are—have not budged an inch either. Kitcher explains the overt cognitive conservatism of creationists as a sign of their underlying cognitive unwholesomeness. Creationists, however, could probably give a comparable array of reasons for their opponents' stubbornness in error: ignorance of the Bible, secular humanist prejudice, modern infatuation with evolutionary theory, plus, perhaps, certain sins of sloth and pride. . . . [F]or all the differences in their favored idioms and authorities, the explanation Kitcher offers for the intellectual obstinacy of his long time adversaries exhibits the same asymmetrical structure as *their* explanation for *his*, which is to say the same tendency toward absolute epistemic self-privileging.[86]

Comments:

(1) Smith has completely misunderstood Kitcher's point. His point is not that creationists have not *changed their position* in response to the criticisms of their adversaries. If that were his point, Smith's claim, that neither have Darwinists changed theirs in response to the criticisms of creationists, would certainly be correct, and perhaps on point. But Kitcher's point is, rather, that *creationists, in quite radical contrast to many Darwinists, do not even acknowledge, respond to, or in any other way attempt to deal with, criticisms by their intellectual adversaries.* Those evolutionists who have addressed themselves to creationism have taken up and responded to the actual arguments used by the leading creationists and presumably stand ready to respond to creationist responses to these responses, were they to be forthcoming. But creationists—and this is Kitcher's point—have refused to respond to Darwinists' response to their anti-Darwinist arguments. Kitcher's point is not that creationists have failed to change their position. Kitcher's example, presented immediately after Smith's quotation of him breaks off, shows this clearly and reveals the magnitude of her misreading:

One important example among many is the creationist use of the second law of thermodynamics. For nearly twenty years, the major exponents of creation science have been declaring that the second law of thermodynamics is incompatible with the evolution of life. Creationists have been in the presence of people who have given lengthy critiques of their objection and there is substantial evidence that their eyes have wandered over some of the pages on which critiques have been printed. How has their thinking adapted to these critiques? Apparently not at all, for they make no replies to them and continue to present their ideas in exactly the same ways.[87]

Thus, as Kitcher's last sentence especially makes clear, he is not criticizing creationists for failing to abandon creationism for Darwinism, or even for abandoning their idea that the latter is incompatible with the second law of thermodynamics. What he is criticizing them for is their failure to reply to criticisms of that favorite argument of theirs—that is, for not saying: "We think that the second law of thermodynamics is incompatible with Darwinism. Now, evolutionists reply that that is not so because . . . , to which we respond . . ."

(2) Once this misreading is corrected, what merit is there to her criticism of Kitcher? Are not those who respond to the criticisms of their critics, *in that respect at least*, truly behaving more rationally and responsibly than are those who blithely ignore all criticisms? And if they are, are they not entitled to *say* that they are?

(3) This brings out the reductionism of her approach. If one person says, "All human beings weigh less than one million pounds, and you are wrong to think otherwise," while another says, "No, in fact all human beings weigh over one million pounds, and you are the one who is wrong to think otherwise," these two statements do indeed have a symmetrical structure. But one is right and the other wrong. Her commitment to symmetry at best obscures, and at worst denies, this highly significant fact. The impetus between science and philosophy, which once were united, is this: There are lots of opinions out there, and they clash with one another. They cannot all be right. So if you really want to know what is what, you need to try to figure your way past the buzzing, cacophonous confusion of opinion. You need criteria, standards, methods, etc. You need science and philosophy. That is what Smith seems to be attacking.

(4) It is not true that Darwinists suffer from the array of deficiencies that Smith thinks creationists could (justly?) attribute to them. For example, a good many Darwinists are quite knowledgeable about the Bible. Do such issues even matter for Smith?

(5) Note the non sequitur of the inference marked by "since" in her second sentence as quoted above. From the premise that Darwinists (allegedly) are inflexible in the face of creationist criticisms of their position, it is supposed to follow that not just anyone can see that *creationists* are inflexible in the face of *Darwinist* criticisms of

their doctrine. But even if it were true that Darwinists are inflexible as charged, this would in no way be incompatible either with its being the case that creationists are inflexible as well, or with that inflexibility being evident to everyone.

Next, let's look at a few of Smith's statements about objectivity. Here is one:

> [T]he idea of objectively good judgments, as distinct from judgments that are good under certain (perhaps quite broad ranges of) conditions and from the perspectives of certain (perhaps highly relevant sets of) people, appears fundamentally untenable. It follows that, no matter what principles we erect or invoke, whether epistemological, ethical, or procedural, "the best judgments" will still always be contingent in their production and operation, and also only contingently and contestibly identifiable as "the best."[88]

Comments:

(1) These very *claims*, then, are good only "under certain conditions and from the perspectives of certain people" and are "contingent in their production and operation, and also only contingently and contestibly identifiable as 'the best.'"

(2) Is this true of claims like "giraffes are taller than ants"?

(3) Perhaps she will try to minimize the force of (1) by referring to her parenthetical asides about the broad ranges of conditions under which some judgments are good, and the "highly relevant" nature of the people from whose perspective they are good. Still, it would be interesting to know under what conditions her anti-objectivist claims would not hold good, and for which people they would not.

(4) On the latter question, she cannot simply say that it does not hold good for people who reject it, as one reading of the word "perspective" might suggest, because that would make clear that her position is one in which validity simply collapses into belief, a position that she explicitly rejects.[89] Nor will it do for her to invoke another meaning of "perspective"—where the term means something closer to "vantage point," in the sense of "angle of vision," than "opinion." To be sure, such a position would let her escape charges of "anything-goes" relativism, since one might have an ideal vantage point from which to appreciate some truth and yet still fail to appreciate it because of, say, a confusion or some other form of intellectual error. But then we recall Smith's strictures against "epistemic self-privi-

leging," and we see that this way is also closed off to her. So who are the people for whom her contingency of value position does not hold good, and why does it not so hold?

(5) Does her contingency thesis go all the way down? That is, does it apply not only to conclusions, but to premises and to reasoning as well? For example, is the logical force of "it follows that" contingent in the same way that her conclusions are? Similarly, she sometimes charges her intellectual antagonists with committing logical fallacies, including those of non sequitur and begging the question.[90] What is the status of all of this? If it seems to me that begging the question is OK, or if my conditioning has led me to this belief, is it OK for me to beg the question? She says that "[n]ot all theories are equal because they . . . can be, and commonly will be, found better or worse than others in relation to measures such as applicability, coherence, connectability, and so forth. These measures are not objective in the classic sense, since they depend on matters of perspective, interpretation, and judgment, and will vary under different conditions."[91] First of all, objectivity is perfectly compatible with a need for interpretation and judgment.[92] More to the point, why should we go by these measures? What is their status? If they are objective, universal, necessary, or context-independent (in the sense that there is no context in which they should not be applied, not in the sense that their application will not vary with context), then we have a self-referential inconsistency. If they are products of her conditioning, and that of people like her, then was not a belief in objective truth also a part of that conditioning? If she rejects that part of her conditioning on the basis of reasoning (appealing to begging the question, etc.), then reasoning is possible after all, and our beliefs are not merely the products of our contingencies, as she ceaselessly claims.

(6) Note that I am not begging the question. I use the same terms and concepts that Smith is using. For example, Smith writes:

> Certainly, the certification of truth and knowledge in their classic senses—as, for example, the accurate affirmation or faithful representation of an altogether autonomous reality—has proved elusive. Meanwhile, alternative conceptions of truth and knowledge—as, for example, the relatively coherent, relatively reliable, and relatively stable products of various social, discursive, and institutional practices—have been proposed in recent years, and have proved relatively coherent, reliable, and stable.[93]

But then this claim itself, insofar as it purports to be passing on knowledge or truth, cannot, on its own terms, be an "accurate affirmation or faithful representation of an altogether autonomous reality," but must rather be understood as a "product of various social, discursive, and institutional practices." To the charge that such an approach renders our preferences for one belief over another merely matters of taste, Smith pleads guilty, adding only the proviso that "[t]he 'merely' would disappear, however, for tastes, understood as contingently shaped preferences, would not, in this account, be distinguished from and opposed to the operation of Reason(s) but would be, rather, a way of reconceptualizing the latter."[94] But note Alexander J. Argyros's response to such a position:

> Consider the radical antifoundationalism that maintains that all values are the contingent and local products of a given performative community. Is it not reasonable to ask how one who argues this position knows that all values are contingent? Has he or she surveyed all real and possible worlds and reached the empirical conclusion that universality is inappropriate? If not, is it not a metaphysical and totalizing act of faith that authorizes such absolute relativism?[95]

Equally objectionable is Smith's definition of "objectivity": "*Objective*, in this tradition [that of classical ethics and epistemology], is understood to mean independent of particular, historical, cultural, or circumstantial conditions, and independent, also, of the perspectives of particular persons."[96] This is incorrect. Consider the sentence "George W. Bush is currently President of the United States." The meaning of this sentence, and its truth, is objective as anything can be, and yet it clearly is not "independent of particular, historical, cultural, or circumstantial conditions." Thus, Smith is setting up a straw man. More to the point, she is making of objectivity a compound, so that refuting the first (straw man) clause can suffice for refuting the whole idea—the second clause need not be attacked directly. And indeed, she quickly proceeds to attack objectivity exclusively by focusing on its alleged commitment to independence from changing and diverse circumstances.[97]

Armed with this questionable definition of objectivity, Smith next argues that in courts of law non-objectivist judges will, all else equal, tend to be better, and in particular more responsible, judges than will those who affirm objectivity. As she explains, "Because, by definition, they believe that every evaluation is a judgment call 'all the way down,' [non-objectivist] judges must take individual responsibility for their rulings. That is, they must be accountable for the particular contexts, perspectives, and considerations in relation to which their rulings are made."[98] But what is usually meant by taking responsibility for a judgment is, among many other things, that you take the blame if you get it wrong, that is, if you judge falsely or incorrectly. But if we are abandoning objectivity altogether, and affirming that "every evaluation is a judgment call 'all the way down,'" then what would it mean to get it wrong? There is an ambiguity to the word "judgment" that may be causing trouble here. Something might be a matter of judgment even on the view that there is an objective truth about the matter. Here judgment would have to be relied upon because in the situation in question, or perhaps due to the nature of the question, there is no way to get access to this objective truth— rather, one must estimate, as best one can, what that truth is. Suppose, for example, that I am estimating, or, in that sense, "judging" the height of a mountain, where I have no way of measuring it or in any other way precisely and accurately determining its height. It is perfectly intelligible, in such an example, to say that my judgment will be either right or wrong, or closer to accurate or further from it, even though we have no way of knowing, immediately following the issuance of my judgment, which it will have been. And if for some reason it is important to people's well-being that my judgment be relatively accurate here, then my responsibility is great indeed. But if we say that there is no objective truth regarding the height of the mountain, it is not clear how this responsibility of judgment is to be understood, and people often do use the word "judgment" in this way, as when saying that it is a matter of judgment, rather than of truth, whether chocolate ice cream is tastier than vanilla.

On the other hand, it may be that Smith's complaint is not with an appeal to objectivity (the idea that something is true or false irrespective of what we may believe about it, so that our beliefs might, in principle, simply be mistaken) but rather with the extremely different idea, which she sometimes equates with objectivity, that "the only reasons that count as 'good' ones are those that are certifiably deduced by pure reason from universally valid, transcendentally necessary principles."[99] Here, as before, a "packed" definition of objectivity is used, so that Smith can attack the whole concept by rejecting one dubious element that she has first grafted onto it.

Let's turn now to one final topic, Smith's efforts at extricating herself from the charge that her assertions are self-referentially inconsistent. One of her strategies is to deny that she is asserting anything at all!: "What I am offering here is neither an 'assertion' . . . nor a 'denial' . . . , but an alternate description of what is *otherwise described* as 'assertion,' 'denial,' and 'truth.' . . . Having designed this verbal/conceptual construct to be of value—interest, use, and perhaps even beauty—to the members of a certain community, I exhibit it here for sale, hoping that some of its readers will, as we say, 'buy it.'"[100]

Comments:

(1) Thus, in order to avoid the implications of Smith's views, one need not bother to refute them, or come to terms with them in any responsible matter. Rather, one can simply refrain from "buying them," as she herself explicitly acknowledges some will do.[101] Moreover, one cannot be wrong in refusing to purchase her "verbal/conceptual construct." A purchase can be wise or foolish, but not "wrong" in the sense of "erroneous," "mistaken," "incorrect." Thus, Smith's attempted escape from self-referential paradoxes is "purchased" (to adopt her metaphor) at the "cost" of: (a) removing from everyone the responsibility to come to terms with her arguments; (b) ensuring that anyone who rejects her views will not be wrong in doing so; and (c) guaranteeing that anyone who does reject her views will, at least for himself or herself, have *refuted* those views (since cogency, and, presumably, its opposite, is, on Smith's understanding, merely a contingent matter of who happens to "buy" what at a given time or place).

(2) The reduction of "truth" to "whatever people are willing to buy at a given time and place" yields the paradoxical implication that one and the same statement can fluctuate back and forth between truth and falsity without anything in the world changing but beliefs about the statement. In other words, the statement "A is taller than B" can be true, then false, then true again, without the height of A or B changing.

(3) How does the move from "assertion" to "description" help here? Are not some of the issues concerning the accuracy of descriptions the same as those concerning the truth of assertions?

(4) When one is buying and selling, are there not ethical issues concerning the quality of what is being offered for sale? And if what is being offered for sale are descriptions, do not these ethical issues concern the accuracy of the descriptions? So, once again, unless Smith wants to remove such ethical considerations from her marketplace, we will have to come to grips with the issue of the accuracy of her characterizations, rather than brush such considerations aside by referring to what in fact people might be willing to "buy."[102]

Here is another example of her tough-minded response to the self-referential inconsistency objection. Commenting on an attempted self-refutation argument concerning the claim that "[s]cientific theories are (mere) reflections of the social interests of those who produce and promote them," Smith argues that "the charge fails if the supposed self-refuter disavows the 'mere,' and the presumably self-*excepting* claim is revealed as (or transformed into) an explicitly and flagrantly self-*exemplifying* one: 'You charge my theory of the social interests of all theories with reflecting social interests? But *of course* it does: it could hardly prosper otherwise!'"[103]

Comments:

(1) The claim that scientific theories are reflections (mere or otherwise) of the social interests of those who produce and promote them has usually been advanced in the cause of debunking science's alleged pretensions to achieving objective knowledge about the world. But this debunking only carries weight if it can lay claim to such pretensions. Were it to turn out to be true that scientific theories are reflections of the social interests of those who produce and promote them, that would be interesting indeed. But now we learn that, in the face of the self-referential inconsistency charge, this is to be construed as saying only that such a claim is itself simply a reflection of the social interests of those who produce and promote *it*. So what? Surely everybody already knows that there are many people who attempt to elevate themselves socially by trying to knock down those who, like scientists, currently enjoy greater prestige and respect. One would have to maintain constantly in mind when reading each one of the claims of these sociologists of science that they should be translated as "It is a reflection of our social interests to maintain that . . . " And if this is not what Smith and others of her ilk mean, then it is not clear what their meaning could possibly be. They cannot mean their doctrines to be objectively true, since they repudiate objective truth. If they mean

their doctrines fallibilistically, this is consistent with objective truth, and they are saying something unremarkable (and are fighting a straw man). If it is something else, what is it? For example, if someone says, "Can you reach the salt?" they probably are not literally inquiring into your reaching ability, and it would indeed show a lack of imagination (or lack of familiarity with English-language idioms) so to construe it. But then we can in this case specify what it does mean—something like, "please pass the salt." How can you paraphrase Smith and her sort? Suppose I say, "I've been murdered in cold blood forty-seven times, no wait, forty-eight counting last Tuesday," and we counter with "Is that true"? Suppose that the reply is then, "No, of course not, I'm obviously very much alive, but anyway, I think I will be murdered again tomorrow." No further explanation of the meaning of these utterances is ever forthcoming. This is what Smith does. She says things that seem to make a kind of sense if taken as literal statements of purported objective truths, but that would defeat her purpose, and she denies that that is what she is doing (and decries those who construe her this way for their blighted imaginations). But she never enlightens us as to what she does mean, except by making fallibilistic noises and taking straw man swipes at defenders of absolutistic, God's-eye-view certainty.

(2) If we were really to take her view of science seriously, it would seem that it would transform the way in which we would argue about scientific issues. The way to show that a given scientific theory was warranted would not be to point to evidence and arguments which would seem to indicate that it is true, but rather to urge that it would further our social interests to adopt it. Before readers are convinced by the sociologists' position, they are likely to say of it, "I don't care whether or not it furthers their social interests; I want to know whether or not it is true." But if they are convinced by it, their response is likely to be "I don't care whether or not it furthers their social interests; I want to know whether or not it will further mine." The view that these sociologists of science present seems to have whatever plausibility it does only on the assumption that the scientists in question are not aware that this is what they are doing. That is, they think that they are making discoveries about the world, when in fact they are attempting to enhance their own social standing. What would happen if we were to get scientists to look at it this way, so that they could feel free to pursue such self-enhancement more nakedly and freely, unencum-

bered by any delusions that they are searching for truth? Would this lead to an improvement in the quality of scientific work?

(3) Note again the reductionism here, and the sweeping claims: "of course it does; it could not be otherwise."

Here is one more formulation of Smith's tough-minded response to the self-referential inconsistency objection:

> The postmodern skeptic thinks that the interest and utility of all theoretical formulations are contingent. She is not disturbed, however, by the idea that, in order to be self-consistent, she must "concede" the "merely" contingent interest and utility of her own theoretical formulations. Nor is she embarrassed by her similar "obligation" to "concede" the historicity—and thus instability and eventual replacement—of the systems and idioms that she finds preferable to traditional epistemology and that she would, and does, recommend to other people. She is not disturbed or embarrassed—or, to her own way of thinking, self-refuted—by these things because she believes, in comfortable accord with the conceptual systems and idioms she prefers, that that's the way all disciplinary knowledge—science, philosophy, literary studies, and so forth—evolves.[104]

Comments:

(1) This is the "no bite" problem. Her position seems to be, then, not only that her postmodern skepticism is not objectively correct, but also that it is interesting and useful only for someone in her circumstances and with her disciplinary training.

(2) What is the status of the claim that it (really?) is interesting and useful for such a person so situated? Is that claim to be construed as an objective claim, or is it to be construed as true only insofar as it is interesting and useful so to construe it? And if the latter, is the claim that it is useful and interesting to view it as useful and interesting, itself to be assented to only insofar as it itself is useful and interesting to do so, and so on ad infinitum?

(3) There is still another ambiguity in this position. When she "'concede[s]' the historicity—and thus instability and eventual replacement—of the systems and idioms that she finds preferable to traditional epistemology," this seems to suggest that circumstances may change in such a way as to make traditional epistemology sound (or sound again?). But if the (first-order) soundness of traditional epistemology is still held to be relative (second-order) to historical

contingencies, then it appears that she is denying (second-order) soundness to traditional epistemology, no matter what the historical circumstances. Thus, her dilemma is that she is holding either that her constructivist epistemology really is absolutely sound at this second level, and thus not sensitive to historical and contextual contingencies at that level, or that such contingencies may one day make it not merely seem but really, objectively, *be* the case not only that traditional epistemology is sound and her constructivist epistemology unsound, but also that traditional epistemology always was right, and her own views always mistaken. She might opt for the latter option but feel unthreatened by it, on the grounds that it seems unlikely that such historical circumstances would ever arrive. Still, she would have to grant that it can only seem that way from the perspective of our current situation.

Smith also suggests that

> the agents/victims of self-refutation are . . . usually philosophical innovators: that is, theorists who have articulated original substantive views on various matters of philosophical interest: knowledge, language, science, and so forth. When their self-refutation is [allegedly] being exposed, however, they are seen primarily in their role of negative critics of orthodox thought: that is, as deniers, rejecters, and abandoners of views that are widely experienced as intuitively correct and manifestly true. Indeed, even prior to and independent of any [attempted] formal demonstration of their self-refutation, the views of such theorists tend to be experienced by disciplinary philosophers—and those whom they have instructed—as self-evidently absurd.[105]

Smith is undoubtedly correct in saying that highly original and unorthodox views will tend to attract a great deal of critical scrutiny and will be dismissed by many simply because they are unorthodox, rather than receiving a fair hearing and being judged on their merits (whatever that might mean to Smith). But surely some unorthodox views are false, and even ridiculous or stupid. Thus, it is question-begging to trot out the originality of the views in question as way of defending them against charges of self-refutation. After all, it may be that such views as she is defending tend to get called "self-refuting" for the same reason that Shaquille O'Neal tends to get called "tall." Moreover, her argument fails to explain why it is precisely this charge that is so often hurled against the views she defends. For there are many other unorthodox positions which draw lots of criticism—the idea that aliens from outer space are continually visiting earth and altering our history, for example—but which are never thought to be self-refuting. And it is an ad hominem argument to imply that such charges, when issued against unorthodox views, must simply be understood as a desperate attempt to keep novelty and innovation at bay.

Equally fallacious is Smith's attempt to rescue Protagorean relativism, the famous doctrine that "man is the measure of all things," from charges of self-referential inconsistency. Those charges are usually presented in something like the following manner. (1) If man is the measure, then the man who says that man is not the measure is just as right as the one who says that man is the measure. So man both is and is not the measure—a contradiction. (2) Reply: no, there is no contradiction, since it should be interpreted this way: "Man is the measure" is true for me; "man is not the measure" is true for you—no contradiction. (3) What does this mean, if not simply that you believe that man is the measure while I do not? More fundamentally, you are still committed to the relativistic thesis enunciated at (2). What can you say to the one who says, "It is false that 'man is the measure' for you while 'man is not the measure' for me"?

Smith misses point (3) above when she argues that Socrates' attempted refutation of Protagoras would not work "if, for example, Protagoras had actually said '*It appears to me* that man is the measure of all things . . . ,' or obviously meant his doctrine to be taken as only *relatively* true, or obviously meant to affirm only that each thing is as it is perceived *to those who perceive it that way*."[106] The first reformulation need not detain us. All parties to the dispute can agree that this is how things appear to Protagoras. The issue concerns the merits of the idea that they are (even if we qualify this with "relatively," or "for him," or "to those who perceive it that way," or what have you) the way they appear to Protagoras. To see that the self-refutation charge remains valid, consider the last formulation, that "each thing is as it is to those who perceive it that way." Now I deny this thesis. I say that this thesis is false. I say that just because you see an elephant as a flying thing, even to or for you (unless all that is meant by this is that you in fact see it that way, a point that no one is disputing) the issue is one of validity, even if only relative validity. So the claim that "each thing is as it is to those who perceive it that way" is itself, on its own terms, only true for those who perceive it as true. For others it is not true. To claim that it is true for everyone is to be guilty of a self-referential inconsistency. Also, note the infinite regress. We start with "man is the measure of all things." Next we get "man is the measure of the issue of whether or not man is the measure of all things." Then it becomes "man is the measure of the issue of whether or not man is the measure of the issue of whether or not man is the measure of all things," and so on infinitely.

Finally, Smith's arguments are fallacious, once again, when she attempts to turn the tables on her opponents and show that they are the one who are guilty of arguing fallaciously. For example, she accuses Harvey Siegel of begging the question: "Siegel argues that the charge by epistemological 'naturalists' that the 'incoherence argument' is question-begging 'founders on the confusion . . . between truth and certainty,' thus appealing (question-beggingly as charged) to the classic conception of 'truth' at issue."[107] While it is question-begging to rely upon, as in the premise of an argument, the very thesis that is under challenge, it is by no means question-begging to "appeal to" the thesis under challenge, if in doing so one is merely distinguishing it from something else. Suppose I affirm x and you deny it. In my defense of x I can make no use of x as a premise in any of my arguments: to do so would be circular and question-begging. But suppose you criticize what you call "x," but I think it is really "y," something easily confused with x, but something which differs from it in such a way that I think your argument, cogent as it may be against y, does not succeed in undermining x. Obviously it would not be question-begging for me merely to point out the distinction between x and y as part of my defense of x, even if, in a sense, this involves "appealing to" x, the very thing I am defending. Moreover, what, from Smith's point of view as an opponent of traditional notions of truth, objectivity, and rationality, can possibly be wrong with begging the question? To be sure, it could be that Smith herself sees nothing wrong with begging the question and recognizes as a logical implication of her own position that it must regard all argumentation as question-begging, so that her point here is that defenders of objectivity, like Siegel, merely fail by their own standards (and not by hers). But no, she explicitly claims that her own position is non-question-begging.[108]

NOTES

1. Ronald Dworkin, "We Need a New Interpretation of Academic Freedom," *Academe* 82, no. 3 (May/June 1996): 11.

2. Here is a small sampling of recent statements on this issue:

[T]he assertion that one cannot describe viewpoints as being true or false, or right or wrong, is becoming commonplace. (Alison Assiter, *Enlightened Women* [New York: Routledge, 1996], p. 5.)

Researchers have almost given up on the quaint notion that there is any such thing as "fact" or "objectivity." (Cynthia Crossen, *Tainted Truth* [New York: Simon & Schuster, 1994], p. 17.)

Given the remarkable variety of theoretical approaches in literary studies today, it is perhaps equally remarkable how little disagreement there is about the concept of truth. Theorists who agree on little if anything else unite to view the word and the concept with suspicion. Anyone who claims truth-value for a statement—so the contemporary orthodoxy has it—is deluded, caught in a system of ideology that has created the discursive structure in which the speaker is operating, and is probably deluding as well, seeking to obtain power over others. A softer version of this would say that to make truth-claims is just a waste of time. . . . The contemporary critique of truth-claims is one with the contemporary critique of objectivity, and the notion that objectivity is a myth plays as important a role in the self-representation of the humanities today as the notion of objectivity has traditionally played in the self-representation of the sciences. (Reed Way Dasenbrock, "We've Done It to Ourselves: The Critique of Truth and the Attack on Theory," in *PC Wars*, ed. Jeffrey Williams [New York: Routledge, 1995], p. 174.)

[A]long with . . . the scepticism that pervades academia, there is a derivative scepticism which has spread beyond academia into the general culture. In that general culture, one finds the sceptical attitude expressed in the use of such phrases as "Who's to say?"; "Everyone's entitled to their own opinion"; "There are no absolutes"; "It's all subjective"; "It's all relative"; "If you believe it, it's true for you"; "Don't judge"; or any number of other related phrases. I would claim that these phrases are the symptomatic expression of a pervasive sceptical attitude. . . . This relativism/ scepticism is constantly reiterated in the phrases mentioned above, which I take to be evidence that the relativism has become a prevailing attitude of many if not most students, and at least some faculty. (Ronald F. Duska, "What's the Point of a Business Ethics Course?" in *Business as Ethical and Business as Usual*, ed. Sterling Harwood [Sudbury, MA: Jones and Bartlett, 1996], p. 13.)

[A] form of intellectual parochialism has triumphed, a style of thinking that its detractors call relativism and its proponents, more clumsily, call perspectivism or standpoint theory. . . . [T]he premise of much thinking in universities and popular lore alike is that how you see is a function of who you are—that is, where you stand. . . . [T]he academy has no monopoly on the decline of the claim to truth. Perspectivists crop up everywhere, from op-ed pages to the Grand Old Oprah of daytime talk shows in which Klansmen and Afrocentrists, anorexics and abusers, rapists and rape victims all get their hearings. . . . There are said to be no privileged positions from which to know anything. Our discussion, or "discourse," is fatally limited to our language, our "interpretive community," our vantage point—by which is usually meant our race, ethnicity, gender. There is no fixed, stable meaning for the very terms with which, imperfectly, we strive to know. There is, instead, a veritable orgy of "discourses" and "knowledges". . . . What there isn't is truth. There are only stories. (Todd Gitlin, *The Twilight of Common Dreams* [New York: Metropolitan Books, 1995], pp. 200–201.)

Anyone who has taught—anyone who has lived in American society—will recognize a truth in the widespread charge of student "relativism." Confronted with unfamiliar stances, outlandish positions, and even inhumane practices, students often shrug their shoulders, unwilling to approve or condemn. "It all depends" comes the irresolute comment, the motto of the relativist. Is foot-binding good or bad? Watching ten hours of television a day? "It all depends." Depends on what? On everything: on who and what and where. This is what might be called relativism or an unwillingness to judge. Everyone and everything is right. . . . I think this; you think that. All have equally valid opinions. It is not necessary to resolve, even pursue questions very far, because all is relative to the individual. (Russell Jacoby, *Dogmatic Wisdom* [New York: Doubleday, 1994], p. 120.)

[T]here are widespread doubts about the very possibility of making absolute or universal judgments that transcend our always limited points of view. New trends in the social sciences and humanities, some of them with popular names like "postmodernism" or "post-structuralism," make much of the fact that all our views about the world are historically and culturally conditioned. We always see things from a particular point of view (a "conceptual framework," or "language game," or "cultural tradition"). How can we therefore show that our point of view, or any other, is the right one and competing views wrong, when we must assume the basic presuppositions of some particular point of view to support our claims? How can we climb out of our historically and culturally limited perspectives to find an Archimedean point, an absolute standpoint above the particular and competing points of view? This problem haunts the modern intellectual landscape. One sees variations of it everywhere in different fields of study, and everywhere it produces doubts among reflective persons about the possibility of justifying belief in objective intellectual, cultural, and moral standards. (Robert Kane, *Through the Moral Maze* [New York: Paragon House, 1994], pp. 1–2.)

If we are certain of anything, it is that we are certain of nothing. If we have knowledge, it is that there can be none. Ours is a world awash with relativism. It has seeped into our culture, it threatens to become our faith. The tide may have begun with the end of belief in a universal morality and religious code, but it has swelled with a recognition of the limited and particular perspective of our culture, our time and our society. Its full force is now being felt in the name of post-structuralism and post-modernity. (Hilary Lawson, "Stories about Stories," in *Dismantling Truth*, ed. Hilary Lawson and Lisa Appignanesi [London: Weidenfeld and Nicolson, 1989], p. xi.)

Our own age has the distinction, perhaps, of being the first age ever in which the basic assumptions of most people, certainly of most educated people, are relativistic. (Norman Melchert, *The Great Conversation*, 4th. ed. [Boston: McGraw-Hill, 2002], p. xiii.)

The conventional wisdom among English professors and graduate students is that "knowledge" is subjective, relative, contingent, culturally determined, [and] political. (Louis Menand, "The Future of Academic Freedom," *Academe* 79, no. 3 [May/June 1993]: 16.)

The philosophy of the modern world is overwhelmingly relativistic. . . . [C]ultural relativism (including moral relativism) seems to be the favoured belief of the day. (J. N. Mohanty, "Philosophy and Today's World," in his *The Self and Its Other* [New York: Oxford University Press, 2000], p. 14.)

What is specifically postmodernist . . . is . . . the . . . far-reaching claim that truth and rationality are always socially and discursively constructed and their validity and applicability are necessarily limited to their particular contexts or situations. They have, it is claimed in principle, no general or universal import. (Satya P. Mohanty, *Literary Theory and the Claims of History* [Ithaca, NY: Cornell University Press, 1997], p. xi.)

[T]he facile subjectivism that now blights many of the humanities and social sciences . . . [holds that] anyone who thinks that some questions have right and wrong answers, which can be confirmed or refuted by evidence and argument, is an epistemological caveman. (Thomas Nagel, "Freud's Permanent Revolution," in his *Other Minds* [New York: Oxford University Press, 1995], p. 40.)

The skeptics are with us again. We are living in the midst of a revival of the attack on normative reasoning and commitment that was a stock-in-trade of Pyrrho's school. This revival enjoys some influence in philosophy but far more in literary theory and, lately, in those parts of legal thought that are influenced by literary theory. It is becoming fashionable to make some of the claims associated with the Pyrrhonist tradition: that to every argument some argument to a contradictory conclusion can be opposed; that arguments are in any case merely tools of influence, without any better sort of claim to our allegiance; [and] that when contradictory claims are asserted there is no rational way to adjudicate between them. (Martha C. Nussbaum, "Skepticism about Practical Reason in Literature and the Law," *Harvard Law Review* 107, no. 3 [January 1994]: 715–716.)

Objectivity has fallen on hard days. . . . To be sure, objectivity has not fallen from philosophical view—various influential philosophers of the day have a good deal to say *about* it. It is just that they generally do not have much good to say *for* it. Feminists see it as a male fetish, new-agers reject it as mere left-brain thinking, radicals dismiss it as a cover for bourgeois self-interest. Most of the fashionable tendencies of the day agree in wanting to topple objectivity from its traditional pedestal. We live in an era where the spirit of the times favors the siren call of subjectivism, relativism, skepticism. . . .

[W]e sophisticates of the present, so [post-modernists] hold, have learned that truth, reason, rational cogency, objectivity, and the like are mere chimeras. (Nicholas Rescher, *Objectivity* [Notre Dame, IN: University of Notre Dame Press, 1997], pp. 1, 42.)

Once upon a time, when students used to respond to a difficult philosophical question in class with statements like "It's all a matter of opinion," or "It's a question of semantics," or "It's all relative," I used to scold them gently. I can no longer do that, for the more knowledgeable among them can now easily cite many of the more prominent practitioners of the craft of philosophy in support of such statements. And they can cite as well no small number of anthropologists, historians, psychologists, sociologists, and literary theorists in the same vein. (Henry Rosemont Jr., "Beyond Post-Modernism," in *Chinese Language, Thought, and Culture*, ed. Philip J. Ivanhoe [Chicago: Open Court, 1996], p. 155.)

Talk . . . against truth has recently gained popularity outside of philosophy. It is now common among literary theorists, sociologists of science, anthropologists, educational theorists, and others to deride classical theories of truth . . . , and even to oppose the very aim of true belief. (Frederick F. Schmitt, *Truth: A Primer* [Boulder, CO: Westview Press, 1995], p. x.)

[T]hat . . . the world does not provide us with a foundational reality, or that we live within the realm of the spectacle, or that it is impossible to authenticate any form of knowledge as truth, or that all knowledges must be understood as productions of particular, situated minds and therefore as incommensurable with the knowledges of differently situated minds . . . all these are familiar if deliberately trivial examples of a recognizably postmodern ethos. (David Simpson, *The Academic Postmodern and the Rule of Literature* [Chicago: University of Chicago Press, 1995], p. 2.)

See also David Edwards, *Burning All Illusions* (Boston: South End Press, 1996), p. 55; James F. Harris, *Against Relativism* (La Salle, IL: Open Court, 1992), p. 1; Larry Laudan, *Science and Relativism* (Chicago: University of Chicago Press, 1990), p. x; and Stephen A. Satris, "Student Relativism," *Teaching Philosophy* 9, no. 3 (September 1986): 199.

Similarly, Barbara Ehrenreich (in "Truth, Justice, and the Left," *Z Papers* 1, no. 4 [October–December 1992]: 58) tells the following, all-too-familiar, story:

I was on a panel, talking about multiculturalism. Afterwards someone in the audience . . . came up to me and said, "that was fine, except I can't believe you used the word 'truth'". . . . It wasn't that we disagreed on the substance of what I'd said, which was very pro-multiculturalism. It was the idea of truth, as in, for example, "the truth about the Spanish conquest." She said the word "truth" as if she were referring to some obscenity I had used. I asked her what she meant, and she said, "Well there is no such thing as truth."

In a letter published in *Z Papers* 2, no. 1 (January–March 1993), Kate Ellis identifies herself as the one who had this exchange with Ehrenreich (p. 4). Ellis does not challenge the accuracy of Ehrenreich's account.

Todd Gitlin (*Twilight of Common Dreams*, p. 157) tells a similar story: "I sat down for lunch . . . with two . . . graduate student activists and pointed out a flock of factual errors . . . in their leaflet. 'There is no "truth,"' one of them, a very intelligent woman, said, 'there are only truth effects.'"

It is important to emphasize, moreover, that this ascendancy of relativism is not confined to writers and professors, but rather permeates the entire culture. Philosophy teachers regularly encounter it in their students. Indeed, Allan Bloom, in *The Closing of the American Mind* (New York: Simon & Schuster, 1987), p. 25, goes so far as to declare that "[t]here is one thing a professor can be absolutely certain of: almost every student entering the university believes, or says he believes, that truth is relative." Bloom is, characteristically, exaggerating. (A minor aim of the present work is to show that one can agree with some of Bloom's complaints about relativism while disagreeing, often violently, with just about everything else he says!) Still, we might well consider Michael P. Zuckert's report on his own attempt to test out Bloom's claim:

I was teaching . . . a course in American Political Thought, discussing . . . the Declaration of Independence. The Declaration claims that certain fundamental moral and political claims about equality and natural rights are "self-evident truths." So I asked my students whether they believed that. The results: YES 7%, NO 77%, NOT VOTING 16%. When I probed beneath the surface of their votes I discovered not that my students were devoted to undemocratic ideas about human inequality but rather that they were convinced there is no such thing as "truth," self-evident or otherwise, in the sphere of claims of the sort raised in the Declaration. ("Two Cheers [at Least] for Allan Bloom," in *Essays on The Closing of the American Mind*, ed. Robert L. Stone [Chicago: Chicago Review Press, 1989], p. 76.)

Similarly, Louis Pojman tells us that

> in polls taken in my ethics and introduction to philosophy classes over the past several years (in three different universities in three areas of the country) students affirmed by a 2 to 1 ratio, a version of moral relativism over moral absolutism with barely 3 percent seeing something in between these two polar opposites. (*Ethics*, 2d ed. [Belmont, CA: Wadsworth, 1995], p. 26.)

It is interesting to note, moreover, that in Bruce Wilshire's *The Moral Collapse of the University*, which is touted in reviewers' comments printed on the back of the paperback copy as constituting "a liberal response to Bloom" (according to Philip L. Smith), and one which takes "a significant step beyond him" (in the words of Edward S. Casey), we find that Wilshire says, seemingly very much in agreement with Bloom, that "many students come to the university with at least one dogma firmly ensconced, and it shields them from disappointments: 'When asked about serious matters of moral concern, one can only think, There is no truth about them'" ([Albany: State University of New York Press, 1990], p. 17). ("I have found," Wilshire goes on to say, "that the response of fellow professors in the university is often on the same swampy, bleary level. Skepticism about truth, tacit or manifest, mindless or half-articulated, is widespread" [p. 18].)

And again, Harry Brod (in an essay that predates Bloom's book, and that advocates, on affirmative action grounds, that teachers should argue for leftist political views in the classroom—not a tactic that Bloom would endorse, I would say) remarks that the increased incidence of relativism among his students has led him to change radically the tone of his introductory remarks at the beginning of a semester:

> In the interests of fostering an atmosphere of objective analysis, I used to stress the need for tolerance, of detachment from adherence to a particular view. I have recently come to see, however, that my undergraduate students are in some sense already overly detached from moral judgments. . . . They tend to talk as if their sole moral obligation was not to pass judgment on others, as if reaching moral conclusions were some sort of totalitarian act against others by imposing one's will on them. In the face of this extreme relativism, I now find myself, to my surprise, stressing in my introductory remarks the need to take a stance, to make moral commitments, to be ethically engaged. ("Philosophy Teaching as Intellectual Affirmative Action," *Teaching Philosophy* 9, no. 1 [March 1986]: 10.)

Finally, let us observe the results of one of Stephen A. Satris's writing assignments for his Introduction to Philosophy course. Each student was to write a short essay "on his or her own idea of human excellence" ("Student Relativism," p. 195). (Note that Satris's essay predates Bloom's book.) Here are eleven short selections from these essays (as quoted in Satris, p. 196, noting that each selection is taken from a different paper; that the total number of papers was twenty-two; that I have abridged Satris's quotations 5 and 10; and that I have followed Satris in quoting the students verbatim, without altering their grammar or spelling):

1. Human excellence in my opinion is a product of an individual's mind. Everyone has different ideas as to what excellence is. Excellence to me can mean a completely different thing to someone else. Excellence can only be measured by an individual.

2. Who's to say what excellence means? . . . Everyone's values, opinions, and standards differ, so how can we separate excellent from good?

3. Excellence in many ways is a relative term. . . . Perhaps . . . an excellent person is one who molds his existence by his own idea of what is right and true. In this way there cannot be a single definition of excellence.

4. I feel that human excellence is excellence with that person . . . it is up to each individual to develop his or her own views of human excellence. . . .

5. Moral values are different to everyone, so what is right for one is wrong for another.

6. Human excellence is a relative term, the definition of which is determined to a large degree by a person's heredity and environment. Stated simply, what is excellence to one person may not be excellence to another person.

7. A person would have to be quite naive to think excellence could exist, for excellence is different in everyone's eyes.

8. . . . if a person feels he has an excellent life then he does, and he has achieved human excellence.

9. The basic problem in defining human excellence is that excellence is a totally subjective state. Like art or beauty, it is determined by the beholder. However, because people are basically social animals, excellence is not so much an individual's opinion as it is the society's opinion. . . . To live an excellent life . . . would be a matter of achieving what one's society considered success.

10. Human excellence is the standard or model which a society imposes. . . .

11. the best someone can do is to follow the guidelines set down by society.

While these quotations, poll results, and essay writing samples are suggestive, and will surprise very few, if any, who have been teaching such courses themselves in recent years, it must be conceded that they constitute merely anecdotal, rather than rigorously scientific, evidence in support of claims like Bloom's.

3. Walter Truett Anderson, *Reality Isn't What It Used to Be* (San Francisco: Harper and Row, 1990), p. 14.

4. Ibid., p. 4.

5. Ibid., p. 75.

6. Ibid., p. 267.

7. Ibid.

8. Ibid., p. 268.

9. Ibid.

10. See chapter 4 above.

11. Anderson, *Reality*, pp. 268–269.

12. Ibid., p. 269.

13. Anderson, "Introduction" to *The Truth about the Truth*, ed. Walter Truett Anderson (New York: G. P. Putnam's Sons, 1995), p. 2.

14. Anderson, "All That Is Solid Melts into Air," in *The Truth about the Truth*, ed. Anderson, p. 69 (emphasis added).

15. Ibid.

16. On the Sapir-Whorf hypothesis, see Steven Pinker, *The Language Instinct* (New York: HarperPerrenial, 1995), pp. 57–82. On Eskimo snow vocabulary, see also Laura Martin, "'Eskimo Words for Snow': A Case Study in the Genesis and Decay of an Anthropological Example," *American Anthropologist* 88, no. 2 (June 1986): 418–423; and Geoffrey K. Pullum, "The Great Eskimo Vocabulary Hoax," in his *The Great Eskimo Vocabulary Hoax and Other Irreverent Essays on the Study of Language* (Chicago: University of Chicago Press, 1991), pp. 159–171. Note that Anderson cites no scholarly source for his claims about Eskimo snow vocabulary, but rather is content to tell us that he has repeatedly been "informed" of this "fact." Note also that Martin's and Pullum's debunking work precedes his, though he does not acknowledge it, let alone attempt to respond to it. (Indeed, there is no reason to suppose that he is aware of it.) This is not surprising, for, as Pullum points out, "[o]nce the public has decided to accept something as an interesting fact, it becomes almost impossible to get the acceptance rescinded. The persistent interestingness and symbolic usefulness overrides any lack of factuality" (p. 159).

17. Indeed, although "[t]here was no word for 'orange' in the Middle English of Chaucer's time," this did not stop him from referring "twice in the *Canterbury Tales* to a shade 'bitwixe yelow and reed.'" Martin Gardner, "Mathematics and the Folkways," in his *The Night Is Large* (New York: St. Martin's Press, 1996), p. 259.

18. Anderson, editorial introduction to Roy Wagner, "The Idea of Culture," in *The Truth about the Truth*, ed. Anderson, p. 53.

19. See, for example, Brent Berlin and Paul Kay, *Basic Color Terms: Their Universality and Evolution* (Berkeley: University of California Press, 1969).

20. Anderson, *Reality Isn't What It Used to Be*, p. 166. Anderson also claims that Reagan "lived in a happy Kantian interaction with the noumena, improvising realities out of them as he went along, and always managing to find a public that liked what he created" (p. 166). This is a travesty of Kant, the full correction of which is beyond the scope of this book. Briefly, however, Kant held that the mind supplies the form of judgments, but not their content. For example, Kant argued that while the *category* "causality" (formal element of judgment) is imposed on reality by the mind, the question of whether it is A which is the cause of B, as opposed to B being the cause of A, or neither, or both (specific content element of judgment), depends upon the world and is not imposed on it by the mind. Moreover, Kant was concerned with universal structures of mind, which we cannot help but employ whenever we think and judge, not idiosyncratic projects of inventing a make-believe world and selling it to others! Kant, who opposed lying more vehemently than did any other philosopher, spins in his grave.

21. Ibid., p. 167.

22. A good collection of Reagan's false statements can be found in Mark Green and Gail MacColl, *Reagan's Reign of Error* (New York: Pantheon, 1987).

23. Anderson, *Reality Isn't What It Used to Be*, pp. 5–6.

24. Ibid., p. 269.

25. Ibid., p. 107.

26. Ruth Benedict, "Anthropology and the Abnormal," *Journal of General Psychology* 10 (1934), as excerpted in *Ethical Theory*, ed. Louis P. Pojman (Belmont, CA: Wadsworth, 2002), p. 36.

27. Thomas Nagel, "MacIntyre versus the Enlightenment," in his *Other Minds* (New York: Oxford University Press, 1995), p. 203. It seems to me that Nagel's criticism applies powerfully against Rorty's position as well. To see this, one need only consult the statements of Rorty's quoted in the second paragraph of chapter 5, section VII above.

28. Michael Bérubé, *Public Access* (New York: Verso, 1994), p. 134, note 8.

29. Bérubé, "Discipline and Theory," in *Wild Orchids and Trotsky*, ed. Mark Edmundson (New York: Penguin, 1993), pp. 182–183.

30. See chapter 5, section IV.

31. For more on Bérubé, see chapter 2, section II A above.

32. Laurie Calhoun, *Philosophy Unmasked* (Lawrence: University Press of Kansas, 1997). See, for example, pp. x, 21–24, and 183.

33. Calhoun, personal communication with the author.

34. Ibid.

35. Calhoun, *Philosophy Unmasked*, pp. 183–184.

36. Ibid., p. 94.

37. Ibid., p. 137.

38. Ibid., p. 188.

39. Ibid., p. 46.

40. Ibid., p. 49.

41. Ibid., pp. 33–34.

42. Ibid., p. 32.

43. See also in this connection p. 197, note 25, where Calhoun writes: "[T]he word 'wrong' used in articulating a meta-thesis could not possibly mean 'morally wrong,' since meta-theories are entirely devoid of normative content." Is this just her perspective, an alleged absolute truth, or what? The same question could be asked about almost everything she says.

44. Richard Campbell, *Truth and Historicity* (New York: Oxford University Press, 1992), p. 6.

45. Stanley Fish, *Is There a Text in This Class?* (Cambridge, MA: Harvard University Press, 1980), p. 369.

46. Fish, "Don't Blame Relativism," *Responsive Community* 12, no. 3 (summer 2002): 28–29.

47. Joshua Cohen, "Who Cares What bin Laden Thinks?" *Responsive Community* 12, no. 3 (summer 2002): 37.

48. Fish, "A Reply to My Critics," *Responsive Community* 12, no. 3 (summer 2002): 63.

49. Ibid.

50. Richard Rorty, *Contingency, Irony, and Solidarity* (New York: Cambridge University Press, 1989), p. 59.

51. Cohen, "Who Cares," p. 38.

52. For more on Fish, see chapter 2, section III B above, and chapter 8, section III below.

53. Frances FitzGerald, *America Revised* (New York: Vintage, 1980), p. 16.

54. Henry Giroux, "Postmodernism and the Discourse of Educational Criticism," *Journal of Education*, 170, no. 3 (1988): 14.

55. Mary E. Hawkesworth, "From Objectivity to Objectification," in *Rethinking Objectivity*, ed. Allan Megill (Durham, NC: Duke University Press, 1994), p. 152.

56. Ruth Hubbard, "Some Thoughts about the Masculinity of the Natural

Sciences," in *Feminist Thought and the Structure of Knowledge*, ed. Mary McCanney Gergen (New York: New York University Press, 1989), pp. 1–2.

57. Peter Davies, ed., *The American Heritage Dictionary of the English Language* (New York: Dell, 1976), p. 256.

58. Kenneth J. Gergen, "Feminist Critique of Science and the Challenge of Social Epistemology," in *Feminist Thought*, ed. Gergen, p. 44. In a similar vein, Gergen also informs us that "the validity of theoretical propositions in the sciences is in no way affected by factual evidence" (ibid., p. 37).

59. Thomas McEvilley, *Art and Otherness* (Kingston, NY: Documentext, 1992), p. 13.

60. Dean Pickard, "Applied Nietzsche," *Auslegung* 19, no. 1 (winter 1993): 20.

61. Ibid., p. 7.

62. Ibid., p. 19.

63. Barry W. Sarchett, "What's All the Fuss about This Postmodernist Stuff?" in *Campus Wars*, ed. John Arthur and Amy Shapiro (Boulder, CO: Westview Press, 1995), p. 19.

64. Ibid., p. 22.

65. Ibid., p. 21.

66. Ibid., pp. 25–26.

67. Ibid., p. 27.

68. Ibid.

69. For more on this point, see chapter 1, section III above.

70. Sarchett, *"What's All the Fuss,"* p. 24.

71. Ibid., p. 22.

72. For more on Sarchett, see chapter 4, section III D above.

73. Barbara Herrnstein Smith, *Belief and Resistance* (Cambridge, MA: Harvard University Press, 1997), pp. xvi–xvii. For other formulations, see pp. 7–8, 79–80, and 131, among others.

74. On her relativism, note also her obvious sympathy, as made manifest in her discussion of contemporary controversies in the philosophy of science and what is now called "science studies," for the view that

there are conditions under which evidently conflicting theories cannot be measured or compared [against a common standard of truth]: when, for example, they assume radically divergent but (arguably) equally credible conceptions of the universe, or, as in the case of these epistemological debates themselves, when part of what divides the parties is how to understand the standards (*truth, rationality, evidence*, and so forth) by which the merits of their divergent theories could be measured—if, indeed, merits, measurements, or even choices, as classically conceived, are relevant to the outcomes of such conflicts (if, indeed, those divergences need be seen as conflicts). (Smith, *Belief and Resistance*, pp. 125–126.)

75. Smith, *Belief and Resistance*, p. xvi. For another formulation of this point, see pp. 7–8.

76. Ibid., p. 5.

77. Ibid., p. 6.

78. Ibid., p. 18.

79. Ibid., p. 156, note 17.

80. Ibid., p. 13.

81. See, for example, the quotation from Tom Bridges immediately prior to section I of chapter 1.

82. Ibid., pp. 79–80.

83. Smith, *Belief and Resistance*, p. 79.

84. For example, see ibid., pp. 73–74.

85. Smith cites Philip Kitcher, *The Advancement of Science* (New York: Oxford University Press, 1993), p. 195.

86. Smith, *Belief and Resistance*, p. 145.

87. Kitcher, *The Advancement of Science*, pp. 195–196.

88. Smith, *Belief and Resistance*, p. 22.

89. Ibid., p. xvi.

90. See, for example, ibid., pp. 77–78.

91. Ibid., p. 78.

92. See, for example, the discussions of objectivity, and especially the criticisms of the journalistic conception of that notion, in chapter 6 above.

93. Smith, *Belief and Resistance*, p. 23.

94. Ibid., p. 41.

95. Alexander J. Argyros, *A Blessed Rage for Order* (Ann Arbor: University of Michigan Press, 1991), p. 311.

96. Smith, *Belief and Resistance*, p. 1.

97. Ibid., pp. 4–5.

98. Ibid., p. 16.

99. Ibid., p. 17.

100. Barbara Herrnstein Smith, *Contingencies of Value* (Cambridge, MA: Harvard University Press, 1988), p. 113.

101. Ibid.

102. In my analysis here I am indebted to J. L. A. Garcia, "The Aims of the University and the Challenge of Diversity," in *An Ethical Education*, ed. M. N. S. Sellers (Providence, RI: Berg, 1994), pp. 30–31.

103. Smith, *Belief and Resistance*, p. 76.

104. Ibid., pp. 86–87.

105. Ibid., pp. 73–74. I have inserted the words "allegedly" and "attempted" above because Smith goes on to make clear that she does not find the self-refutation charge convincing when applied against the philosophical innovators she is discussing here.

106. Ibid., p. 76.

107. Ibid., p. 184, note 24. Smith quotes here from Harvey Siegel, *Relativism Refuted* (Dordrecht: Reidel, 1987), p. 187.

108. Smith, *Contingencies of Value*, p. 153. For further discussion of Smith's dubious attempt to escape charges of self-referential inconsistency by accusing her critics of begging the question, see David L. Roochnik, "Can the Relativist Avoid Refuting Herself?" *Philosophy and Literature* 14, no. 1 (April 1990): 92–98.

Chapter 8

THE LIMITATIONS OF RATIONALITY AND SCIENCE?

NOAM CHOMSKY, O. J. SIMPSON, AND ALAN SOKAL

As we have seen, "truth," "science," "rationality," "objectivity," "logic," and related notions are currently under widespread attack. Many contemporary thinkers simply reject these concepts out of hand, regarding them as pointless and passé at best, and as thoroughly discredited and politically harmful at worst. Other thinkers, undoubtedly significantly greater in number, do continue to make use of these notions, but only after first subjecting them to a deflationary analysis, wherein their weaknesses and limitations are emphasized. Indeed, these terms are now often modified by "Western," so as to rein in their pretensions of universality and to mark their embeddedness in specific geographical and historical contingencies. Thus, while it is true (if I may say so) that most contemporary "postmodern" thinkers do not assert (though some do) that science and logic are destructive and dispensable, they nonetheless still tend to insist that logic is just one way of thinking, and science just one set of stories and social practices, among others, with no entitlement to claims of unique or special merit.

An important feature of this postmodern critique of science, rationality, and other "Enlightenment" ideas is that it is often couched substantially in moral and political terms. That is, the concepts (and related practices) in question are seen not just as intellectually bankrupt, but as ethically pernicious as well. In particular, they are seen as obstacles to the development of a more humane, progressive, and radical politics.[1]

Many of those claiming to defend traditional conceptions of truth, science, rationality, and objectivity (and here I have in mind primarily the authors of best-selling potboilers attacking multiculturalism, "political correctness," and kindred phenomena),[2] have, in turn, tended to reject not only the postmodernists' critique of the Enlightenment, but their politics as well. Noam Chomsky's criticism of the postmodern attack on science and rationality is different, however, in that he, as a leading figure in contemporary radical political thought, is largely sympathetic to many of the political aspirations underlying this postmodern attack. But while he does regard the postmodern critique of Enlightenment concepts as wrong in principle, for reasons having little directly to do with politics, Chomsky too brings political considerations to bear on the debate over science and rationality, maintaining that the position defended by his opponents is ill-suited to any program of meaningful political change.

Chomsky's defense of rationality and science against their recent critics is relatively unknown, however, perhaps because it has been published in extensive form only in an obscure journal, called *Z Papers*, which has since ceased to exist. One of my goals in this chapter, accordingly, is to help bring Chomsky's critique of postmodernism and defense of rationality and science to the attention of readers, so as to facilitate the discussion and critical evaluation of his arguments.

Naturally, I also wish to participate in that discussion and critical evaluation, and will do so, at least in part, by the seemingly bizarre means of a consideration of the recent O. J. Simpson murder trial (I refer to the first, criminal, trial, rather than the second, civil, one) and of the many public discussions concerning both the trial itself and the issues surrounding it. For it has turned out, I shall argue, that the abstract theoretical positions staked out by Chomsky and his opponents have since been manifested concretely in the arguments of those who have disputed publicly over the Simpson trial.

And they have received yet another public hearing during the acrimonious debate about science and "science studies" that has been provoked by the "Sokal hoax." The chapter concludes with a consideration of that notorious public event.

I. Chomsky's Defense of Rationality and Science

Chomsky offers several arguments in support of science and Enlightenment conceptions of rationality. The first one flows from a simple consideration of what is involved in entering into such a debate in the first place:

> [T]o take part in a discussion, one must understand the ground rules. In this case, I don't. In particular, I don't know the answers to such elementary questions as these: Are conclusions to be consistent with premises (maybe even follow from them)? Do facts matter? Or can we string together thoughts as we like, calling it "argument," and make up facts as we please, taking one story to be as good as another? There are certain familiar ground rules: those of rational inquiry. They are by no means entirely clear, and there have been interesting efforts to criticize and clarify them; but we have enough of a grasp to proceed over a broad range. What seems to be under discussion here is whether we should abide by these ground rules at all (trying to improve them as we proceed). If the answer is that we are to abide by them, then the discussion is over: we've implicitly accepted the legitimacy of rational inquiry. If they are to be abandoned, then we cannot proceed until we learn what replaces the commitment to consistency, responsibility to fact, and other outdated notions. Short of some instruction on this matter, we are reduced to primal screams.[3]

Thus, wholesale attempts to reject what Chomsky is calling "rational inquiry" appear to be trapped within a dilemma. Either such attempts themselves substantially conform to the canons of rational inquiry or they do not. To the extent that they do, they are self-referentially inconsistent (e.g., they use logical arguments to prove that we should abandon logic, appeal to facts in order to show that facts carry no weight, and so on). Moreover, they place their opponents in the untenable position of having to beg the question (by using rational arguments, when the very issue at stake is whether that is the right way to proceed) at the very outset of the debate.

On the other hand, to the extent that attempts to overthrow rational inquiry do not themselves make use of the principles of rational inquiry, it is unclear why they should be taken seriously. At the very least, attempts at pursuing this latter path need to be accompanied by some sort of fairly well worked-out conception of what the alternatives to rational inquiry are to be, and of what the criteria are by which the attempts themselves are to be evaluated.

But for the most part such conceptions are lacking, as critics are content simply to point out alleged weaknesses of rational inquiry. Occasionally, however, an alternative is sketched. Consider the following:

> [R]eality can be shaped by any series of myths and I choose the shared consciousness of things and beings as the definition of reality and the project which human beings should accept, just because there is no set of laws about reality which can be known but there is a common consciousness which we need to make the dominant expression of this period. . . . [R]eality cannot be known and social reality can be constructed. . . . [I]t is made.[4]

In response, Chomsky points out, borrowing a phrase from Bertrand Russell, that such a proposal "has all the advantages of theft over honest toil."[5]

Another of Chomsky's arguments is a *reductio ad absurdum* of a standard antiscience argument. Chomsky presents the antiscience argument as follows (note that all of the quotations are drawn from the six critics to whom Chomsky is responding, and that he has replaced the term "science" with "X" to mark his conviction that his critics are caricaturing science):

> X is dominated by "the white male gender." It is "limited by cultural, racial and gender biases," and "establishes and perpetuates social organization [with] hidden political, social and economic purposes." "The majority in the South has waited for the last four hundred years for compassionate humane uses of X," which is "outside and above the democratic process." X is "thoroughly embedded in capitalist colonialism," and doesn't "end racism or disrupt the patriarchy." X has been invoked by Soviet commissars to bring people to "embrace regimentation, murderous collectivization, and worse." . . . X's dominance "has gone unchallenged." It has been "used to create new forms of control mediated through political and economic power." Ludicrous claims about X have been made by "state systems" which "used X for astoundingly destructive purposes . . . to create new forms of control mediated through political and economic power as it emerged in each system."

Conclusion: there is "something inherently wrong" with X. We must reject or transcend it, replacing it by something else; and we must instruct poor and suffering people to do likewise.[6]

Chomsky's *reductio*:

It follows that we must abandon literacy and the arts, which surely satisfy the conditions on X as well as science. More generally, we must take a vow of silence and induce the world's victims to do likewise since language and its use typically have all these properties, facts too well-known to discuss.[7]

The fact that the critics advocate rejecting science on the grounds that it is dominated by white males, used to justify atrocious political practices, and so forth, but do not advocate rejecting the thousands of other practices which share these same features certainly appears, in the absence of any argument explaining why science should be regarded differently in this respect, to constitute a glaring inconsistency. Still, as Chomsky points out, in a call-back to the argument about ground rules discussed above, "if consistency is to be abandoned or transcended, there is no problem."[8]

What Chomsky's *reductio* shows, though he does not put it this way, is that the antiscience critics are committing an elementary causal fallacy. From the simple fact that science is often put to odious political use, or used to justify odious political practices, it does not even begin to follow that there is something in the nature of science or scientific rationality which leads to such objectionable consequences. Indeed, the critics have failed even to establish a correlation between science and bad politics, much less a causal connection flowing from the one to the other. To establish a correlation, the critics would have to show that scientific thinking and practices, on the one hand, and odious politics, on the other, tend to vary together. That is, they would need to show that where we find more of the one, we tend to find more of the other, and that when we find less of the one, we find less of the other. To make a causal connection even plausible, much less actually to establish such a connection, they would have to do even more. They would have to do something along the lines of, for example, conducting experiments in which a population is divided into two groups which, at the outset of the experiment, are equally ignorant of science and comparable in their political beliefs and practices. One of the groups would then receive training in science and logic. The two groups would then be evaluated, using blind judging techniques, to see whether or not the scientifically aware group would have in the interim developed vile political convictions. More realistically, the antiscience critics might be expected to explain (1) which of the intrinsic features of science might be the culprit(s) in bringing about the bad political effects; (2) what is it about these features, and on the basis of what evidence, that makes them good candidates for suspicion; and (3) why we should not suppose that other factors, quite unconnected with the intrinsic nature of science, are more plausibly to be viewed as explaining the objectionable political uses to which science is often put.

Several factors suggest grounds for doubting that such explanations will be forthcoming. First, as Chomsky's *reductio* suggests, the objectionable political features present in much scientific thought and practice seem also to be powerfully present in thousands of other arenas of thought and practice. Second, there is no shortage of familiar economic, social, and cultural pressures which appear more than adequate to explain the presence of such features both in science and elsewhere. Finally, the distinguishing characteristics of science seem, if anything, to be of such a nature as to stand as obstacles, albeit obviously often insufficiently powerful, to the growth of detestable political ideas and practices.

Let us take up these last two points. With regard to the economic, social, and cultural pressures which might be operating on science, distorting it and pushing it in politically detestable directions, consider the following anecdote. Dr. Douglas Gildersleeve, a medical researcher, reports that a paper he had written, which argued that vitamin supplements are effective in treating the common cold, was rejected by every one of the eleven professional journals to which it had been submitted. An editor for one of the journals had the candor to tell Dr. Gildersleeve that it would be economically harmful for any medical journal to publish his article, since such journals depend for their existence on the support of advertisers, and that over 25 percent of the advertisements in the journals are for patented drugs to be used for the alleviation of cold symptoms. Dr. Gildersleeve concludes that such practices tend to block research into, and consequent development and availability of, effective vitamin therapies, since vitamins cannot be patented, and thus their widespread medical use would result in "monetary losses that would be inflicted on pharmaceutical manufacturers, professional journals, and doctors themselves."[9]

Will anyone suggest that this disaster is to be attributed to the intrinsic features of science, rather than to economic factors quite independent from science? And will anyone deny that such factors permeate all sectors of society and instead insist that science is unique in allowing itself to be influenced by them? Finally, will anyone claim that this case is atypical and deny that similar examples could be cited ad nauseam?

A critic of science might reply that this reasoning is unfair, since it seems capable of absolving science in advance of any and all sins: the defender of science can always simply blame any defects of actual scientific practices on deviations, typically brought about by economic, political, or social pressures, from "proper" scientific methods. But the way remains clear for antiscience critics to refute such reasoning by providing some sort of plausible argument both that such pressures are not sufficient to explain the politically abhorrent aspects of some scientific arguments and practices, and that the intrinsic features of science (e.g., experimental testing; rules requiring logical consistency and attention to evidence; a willingness to overthrow old ideas in the light of new evidence, rather than hold on to them as fixed dogmas; an appeal to experience as the prime arbiter of disputes; a disregard for credentials and authority in evaluating a person's claims, etc.) are adequate to explain them. It would seem, however, not only that such arguments are not likely to be forthcoming, but also that the shoe is on the other foot. For surely the distinguishing characteristics just mentioned are, if anything, antithetical to the political ideas and practices they are touted as causing. The case is much different with other social institutions, such as religion, at least in some of its forms. For there one can point to specific features—obedience, authority, fixed dogma, etc.—which can plausibly be pointed to as possible causes of odious political phenomena associated with the social institution in question. The fact that it is much easier to do this in the case of religion than it is in the case of science itself suggests that the present argument does not suffer from vacuous a priorism.

In any case, the antiscience critics rarely discuss what I am calling the distinguishing characteristics of science. Instead, and this is another argument of Chomsky's, the antiscience arguments rest on inaccurate characterizations of science:

X is "E-knowledge," "obtained by logical deduction from firmly established first principles." The statements in X must be "provable"; X demands "absolute proofs." The "most distinctive component of [X]" may be its "elaborate procedures for arriving at acceptable first principles." . . .

Furthermore, X "claims to a monopoly of knowledge." It thus denies, say, that I know how to tie my shoes, or know that the sky is dark at night, or that walking in the woods is enjoyable, or know the names of my children and something about their concerns, etc.; all such aspects of my (intuitive) knowledge are far beyond what can be "obtained by logical deduction from firmly established first principles," . . . and is therefore mere "superstition, belief, prejudice," according to advocates of X. Or if not denying such knowledge outright, X "marginalizes and denigrates" it. . . . X is "arrogant" and "absolutist." What doesn't fall "within the terms of its hegemony . . . —anger, desire, pleasure, and pain, for example— becomes a site for disciplinary action." . . .

I quite agree that X should be confined to the flames. But what that has to do with our topic escapes me, given that these attributes scarcely rise to the level of a caricature of rational inquiry (science, etc.), at least as I'm familiar with it.

Take the notion of "E-knowledge." . . . Not even set theory . . . satisfies the definition offered. Nothing in the sciences even resembles it. As for "provability," or "absolute proofs," the notions are foreign to the natural sciences. . . . If "elaborate procedures," or any general procedures, exist "for arriving at acceptable first principles," they have been kept a dark mystery.

Science is tentative, exploratory, questioning, largely learned by doing. . . .

As for the cited properties of X, they do hold of some aspects of human thought and action: elements of organized religion, areas of the humanities and "social sciences" where understanding and insight are thin and it is therefore easier to get away with dogmatism and falsification, perhaps others. But the sciences, at least as I am familiar with them, are as remote from these descriptions as anything in human life.[10]

The antiscience critics thus seem to be caught within a dilemma of their own making. On the one hand, many of their criticisms of "science" are based upon pointing out specific instances in which science is put to the service of odious politics. Here, though the critics undeniably often make excellent points, they ultimately fail (1) to distinguish "science" conceived normatively from "science" understood as a social institution situated within a particular social, political, and economic framework; (2) to address the normative conception of science at all, even though this is obviously an important task if we are attempting to determine not merely how science is in fact practiced, but also how it should be practiced, and what we can do to see that it is so practiced; (3) to show that the examples presented are adequately representative of science as it is actually practiced; (4) to demonstrate that science is more entangled with oppressive politics than are other social practices or ways of thinking and inquiring; and, most important, (5) to show that when science does involve itself with odious politics the reason for this flows from the nature of science itself, rather than from other factors that are at work bringing about the same effects throughout the culture generally.

On the other hand, and this is the other horn of the dilemma, when the critics do attempt a deeper critique of the very nature of science, as opposed to its instantiation in various (and typically nefarious) instances of its practice, they discuss instead a crude caricature.

Finally, let us briefly consider Chomsky's political objections to those who would attempt to defend radical politics by renouncing or eviscerating truth, rationality, and science. One point is simply that, in any program of political change, there can be no substitute for operating from an accurate understanding of how the world (or at least those parts of it that are relevant to one's project) really works. With this in mind, consider Chomsky's reply to Marcus Raskin's call for a repeal of the law of contradiction, and for an overthrowing of science in favor of personal myths and "the social construction of reality." In addition to pointing out that "[r]easonable people will be concerned with consistency; they will, for example, be troubled if they find that their conclusions contradict their premises," Chomsky asks

> who could possibly be interested . . . in the lines of thinking that Mark suggests[?] Surely not people with intellectual curiosity: who want to know why metals keep their shape; or why the sun is hot and the sky dark at night; or why a chicken embryo develops along its particular course while a human embryo becomes a person with intricate and curious characteristics, including specific ways of creating, interacting, expressing thoughts, interpreting and evaluating; or why Kennedy sent the U.S. Air Force to bomb Vietnamese villages; and so on. For people who want to understand the world,

there is no alternative to the common sense procedures that we come to call "science" as they are pursued with greater care and reach deeper insight: try to construct explanatory principles that yield insight and understanding, test them against relevant evidence, keep an open mind about alternatives, work cooperatively with others, etc.[11]

Or again, consider the practical consequences of renouncing science, logic, and robust conceptions of truth, on the grounds that these are often put in service of political oppression. Michael Albert, another participant in the *Z Papers* debate, bluntly exposes the central problem with such a strategy: "[I]n the struggle over how to improve society, activists confront established power with, essentially, our minds and bodies. Anti-rationalism says let's not use a significant portion of our minds, thereby giving away a chief asset before the contest even begins. Elites not only have the guns and money, now we let them have 'truth' too. That's pathetic."[12] Chomsky concurs:

It strikes me as remarkable that [left intellectuals] today should seek to deprive oppressed people not only of the joys of understanding and insight, but also of tools of emancipation, informing us that the "project of the Enlightenment" is dead, that we must abandon the "illusions" of science and rationality—a message that will gladden the hearts of the powerful, delighted to monopolize these instruments for their own use.[13]

Clearly, on Chomsky's view there is no need to abandon Enlightenment conceptions of evidence, rationality, logic, and so forth, in order to make cogent radical political points. Rather, what is needed for the job is simply a scrupulous and critical attention to relevant evidence, together with an appeal to principles of consistency, parsimony, plausibility, and the like.

In my view, Chomsky has demonstrated this convincingly through his own analyses of political phenomena. Though he has presented thousands of these analyses in his many books and articles, I will have to content myself with a brief discussion of one, that concerning the reaction within respectable mainstream political circles in the United States to President Clinton's 26 June 1993 bombing of Baghdad.

The official line held that this bombing was justified as a proper retaliatory response to an alleged assassination attempt against George Bush, since any attempt to assassinate a (former) president can only be regarded as "loathsome and cowardly" (President Clinton), "an outrageous crime" (*Washington Post*), and "an act of war" (*New York Times*). As William Safire further elaborated, it is "an act of war . . . when one head of state tries to murder another. If clear evidence had shown that Fidel Castro ordered the killing of President Kennedy, President Johnson would surely have used military force to depose the regime in Havana."[14]

Now, as Chomsky points out, this "hypothetical example reverses the actual historical record," since, as should by now be well known, it is the Kennedy administration which repeatedly attempted to assassinate Castro.

"But a truly refined imperial arrogance," Chomsky continues,

> permits the bland inversion of the facts, with confidence that colleagues and the educated community generally will not "notice" that according to the preaching of the Western moralists, US attempts to assassinate Castro were "loathsome and cowardly acts of war" which entitled Castro to use military force to depose the regime in Washington, had that been possible, and surely justified bombs in Washington in retaliation for Kennedy's "outrageous crime."[15]

Notice that here, as elsewhere, Chomsky is able to draw radical political conclusions, and to defend them powerfully, simply by appealing to the relevant historical facts and to principles of simple consistency, resources which postmodern attacks on Enlightenment principles would either weaken or take away from him entirely. Furthermore, given the obviousness of Chomsky's point, together with the rarity of its comprehension, whether within mainstream media and scholarly circles or within the thinking of the general public, it seems fair to say that the Enlightenment project, far from merely standing in need of completion (and much less having exhausted itself in failure), has in fact as of yet scarcely gotten off the ground.

II. O. J. SIMPSON

Some might counter, however, that the public reaction to the recent O. J. Simpson trial demonstrates just how impotent these Enlightenment principles, much prized by Chomsky, really are. After all, do not the disparate reactions of white and black Americans to the verdict strongly suggest that no "reason" is available to us that is not deeply embedded in experiential contingencies, which may often vary along race (or, for that matter, class or gender) lines? And if this is so, who is to say what is "real" or "true"?

I will limit myself to three points by way of reply. First, a murder trial puts in sharp relief what is morally problematic about replacing the notion of truth with a cheerful acceptance of multiple interpretations, or perhaps social constructions. For consider that it is possible that O. J. Simpson took a knife one night and slaughtered two people. Another possibility is that he had nothing to do with their deaths. There are other possibilities as well: that he paid someone else to commit the crimes, participated in them as a member of a team of killers, and so forth. What does not seem possible is that he both did and did not (or either did or did not) commit these murders, depending upon the life experiences and cultural frame of reference of the person considering the issue. For how can anyone's thinking about the crimes, after the fact, affect what had already taken place? What we need to be able to figure out is what really happened. If the response is that the embeddedness of reason in diverse experiential contingencies rules out a priori any possibility of determining what really happened, or renders the very concept of "what really happened" incoherent, we should realize that we have arrived at a disabling skepticism, not a robust, exciting alternative to outworn notions of "truth." If the best evidence and arguments suggest that such a conclusion is warranted, then so be it, but we should recognize that it is nothing to celebrate. For we would then have to acknowledge not only our inability to determine who has and has not committed a murder, a matter of no small moral seriousness, but also that we can never figure out what anyone has ever done. What then becomes of the notion of responsibility?

Let me put the point another way. Either we can legitimately draw a distinction between what really happened to Nicole Brown and Ronald Goldman, on the one hand, and what people might happen to *think* happened to them, on the other, or we cannot. If the latter, then there is no such thing as real political oppression, or even real events and states of affairs that we might judge to be politically objectionable. We could then eliminate political oppression simply by changing how we think about things. But if there is a valid distinction to be drawn (in principle) between what really happens and what we think happens, it follows that interpretation can never be a substitute for truth, that mutually inconsistent interpretations cannot both be true, and that reality can be inconsistent with some interpretations. People think there is a relativism of truth. Instead, perhaps there is a relativism of error—different people in different situations tend to have different disadvantages in connection with the difficult task of discovering the truth, and thus tend to make different errors. Moreover, people tend to err in a self-interested way, and thus, insofar as people who are differently situated culturally tend to have different interests, their errors will tend to differ accordingly.

The second problem I see with regard to the reduction of truth and rationality to multiple perspectives in connection with the Simpson case is that, at least in the commentary I have read and heard, but in *all* of that, the argument consists of drawing a hasty conclusion from a truism. The truism is that people's initial visceral response to evidence is strongly influenced by their own life experiences. The hasty conclusion is that no one can (or perhaps, rather, because we should "respect people's different life experiences," no one should be expected to) transcend the limitations of personal experience.

In this connection, consider attorney Gerry Spence's analogy.[16] Spence suggests that a person whose first experience riding a horse is with a gentle, slow-moving, unthreatening animal will from then on love and trust horses, but that someone who is thrown the first time will, by contrast, forever more fear and dislike them. Similarly, Spence reasons, those who have had firsthand experience with police misconduct, as many blacks have, will be quite ready to give credence to accusations of, for example, evidence planting by a few police officers, and a wider police conspiracy to cover it up, while those who have had no such experience, as is the case with many whites, will regard any such accusations as preposterous.

While I find the spirit of tolerance and patient understanding underlying this analogy admirable, I confess that I nonetheless react to it with a certain impatience. Granting that our personal firsthand experiences often serve as the starting point from which we must make our way in attempting to understand the world, are we really stuck with the limitations, flowing primarily from their puny scope, of such experiences? Wouldn't it really be an irrational prejudice to conclude, on the basis of one's own unfortunate experiences with horses, that all of them are untrustworthy (and vice versa)? Wouldn't such a conclusion merit criticism as false, and as flowing from an objectionably narrow perspective, as opposed to deserving respect as merely one perspective among others, flowing from one set of experiences among others?

Moreover, and especially with respect to more serious matters, such as police misconduct, is there no obligation to learn something about the world beyond what one can glean from firsthand experience? Is there nothing morally objectionable about willful ignorance, especially when one is called upon, as we all are, to undertake actions and to make decisions affecting other people's lives?[17] What possible excuse can anyone have, for example, for being so unaware of the existence of police misconduct, especially in the wake of the Rodney King incident, as to reject out of hand accusations of such misconduct as wildly implausible?

But recognition of the general prima facie plausibility of charges of police misconduct does not resolve the Simpson issue in favor of reasonable doubt, as several commentators have suggested.[18] For one thing, one would still have to inquire as to whether such misconduct is plausible in this particular case. More importantly, just as we know that police sometimes plant evidence, especially when this is to the detriment of a black defendant, so do we know that ex-husbands often kill their ex-wives. (Indeed, the Simpson defense team insisted upon this very point, using it to bolster their theory that even the honest—non-evidence-planting, non-conspiring-to-cover-up—police officers in the case still were guilty of a "rush to judgment" that the ex-husband must be the guilty party.) Thus, we have two prima facie plausible scenarios to consider: Either Simpson murdered his ex-wife and a man who had the misfortune to be present at the scene, or someone else committed the murders and racist cops planted evidence to frame him. What is to be done to choose between these two possibilities?

One possibility would be to look to see whether or not there might be some evidence capable of discriminating between the two possibilities. While this would seem a tough task, since much of the evidence, especially the seemingly powerful physical evidence, is capable, at first blush, of being equally explained either by the theory that Simpson committed the murders (dropping his blood, fibers, cap, hairs, and glove at the crime scene, and bringing back the victims' blood to his car and to his home, where he also drops more of his own blood and another glove) or by the theory that the police planted the blood, fibers, cap, hairs, and gloves. But before concluding that the case must be resolved in favor of reasonable doubt, consider one more piece of evidence: the interview that Simpson gave to police detectives Lange and Vannatter, after having been read his Miranda rights, the day after the murders. Here are a few excerpts:[19]

Vannatter: We found some [blood] in your house. Is that your blood that is dripped there?

Simpson: If—if it's what I dripped running around trying to leave.

Vannatter: How did you get the injury on your hand?

Simpson: I don't know. The first time, when I was in Chicago, and all, but at the house I was just running around.

Lange: Do you recall bleeding at all in your truck, in the Bronco?

Simpson: I recall bleeding at my house, then I went to the Bronco. The last thing I did before I left, when I was rushing, was went and got my phone out of the Bronco.

Finally, in response to one more question about blood spattered at his house, Simpson again discussed having an open wound there the night of the murders:

Lange: We found some [blood] in your house. Is that your blood that's there?

Simpson: If it's dripped, it's what I dripped around trying to leave. . . . I wasn't aware that it was . . . I was aware that I, you know, I was trying to get out of the house, I didn't—didn't pay any attention to it. I saw it when I was in the kitchen and I grabbed a napkin or something, and that was it. I didn't think about it after that.

Now let us go back to our two possible scenarios. This evidence clearly discriminates between them. We know from this evidence that at least some of Simpson's blood that was at his home and in his car the night of the murders was not planted by police, because Simpson himself admitted, before his reference blood sample had been drawn from his arm, and thus before the police would have had any of his blood to plant, that his hand was cut that night and that he was dripping blood at his residence. Now, if Simpson committed two murders with a knife on the night in question, it is easy to understand why he would have been cut and dripping blood: He would have been cut by his own knife in committing the murders; he would have dripped blood in his vehicle leaving the murder scene; and he would have continued to drip blood at his residence in several locations, either because he was too agitated and panic-stricken to notice that he was bleeding, or, more likely, because he was frantically trying to get ready to make his scheduled flight to Chicago—for how would it look if it were discovered that he had missed his flight on the night of the murders?—and thus did not have time to take the first-aid measures necessary to stop the bleeding.

If, on the other hand, we are to go along with the planting of evidence theory, we will have to assume the following coincidences: (1) that on the very night, and at approximately the same time, that two people are murdered with a knife, the very person who by all accounts, including that of his own lawyers, would be the logical prime suspect happens to cut his own hand; (2) that this suspect cannot recall how he cut his hand, in spite of the fact that he is asked about it only half a day after it happened; and (3) that he is for some reason either unable or unwilling to do what people ordinarily do when they cut themselves at home—stop the bleeding and apply a bandage before they drip blood in several mutually remote locations (driveway, foyer, bathroom, car, etc.) of their residence. I fail to see how it could possibly be rational to believe these coincidences, or even, more modestly, to believe that their likelihood is sufficiently robust as to constitute reasonable doubt.[20]

It would be beyond the scope of this discussion to go through the rest of the evidence. I would, however, make this general comment. It is easy to see how murder cases could be based entirely upon planted evidence when the total physical evidence in the case is limited in kind and quantity—when there is, for example, one (planted) murder weapon, or fingerprint, or blood drop. Here we have: (1) Simpson's blood at the crime scene; (2) the victims' blood in his car and at his home; (3) bloody shoe impressions walking away from the crime scene in Simpson's size (worn by only 9 percent of American men), of an extremely expensive style of shoe (Simpson was rich) that is sold in only forty U.S stores (at one of which Simpson regularly purchased his shoes);[21] (4) fibers consistent with those from Simpson's car (and inconsistent with those from the vast majority of cars) at the crime scene; (5) a cap at the crime scene containing hairs consistent with Simpson's; (6) hair consistent with Simpson's on the body of Ron Goldman (allegedly a stranger to Simpson); (7) blue-black cotton fibers at the crime scene (consistent with non-police testimony, including that of a Simpson friend, that he was wearing dark clothing on the night of the murders); (8) an Aris Leather Light glove (not sold west of the Mississippi—recall that the murders took place in Los Angeles) at the crime scene, and a matching one at Simpson's home, to be juxtaposed with the introduction into evidence of a receipt for two pairs of just such gloves, signed by Nicole Brown Simpson, from a New York City store (note also in this connection the fact that the defense did not produce these two pairs of gloves in court); (9) the testimony of Simpson's limousine driver—and notice that his is not police testimony—that Simpson failed to respond to his buzzer for twenty minutes when the driver arrived on the night of the murders to take Simpson to the airport; and (10) a significant wound and several smaller cuts on Simpson's left hand, photographed shortly after the murders and testified to by Simpson's doctor, who examined his injuries (consistent with the fact that the blood drops at the crime scene are all to the left of the footprints leaving the scene). Are all of these also to be explained in terms of planting, coincidences, or some combination of the two (and there are many similar pieces of evidence which could easily be added to this list)?[22] Is there anything in human experience or history to be found which would be comparable to such a massive conspiracy, string of coincidences, or combination of the two? Just think of the logistical problems involved in pulling it off and keeping everybody quiet, and/or the stupendous luck required (e.g., Simpson cooperates by cutting himself, forgetting how, doing so on the correct hand, failing to stop the bleeding, dripping blood in several places, not responding to the limousine driver, etc. etc.) in having all of these coincidences fall in line with your nefarious scheme!

The prima facie plausible police conspiracy thus collapses. Reason—simple procedures of synthesizing discrete pieces of evidence and subjecting them to principles of logic, especially consistency and parsimony—is adequate to determine that O. J. Simpson is guilty of murder.

These are the very same principles that Noam Chomsky uses to show that the claims of the U.S. government to support democracy and foreign rights around the world are hollow (e.g., while a given instance of support for a tyrant might be explained by the argument that the alternative would be a worse tyrant, what is to be done with the fact that there is a substantial positive correlation between a nation's use of torture and its receipt of U.S. money, weapons, and other forms of aid?).[23] And if these principles are adequate to tell us so much about the world—from the hidden motives of U.S. foreign policy to the identity of the perpetrator of an unseen murder—why should we want to abandon them? Perhaps we should instead begin to use them.

III. The Sokal Hoax

In May 1996 physicist Alan Sokal published an article in *Social Text*, an academic cultural studies journal that frequently publishes postmodern criticisms of science. Sokal's article, "Transgressing the Boundaries: Toward a Transformative Hermeneutics of Quantum Gravity,"[24] fit the bill nicely. In its very first paragraph Sokal denounces

> the dogma imposed by the long post-Enlightenment hegemony over the Western intellectual outlook, which can be summarized briefly as follows: that there exists an external world, whose properties are independent of any individual human being and indeed of humanity as a whole; that these properties are encoded in "eternal" physical laws; and that human beings can obtain reliable, albeit imperfect and tentative, knowledge of these laws by hewing to the "objective" procedures and epistemological strictures prescribed by the (so-called) scientific method.

As against this "dogma," Sokal goes on to argue that

> [i]t has . . . become increasingly apparent that physical "reality," no less than social "reality," is at bottom a social and linguistic construct; that scientific "knowledge," far from being objective, reflects and encodes the dominant ideologies and power relations of the culture that produced it; that the truth claims of science are inherently theory-laden and self-referential; and consequently, that the dis-

course of the scientific community . . . cannot assert a privileged epistemological status.[25]

But the article is a hoax. It offers no argument in support of these claims—or at least none that would even begin to persuade anyone in possession of minimum standards of clarity or logic, or who had a good high-school graduate's knowledge of physics and mathematics. For the article, in Sokal's own words (published later, in articles explaining his hoax),

> is a mélange of truths, half-truths, quarter-truths, falsehoods, non sequiturs, and syntactically correct statements that have no meaning whatsoever. . . . I also employed some other strategies that are well-established . . . in the genre: appeals to authority in lieu of logic; speculative theories passed off as established science; strained and even absurd analogies; rhetoric that sounds good but whose meaning is ambiguous; and confusion between the technical and everyday senses of English words. . . . [26] Nowhere in all of this is there anything resembling a logical sequence of thought; one finds only citations of authority, plays on words, strained analogies, and bald assertions.[27]

Here are three examples of the intentional scientific errors and confusions in Sokal's articles. He claims that the famous constants pi (from Euclidean geometry) and G (Newton's Gravitational Constant) are variables.[28] He calls complex number theory "a new and still quite speculative branch of mathematical physics,"[29] when it is in fact a branch of pure mathematics, dating to the early nineteenth century, which is regularly taught to undergraduate mathematics and physics majors. And he praises a quotation from Jacques Lacan in which Lacan confuses imaginary and irrational numbers.[30]

But even more telling, perhaps, is his habit, throughout the article, of claiming to derive political conclusions from scientific and mathematical concepts and theories that are, in fact, irrelevant to the political issues in question. Here is an example.

> Just as liberal feminists are frequently content with a minimal agenda of legal and social equality for women and are "pro-choice," so liberal (and even some socialist) mathematicians are often content to work within the hegemonic Zermelo-Fraenkel framework (which, reflecting its nineteenth-century liberal origins, already

incorporates the axiom of equality) supplemented only by the axiom of choice. But this framework is grossly insufficient for a liberatory mathematics, as was proven long ago by Cohen (1966).[31]

This is nonsense. The axiom of equality merely provides a definition of when it is that two sets are the same. It says that they are equal if and only if they have the same members. Clearly this has nothing to do with liberalism, political equality, or political philosophy of any kind. "Similarly, the axiom of choice simply says that given any collection of mutually exclusive sets, there is always a set consisting of exactly one member of each of those sets."[32] Obviously this has nothing to do with the abortion debate; the only connection is that the word "choice" is used in both contexts, just as "equality" is both a mathematical and a political concept. As for the final sentence from the quoted passage above, the point of Cohen's article is to show that "neither the axiom of choice nor its negation can be deduced from the other axioms of set theory."[33] If you can derive political implications from that, you're way ahead of me!

Why did Sokal do it? He reports that he had been troubled for some years by the poor intellectual quality of many postmodernist and social constructionist contributions to debates about science. Even many of the most revered and frequently cited figures in this movement seemed to make grotesque errors of logic, to betray a poor understanding of their subject matter, to write in a torturously obscure style, and to arrive at preposterous conclusions.[34] Moreover, as a leftist, Sokal had been concerned that all of this was harming the left, both because the silliness was primarily emanating from the self-professed left (and thus giving the left a bad name), and because of his conviction that "rational thought and the fearless analysis of objective reality (both natural and social) are incisive tools for combating the mystifications promoted by the powerful—not to mention being desirable ends in their own right"[35]—tools which, furthermore, tend to get buried in certain intellectual precincts under a lot of epistemic relativism and talk about "the social construction of reality."[36]

Well, then, why not simply write a straightforward critique of these postmodern trends in contemporary science studies? Why resort to parody? Sokal reports that he did so

for a simple pragmatic reason. The targets of my critique have by now become a self-perpetuating academic subculture that typically ignores (or disdains) reasoned criticism from the outside. In such a situation, a more direct demonstration of the subculture's intellectual standards was required. But how can one show that the emperor has no clothes? Satire is by far the best weapon; and the blow that can't be brushed off is the one that's self-inflicted. I offered the *Social Text* editors an opportunity to demonstrate their intellectual rigor. Did they meet the test? I don't think so.[37]

Sokal's claim that his targets don't take kindly to reasoned criticism is an understatement. Indeed, a delicious irony of the Sokal hoax episode is that the *Social Text* editors chose to publish his essay in a special edition of their journal, entitled "Science Wars," devoted largely to a protracted lashing out at such critics as Gerald Holton[38] and Paul Gross and Norman Levitt,[39] who have attempted, in a more straightforwardly scholarly fashion, to criticize the logic and the science scholarship of those in the postmodern science studies movement.

Immediately after the special issue of *Social Text* hit the newsstands, Sokal revealed the hoax in an article for *Lingua Franca*, a now defunct academic affairs magazine.[40] (In yet another delicious irony, *Social Text* declined to publish Sokal's account of the hoax in their own journal, claiming that this new, nonhoax, article, failed to "meet their intellectual standards.")[41] The hoax became a major news story, carried on the front page of the *New York Times*, the *International Herald Tribune*, the [London] *Observer*, *Le Monde*, and several other major newspapers.[42] It has also been much discussed in political and public affairs journals,[43] and in several public forums, "including packed sessions at Princeton, Duke, the University of Michigan, and New York University."[44]

But what, ultimately, does the hoax prove? Not much, it seems to me. It definitely proves something about the carelessness and incompetence of the editors at *Social Text* who chose to publish Sokal's article, and it very strongly suggests that these editors are way out of their depth when they attempt to discuss science (unless, of course, they simply published the piece without reading it, but that seems unlikely). And, while it is tempting to see this as symptomatic of the state of intellectual affairs within the genre of postmodern science studies, this would, I think, be unfair. We don't know what would have happened had Sokal submitted his article to other editors at other journals who are located within this camp. Perhaps they would have recognized that Sokal's piece was a parody (or, failing that, regarded it as rubbish). The sample is just too small to permit the drawing of definite conclusions.

Moreover, one can imagine scenarios whereby even the editors at *Social Text* might come off not looking so terribly bad. Suppose they had been in a position to say (truthfully), after the hoax was revealed, something like the following: "Gosh, folks, are we ever embarrassed! We should have been more careful! The truth is, we're all busy academics, and we just didn't read Sokal's article as carefully as we should have. We're not physicists or mathematicians, and a lot of this stuff just went right over our heads. And remember, we're not a refereed journal. But we've learned our lesson. From now on, when we get an article on physics, or mathematics, or some other technical field beyond our competence, we'll be sure to run it by a competent practitioner in that field to make sure that the technical stuff is right."

Moreover, the editors might have argued that their ignorance of much that is well known to college physics and mathematics majors does not necessarily prove that their criticisms of scientific methodology and epistemology are unsound. To suggest otherwise would be to engage in fallacious ad hominem argumentation. The issue is not the ignorance of an argument's author, but rather the cogency, or lack thereof, of his or her argument.

But if Sokal's aim was to call attention to what's going on in postmodern science studies, and to get a conversation about it going, he succeeded brilliantly. Unfortunately, however, the editors of *Social Text* (and their defenders), rather than offering the sorts of points I've just been sketching, have tended, through their public utterances on the matter, only to make things vastly worse for themselves and for their cause.

Many of them immediately resorted to name-calling attacks against Sokal. For example, one of the editors, Stanley Aronowitz, pronounced Sokal "ill-read and half-educated."[45] Two other editors, Bruce Robbins and Andrew Ross, in denouncing Sokal's claim to have shown "that something is rotten in the state of cultural studies," did not content themselves with calling that claim "wobbly." Rather, they said that it is "as wobbly as the [original] article itself" and claimed that they knew all along that Sokal's essay was "a little hokey."[46] In making these statements the editors only exposed themselves to further ridicule, because one now wants to know how it is that someone who is "ill-read and half-educated" could have fooled them, and why it is that they decided to publish a "wobbly" article that is "a little hokey."

Perhaps even worse, at least one of the editors (who appears to be claiming to speak for others of them as well, given his use of the word "we") refuses to acknowledge that *Social Text* was the victim of a hoax: "When Sokal said his essay was nonsense, most reporters instantly followed his lead. After all, he should know, right? But we thought Sokal had a real argument, and we still do."[47] And Steve Fuller (not one of the editors, but a leading figure in science studies and a contributor to the "Science Wars" issue of *Social Text* containing Sokal's hoax article) argues that

> the first mistake the editors made was to grant Sokal the authority to speak on behalf of his text and thereby accept the verdict that they had indeed been hoaxed. Instead, they should have stuck to the postmodernist tenet of not privileging the author's intention when conferring meaning on a text. Since the author is only one of many possible voices that constrains how the text "speaks," ultimately the text's meaning is determined by the community of readers that the text attracts.[48]

While it is quite true that an author need not be regarded as the ultimate authority on his or her own work, there is still the matter of the actual content of Sokal's article. Are Robbins and Fuller saying that it is not wrong to assert that pi and G are variables? Or that complex number theory is new or speculative? Or that the axiom of choice in set theory has implications for political liberalism? Or that the axiom of choice is relevant to the abortion debate? Perhaps they are, since Robbins and Ross refuse to concede that Sokal's article "would have been declared substandard by a physicist peer reviewer."[49]

And what of the deliberate obfuscation in Sokal's hoax article? Robbins and Ross claim to "share Sokal's . . . concerns about obscurantism"[50] but express bafflement at finding their own journal to be receiving criticism on this score. And Ross elsewhere puts the point even more strongly: "There is no excuse for obscurantism, just as there are no critical insights that cannot be phrased in a readily intelligible manner, without causing eyes to glaze over."[51]

Why, then, did Robbins and Ross choose to publish an article that was larded with such gaseous passages as the following:

In mathematical terms, Derrida's observation relates to the invariance of the Einstein field equation $G\mu\nu = 8\pi GT\mu\nu$ under non-linear space-time diffeomorphisms (self-mappings of the space-time manifold which are infinitely differentiable but not necessarily analytic). The key point is that this invariance group "acts transitively": this means that any space-time point, if it exists at all, can be transformed into any other. In this way the infinite-dimensional invariance group erodes the distinction between observer and observed; the π of Euclid and the G of Newton, formerly thought to be constant and universal, are now perceived in their ineluctable historicity; and the putative observer becomes fatally de-centered, disconnected from any epistemic link to a space-time point that can no longer be defined by geometry alone.[52]

In evaluating the degree to which this is objectionably obscurantist, it must be recalled that *Social Text* is not a scientific journal. For example, Sokal is the only representative of the physical sciences among the authors of the special "Science Wars" issue in which his parody article appears. The journal is clearly aimed at scholars and students in the humanities and social sciences. Thus, this jargon, leaving aside its deliberate errors and howlers, cannot be excused as shorthand for the cognescenti. The article presents itself as a physicist's attempt to communicate with nonscientists interested in postmodern social constructionist science studies. Well, according to Fuller, Sokal's style in his hoax article (which, you'll recall, Fuller refuses to acknowledge is really a hoax) is "unexceptionable in postmodernist circles." Indeed, Fuller informs us that Sokal's article "was rather clearly presented by current standards."[53]

Nor does Stanley Fish find anything askew in Sokal's original article. (It goes without saying, of course, that he violently objects to just about everything Sokal has said after he revealed his hoax.) No, he declares that the editors of *Social Text* "could not have anticipated" that Sokal's article would be revealed as a hoax, since Sokal had "carefully packaged his deception so as not to be detected except by someone who began with a deep and corrosive attitude of suspicion."[54] Unfortunately, the rest of Fish's article on the Sokal hoax undermines these claims. Let's see why.

Fish almost immediately (the second paragraph of his article) singles out for criticism the following statement of Sokal's, originally published in his article declaring the *Social Text* piece to have been a hoax: "There *is* a real world; its properties are *not* merely social constructions; facts and evidence do matter. What sane person would contend otherwise?"[55] Fish's comment: "Exactly! Professor Sokal's question should alert us to the improbability of the scenario he conjures up: Scholars with impeccable credentials making statements no sane person would credit. The truth is that none of his targets would ever make such statements."[56] The rest of Fish's article is devoted to giving Sokal an education into just what it is that his targets do say. For example, according to Fish, "[w]hat sociologists of science say is that of course the world is real and independent of our observations but that accounts of the world are produced by observers and are therefore relative to their capacities, education, training, etc. It is not the world or its properties but the vocabularies in whose terms we know them that are socially constructed."[57]

Now, let's recall one of the claims Sokal makes in his hoax article (early on, in the second paragraph): "It has thus become increasingly apparent that physical 'reality' . . . is at bottom a social and linguistic construct."[58] Note that Sokal explicitly states in his hoax article that "reality" (which he doesn't forget to put in scare quotes) "is at bottom a social and linguistic construct." "Not our *theories* of physical reality, mind you, but the reality itself."[59]

So we are left with the following. (1) Sokal said in his hoax article something that Fish concedes "no sane person" would say. (2) Sokal's insane statement raised no eyebrows, or at least provoked no questions, among the *Social Text* editors, who published the article, despite its insane claim. (3) Fish nonetheless claims that Sokal's deception could not be detected "except by someone who began with a deep and corrosive attitude of suspicion." It's beginning to look as if there is, indeed, something rotten in the state of postmodern science studies.

NOTES

1. The views described above may be found in many sources. For the purposes of this discussion, the most important are: Ashis Nandy, "Oh What a Lovely Science"; Kate Ellis, "Life without Father: A 'Postmodern' Political Practice"; Stephen Marglin, "Why Is So Little Left of the Left?"; Wahneema Lubiano, "To Take Dancing Seriously Is to Redo Politics"; Frederique Apffel Marglin, "Rationality and the Lived World"; and Marcus Raskin, "Story

Telling Time"; all in *Z Papers* 1, no. 4 (October–December, 1992). I focus on these essays because they are the ones explicitly addressed by Chomsky in what is to my knowledge his only extended discussion of these matters: Chomsky, "Rationality/Science," published in this same issue of *Z Papers*.

2. See, for example, Martin Anderson, *Impostors in the Temple* (New York: Simon & Schuster, 1992); Richard Bernstein, *Dictatorship of Virtue* (New York: Knopf, 1994); Allan Bloom, *The Closing of the American Mind* (New York: Simon & Schuster, 1987); Dinesh D'Souza, *Illiberal Education* (New York: Vintage, 1992); Roger Kimball, *Tenured Radicals* (New York: Harper & Row, 1990); Thomas Sowell, *Inside American Education* (New York: Free Press, 1993); and Charles Sykes, *Profscam* (Washington, D.C.: Regnery Gateway, 1988).

3. Chomsky, "Rationality/Science," p. 52.

4. Raskin, "Story Telling Time," p. 38.

5. Chomsky, "Rationality/Science," p. 56.

6. Ibid., pp. 52–53.

7. Ibid., p. 53.

8. Ibid.

9. Douglas Gildersleeve, "Why Organized Medicine Sneezes at the Common Cold," *Fact* (July–August, 1967): 21.

10. Chomsky, "Rationality/Science," pp. 53–54.

11. Noam Chomsky, "Chomsky Replies," *Z Papers* 2, no. 3 (July–September 1993): 12.

12. Michael Albert, "Not All Stories Are Just Stories," *Z Papers* 1, no. 4 (October–December 1992): 51.

13. Chomsky, "Rationality/Science," p. 57.

14. William Safire, quoted in Noam Chomsky, *Enter a World That Is Truly Surreal: President Clinton's Sudden Use of International Violence* (Westfield, NJ: Open Media, 1993), p. 8.

15. Chomsky, *Enter a World That Is Truly Surreal*, p. 8.

16. I have heard Spence give this analogy on several television programs devoted to the Simpson case. Unfortunately, I have no tape or transcript of any of these appearances and thus am paraphrasing from memory.

17. In this connection it is perhaps noteworthy that Judge Ito, the judge presiding over the Simpson trial, chose to exclude any potential juror who admitted, on a questionnaire, to reading newspapers or visiting bookstores regularly. M. L. Rantala, *O. J. Unmasked* (Chicago: Catfeet Press, 1996), p. 178.

18. I have in mind those television commentators, and there were many of them, who regularly asserted that whites who rejected the police conspiracy did so because nothing in their personal experience suggested that such a thing was possible. Regularly ignored was the possibility, discussed below, that such a conspiracy might be viewed as perfectly plausible in prin-

ciple, and yet rejected in this specific case on the grounds that it is virtually ruled out by the evidence.

19. A complete transcript of this interview can be found in Vincent Bugliosi, *Outrage* (New York: Norton, 1996), pp. 291–305. The passages quoted here appear on pp. 297 and 303–304.

20. One attempt to argue otherwise is that of Nikol G. Alexander and Drucilla Cornell, who promise to illustrate "how the jurors' careful consideration on the legal issues presented to them contradicts the common rhetoric about their lack of sophistication" and to "expose the racial fantasies behind the characterizations of the jurors as both unreasonable and irrational." "Dismissed or Banished? A Testament to the Reasonableness of the Simpson Jury," in *Birth of a Nation'hood: Gaze, Script, and Spectacle in the O. J. Simpson Case*, ed. Toni Morrison and Claudia Brodsky Lacour (New York: Pantheon, 1997), p. 59. They do so principally by relaying to their readers the jurors' own account of the reasons underlying their verdict, as these are presented in a book coauthored by the jury foreman and two of her colleagues on the jury (Armanda Cooley et al., *Madam Foreman* [Beverly Hills, CA: Dove Books, 1995]). Alexander and Cornell rightly point out that it is regrettable that "this book has been given little public attention, even though it provides one of the few lengthy and systematic discussions by actual jurors of the reasons for their verdict" (p. 60). The problem, however, is that Alexander and Cornell do not subject the book even to the most minimal of critical scrutiny, but rather simply pass along its errors as fact, and then, on that basis, proceed to claim to have "demonstrated" that "the jurors had a more than adequate grasp of the key legal concepts and evidentiary considerations used during the trial" (p. 91), and to attribute criticism of the jurors to various cognitive and moral shortcomings of their critics.

Let's look at just one example of the jurors' (and Alexander and Cornell's) incompetence. Alexander and Cornell present, as an instance of the jury's reasonableness, the fact that "[t]he jurors . . . raised questions as to why, when Simpson purportedly had such a bad cut on his hand, there was no blood on the glove found at Rockingham" (p. 67). They are referring to the following observations of juror Carrie Bess, as presented in *Madam Foreman*: "Had the cut [on O. J.'s hand] been as bad as they say it should have been, some of his blood should have been on the Rockingham glove somewhere, but none of his blood was on it. . . . I would say if his finger was cut and he was handling these things—if he was wearing them—his blood should be on one of those gloves. And his blood wasn't on either one of those gloves" (p. 124). One has to admit that Alexander and Cornell seem to have a point—that sounds pretty reasonable.

The problem, however, is that it simply isn't true. M. L. Rantala (*O. J. Unmasked*) comments as follows:

Did Bess fail to hear the testimony that DNA tests on three different portions of this glove yielded a match to Simpson? Wasn't she listening when Scheck vigorously cross-examined analyst Collin Yamauchi, suggesting that Yamauchi's careless handling of the glove near Simpson's reference blood might have been the explanation for Simpson's DNA being on the glove? Did she think it odd for Dr. John Gerdes to testify that cross-contamination might account for Simpson's blood on the Rockingham glove, since she thinks none of Mr. Simpson's blood is on it? Why did she think Barry Scheck spoke so passionately in closing argument, explaining how he thought the defendant's blood might have gotten on the glove well after the murders?

Bess obviously didn't listen to Marcia Clark, either. In closing argument Clark pointed out that Simpson's blood was on that glove . . . :

> So what do we find on the Rockingham glove, the one he [Simpson] drops? We find everything. Everything.
>
> We find fibers consistent with Ron Goldman's shirt. We find the hair of Ron. We find the hair of Nicole. We find the blood of Ron Goldman. We find the blood of Nicole Brown. And we find the blood of the defendant. And we find Bronco fiber from the defendant's Bronco. We find blue black cotton fibers just like those found on the shirt of Ron Goldman and on the socks of the defendant in his bedroom.
>
> And on this glove he is tied to every aspect of the murder; to Ron Goldman, to Nicole Brown, to the car, and of course that is why the defense has to say that the glove is planted, because if they don't, everything about this glove convicts the defendant, where it is found, what is found on it, what is found in it. . . . Everything about it convicts him" (Trial Transcript, September 26, 1995).

One of the few things the two sides did not disagree about was the presence of Simpson's blood on the glove. The dispute was over how the blood got there, how little of Simpson's was present, and how the defense thought it was peculiar that Simpson's blood was only near the wrist area. The defense maintained Simpson's blood found its way onto the glove in the testing laboratory of the LAPD, as a result of cross-contamination. The prosecution argued that Simpson spilled his own blood on it either during or after the commission of the two murders.

Yet the vital fact that Simpson's blood was on the Rockingham glove was not known to juror Carrie Bess. (pp. 179–180)

Nor, one might add, was it known to Nikol Alexander and Drucilla Cornell.

21. Too late for the criminal trial, but in time for the later civil trial, important new evidence emerged concerning the shoes. Because of their unique soles, experts had been able to determine by the time of the criminal trial that bloody shoe impressions at the crime scene had been made by Bruno Magli shoes. Despite the suggestive considerations already noted in the text, however, there was no proof at that time that Simpson had ever worn such shoes. Then, after Simpson had denied, during his deposition for the civil trial, that he ever had or ever would wear such "ugly-ass" shoes, a photograph was discovered in which Simpson was shown wearing Bruno Magli shoes while working as a broadcaster at a football game played less than a year prior to the murders. While the defense mounted an argument that the photo was a fake, this argument collapsed when yet another photographer came forward with a roll of over thirty photographs, taken on the same day and at the same game, in which the Bruno Magli shoes were clearly discernible on Simpson's feet. The decisive refutation to the argument that these might have been faked after the fact: one of the photos had been _published_ seven months prior to the murders. Daniel Petrocelli with Peter Knobler, _Triumph of Justice: The Final Judgment on the Simpson Saga_ (New York: Crown, 1998), pp. 160–179, 305–316, 579–594.

22. Here I am indebted to the discussion in Rantala, _O. J. Unmasked_, especially pp. 208–211. I recommend this book as the finest presentation and analysis known to me of the evidence in the Simpson case.

23. See, for example, Chomsky, _Terrorizing the Neighborhood: American Foreign Policy in the Post–Cold War Era_ (San Francisco: Pressure Drop Press, 1991), p. 35.

24. Alan D. Sokal, "Transgressing the Boundaries: Toward a Transformative Hermeneutics of Quantum Gravity," _Social Text_ 14, nos. 1 and 2 (spring/summer 1996): 217–252. This article is also available in _The Sokal Hoax_, the editors of _Lingua Franca_ (Lincoln: University of Nebraska Press, 2000), pp. 11–45; and in Alan Sokal and Jean Bricmont, _Fashionable Nonsense_ (New York: Picador, 1998), pp. 212–258. Subsequent citations will be to the Sokal and Bricmont volume.

25. Sokal, "Transgressing the Boundaries: Toward a Transformative Hermeneutics of Quantum Gravity," in Sokal and Bricmont, _Fashionable Nonsense_, pp. 212–213.

26. Sokal, "Transgressing the Boundaries: An Afterword," _Dissent_ 43, no. 4 (fall 1996): 93–99. This article is also available in Sokal and Bricmont, _Fashionable Nonsense_, pp. 268–280. Subsequent citations will be to the Sokal and Bricmont volume. The quotation here cited is on pp. 268–269.

27. Alan Sokal, "Revelation: A Physicist Experiments with Cultural

Studies," in *The Sokal Hoax*, ed. the editors of *Lingua Franca*, p. 51.

28. Sokal, "Transgressing the Boundaries: Toward a Transformative Hermeneutics of Quantum Gravity," pp. 223–224.

29. Ibid., p. 239, note 86.

30. Ibid., p. 240, note 89.

31. Ibid., p. 245, note 105.

32. Paul Boghossian, "What the Sokal Hoax Ought to Teach Us," in *The Sokal Hoax*, ed. the editors of *Lingua Franca*, p. 175.

33. Sokal and Bricmont, *Fshionable Nonsense*, p. 267.

34. Sokal, "Revelation: A Physicist Experiments," pp. 49–53.

35. Ibid., p. 52.

36. Ibid., pp. 51–52.

37. Ibid., p. 53.

38. See, for example, Gerald Holton, *Science and Anti-Science* (Cambridge, MA: Harvard University Press, 1993).

39. See, for example, Paul Gross and Norman Levitt, *Higher Superstition* (Baltimore: Johns Hopkins University Press, 1994).

40. Sokal, "Revelation: A Physicist Experiments," pp. 49–53.

41. The article is Sokal, "Transgressing the Boundaries: An Afterword," pp. 268–280. The information about the article's having been rejected by *Social Text* is on p. 268.

42. Sokal and Bricmont, *Fashionable Nonsense*, p. 2, note 3. Full bibliographical information for these articles can be found there.

43. Ibid. Once again, full bibliographical information can be found here. Some of the articles are included in *The Sokal Hoax*, ed. the editors of *Lingua Franca*.

44. Boghossian, "What the Sokal Hoax Ought to Teach Us," p. 172.

45. Aronowitz is quoted in Janny Scott, "Postmodern Gravity Deconstructed, Slyly," in *The Sokal Hoax*, ed. the editors of *Lingua Franca*, p. 76.

46. Bruce Robbins and Andrew Ross, "Response: Mystery Science Theater," in *The Sokal Hoax*, ed. the editors of *Lingua Franca*, pp. 54–55.

47. Robbins, "Anatomy of a Hoax," *Tikkun* 11, no. 5 (September–October 1996): 58.

48. Steve Fuller, "Science Studies through the Looking Glass," in *Beyond the Science Wars*, ed. Ullica Segerstråle (Albany: State University of New York Press, 2000), p. 206.

49. Robbins and Ross, "Response," p. 55.

50. Ibid., p. 57.

51. Andrew Ross, "Reflections on the Sokal Affair," in *The Sokal Hoax*, ed. the editors of *Lingua Franca*, p. 247.

52. Sokal, "Transgressing the Boundaries: Toward a Transformative

Hermeneutics of Quantum Gravity," p. 224.

53. Fuller, "Science Studies," p. 202.

54. Stanley Fish, "Professor Sokal's Bad Joke," in *The Sokal Hoax*, ed. the editors of *Lingua Franca*, pp. 81, 84.

55. Sokal, "Revelation: A Physicist Experiments," p. 51.

56. Fish, "Professor Sokal's Bad Joke," p. 81.

57. Ibid.

58. Sokal, "Transgressing the Boundaries: Toward a Transformative Hermeneutics of Quantum Gravity," p. 213.

59. Sokal, "Revelation: A Physicist Experiments," p. 50.

Chapter 9

CHOMSKY, "POLITICAL CORRECTNESS," AND THE POLITICS OF TRUTH

Who are the current defenders of "rationality," "objectivity," "logic," "truth," "science," and similar allegedly outdated and discredited Enlightenment notions? The authors of the many recent best-selling potboilers attacking multiculturalism, "political correctness," and kindred phenomena[1] appear—paradoxically enough, given their traditionalism and other conservative, anti-Enlightenment characteristics—to be offering themselves as candidates to fulfill this important cultural function. For while these authors are primarily known for defending mainstream politics against what they regard as an ascendant orthodoxy of leftist dissent, it cannot be denied that they also expend considerable energy in defending mainstream epistemology against deconstructive, feminist, and postmodernist attacks. They do so because, as they see it, it is no accident that many of the same people who are currently advocating leftist politics are also simultaneously attacking Enlightenment principles. The explanation for this coincidence, according to the anti–political correctness forces, lies in the fact that science, rationality, and truth support their own mainstream politics, and precisely not the leftist political fantasies of the "politically correct." It is thus no wonder, the argument continues, that the project of promulgating politically correct ideas can only be built upon a platform of opposition to science, rationality, and truth. Defenders of anti–politically correct politics are accordingly well advised to defend these Enlightenment conceptions, as the authors of the potboilers have done, so as to prevent the politically correct argument from getting off the ground.

Noam Chomsky's position with respect to these epistemological and political debates is distinctive. On the one hand, he rejects as ludicrous the recent campaign against "political correctness." But on the other hand, he finds equally objectionable any attempt to defend leftist politics by renouncing or eviscerating rationality and science. Moreover, while most of his arguments in defense of Enlightenment principles are not explicitly political in character,[2] he does also suggest, on straightforwardly political grounds, that the proposed epistemological changes are at best unnecessary and at worst potentially harmful to the cause of progressive politics. For, on his view, Enlightenment conceptions of evidence, rationality, logic, and the like are quite adequate to, and indeed are probably indispensable for, the task of making and defending the relevant political points. Accordingly, they are not to be surrendered without a fight.

In this chapter I propose to explore these issues not by examining Chomsky's explicitly theoretical arguments on the epistemological issues,[3] but rather by examining how he makes use of those arguments in his many concrete analyses of political phenomena. I will then offer an argument of my own in support of Chomsky's position, based upon a consideration of the recent controversy surrounding the Columbus quincentennial.

I. CHOMSKY AND THE POLITICS OF "POLITICAL CORRECTNESS"

Chomsky's response to the recent "political correctness" brouhaha is noteworthy in at least two respects. First, as already noted, Chomsky's critique of the anti–political correctness forces does not in any way rely upon an abandonment of Enlightenment conceptions of evidence, rationality, logic, and the like. Second, Chomsky uses these conceptual tools in an attempt to show not only that the anti–political correctness criticisms misfire, but that in fact they would be more appropriately directed against the mainstream political culture of the United States. For he argues that any competent acquaintance with the relevant evidence would show that it is within this political culture, as opposed to the one derided as "politically correct," that one finds all of the alarming phenomena that the anti–political correctness forces claim to deplore: a stifling conformity of political opinion, an insistence upon using words in politically loaded ways unwarranted by the dictionary, a viewing of even a tiny deviation from orthodoxy as a cause for alarm, a politicization of the university, an intolerance of free speech, and so on.[4]

To illustrate this point, Chomsky provides the following analysis of the use of key political terms in mainstream discourse, which he here ironically calls "PC":

> [T]ake the term *peace process*. The naive might think that it refers to efforts to seek peace. Under this meaning, we would say that the peace process in the Middle East includes, for example, the offer of a full peace treaty to Israel by President Sadat of Egypt in 1971, along lines advocated by virtually the entire world . . . ; the Security Council resolution of January 1976 introduced by the major Arab states with the backing of the PLO, which called for a two-state settlement of the Arab-Israel conflict in the terms of a near-universal international consensus; PLO offers through the 1980s to negotiate with Israel for mutual recognition; and annual votes at the UN General Assembly . . . calling for an international conference on the Israel-Arab problem, etc.
>
> But the sophisticated understand that these efforts do not form part of the peace process. The reason is that in the PC meaning, the term *peace process* refers to what the US government is doing—in the cases mentioned, this is to block international efforts to seek peace. The cases cited do not fall within the peace process, because the US backed Israel's rejection of Sadat's offer, vetoed the Security Council resolution, opposed negotiations and mutual recognition of the PLO and Israel, and regularly joins with Israel in opposing—thereby, in effect, vetoing—any attempt to move towards a peaceful diplomatic settlement at the UN or elsewhere.[5]

As evidence in support of Chomsky's claim, I would point out that one never hears the phrase "the United States opposes the peace process" in mainstream journalism or in other circles of respectable opinion. Nor are any arguments ever given in such circles in defense of the policies, definitions, and ideas described above. Rather, as Chomsky puts it, they

> are givens; they are subject to no challenge and no debate. It would be misleading to say that there is near unanimity on these matters in Congress, the media and the intellectual community. More accurately, the basic doctrines are out of sight, out of mind, like the air we breathe, beyond the possibility of recognition, let alone discussion.[6]

In such an atmosphere it is perhaps understandable that even the smallest deviation from orthodoxy would result in panic, and that is what we indeed find in our mainstream political culture. Chomsky cites the example of Accuracy in Academia, an organization which decries the (alleged) fact that there are 10,000 Marxist professors on the campuses of America's colleges and universities out of a total number of 600,000 professors:

> To combat this threat, they propose to monitor these dangerous creatures, using student spies, the aim being "to promote greater balance," according to director Laslo Csorba. The idea that an advantage of 60 to 1 does not suffice for "balance" captures well the totalitarian mentality of these elements, as does the very idea, which would be abhorrent to people who had even the most remote conception of the notion of a free society.
>   One might observe, however, that the paranoid vision of Marxist-controlled universities, which barely merits the term "comical," is not limited to the totalitarian right. One can read in the *New York Times Book Review* that Marxism "has come close to being the dominant ideology in the academic world"; this, from a respected liberal intellectual historian who has surely set foot in American universities more than once. The concept is so remote from reality as to defy rational discussion. It can only be understood as a reflection of the fear that if heresy is granted even a tiny opening, then all is lost.[7]

I would only add that the claim of Marxist domination, ludicrous as it is when it is suggested with regard to humanities departments, becomes even more so when it is understood as applying to colleges and universities as a whole (as here it does) with their departments of economics, business, advertising, public relations, and so forth.

Finally, with regard to the issue of the "politicization" of the university, one might well inquire as to why the introduction of multiculturalist or feminist concerns into the study of literature or philosophy should count as politicization, if the introduction of Pentagon concerns into scientific research—Chomsky in the 1960s had advocated truth in advertising in this connection, so that we might refer to some departments as "Department of Death" or as "Department of Bacteriological Warfare"[8]— should not.

Perhaps this is sufficient to clarify, at least in general outlines, Chomsky's position on the recent "political correctness" debates. Still, it might prove useful before moving on to look at one of his few explicit statements on the subject, if only to confirm the sketch presented above:

> [I]f you look over history, you can see definite improvement in the past twenty or thirty years. I think there's been a cultural revolution in this country, and people in power are scared to death of it.
>
> That's why there's all this comical stuff about political correctness. It's a kind of joke; it's so silly. Here are people who have run the ideological system with an iron hand, and then in some literature department somewhere, somebody says something that isn't orthodox, and they go crazy. . . .
>
> This stuff about the quincentennial is interesting in this respect. There's a big fuss now about the "left fascists," who are dumping on Columbus and denying all the wonderful things Columbus brought. What they're saying is, for 500 years we went along, denying two of the worst acts of genocide in human history, maybe *the* worst act—the destruction of the Native Americans, which was tens of millions of people—and the destruction of large numbers of Africans through the slave trade, both of which got their start through Columbus. We've been celebrating genocide for 500 years, and that's not a problem. The problem is that the left fascists are now reversing it.
>
> Anyone with a gray cell ought to be saying, "Thank God the left fascists are taking over and trying to get this straight." Virtually no one is saying that, of course. Our more educated circles are as retrograde as they ever were. That the controversy is taking place now is a reflection of a very substantial improvement in the cultural climate.[9]

II. COLUMBUS AND THE POLITICS OF TRUTH

Chomsky's defense of the "politically correct" position on Columbus should not, however, be taken as evidence that he endorses the deflationary epistemologies which are often invoked in support of that position. Rather, that Columbus initiated two of the worst acts of genocide in human history is, according to Chomsky, the simple truth, available as such to anyone who takes the trouble to consult the relevant evidence. It is precisely *not* merely a "perspective" of Native Americans or of the descendants of African slaves.

It might be protested at this point that the traditional view of Columbus also is "true," as far as it goes. After all, Columbus's reputation as an accomplished explorer does not rest substantially on lies. The problem with the traditional view thus has little to do with issues of truth and falsehood, and everything to do with issues of emphasis and omission.[10] Indeed, recognition of this, and of the inevitability of considerations of omission and emphasis in *any* situation in which *anyone* is called upon to give an account of *anything*, shows how absurd is the charge that the introduction of information concerning Columbus's genocidal activities constitutes a "politicization" of scholarship and teaching. For how can it be claimed that an emphasis on Columbus's feats as a navigator and explorer, at the expense of a consideration of his involvement in slavery and murder, is nonpolitical?

One might be tempted to conclude on the basis of such considerations that neither the traditional nor the newer, "political correct," position on Columbus is "true," but rather that each is merely a partial (both in the sense of "incomplete" and in the sense of "biased") perspective. Moreover, given the inevitability of omission and emphasis in any account, and given further the typically political motivations for, and consequences of, such partiality, perhaps we should simply drop all talk of truth and falsity, acknowledge that we are always dealing merely with different perspectives, and use frankly political criteria in choosing among these different perspectives.

But this gives far too much away to the defenders of the traditional evaluation of Columbus. For, in the first place, the traditional view is political in a sense—and it is a bad sense—in which the "politically correct" view is not. This becomes clear when one notices that Columbus's accomplishments as an explorer seem to have a special relevance and importance to one group of people (in addition to those who simply take a great interest in exploration and navigation), namely, the descendants of Europeans. Genocide is, in quite radical contrast, presumably a subject of universal human concern. Thus, it is the old, traditional, manner of teaching and writing about Columbus that is "political" in the more narrow and parochial sense. One needs to have a special bias to think that Columbus "discovered America"; one need only be human to be concerned about genocide.

If this reasoning is correct, it is a mistake to regard the traditional view of Columbus as one perspective among others, to be accepted or rejected primarily on the basis of political considerations, the salience of which depends upon one's particular perspective. To conceive matters in this way is to concede too much to the traditional view. Moreover, since there are currently far more Americans of European than of African or Native American descent, such a concession paves the way for the traditional view to remain dominant.

A more fundamental problem, however, is that the perspictivist understanding of these matters seems to rest in part on a conflating of issues of truth and falsity with issues of emphasis and omission. To ask whether a given account is true is one thing. To ask what it leaves out and what it stresses is something quite different. One of the great benefits of multiculturalism, and of the changing, increasingly inclusive, demographics of contemporary teaching and scholarship, is that issues are being examined from a greater variety of perspectives, with the result that fewer things are omitted from, or deemphasized in, *all* accounts than has ever been the case previously. But this has little or nothing to do with issues of truth and falsity. That Columbus was an accomplished explorer is a fact, as is his involvement in slavery and genocide. Any "perspective" which would deny these would simply be mistaken, as would one that asserted that Columbus was, say, a great basketball player. Thus, considerations of omission and emphasis constitute a valuable supplement to, rather than replacement for, considerations of truth and falsity.

III. CONCLUSION

In conclusion, it should be noted that, if Chomsky is right, there are special reasons why the retention of a robust conception of truth and falsity is needed to understand contemporary political realities in

this, the age of propaganda, obfuscation, advertising, public relations—in short, the age of political lying in defense of the indefensible. As Chomsky puts it,

> I think most Americans would be horrified if they knew what they
> were doing in the world. And I think that's the reason for this whole
> edifice of lies.
>
> It's an obvious question: Why don't our leaders tell the people
> the truth? When they're going to destroy Iraq, say, why don't they
> announce: "Look, we want to control the international oil system.
> We want to establish the principle that the world is ruled by force,
> because that's the only thing that we're good at. We want to prevent
> any independent nationalism. We've got nothing against Saddam
> Hussein. He's a friend of ours. He's tortured and gassed people. That
> was fine. But then he disobeyed orders. Therefore, he must be
> destroyed as a lesson to other people: Don't disobey orders."
>
> Why don't they just say that? It has the advantage of being true.
> It's much easier to tell the truth than to concoct all sorts of crazy
> lies. Much less work. Why don't they say that? Because they know
> that people are basically decent. In fact, that's the only reason for
> all the fabrication. Our leaders believe that people are decent and
> that there is hope. And I think they're right.[11]

But if, rather than following Chomsky's lead in ferreting out the
relevant facts, using our logical powers in tracing out their implications, and then taking appropriate action, we instead follow Walter
Truett Anderson's counsel and "choose to live within a belief system
for the simple comfort it brings,"[12] or heed Richard Rorty's advice
that we should adopt a position which "makes it impossible to ask the
question 'Is ours a moral society?'"[13] we will only end up doing our
leaders' nefarious bidding. Those choices carry with them the less-
ening of hope and the continuance, indeed perhaps the increasing, of
human suffering around the world. Let us make a different choice.

NOTES

1. See, for example, Martin Anderson, *Impostors in the Temple* (New
York: Simon & Schuster, 1992); Richard Bernstein, *Dictatorship of Virtue*
(New York: Knopf, 1994); Allan Bloom, *The Closing of the American Mind*
(New York: Simon & Schuster, 1987); Dinesh D'Souza, *Illiberal Education*

(New York: Vintage, 1992); Roger Kimball, *Tenured Radicals* (New York: Harper & Row, 1990); Thomas Sowell, *Inside American Education* (New York: Free Press, 1993); and Charles Sykes, *Profscam* (Washington, D.C.: Regnery Gateway, 1988).

2. See, for example, Noam Chomsky, "Rationality/Science," *Z Papers* 1, no. 4 (October–December, 1992): 52–57.

3. I have examined these arguments in chapter 8 above.

4. For example, consider the reaction within mainstream political opinion in the U.S. to President Clinton's 26 June 1993 bombing of Baghdad, discussed toward the end of section I in chapter 8, above.

5. Noam Chomsky, *What Uncle Sam Really Wants* (Berkeley, CA: Odonian Press, 1992), pp. 88–89.

6. Chomsky, *Terrorizing the Neighborhood: American Foreign Policy in the Post-Cold War Era* (San Francisco: Pressure Drop Press, 1991), pp. 34–35.

7. Chomsky, *Turning the Tide: U.S. Intervention in Central America and the Struggle for Peace* (Boston: South End Press, 1985), p. 229. Laslo Csorba is quoted from an article by Steve Curwood in the *Boston Globe*, 3 October 1985. The "respected liberal intellectual historian" to whom Chomsky refers is John Patrick Diggins. He is quoted from the 20 October 1985 issue of the *New York Times Book Review*.

8. See, for example, Chomsky, "Linguistics and Politics" (a 1969 interview) in his *Language and Politics*, ed. C. P. Otero (New York: Black Rose Books, 1988), pp. 138–139.

9. Chomsky, from an interview with Charles M. Young in *Rolling Stone*, 28 May 1992, pp. 70–71.

10. Howard Zinn, in *A People's History of the United States* (New York: Harper & Row, 1980), pp. 7–8, makes this point quite effectively in his discussion of the distinguished Harvard historian Samuel Eliot Morrison's book *Christopher Columbus, Mariner* (Boston: Little Brown, 1955). Zinn points out that Morrison neither lies about nor omits the facts concerning Columbus's involvement in slavery and murder. Nor does he mince words. Rather, he forthrightly states that "[t]he cruel policy initiated by Columbus and pursued by his successors resulted in complete genocide." The problem, however, is that he buries this statement halfway through what Zinn terms a "grand romance," in which Columbus's exploits as a sailor and explorer are emphasized, along with the more attractive aspects of his personality.

11. Chomsky, from the Charles M. Young interview in *Rolling Stone*, p. 73.

12. Walter Truett Anderson, *Reality Isn't What It Used to Be* (San Francisco: Harper and Row, 1990), p. 268.

13. Richard Rorty, *Contingency, Irony, and Solidarity* (New York: Cambridge University Press, 1989), p. 59.

INDEX